I0824360

(!x==[33])

.UNFO

Book 1

Volume 1

Blanc
Press
Los Angeles, California

(!x==[33]) BOOK 1 VOLUME 1
Blanc Press November, 2011
Los Angeles, California

ISBN 13: 978-0-9814623-9-4

Author & Publisher Edition

.UNFO wishes to thank Mathew Timmons and Blanc Press.

(!x==[33]) is curated by UNFO (Unauthorized Narrative Freedom Organization), an unofficial and temporary coalition of coders and writers, including Dan Richert and Harold Abramowitz.

Source text was accessed from project gutenberg australia at http://gutenberg.net.au/ebooks02/0200601.txt

Forthcoming .UNFO Titles from Blanc Press:

(!x==[33]) Book 2 - Volume 2
(!x==[33]) Book 1 - Volume 2
(!x==[33]) Book 2 - Volume 1

(!x==[33])

[33]
DEDICATION ON NOVEMBER 9, 1923, at 12.30 in the afternoon, in front of the Feldherrnhalle as well as in the courtyard of the former

[33]
War Ministry, the following men, steadfast in their belief in the resurrection of their people, were killed : ALFARTH, Felix,

[33]
businessman, b. July 5, 1901 BAURIEDL, Andreas, hatter, b. May 4, 1879 CASELLA, Theodor, bank employee, b. August 8, 1900 EHRLICH, Wilhelm, bank employee, b. August 19, 1894 FAUST,

[33]
Martin, bank employee, b. January 27, 1901 HECHENBERGER, Anton, locksmith, b. September 28,; 1902 KOERNER, Oskar, businessman, b. January 4, 1875 KUHN, Karl,

[30]
headwaiter, b. July 26, 1897 LAFORCE, Karl, student of Engineering, b. October 28, 1904 NEUBAUER, Kurt, valet, b. March 27, 1899 PAPE, Claus von,

[32]
businessman, b. August 16, 1904 PFORDTEN, Theodor von der, County Court Council- lor, b. May 14, 1873 RICKMERS, Johann, retired Cavalry Captain, b. May 7, 1881

[33]
SCHEUBNER-RICHTER, Max Erwin von, Doctor of Engineering, b. January 9, 1884 STRANSKY, Lorenz Ritter von, Engineer, b. March 14, 1889 WOLF, Wilhelm,

[32]
businessman, b. October 19, 1898 So-called national authorities denied these dead heroes a common grave. Therefore

[31]
I dedicate to them, for common memory, the first volume of this work, as the blood witnesses of which they may

[32]
continue to serve as a brilliant example for the followers of our movement. ADOLF HITLER LANDSBERG ON THE LECH

[33]
PRISON OF THE FORTRESS October 16, 1924 PREFACE ON APRIL I, 1924, because of the sentence handed down by the People's Court of

[33]
Munich, I had to begin that day, serving my term in the fortress at Landsberg on the Lech. Thus, after years of uninterrupted

[33]
work, I was afforded for the first time an opportunity to embark on a task insisted upon by many and felt

[33]
to be serviceable to the movement by myself. Therefore, I resolved not only to set forth, in two volumes,

[33]
the object of our movement, but also to draw a picture of its development. From this more can be learned than from

[30]
any purely doctrinary treatise. That also gave me the opportunity to describe my own

[33]
development, as far as this is necessary for the understanding of the first as well as the second volume, and which

[33]
may serve to destroy the evil legends created about my person by the Jewish press. With this work I do not address myself

[32]
to strangers, but to those adherents of the movement who belong to it with their hearts and whose reason now seeks a more

[33]
intimate enlightenment. I know that one is able to win people far more by the spoken than by the written word,

[30]
and that every great movement on this globe owes its rise to the great speakers and not to the great writers.

[33]
Nevertheless, the basic elements of a doctrine must be set down in permanent form in order that it may be repre-

[32]
sented in the same way and in unity. In this connection these two volumes should serve as building stones which

[31]
I add to our common work. THE AUTHOR LANDSBERG ON THE LECH PRISON OF THE FORTRESS CONTENTS Volume I PUBLISHERS' NOTE v

[32]
INTRODUCTION vii DEDICATION xiii PREFACE xv Chapter I AT HOME 3 The Young Ringleader 7 Enthusiasm for War 8

[32]
Drawing Talent IO Never State Official 12 But Painter 13 The Young Nationalist 15 The German Ostmark 15 The Fight for the German

[33]
Nationality 16 History Lessons 18 History Favorite Subject 2O The Habsburgs' Policy of Slavization 21 The Young

[32]
983 Not Weapons, but Will, Decides! 987 Cuno's Road 987 The 'United Front' 988 Passive Resistance 989 The Position of the National

[33]
Socialists 990 November 1923 992 Our Dead as Monitors of Duty 993 ' CONCLUSION 994 INDEX 995 Volume One AN ACCOUNTING This translation

[33]
was prepared under the auspices of Dr. Alvin Johnson, of The New School for Social Research. The typography of the text of

[31]
this book follows that of the first German edition. Both italics and bold-faced type are used wherever they

[32]
occurred in the original. The more important portions of this book, omitted from the Dugdale Abridgment or

[33]
condensed in that version, are indicated by a dagger at the beginning of such passages and by an arrow at

[33]
the end. CHAPTER I AT HOME TODAY I consider it my good fortune that Fate designated Braunau on the Inn as

[33]
the place of my birth. For this small town is situated on the border between those two German States, the reunion of which

[29]
seems, at least to us of the younger generation, a task to be furthered with every means our lives long.

[32]
German-Austria must return to the great German motherland, and not because of economic considerations of

[34]
any sort. No, no: even if from the economic point of view this union were unimportant, indeed, if it were harmful,

[33]
it ought nevertheless to be brought about. Common blood belongs in a common Reich. As long as the German nation is unable

[33]
even to band together its own children in one common State, it has no moral right to think of colonization as

[33]
one of its political aims. Only when the boundaries of the Reich include even the last German, only when it is

[34]
no longer possible to assure him of daily bread inside them, does there arise, out of the distress of the nation,

[34]
the moral right to acquire foreign soil and territory. The sword is then the plow, and from the tears of war there grows the daily

[33]
bread for generations to come. Therefore, this little town on the border appears to me the symbol of a great task. But

[33]
in another respect also it looms up as a warning 4 MEIN KAMPF to our present time. More than a hundred years ago, this

[33]
insignificant little place had the privilege of gaining an immortal place in German history at least by

[32]
being the scene of a tragic misfortune that moved the entire nation. There, during the time of the deepest

[33]
humiliation of our fatherland, Johannes Palm, citizen of Nurnberg, a middle- class book dealer, die-hard ‘nationalist,

[33]
1 an enemy of the The idealism of the Wars of Liberation, waged by Prussia against Napoleon, is reflected

[31]
in the career of Johann Phillip Palm, Nurnberg book-seller, who in 1806 issued a work entitled, Deutschland in seiner tiefsten

[33]
Erniedrigung (Germany in the Hour of Its Deepest Humiliation). This was a diatribe against the Corsican. Palm was

[33]
tried by a military tribunal, sentenced to death, and shot at Braunau on August 26, 1806. During the centenary year (1906) a play

[33]
in honor of Palm was written by A. Ebenhoch, an Austrian author. It is possible that Hitler may have seen or read

[31]
this drama. Leo Schlageter, a German artillery officer who served after the World War in the Free Corps with which

[32]
General von der Goltz attempted to conserve part of what Germany had gained by the Treaty of Brest-Litovsk, was found

[33]
guilty of sabotage by a French military tribunal during the Ruhr invasion of 1923. He had blown up a portion of

[33]
the railway line between Dusseldorf and Duisburg, and had been caught in the act. The assertion that he was 'betrayed' to the French is

[30]
without historical foundation. It was the policy of the German government to discountenance open

[33]
military measures and to place its reliance upon so-called 'passive resistance.' Karl Severing, then

[34]
Social Democratic Minister of the Interior in Prussia, was a zealous though cautious patriot whose firm defense of

[33]
the democratic institutions of Weimar angered extremists of all kinds. He was thus a favorite Nazi target.

[33]
The governments of the Reich and of Prussia made every effort to save Schlageter. The Vatican intervened

[33]
in his behalf, and it is generally supposed that the French authorities would have commuted the sentence had it

[34]
not been for a sudden wave of opposition to AT HOME 5 French, was killed for the sake of the Germany he ardently

[32]
loved even in the hour of its distress. He had obstinately refused to denounce his fellow offenders, or

[31]
rather the chief offenders. Thus he acted like Leo Schlageter. But like him, he too was betrayed to France by a

[33]
representative of his government. It was a director of the Augsburg police who earned that shoddy glory, thus

[33]
setting an example for the new German authorities of Heir Severing's Reich, In this little town on the river Inn, gilded

[33]
by the light of German martyrdom, there lived, at the end of the eighties of the last century, my parents, Bavarian

[32]
by blood, Austrian by nationality: the father a faithful civil servant, the Poincare's policy in the Chamber. That

[33]
induced the government to make a show of firmness. Schlageter, whose last words are said to have been, 'Germany must

[34]
live,' was executed on May 26, 1923. Immediately he became a German national hero. His example more than

[33]
anything else hallowed the tradition of the Free Corps in the popular mind and thus strengthened pro- militaristic

[33]
sentiment. One of the first cultural activities of the Nazi regime was a tribute to Schlageter. Hitler's

[33]
family background has been a subject for much research and speculation. The father, Alois Hitler (1837-1903), was the illegitimate

[32]
son of Maria Anna Schicklgruber; and it is generally assumed that the father was the man she married Johann

[32]
Hiedler. Until he was forty, he bore the name of his mother, being known as Alois Schicklgruber. Then on January 8, 1877, he

[33]
legally changed the name to Hitler, which had been that of his maternal grandmother. His third wife was Klara Poelzl (1860-1908), who on

[33]
April 20, 1889, gave birth to Adolf Hitler. There may have been a brother or half-brother if reports current in Nazi circles

[31]
are to be credited. At any rate, Hitler has a living sister and a half-sister. The first has lived in

[33]
retirement, but the second a woman of considerable charm and ability is known to have exercised no

[32]
little influence at times. 6 MEIN KAMPF mother devoting herself to the cares of the household and looking after her

[33]
children with eternally the same loving kindness. I remember only little of this time, for a few years later my

[31]
father had again to leave the little border town he had learned to like, and go down the Inn to take a new

[33]
position at Passau, that is in Germany proper. But the lot of an Austrian customs official of those days frequently

[32]
meant 'moving on.' Just a short time afterwards my father was transferred to Linz, and finally retired on a pension

[33]
there. But this was not to mean ' rest' for the old man. The son of a poor cottager, even in his childhood he had not been able

[32]
to stay at home. Not yet thirteen years old, the little boy he then was bundled up his things and ran away from his homeland, the

[33]
Waldviertel. Despite the dissuasion of 'experienced' inhabitants of the village he had gone to Vienna to

[33]
learn a trade there. This was in the fifties of the last century. A bitter resolve it must have been to take to

[31]
the road, into the unknown, with only three guilders for traveling money. But by the time the thirteen- year-old lad was

[31]
seventeen, he had passed his apprentice's examination, but he had not yet found satisfaction. It was rather the

[33]
opposite. The long time of hardship through which he then passed, of endless poverty and misery, strengthened his resolve

[32]
to give up the trade after all in order to become something 'better.' If once the village pastor had

[31]
seemed to the little boy the incarnation of all obtainable human success, now, in the big city which had so

[33]
widened his perspective, the rank of civil servant became the ideal. With all the tenacity of one who had

[33]
grown 'old' through want and sorrow while still half a child, the seventeen-year-old youth clung to his decision . . . and became a civil

[34]
servant. The goal was reached, I believe, after nearly twenty-three years. Now there had been realized the premise of the vow

[33]
that the poor boy once had sworn, not to return to his dear native village before he had become something. AT

[33]
HOME 7 Now the goal was reached, but nobody in the village remembered the little boy of long ago, and the village

[33]
had become a stranger to him. When he retired at the age of fifty-six, he was unable to spend a single day

[32]
in 'doing nothing.' He bought a farm near Lambach in Upper Austria which he worked himself, thus returning, after a long and

[33]
active life, to the origin of his ancestors. It was probably at that time that my first ideals were formed.

[32]
A lot of romping around out-of-doors, the long trip to school, and the companionship with unusually 'robust boys, which at

[34]
times caused my mother much grief, made me anything but a stay-at-home. Though I did not brood over my future career

[33]
at that time, I had decidedly no sympathy for the course my father's life had taken. I believe that even

[32]
then my ability for making speeches was trained by the more or less stirring discussions with my comrades. I had

[32]
become a little ringleader and at that time learned easily and did very well in school, but for the rest I was

[33]
rather difficult to handle. Inasmuch as I received singing lessons in my spare time in the choir of the Lambach

[32]
Convent, I repeatedly had an excellent opportunity of intoxicating myself with the solemn splendor of the

[34]
magnificent church festivals. It was perfectly natural that the position of abbot appeared to me to be the highest

[32]
ideal obtainable, just as that of being the village pastor had appealed to my father. At least at times this was the

[33]
case. For obvious reasons my father could not appreciate the talent for oratory of his quarrelsome son

[33]
in the same measure, nor could he perceive in it any hope for the future of the lad, and so he showed no

[30]
understanding for these youthful ideas. Sadly he observed this dissension of nature. Actually, my

[33]
occasional longing for this profession disappeared very quickly and made way for aspirations more in keeping

[32]
with my temperament. Rummaging through MEIN KAMPF my father's library, I stumbled upon various books on military

[31]
subjects, and among them I found a popular edition dealing with the Franco-Prussian War of 1870-71. These were two

[34]
volumes of an illustrated journal of the period which now became my favorite reading matter. Before long

[34]
that great heroic campaign had become my greatest spiritual experience. From then on I raved more and more about

[33]
everything connected with war or with militarism. Since Hitler's outlook and policies are rooted in Austrian

[34]
experience (it is sometimes said that he 'made Germany an Austrian's province') some remarks on the general

[32]
situation in his home land may be helpful. The Austria-Hungary of the last three decades of the nineteenth

[32]
century was only the remnant of a Habsburg Empire that had once included most of western Europe. It was

[33]
a 'dual monarchy,' the crown belonging to the monarch as Emperor of Austria and King of Hungary. Since most of

[34]
Germany had been welded together (1871) by Bismarck in an empire ruled by the Hohenzollern kings of Prussia, the Germans

[29]
who remained in Austria-Hungary constituted a minority, even though most of the important

[33]
bureaucratic positions were still in their hands. The position obtained by Hungary made their lot no easier. For

[33]
soon every 'nationality' wished to secure comparable advantages for itself. The monarchy itself had

[32]
suffered many a reverse. Under Frederick the Great and Bismarck, the Prussians had inflicted several major

[34]
defeats upon their Austrian rivals. While the revolutionary liberalism of 1848 was successfully put down at the cost

[31]
of severe fighting, the power of the bureaucratic State was none the less seriously undermined and the

[33]
eventual triumph of 'constitutionalism' in 1860-61 was assured. In addition the unification of Italy was

[33]
achieved at the cost of Austrian prestige and possessions. And though the Partition of Poland had added Galicia to

[34]
the Habsburg domains, it was always doubtful who ruled the province the Poles or the Austrians. Galicia was also the home

[33]
of large Jewish communities, from which strong contingents moved to Vienna and other important cities. AT HOME 9 But this

[33]
was to prove of importance to me in another direction as well. For the first time the question confronted me I

[34]
was a bit confused, perhaps if and what difference there was between those Germans fighting these battles and the others.

[33]
Why was it that Austria had not taken part also in this war, why not my father, and why not all the others? Are we not

[33]
the same as all the other Germans? Do we not all belong together? This problem now began to whirl through my little head for

[33]
the first time. After cautious questioning, I heard with envy the reply that not every German was fortunate enough

[30]
to belong to Bismarck's Reich. This I could not understand. I was to become a student. From 1880 onward, the problem of

[33]
'nationalities' dominated Austrian life. On the one hand, the Hungarians were concerned lest the Slavic groups

[33]
Czechs, Croats, Poles, etc. extend their demand for autonomy to the point where the Empire would become a ' federation'

[33]
of States, and therefore made common cause with the Germans on issues affecting the status quo. But a good many

[32]
Germans, for their part, felt aggrieved at having been excluded from the Bismarckian Empire and saw no future for

[33]
themselves in a predominantly Slavic State. On the other hand, the Czechs and kindred 'nationalities' con- tinued to

[33]
urge the idea of a federation, and to insist upon the right to foster their own languages and cultures. The Habs-

[31]
burg rulers had no choice save recourse to continual compromise. In the Austrian parliament common

[32]
national interests, for example the army, were always being subordinated to hotly debated matters of

[33]
domestic 'nationality' policy. Doubtless there was no way out except the establishment of a federation. To

[33]
this idea Franz Ferdinand, the Crown Prince whose murder at Saravejo was the immediate cause of the World War,

[31]
seems to have committed himself. 10 MEIN KAMPF Because of my entire nature, even more because of my

[34]
temperament, my father thought he was right in concluding that attendance at the humanistic Gymnasium would not be in

[33]
keeping with my ability. He thought that the Realschule [a German secondary school for modern subjects and sciences] seemed

[33]
more suitable. This opinion was strengthened by my obvious talent for drawing; this subject, he thought, had been neglected in

[31]
the Austrian schools. Per- haps his own lifetime of hard work was a decisive factor and made him appreciate

[33]
humanistic studies to a lesser degree, for to him they appeared impractical. As a matter of principle, he was

[30]
determined that like himself his son should, nay must, become an official. It was natural that the bitter

[34]
experiences of his own youth made his later achievements appear so much greater, especially since they were exclu-

[32]
Some Germans protested strongly against these tendencies. Nevertheless, the effort to create a party openly

[31]
favorable to the separation of German Austria from the Austro-Hungarian Empire and its merger in the

[33]
Bismarckian State was far less successful than might have been anticipated. The early Nationalists of the

[33]
eventually gave rise to the Grossdeutsch Partei of Hitler's youth, which was violently critical of the Habsburgs and

[33]
of all concessions made to the Slavs during the years 1879-1900. Perhaps it would have gained more ground if Bismarck had been vitally

[33]
interested in the problem. But in addition to the dynastic question of the status of the Habsburgs, he had after 1871 to

[31]
avoid giving the impression that Prussia was an expansion-hungry State. He also realized that the Vienna

[32]
monarchy was a source of unity in the chaotic southeast of Europe, in the affairs of which he did not wish to

[33]
involve Germany. Accordingly, the Grossdeutsch people got little sympathy from him. When he was dismissed from his post by

[34]
Emperor Wilhelm II, the sole group remaining in Germany that could have given much support to the separationist

[33]
movement in German Austria was the Audeutscher Verband (Pan- AT HOME 11 sively the result of his own industry and

[31]
energy. It was the pride of the self-made man which moved him to endeavor to bring his son to a similar

[33]
position in life, if not a better one, and all the more since he hoped to make things easier for the child through

[33]
his own industry. It was unthinkable that that which had become the content of his whole life could be rejected. Thus

[33]
the father's decision was matter-of-fact, simple, exact, and clear, quite comprehensibly in his own eyes. His domineering

[34]
nature, the result of a lifelong struggle for existence, would have thought it unbearable to leave the ultimate

[33]
decision to a boy who, in his opinion, was inexperienced and irresponsible. What is more, this would have been

[31]
inconsistent with his idea of duty, a wicked and reprehensible weakness in exercising his paternal

[29]
authority as he saw it in his responsibility for the future of his son. German League, an

[33]
organization of chauvinists and expansionists. They, however, looked upon Austria-Hungary as a powerful

[33]
ally and as a diving-board for the plunge eastward which they looked upon as the German destiny. In Austria itself

[33]
the Grossdeutsch elements adopted a policy calculated to insure failure. They sponsored a little Kultur-

[33]
kampf (religious war) of their own, attacking the clergy and the Church; they disassociated themselves from all social re- form

[33]
and all concessions to other groups; and they were given to rabid attacks on the monarchy. As a consequence, the Ger-

[33]
man group was more seriously divided than ever. These mistakes all made, as is evident from the text of Mein

[33]
Kampf , a deep and lasting impression upon Hitler. Just as he was disgusted with the wrangling about 'nationality' problems

[33]
that characterized the Austrian parliament, so was he conscious of the mistakes which the pro-Prussia leaders had made.

[34]
He never disassociated himself from the principles adopted by those leaders, but he learned to look askance at

[33]
their methods. The extent of Austrian yearning for incorporation in the 12 MEIN KAMPF And yet the course of events was to take

[33]
a different turn. For the first time in my life, I was barely eleven, I was forced into opposition. No

[33]
matter how firm and determined my father might be in carrying out his plans and intentions once made, his son was just as

[33]
stubborn and obstinate in rejecting an idea which had little or no appeal for him. I did not want to become an

[33]
official. Neither persuasion nor 'sincere' arguments were able to break down this resistance. I did not want to

[33]
become an official, no, and again no! All attempts to arouse my interest or my liking for such a career by

[33]
stories of my father's life had the opposite effect. The thought of being a slave in an office made me ill ; not

[33]
to be master of my own time, but to force an entire lifetime into the filling-in of forms, What ideas this

[34]
must have awakened in a boy who was anything but 'good' in the ordinary sense of the word ! The ridiculously

[33]
easy learning at school left me so much spare German Empire or, after 1918, the German Republic, is a moot question. Prior to

[32]
the War, anti-Prussian sentiment was probably just as vigorous among the people generally as pro- Habsburg

[33]
sentiment. After the defeat there was a general feeling that the little independent State of Austria could not

[33]
survive. Even so it is very doubtful whether the demand for Anschluss was as 'elemental 1 as Hitler says it was. Some

[30]
Austrians notably Professor Ludo Hartmann sponsored it with vigor and eloquence. A few unofficial

[33]
plebiscites were held in Salzburg and elsewhere and seemed to show that sentiment was overwhelmingly in favor

[33]
of Anschluss; but individually and collectively they have little value as evidence. Other sources of

[33]
information (e.g., records of party deliberations) give a different impression. Undoubtedly the desire for

[31]
union grew during the following years, but it is nonetheless doubtful whether an honest plebiscite in 1938 would have

[33]
favored absorption of Austria into the Third Reich. AT HOME 13 time that the sun saw more of me than the four walls of

[32]
my room. When today my political opponents examine my life down to the time of my childhood with loving

[32]
attention, so that at last they can point with relief to the intolerable pranks this Hitler 1 carried out even in his youth,

[33]
I thank Heaven for now giving me a share of the memories of those happy days. Woods and meadows were the battlefield

[32]
where the ever-present 'conflicts' were fought out. My attendance at the Realschule, which now followed, did little to

[33]
deter me. But now it was a different conflict that had to be fought. This was bearable as long as my father's intention to

[31]
make an official of me was confronted by nothing more than my dislike of the profession on general

[33]
principles. I could restrain my private views and, after all, it was not always necessary for me to contradict. My own

[31]
firm intention not to become an official was sufficient to set my mind at rest. This decision, however, was

[33]
irrevocable. The question be- came more difficult as soon as my father's plan was met by one of my own. This took

[32]
place when I was twelve years old. I do not know how it happened, but one day it was clear to me that I would become

[33]
a painter, an artist. My talent for drawing was obvious and it was one of the reasons why my father had sent me to

[32]
the Realschule, but he never would have thought of having me trained for such a career. On the contrary. When, after a

[34]
renewed rejection of my father's favorite idea, I was asked for the first time what I intended to be after

[33]
all, I unexpectedly burst forth with the resolve I had irrevocably made; in the meantime my father at first

[33]
was speechless. 'A painter? An artist?' He doubted my sanity, he did not trust his own ears or thought that he had misunderstood. But

[31]
when it had been explained to him and when he had sensed the sincerity of my intentions, he opposed me with the

[33]
resoluteness of his 14 MEIN KAMPF entire nature. His decision was quite simple, and any con- sideration of

[33]
those actual talents that I might have possessed was out of the question. 'An artist, no, never as long as I live'

[34]
But as his son had undoubtedly inherited, amongst other qualities, a stubborn- ness similar to his own, he received

[33]
a similar reply. Only its meaning was quite different. So the situation remained on both sides. My father

[32]
did not give up his 'never' and I strengthened my 'nevertheless/ Obviously the consequences were not very

[33]
enjoyable. The old man became embittered, and, much as I loved him, the same was true of myself. My father forbade

[33]
me to entertain any hope of ever becoming a painter. I went one step farther by declaring that under these

[33]
circumstances I no longer wished to study. Naturally, as the result of such 'declarations' I got the 'worst of it,'

[33]
and now the old man relentlessly began to enforce his authority. I remained silent and turned my threats into

[34]
action. I was certain that, as soon as my father saw my lack of progress in school, come what may he would let me seek the happiness

[32]
of which I was dreaming. I do not know if this reasoning was sound. One thing was certain: my apparent failure in school.

[33]
I learned what I liked, but above all I learned what in my opinion might be necessary to me in my future

[31]
career as a painter. In this connection I sabotaged all that which seemed unimportant or that which no longer

[33]
attracted me. At that time my marks were always extreme depending upon the subject and my evaluation of

[33]
it. 'Praiseworthy' and 'Excellent' ranked with 'Sufficient' and 'Insufficient'. 1 My best efforts were in geography and perhaps

[32]
even more so in history. These were my two favorite subjects and in them I led my class.-' Now, after so

[33]
many years, when I examine the results of that period, I find two outstanding facts of particular importance:

[31]
AT HOME 15 First, / became a nationalist. Second, / learned lo grasp and to understand the meaning of history. Old

[33]
Austria was a 'State of nationalities. A citizen of the German Empire, at that time at least, could hardly

[33]
understand the bearing of this fact upon the daily life of the individual in such a State. After the amaz-

[34]
ingly victorious campaign of the heroic German armies during the Franco- Prussian War, one had become more and

[33]
more estranged from the Germans abroad, partly because one no longer knew how to appreciate them or perhaps

[32]
because one was unable to do so. As far as the Austro German was concerned, it was easy to confuse the

[33]
decadent dynasty with a people who were sound at heart. It was hard to understand that, were the German in Austria

[33]
not actually of the best stock, he never would have been able to impress his mark upon a State of fifty-two mil-

[32]
lion people in such a manner as to create even in Germany the erroneous impression that Austria was a

[32]
German State. This was nonsensical, with the gravest of consequences, but brilliant testimony for the ten million

[31]
Germans in the Ostmark. Only a very few Germans in the empire had any idea of the continuous and

[33]
inexorable struggle waged for the German language, the German schools, and the German mode of existence. Only

[32]
today, when this misery has been forced upon millions of our people outside of the Reich proper, who, under foreign

[33]
domination, dream of a common fatherland and in their longing for it strive to preserve their most sacred claim their mother

[34]
tongue only today wider circles understand what it means to fight for one's nationality. It is now perhaps that the one

[31]
or the other will be able to realize the greatness of the Germans abroad in the old East of the Reich who at first,

[33]
dependent upon themselves, for centuries protected the Reich in the East, and at last guarded the German language frontier

[33]
in a war of 16 MEIN KAMPF attrition at a time when the Reich was greatly interested in colonies but not in its own flesh

[32]
and blood outside its very doors. As everywhere and always, as in every struggle, there were also in the

[33]
language struggle of the old Austria three groups: The fighters, the lukewarm, and the traitors. Even in school this segregation

[32]
was apparent. It is significant for the language struggle on the whole that its ways engulf the school, the seed bed of the

[33]
coming generation. The child is the objective of the struggle and the very first appeal is addressed to it: 'German

[33]
boy, do not forget that you are a German.' 'German maid, remember that you are to be a German mother/ + Those who know

[33]
the soul of youth will understand that it is youth which lends its ears to such a battle-cry with the greatest joy. In hundreds of forms, in

[33]
its own way and with its own weapons, it carried on the battle. It refuses to sing non-German songs; the more one tries to

[34]
estrange it from German heroic grandeur, the more enthusiastic it waxes; it stints itself to collect pennies for the fund

[33]
of the grown-ups; it has an unusually fine ear for all that the non-German teacher says to it; it is rebellious;

[33]
it wears the forbidden emblem of its own nationality and rejoices in being punished or even in being beaten for

[32]
wearing that emblem. On a smaller scale youth is a true reflection of its elders, but more often with a deeper and

[32]
a more honest conviction. At a comparatively early age I, too, was given the opportunity to

[32]
participate in the national struggle of old Austria. Money was collected for the Sildmark and the school club; our

[31]
conviction was demonstrated by the wearing of corn-flowers and the colors black, red, and gold; the greeting was 1 Hei ' ; ' Deutschland

[33]
iiber alles f was preferred to the imperial anthem, despite warnings and punishments. In this man- AT HOME 17 ner

[34]
the boy was trained politically at an age when a member of a so-called national State knows little more of

[33]
his nationality than its language. It is obvious that already then I did not belong to the lukewarm. In a short

[33]
time I had become a fanatical 'German nationalist/ a term which is not identical with our same party

[31]
name of today. My development was quite rapid, so that at the age of fifteen I already understood the

[33]
difference between dynastic 'patriotism' and popular 'nationalism'; at that time the latter alone existed

[32]
for me. Those who have never taken the trouble to study closely the internal situation of the Habsburg

[31]
monarchy may not be able to understand the full meaning of these events. In this State the origin for this

[31]
development was to be found in the lessons in world history taught in the schools, since there is practically no

[34]
specific Austrian history as such. The conservative cabinet headed (1879-1893) by Taafe attempted to solve the problems

[31]
of the Empire by winning the support of the Slavic groups. In 1895-1897 Count Casimir Badeni sponsored legislation

[32]
favoring the Czechs in linguistic and cultural matters; and violent opposition to these measures was aroused

[33]
among the nationalistic Germans. The Deuischer Schulverein (German School Society), an organization founded in 1880 to

[34]
promote German schools in foreign countries, was a center of resistance particularly in Carinthia, where the Slavs

[33]
were looked upon as especially menacing. The corn-flower was a patriotic symbol in Wilhelmian days. Deutschland,

[33]
DeiUsth- land uber alles, a lyric written by Fallersleben in 1841, was sung by the nationalistic groups in Austria

[33]
to the tune written by Hayden for the Imperial hymn. Singing it was, therefore, an insult to the Habsburgs. The 'HeiF

[33]
an old German form of greeting was used by Austrian nationalists instead of the native forms (e.g., Griiss Gotf), and had

[33]
an anti-Semitic undertone. It required little manipulation to transform all these things into the Nazi

[32]
practices now current. 18 MEIN KAMPF The fate of this State is so closely bound up with the life and growth of the entire

[32]
German nationality that it is unthinkable to separate its history into German and Austrian. As

[33]
a matter of fact when Germany began to split into two supreme powers, this very separation became German

[32]
history. The imperial crown jewels kept in Vienna, reminders of the old realm splendor, still seem to exercise a

[34]
magic spell, a pledge of eternal communion. The German-Austrian's elementary outcry for a reunion with the German

[33]
motherland during the days of the breakdown of the Habsburg State was merely the result of a feeling of nostalgia

[33]
slumbering deep in the hearts of the entire nation for a return to the paternal home which had never been forgotten.

[32]
This would be inexplicable had not the political education of each individual German-Austrian been the

[34]
origin of that common longing. In it there lies a longing which contains a well that never dries, especially in time of

[32]
forgetfulness and of temporary well-being it will again and again forecast the future in recalling the past.

[32]
Even today, courses in world history in the so-called secondary schools are still badly neglected. Few teachers

[33]
realize that the aim of history lessons should not consist in the memorizing and rattling forth of historical facts and

[33]
data; that it does not matter whether a boy knows when this or that battle was fought, when a certain military leader was born,

[33]
or when some monarch (in most cases a very mediocre one) was crowned with the crown of his an- cestors. Good God, these

[34]
things do not matter. To 'learn' history means to search for and to find the forces which cause those effects which we later face as

[32]
historical events. Here, too, the art of reading, like that of learning, is to remember the important, to forget the

[34]
unimportant. AT HOME 19 It was perhaps decisive for my entire future life that I was fortunate enough

[30]
to have a history teacher who was one of the few who understood how essential it was to make this the

[32]
dominating factor in his lessons and examinations. At the Realschule in Linz my teacher was Professor Doctor

[33]
Ludwig Poetsch, who personified this requisite in an ideal way. The old gentleman, whose manner was as kind as it was

[33]
firm, not only knew how to keep us spellbound, but actually carried us away with the splendor of his eloquence. I am

[32]
still slightly moved when I remember the gray-haired man whose fiery descriptions made us forget the present and who

[33]
evoked plain historical facts out of the fog of the centuries and turned them into living reality. Often we would

[32]
sit there enraptured in enthusiasm and there were even times when we were on the verge of tears. Our

[33]
happiness was the greater inasmuch as this teacher not only knew how to throw light on the past by utilizing the present,

[31]
but also how to draw conclusions from the past and applying them to the present. More than anyone else he showed

[33]
understanding for all the daily problems which held us breathless at the time. He used our youthful na- The educational

[33]
ideas here expressed are in part the common property of all who have gone to school and in part the legacy

[32]
of Turnvater Jahn, the founder of the Turnvereine, or gymnastic societies, whose Deutsches Volkstum (German Folkishness)

[33]
appeared in 1810, and whose part in rallying Prussian youth against Napoleon was a most estimable one. When Hitler speaks

[33]
of the girl who ought to remember that her duty is to become a German mother, or of history as the science which

[33]
demonstrates that one's own people is always right, he is echoing Jahn in the first instance. The best discussion in English

[33]
of this interesting pedagogue is still an essay which appeared in the London Magazine during 1820, when these new

[33]
Prussian ideas of education seemed important but strange to Englishmen. 20 MEIN KAMPF tional fanaticism as a means

[33]
of education by repeatedly appealing to our sense of national honor, and through this alone he was able

[33]
to manage us rascals more easily than would have been possible by any other means. He was the teacher who made

[31]
history my favorite subject. Nevertheless, although it was entirely unintentional on his part, I

[33]
already then became a young revolutionary. Who could possibly study German history with such a teacher and

[32]
not become an enemy of the State which, through its ruling dynasty, so disastrously influenced the state of the

[32]
nation? And who could keep faith with an imperial dynasty which betrayed the cause of the German people for its own ig-

[33]
nominious ends, a betrayal that occurred again and again in the past and in the present? Boys though we were, did we not

[33]
already realize that this Austrian State did not and could not harbor love for us Germans? Our historical knowledge

[33]
of the influence of the House of Habsburg was supported by daily experiences. In the North and the South the poison of

[33]
foreign nationalities This is probably one of the most revealing passages in the book. Hitler has consistently

[33]
considered himself a 'Revolutionary,' but has added little to the interpretation of the term given here.

[33]
The longing to change the structure of society developed, in his case, not out of the consciousness of real or fan-

[33]
cied social and economic injustices, but out of the feeling that the Ruling House did not adequately support

[32]
the demands of the German groups. After the War he took an identical point of view in Germany itself, laying siege to the

[33]
Weimar Republic because its policy of international conciliation seemed to him a duplicate of

[33]
the policy of making concessions to Slavic groups which Habsburg governments had sponsored. Cf . Adolf Hitter, by Theodor Heuss (1932). AT

[33]
HOME 21 eroded the body of our own nationality, and it was apparent how even Vienna became less and less

[32]
a German city. The Royal House became Czech wherever possible, and it must have been the hand of the goddess of

[33]
eternal justice and inexorable retribution which caused Archduke Franz Ferdinand, the most deadly enemy

[31]
of Austrian-Germanism, to fall by the very bullets he himself had helped to mold. For was he not the patron of

[33]
Austria's Slavization from above! The burdens which the German people had to bear were enormous, its sacrifices

[33]
in taxes and blood unheard of, and yet, everyone who had eyes to see realized that all this would IDC in vain. What grieved us

[32]
most was the fact that the whole system was morally protected by the alliance with Germany, and thus Germany

[31]
herself, in a fashion, sanctioned the slow extermination of the German nationality in the old monarchy. The

[32]
hypocrisy of the Habsburgs, who knew well how to create the impression abroad that Austria was still a German State,

[34]
fanned the hatred against this house into flaming indignation and contempt. It was only in the Reich itself that the 'chosen

[33]
ones' saw nothing of all this. As if stricken with blindness, they walked by the side of the corpse, and in the indications

[32]
of decomposition they thought they detected signs of 'new' life. The tragic alliance between the young Reich and the old

[33]
Austrian sham State was the source of the ensuing World War and of the general collapse as well. In the course of this

[32]
book I shall find it necessary to deal further with this problem. It suffices to state here that from my earliest youth

[33]
I came to a conviction which never deserted me, but on the contrary, grew stronger and stronger: That the protection of

[33]
the German race presumed the destruction of Austria, and further, that national feeling is in no way identical

[33]
with dynastic patriotism; that above all else, the 22 MEIN KAMPF Royal House of Habsburg was destined to bring misfortune

[34]
upon the German nation. Even then I had drawn the necessary deductions from this realization: an intense love for

[33]
my native German- The picture Hitler draws of his early youth is, therefore, one of idle years spent fighting off

[33]
formal education under the pre-text that he wanted to become an artist. That he has ever since considered

[32]
himself brilliantly gifted as a painter and architect is indubitable. The flags, uniforms and insignia of the

[32]
Party were designed by him. The 'senate chamber' and study in the Brown House, Munich, are proudly displayed as

[33]
examples of the Fuhrcr's (Leader's) work. In the first, which is primarily a study in red leather, the swastika serves as an

[31]
allusion to the SPQR of ancient Rome. Later on his views were influenced by his Bavarian environment, more

[31]
particularly it would seem by the art theories of Schulze-Naumburg, who in the Thuringia of 1930 led the attack on

[32]
modernistic art and architecture. During 1937 Munich was stirred by an exposition of 'De-generate Art,' which

[31]
gathered from the museums pictures adjudged not to be in the strict Aryan tradition. Meanwhile there had been

[33]
erected in the same city a Kunsthalle adorned with a row of simple classical pillars; and this structure is

[32]
generally accepted as embodying Hitler's ideal of what a building ought to be. The example of Mussolini

[33]
also had its effect. In order to provide a suitable approach to the Kunsthalle, one of King Ludwig's ancient streets

[33]
was torn down and widened. Down this avenue, festooned with countless flags and abundant drapery, II Duce proceeded

[33]
upon the occasion of his historic trip to Munich in 1937. More recently the new Chancellery in Berlin has been com-

[33]
pleted. A skyscraper, taller than any in New York, was projected for Hamburg. Hitler is also known to have devised

[33]
models of a Vienna and Berlin reconstructed according to his ideas of what a city ought to be. Enormous sums have

[31]
already been diverted into building operations. AT HOME S3 Austrian country and a bitter hatred against the

[33]
'Austrian' State. The art of historical thinking, which had been taught me in school, has never left me since. More and more,

[33]
world history became a never-failing source of my understanding of the historical events of the present, that

[30]
is, politics. What is more, I do not want to 'learn' it, but I want it to teach me. Since I had become a

[32]
political 'revolutionary' at so early a stage, it was not much later that I became an 'artistic'

[33]
one. At that time the capital of Upper Austria had a theater of fairly high standing. Almost everything was

[32]
performed there. At the age of twelve I saw 'Wilhelm Tell' for the first time, and a few months later, I saw the first

[33]
opera of my life, 4 Lohengrin.' I was captivated at once. My youthful enthusiasm for the master of Bayreuth

[32]
knew no bounds. Again and again I was drawn to his works and today I consider it particularly fortunate that the

[32]
modesty of that provincial performance reserved for me the opportunity of seeing increasingly better

[33]
productions. All this served to confirm my deep-rooted aversion for the career my father had chosen for me, especially

[34]
after I had left childhood behind and approached manhood a painful experience. I was more definitely convinced

[33]
that I could never be happy as an official. And now that my talent for drawing had also been recognized in school, my

[32]
resolve was even more firmly established. Neither pleas nor threats could influence me. I wanted to become a

[33]
painter, and no power on earth could ever make an official of me. But it was strange that as the years passed, I demon-

[33]
strated more and more interest in architecture. At that 24 MEIN KAMPF time I took it for granted that this was merely

[31]
an augmentation of my talent for painting and secretly I was delighted at this widening of my artistic

[33]
horizon. I had no idea that things were to turn out so differently. The question of my career was to be settled more

[33]
quickly than I had anticipated. When I was thirteen my father died quite suddenly. The old gentleman, who had always

[32]
been so robust and healthy, had a stroke which painlessly ended his wanderings in this world, plunging us all in the depths of

[32]
despair. His dearest wish, to help his son to build up his existence, thus safe-guarding him against the pitfalls of his own

[33]
bitter experience, had apparently not been fulfilled. But unconsciously he had sown the seed for a future which

[33]
neither he nor I would have grasped at that time. At first nothing changed in my daily life. My mother probably felt

[32]
the obligation to continue my education in accordance with my father's wishes, in other words, to have me

[33]
continue my studies for the career of an official. But I was determined more than ever not to become an

[32]
official. My attitude became more and more indifferent in the same measure that the subjects and the

[34]
education which school afforded me deviated from my own ideal. Suddenly an illness came to my aid, and in the course

[31]
of a few weeks, settled the perpetual arguments at home and, with them, my future. Because of a severe

[32]
pulmonary illness, the doctor strongly advised my mother not to place me in an office later on under

[33]
any circumstances. I was also to give up school for at least one year. With this event, all that I had fought for, all that

[33]
I had longed for in secret, suddenly became reality. Impressed by my illness, my mother agreed at long last to

[33]
take me out of school and to send me to the Akademie. AT HOME 25 These were my happiest days; they seemed like a

[33]
dream to me, and so they were. Two years later my mother's death put a sudden end to all these delightful plans. It was the end

[33]
of a long and painful illness that had seemed fatal from the very beginning. Nevertheless it was a terrible shock to

[33]
me. I had respected my father, but I loved my mother. Necessity and stern reality now forced me to make a

[33]
quick decision. My mother's severe illness had almost exhausted the meager funds left by my father; the orphan's pension which

[33]
I received was not nearly enough for me to live on, and so I was faced with the problem of earning my own daily

[31]
bread. I went to Vienna with a suitcase, containing some clothes and my linen, in my hand and an unshakable

[32]
determination in my heart. I, too, hoped to wrest from Fate the success my father had met fifty years earlier; I, too,

[33]
wanted to become 'something' but in no event an official. CHAPTER II YEARS OF STUDY AND SUFFERING IN VIENNA

[34]
t% ^W^ JTHEN my mother died, Fate had cast the die in \J\X one direction at least. T T During the last months of her suffering, I had gone to

[33]
Vienna to take my entrance examination to the Akademic. I had set out with a lot of drawings, convinced

[33]
that I would pass the examination with ease. At the Realschule I had been by far the best artist in my class; and since then

[34]
my ability had improved greatly, so that my self-satisfaction made me hope both proudly and happily for the best.

[33]
There was but one cloud which occasionally made its appearance; my talent for painting sometimes seemed to

[33]
overshadow my ability for drawing, especially in nearly all of the branches of architecture. Also my

[34]
interest in the art of building as a whole grew steadily. This was stimulated, when I was not quite sixteen, by the fact

[33]
that I was allowed for the first time to spend a two weeks' vacation in Vienna. I went there especially to study

[33]
the picture gallery of the Hofmuseum, but I had eyes for nothing but the buildings of the museum itself. All day long, from

[33]
early morn until late at night, I ran from one sight to the next, for what attracted me most of all were the buildings. For

[32]
hours on endYEARS OF STUDY AND SUFFERING 27 I would stand in front of the opera or admire the Parliament Building; the

[31]
entire Ringstrasse affected me like a fairy tale out of the Arabian Nights. And now I was in this

[32]
beautiful city for the second time, burning with impatience; I waited with pride and confidence to learn the

[34]
result of my entrance examination. I was so convinced of my success that the announcement of my failure came

[32]
like a bolt from the blue. And yet it was true. When I had obtained an interview with the director and asked him to

[33]
explain why I had not been admitted to the general painting school at the Akademie, he assured me that the drawings

[32]
I had submitted clearly showed my lack of painting ability, but that my talents obviously lay in the field of

[31]
architecture; it was the school of architecture and not the school of painting where I belonged. They could not

[33]
understand why I had not attended a school for architecture or why I had not been given any instruction in this

[33]
art. Downcast, I left von Hansen's magnificent building on the Schillerplatz, dissatisfied with myself for the first time in my

[33]
life. What I had been told about my ability was like a bright flash of lightning which seemed to illuminate a

[32]
dissonance from which I had long suffered, but as yet I had not been able to give myself a clear account of its

[33]
wherefore and whyfore. A few days later I, too, knew that I would become an architect. However, the way was to

[33]
be an extremely difficult one, for all that which I had stubbornly neglected at the Realschule was to take its

[33]
vengeance now. The admission to the school of architecture of the Akademie was dependent on attendance at

[34]
the Polytechnic's building school, and admission to this was only possible after having received a certifi- cate of

[31]
maturity at a secondary school. I was without all this. In all human probability it seemed as though the

[33]
realization of my artist dreams was no longer possible. 28 MEIN KAMPF When, after my mother's death, I went to Vienna for the third

[32]
time and this time to remain there for many years, I had in the meantime regained my peace and my confi-

[33]
dence. My former obstinacy had returned and my goal was finally fixed before my eyes. I wanted to become

[33]
an architect, and one should not submit to obstacles but overcome them. And I would overcome these obstacles,

[33]
always bearing in mind my father's example, who, from being a poor village boy and a cobbler's apprentice, had made his

[32]
way up to the position of civil servant. Now I was on surer ground and the chances for the struggle were better; what

[32]
I then looked upon as the cruelty of Fate, I praise today as the wisdom of Providence. When the Goddess of

[32]
Misery took me into her arms more than once and threatened to Hitler's mother died on December 21, 1908, leaving him vir-

[33]
tually penniless. He left Vienna again in the spring of 1912. During the period intervening, he lived generally

[31]
in the Refuge for Men, in Vienna-Brigittenau, Information concerning his activities has been supplied by

[33]
various people who then knew him, primarily Rudolf Hanisch, a designer, whose memoirs have been evaluated

[33]
by Heiden. It is often difficult to determine whether these traditions are historically accurate,

[33]
since the Hitler of Vienna days was a bit of human flotsam who in addi- tion kept pretty much to himself. But we know that

[33]
he slept in a ward with other derelicts, that he was fed at the gate of the monastery in the Gumpendorferstrasse;

[32]
that in winter he earned an occasional schilling with a snow shovel; and that he drew little water-colors and sketches

[29]
whicii Hanisch peddled around at the humbler art shops. It has been proved that at the time he had Jewish

[34]
acquaintances and a number of Jewish friends. More important, however, is the fact that he spent much time in the cafes,

[33]
reading the newspapers constantly available there. He was never, then, a house painter, 1 but remained a young man with

[33]
a poor scholastic record who had time to read political journalism. YEARS OF STUDY AND SUFFERING 29 crush me, the will to

[32]
resist grew and was finally victorious. I owe much to the time in which I had learned to become hard and

[33]
also that I know now how to be hard. I praise it even more for having rescued me from the emptiness of an easy

[33]
life, that it took the milksop out of his downy nest and gave him Dame Sorrow for a foster mother, that it threw him out

[33]
into the world of misery and poverty, tnus making him acquainted with those for whom he was later to fight. During

[33]
this time my eyes were to be opened to two dan- gers which hitherto I had barely known by name; but I did not

[33]
perceive their terrible bearing upon the existence of the German race to its fullest extent. Vienna, the city

[33]
that to so many represents the idea of harmless gaiety, the festive place for merry-making, is to me only

[33]
the living memory of the most miserable time of my life. Even today it can waken only depressing thoughts

[33]
in my mind. The name of this Phaeacian city means five years of sorrow and misery. Five years in which I had to

[33]
make my living, first as a worker, then as a painter; a truly scanty living, for it was barely enough to appease

[33]
even my daily hunger. Hunger was then my faithful guard; he was the only friend who never left me, who shared everything

[33]
with me honestly. Every book I bought aroused his sympathy; a visit to the opera made him my companion

[32]
for days; it was a constant struggle with a pitiless friend. And yet, during this time, I learned as I had never learned

[33]
before. Apart from my interest in architecture and my visits to the opera for which I had to stint myself,

[33]
books were my only pleasure. At that time I read endlessly, but thoroughly. The spare time my work left to me I

[33]
spent entirely in study. So in a few years I built a foundation of knowledge from which I still draw nourishment today.

[32]
30 MEIN KAMPF But much more than that. At that time I formed an image of the world and a view of life which became the

[33]
granite foundation for my actions. I have had to add but little to that which I had learned then and I have had to

[32]
change nothing. On the contrary. Today it is my firm belief that in general all creative ideas appear in youth,

[31]
provided they are present at all. Here I distinguish between the wisdom of old age, which, as the result of the

[31]
experiences of a long life, is of value only in the form of a greater thoroughness and carefulness as

[33]
contrasted with the genius of youth whose inexhaustible fertility pours forth thoughts and ideas without being able to

[31]
digest them because of their abundance. Youth furnishes the building material and the plans for the future;

[33]
maturity takes and cuts the stones and constructs the building, provided the so-called wisdom of old age has not suf-

[33]
focated the genius of youth. The life I had known in my father's house showed little or no difference from that

[34]
of other people. I looked forward to each new day without a care and social problems were unknown to me. The surroundings

[33]
of my childhood were the circles of the bourgeoisie, a world which had but very few connections with the working classes. Though

[33]
at first sight Here Hitler describes very well the feeling which was later on to swell the ranks of the National-Socialist

[33]
Party. 'The bourgeois and peasant middle classes still constitute forty-five per cent of the total population of

[33]
Germany,' wrote Guenter Keiser in June, 1931. 'Today they have a mass movement, the beginnings of a program, the nucleus

[33]
of a leadership, a firm determination to have their way, a contagious activism, and a myth of the Third Reich. All these

[31]
things are necessary YEARS OF STUDY AND SUFFERING 31 it may seem absurd, yet the difference between these two,

[34]
unfavored as they are by economic conditions, is greater than one realizes. The reason for that which one could

[32]
almost call 'hostility' is the fact that a social class, which has only recently worked its way up from the level of

[32]
manual labor, fears to fall back into the old, but little esteemed, class, or at least fears being counted in with that class. In

[32]
addition many remember with disgust the misery existing in the lower class; the frequent brutality of their

[34]
daily social contacts; their own position in society, however small it may be, makes every contact with the state of

[33]
life and culture, which they in turn have left behind, unbearable. This explains why members of the higher social class can

[34]
frequently lower themselves to the humblest of their fellow outgrowths of historical development and cannot be disposed

[34]
of with an allusion to " demagogues." These masses are neither pro- nor anti-capitalistic. They are opposed

[32]
to certain especial aspects of high capitalism and to certain particular ways in which capitalism manifests

[34]
itself. Before the War . . . the handicrafts prospered, retail merchants profited by reason of expanding markets, and the peasants

[34]
were benefited by the rise in the standard of living. But today, inside the far narrower boundaries of the post-

[32]
War economy, the expansionist impulse latent in capitalism is carrying that capitalism into the dis-

[33]
tribution process. Department stores, branch concerns, ten- cent stores, direct sales by the manufacturer, etc., are now nor-

[33]
mal. Technical progress is also making it possible to organize on a wholesale, capitalistic basis

[32]
what until now have been typical handicraft industries, e.g., baking, butchering, tailoring, building. . . . Finally, the more

[30]
bureaucratic the corporative enterprise becomes, the more dependent does the status of its

[32]
white-collar employee become. That is the economic fundament upon which National Socialism rests. The middle

[32]
classes, the peasants, and the white-collar employees want the economic situation which existed in pre-War days: a

[32]
healthy 32 MEIN KAMPF beings with less embarrassment than seems possible to the 'upstarts/ For an upstart is anyone who, through his own

[33]
energy, works his way up from his previous social position to a higher one. Finally, this relentless struggle kills all

[34]
pity. One's own painful scramble for existence suffocates the feeling of sym- pathy for the misery of those left

[33]
behind. In this respect Fate took pity on me. By forcing me back into this world of poverty and uncertainty, a world

[33]
from which my father had emerged in the course of his own life, the blinders which a narrow bourgeois education had

[33]
given me were cast off. It was only now that I learned to know man; I learned to distinguish between sham or the brutal

[32]
appearance of human lives and their inner being. At the turn of the century Vienna was already a city with

[33]
unfavorable social conditions. Glamorous wealth and repulsive poverty were mixed in sharp contrast. In the heart

[33]
of the city and in the inner districts, one could well feel the pulse of a realm of fifty-two million people, for all its

[33]
doubtful charm, as a State of nationalities. Like a magnet, the Court with all its brilliant balance between big and

[31]
little industry, and between agricul- ture and industry as a whole. Therefore they are against "High

[33]
Capitalism" and "Marxism" alike. The second is held to encourage competition through fostering the development

[34]
of co-operatives, and accused, beyond that, of having helped the worker to climb the social ladder faster than the other

[34]
classes an insupportable fact.' (Cf. Neue Blaetter fuer den Sozial- ismus, Vol. II, nr. 6.) The list of Nazis who fell during the putsch

[33]
of 1923 is a striking demonstration of all this. It includes intellectuals, white-collar employees, students and artisans,

[33]
but no workers. And, of course, no 'capitalists.' YEARS OF STUDY AND SUFFERING 33 splendor attracted the wealth and intelligence

[32]
from the rest of the State. To this was added the strong centralizing policy of the Habsburg monarchy in itself. This

[32]
offered the only possibility of keeping this porridge of nations together. The result, however, was a

[31]
concentration of the higher and highest authorities in the capital and Court city. But Vienna was not only

[32]
politically and intellectually, but also economically, the center of the old Danubian mon-

[34]
archy. The host of high officers, civil servants, artists and savants was confronted by a still greater number of workers; the wealth

[33]
of aristocracy and commerce was contrasted with a dismal poverty. Thousands of unemployed loitered about in

[33]
front of the palaces in the Ringstrasse, and below that via triumphalis of the old Austria, in the twilight and the mud

[34]
of the canals, the homeless sought shelter. There was hardly any other German city where social questions could have been

[34]
studied better than in Vienna. But we must not deceive ourselves. This 'study' cannot be carried out from above. Those who

[32]
have never felt the grip of this murderous viper will never know its poisonous fangs. On the other hand, the result is

[32]
nothing but a superficial babbling or hypocritical sentimentality. Both are equally evil. The first,

[33]
because it never penetrates into the nucleus of the problem; the second, because it passes it by. I do not

[33]
know which is worse: the ignoring of the social misery by the majority of the fortunate, or by those who

[33]
have risen through their own efforts, as we see it daily, or the graciously patronizing attitudes of a certain part

[32]
of the fashionable world (both in skirts and trousers) whose 4 sympathy for the people 1 is at times as haughty as it is

[30]
obtrusive and tactless. These people do more harm than their brains, lacking in all instinct, are capable of

[33]
imagining. Therefore they are astonished to find that the response to their helpful social 'disposition' is

[33]
always nil and frequently causes indignation 34 MEIN KAMPF and antagonism ; this, of course, is taken to prove the people's

[32]
ingratitude. These minds fail to see that social work has nothing to do with this: that above all it must not expect

[33]
gratitude, since it should not deal out favors but restore rights. I was prevented from learning the social question in this

[33]
fashion. Because I was drawn into the confines of its suffering, it seemed to invite me not to 4 learn/ but rather

[33]
to use me for experimentation. It was none of its doing that the guinea pig recovered from the operation.

[32]
If I were to try now to describe chronologically my various stages of feeling, I could never fully

[33]
accomplish it; I wish to present only those impressions which seemed most important and frequently those most moving for

[34]
me, together with the few lessons they had given me then. In general, I did not find it very difficult to secure work,

[33]
because I was not a skilled laborer, but only a handy man, and I had to earn my living by doing occasional

[33]
work. I had the point of view of all those who wish to shake Europe's dust from their feet with the firm resolve to create a

[33]
new existence in the new world, to conquer a new home- land. Severed from all the paralyzing conceptions of class and

[33]
profession, of surrounding and tradition, they seize any opportunity which is offered, take any kind of work,

[32]
and gradually they come to realize that honest work is no disgrace no matter what it may be. So I, too, had

[33]
resolved to jump with both feet into the new world and to fight my way through. I soon learned that there is always work to be found

[33]
and that it is lost just as easily. YEARS OF STUDY AND SUFFERING 35 The uncertainty of earning one's daily bread seemed

[33]
to me to be the darkest side of my new life. Of course the 'skilled' worker is not dismissed quite so frequently

[32]
as the unskilled; but even he is not completely protected against such a fate. Instead of losing his income

[30]
because of a shortage of work, he is confronted with a lock- out or a strike of his own choosing. Here the

[34]
uncertainty of the daily income takes its most bitter revenge on the whole of economic life. The farmer's

[33]
boy who comes to town, attracted by easier work, be it real or imaginary, by the shorter working hours, but most of all

[30]
by the dazzling bright lights which the city sheds forth, is still accustomed to a certain security of in- come. He

[33]
usually only gives up his job if there is at least another in sight. Finally, the shortage of farm hands is

[33]
great and therefore the probability of long periods of unemployment is very slight. It is a mistake to

[33]
assume that the young people who come to town are of inferior material to those who continue making

[33]
their living by cultivating the soil. No, on the contrary: experience teaches that all migratory individuals

[32]
consist of energetic and healthy elements rather than the reverse. But among those 'immigrants' one counts not

[33]
only the American immigrant, but also the young farmer boy who makes up his mind to leave his native village

[33]
to come to town. He, too, is ready to chance an uncertain destiny. Frequently he brings a little money with him to

[31]
the big city so that he need not despair the very first day if he has had no luck in finding work for a pro- longed

[34]
period of time. But the situation is more difficult when shortly thereafter he has to give up the job that he found.

[33]
It is especially hard in winter, if not almost impossible, to find a new home. The first few weeks may go well enough.

[33]
He draws relief from the treasury of his union and he manages as best he can. But once he has spent his last cent and in

[32]
consequence of his long period of unemployment 36 MEIN KAMPF the treasury suspends its relief payments, then the distress

[33]
becomes great. Now he loiters about hungrily, he pawns or sells the last of his belongings, his clothes get shabbier day by day,

[33]
and he sinks into surroundings which, apart from the material misery he experiences, also poison his spirit. If

[31]
then he becomes homeless, and if this happens (as is often the case) in winter, then his misery becomes

[33]
acute. Finally he finds work of some kind. But the game repeats itself. He is hit the same way a second time,

[32]
a third time perhaps more severely, so that by and by he learns to endure the uncertainty of life with

[33]
indifference. Finally the repetition becomes a habit. Thus the entire concept of life of a fellow

[34]
who is otherwise industrious is demoralized and he is gradually transformed into a tool for those who

[33]
use him for their own ends. He has been out of work so many times through no fault of his own that one time more or less

[33]
no longer matters; it may be no longer a question of fighting for economic rights, but the destruction of political,

[33]
social, or cultural values in general. Though he may not like strikes, he is probably indifferent to them. I was

[33]
able to observe this process with my own eyes in thousands of cases. The longer I observed the game, the more my

[33]
aversion grew against the metropolis which so greedily sucked the people in only to destroy them. When they arrived,

[32]
they still belonged to their people; if they remained, they were lost to them. I had been knocked about by my life in the

[33]
metropolis in a similar manner and I was able to test the effect of such a fate on my own person and to

[33]
experience it spiritually. I saw one thing more there: the rapid change from working to unemployment and

[32]
vice versa; the repeated changes in income and expenditure destroyed in many people the desire for

[33]
saving and the realization of a balanced mode of living. The body apparently becomes accustomed to

[33]
good YEARS OF STUDY AND SUFFERING 37 living in times of plenty and to going hungry in times of need. Even in times of

[32]
better income, hunger often overthrows every resolve for a future balanced distribution, for, like

[33]
a perpetual mirage, hunger conjures up before the eyes of its victim visions of a life of abundance

[32]
and embellishes his dream until such a state of longing is achieved that it puts an end to all self-denial once

[31]
earnings and income permit it. This is the reason why a laborer, as soon as he has found work, forgets to budget

[34]
intelligently and becomes a spendthrift instead. This even leads to discarding the small household budget, because even

[33]
here wise distribution is neglected; in the beginning there may be enough for five days out of seven, later

[33]
only for three, finally hardly enough for one day, and at last the money is spent on the very first night. At home there

[33]
are often wife and children. Sometimes they are drawn into this sort of life, especially if the man treats them

[33]
well on the whole and loves them after a fashion. Then the weekly salary is spent jointly at home during the first two

[33]
or three days; they eat and drink as long as there is some money left, and the remaining days of the week are spent in hunger.

[33]
Then the wife sneaks away into the neigh- borhood and the surroundings, borrowing a little, making small debts at the grocer's so

[33]
that the remaining lean days can be endured. At noon they are all gathered around meager dishes and sometimes there

[33]
is nothing at all, and they await the next payday, talk of it and make plains, and while they are hungry, they already dream

[33]
of the good fortune to come. So, from their earliest days, the young children become familiar with misery. But things end

[33]
badly indeed when the man from the very start goes his own way and the wife, for the sake of her children, stands up against him.

[33]
Quarreling and nagging set in, and in the same measure in which the husband be- 38 MEIN KAMPF comes estranged from his wife,

[33]
he becomes familiar with alcohol. Now he is drunk every Saturday, and in her instinct of self-preservation

[34]
for herself and her children, the wife fights for the few pennies which she wangles from him, and frequently her sole opportunity

[33]
is on his way from the factory to the saloon. When he finally comes home on Sunday or Monday night, drunk and brutal,

[31]
but always without a last cent and penny, then God have mercy on the scenes which follow. I witnessed all of this

[33]
personally in hundreds of scenes and at the beginning with both disgust and indignation; but later I began to grasp

[31]
the tragic side and to understand the deeper reasons for their misery. Unfortunate victims of poor social

[32]
conditions. Almost sadder were the housing conditions in those days. The housing distress of the Viennese unskilled

[34]
workers was dreadful. Even now I shudder when I think of those pitiful dens, the shelters and lodging houses, those sinister

[33]
pictures of dirt and repugnant filth, and worse still. How would it be, and how will it be, when one day there pours forth the mass

[31]
of unleashed slaves out of these mis- erable dens, overflowing the other so thoughtless fellow creatures and

[33]
contemporaries! For this other world is thoughtless. Thoughtlessly it allows things to go as they will with- out foreseeing, in their

[33]
lack of intuition, that sooner or later Fate will take its revenge if Fate is not reconciled in time. How

[32]
grateful I am today to Providence which bade me go to this school ! There I could not sabotage what I dis-

[33]
liked. It educated me quickly and thoroughly. If I were not to despair of the people of my surroundings, I had

[32]
to learn to distinguish between their external ap- pearance and manners and the origins of their develop- ment. This was the

[33]
only way possible to bear all this YEARS OF STUDY AND SUFFERING 39 without despairing. What grew out of this unhappiness and

[33]
misery, of this filth and external decay, were no longer human beings, but the deplorable results of deplorable

[33]
laws; however, the pressure of my own hard and no less easy struggle for life prevented me from capitulating in

[31]
miserable sentimentality before the final results of this process of development. No, it must not be

[34]
interpreted like that. I saw then that only a twofold way could lead to the goal for the improvement of these conditions:

[32]
A deep feeling of social responsibility towards the estab- lishment of better foundations for our development,

[33]
combined with the ruthless resolution to destroy the incurable social tumors. Just as Nature concentrates, not

[33]
on safeguarding that which exists, but on breeding the coming generation as the representative of the species, so

[34]
in human life it is less a question of artificially cultivating the existing evils which, human nature being

[34]
what it is, would be ninety-nine per cent impossible, but rather to assure healthier paths for future development

[33]
from the start. Already during my struggle for life in Vienna, it had become clear to me that: Social activity must

[33]
never see its task in the sentimental conception of welfare work which is as ridiculous as it is futile, but

[31]
rather in the abolition of those fundamental defects in the organization of our economic and

[33]
cultural life which must lead to, or at least encourage, the degradation of the individual. The difficulty

[33]
of applying the most extreme and brutal means against the criminality endangering the State is to be found, above

[31]
all, in the prevailing uncertainty concern- ing the inner motives or causes of the symptoms of our time. This

[30]
uncertainty is only too deeply rooted in one's own 40 MEIN KAMPF feeling of being guilty of such tragedies of

[31]
demoralization; it paralyzes every sincere and firm decision, thus adding to the wavering and

[33]
half-heartedness with which even the most urgent measures of self-preservation are applied. Only when the time comes

[32]
when a race is no longer over- shadowed by the consciousness of its own guilt, then it will find internal peace and

[33]
external strength to cut down regardlessly and brutally the wild shoots, and to pull up the weeds. These pages indicate a

[33]
possible debt to Karl Freiherr von Vogelsang, one of the founders of the Christian Social Movement in Austria, and one of

[33]
the editors of the journal Vaterland. A conservative nobleman of Prussian ancestry, he had been received

[33]
into the Catholic Church by Bishop Emanuel von Ketteler, the first German Catholic apostle of social reform, and

[32]
had then migrated to Vienna. His group taught that the rights of all take precedence over the rights of the few (which Hitler

[32]
phrases, Gemeinnutz geht vor Eigennutz), demanded legislation to protect the worker against exploitation (a precept

[31]
developed later on by Franz Hitze and others in Germany into a code of labor protection laws), and

[34]
sponsored a type of economic organization akin in some ways to the kind of 'corporative society'

[30]
endorsed in the Papal Encyclical, Quadragesima Anno (i.e., not the 'corporative state' of

[31]
Italian Fascism). Of especial concern to Vogelsang were the moral consequences of the liberalistic

[32]
economy intemperance, improvidence, etc. He also attacked the taking of interest and the grip on

[33]
industry exercised by the 'money lenders/ (Cf. the biography of Vogelsang by Wiard Klopp, Vienna, 1930.) A more modern

[32]
and very much more radical statement of the same views can be found in Economia Perennis, by Anton

[32]
Orel (Graz, 1928). It seems probable that Hitler saturated himself at one time with Vaterland editorials, which

[32]
afford interesting parallels to what he writes here. But he subordinates the Vogelsang teaching to hifc own

[33]
chauvinistic Pan-German outlook. YEARS OF STUDY AND SUFFERING 41 Since the Austrian State hardly knew social justice and

[33]
social laws, its weakness in fighting even the worst excrescences was glaringly obvious. I do not know what shocked me more

[32]
at that time: the economic distress of my erstwhile comrades, their ethical and moral crudity, or the low

[34]
level of their spiritual development. Does not our bourgeoisie rise in moral indignation when it hears from the lips

[33]
of some miserable tramp that he doesn't care whether he is German or not, that he feels at home anywhere, as long

[33]
as he has enough to live on? This lack of 'national pride' is deeply deplored and the horror at such an attitude

[33]
is expressed in strong terms. But how many people ask themselves the question, what in their own case was the reason for their own

[33]
better way of thinking? How many are there who understand the numerous memories of the greatness of the fatherland,

[32]
of the nation, in all fields of cultural and artistic endeavor which, when summoned up, justify their pride in being

[33]
privileged to belong to such a blessed nation? How many know how dependent their pride in their country is upon their

[33]
knowledge of its greatness in all these domains? f Does our bourgeoisie realize to what a ridiculously small extent

[33]
this assumption of pride in the fatherland is transmitted to the 'people'? We cannot excuse ourselves by saying' it is

[33]
not different in the other countries'; that 'in spite of this' the workers there stand up for their nationality. Even if

[31]
this were so, it could not serve as the excuse of our own negligence. But it is not so. What we always term

[33]
'chauvinistic' education, that of the French nation, for example, is nothing but the 42 MEIN KAMPF stress upon France's greatness in

[33]
all fields of culture or, as the French say, 'civilization.' The young Frenchman is not educated with an objective, but

[32]
a subjective, point of view, which we can only understand as far as the political or cultural greatness of his

[33]
country is concerned. This education should be limited to general and im- portant points of view, which, if necessary,

[31]
should be impressed on the minds and feelings of the people by constant repetition. But to our negative sin of

[34]
omission, we add the positive sin of destroying the little the individual is lucky enough to learn in school. The rats

[34]
of the political poisoning of our nation gnaw away the little that is left in the hearts and the memories of the masses,

[32]
if misery and distress have not already done so. Now let us imagine the following: In a basement

[33]
apartment of two stuffy rooms lives a worker's family of seven people. Among the five children there is a boy,

[33]
let us say, of three. This is the age at which a child becomes conscious of his first impressions. In many intelligent people,

[33]
traces of these early memories are found even in old age. The smallness and the overcrowding of the rooms do not

[34]
create favorable conditions. Quarreling and nagging often arise because of this. In such circumstances people do

[33]
not live with one another, but on top of one another. Every argument, even the most unimportant, which

[30]
in a larger apartment would take care of itself for the reason that one could step aside, leads to a

[31]
neverending, disgusting quarrel. Among the children this does not usually matter; they often quarrel under such

[33]
circumstances and forget completely and quickly. But when the parents fight almost daily, their brutality leaves nothing

[31]
to the imagination; then the results of such visual education must slowly but inevitably become

[33]
apparent in the little ones. Those who are not familiar with such con' YEARS OF STUDY AND SUFFERING 43 ditions can

[33]
hardly imagine the results, especially when the mutual differences express themselves in the form of brutal

[33]
attacks on the part of the father towards the mother or to assaults due to drunkenness. The poor little boy, at the age of

[33]
six, senses things which would make even a grown-up person shudder. Morally infected, undernourished, his poor little head

[33]
covered with lice, the young 'citizen' wanders off to the elementary school. He may learn to read and to write only

[32]
with the greatest difficulty, and nothing more. Learning at home is out of the question. On the contrary. In front of the

[32]
children, father and mother often speak about school and the teachers in a manner one cannot possibly repeat, and are

[33]
inclined them; instead of placing the spanking some sense into The other things the litt tend to further his r single good shred

[33]
is left tution is left unattacked; the head of the State, be be it the State or society, abused, everything

[33]
is pulled into the filth of a depraved of fourteen, the young lad is dismissed from school, it is difficult to say which is

[32]
worse: his unbelievable ignorance as far as knowledge and ability are concerned, or the biting

[33]
impudence of his behavior, combined with an immorality which makes one's hair stand on end, considering

[32]
his age. But what place in society will the young man for almost nothing is sacred to him; having learned nothing of

[33]
greatness, he but guesses and knows all the meanness of life now take when he enters into life? The three-year-old child has now

[33]
become a youth of fifteen who despises all authority. Familiar with nothing things about knee and them. do not Not

[34]
a insti- up to such, ing is manner at the age 44 MEIN KAMPF other than dirt and filth, the young fellow knows nothing that could rouse his

[33]
enthusiasm for higher things. But now for the first time he enters the high school of life. Now the same mode of living,

[32]
which he learned from his father during childhood, begins. Now he loiters about, and God only knows when he comes home; for

[32]
a change he may even beat the poor creature who was once his mother, curses God and the world, and finally, for some

[31]
reason or other, he is sentenced to a reformatory. There he receives the final polish. But his dear

[33]
bourgeois fellow men are truly astonished at the lack of 'national' enthusiasm in this young 'citizen.' They see

[33]
how theaters and movies, worthless literature and tabloid newspapers pour poison into the masses by the bucketful, and

[33]
are surprised by their low 'morality,' their national 'indifference.' As though movie sentimentality, tabloid

[32]
newspapers, and similar rubbish could lay the foundation for a realization of national greatness! To say nothing of the

[33]
previous education of the individual. What I had never guessed before, I learned to understand now: quickly

[32]
and thoroughly. The question of the nationalization of a people is first of all a question of creating sound social

[32]
conditions as the fundamental possibility for educating the individual. For only those who, through

[33]
education and schooling, get to know the cultural and economic, and above all the political, greatness of their

[33]
own country, can and will be proud of being allowed to call themselves members of this nation. Moreover, I can only fight for

[33]
what I love; only love what I can respect; only respect what I know. Now that my interest for the social question was

[32]
awakened, I began to study it in all thoroughness. It was a YEARS OF STUDY AND SUFFERING 45 new and hitherto

[33]
unknown world which opened itself before my eyes. In 1909-10 my own situation had changed somewhat, as I no longer had

[31]
to earn my daily bread as an unskilled worker. I worked independently as a modest draftsman and painter of

[33]
aquarelles. Though this was bitter as far as my earnings were concerned it was really barely enough for a living

[33]
it was good for the career I had chosen. Now I was no longer dead tired as formerly when coming home from my work in

[33]
the evening, unable to open a book without falling asleep after a short time. The work I was doing went hand in hand

[32]
with my future profession. I was also master of my own time and I was able to arrange it better than

[33]
before. I painted in order to earn a living and I learned for enjoyment. Thus I was enabled to supplement my

[32]
practical experiences concerning social problems with the necessary theory. I studied almost every book on the

[33]
subject I could get hold of, and for the rest I was steeped in thoughts of my own. I believe that those who knew me then must have

[32]
thought me a queer fellow. But with all this it was natural that I devoted myself enthusiastically to my

[33]
passion for architecture. Along with music, architecture appeared to me to be the queen of the arts: under

[34]
such circumstances my occupation with it was not 'work,' but the greatest happiness. I was able to read or draw late into

[33]
the night; I was never tired. Thus my belief, that my beautiful dream of the future would become reality, perhaps

[31]
only after many years, was strengthened. I was firmly convinced that some day I would make a name as an

[33]
architect. 1 did not place much importance on the fact that in addition I took the greatest interest in everything

[33]
con- 46 MEIN KAMPF nected with politics. On the contrary; to me this was the natural duty of every thinking human being

[33]
anyway. He who had no understanding for this simply had no right to criticize or to complain, Here, too, I also

[34]
read and learned a lot. But by 'reading' I may possibly mean something entirely different from the great average of

[33]
our so-called 'intelligentsia/ I know people who endlessly 'read' a lot, book after book, letter for letter, yet I would

[32]
not call them 'well read.' Of course, they possess a wide 'knowledge,' but their intellect does not know how to distribute and

[33]
register the material gathered. They lack the ability to distinguish in a book that which is of value and that

[32]
which is of no value to them; to keep the one in mind forever, and to Hitler was never more candid than in these

[33]
pages, which must not be read, however, as a mere defense against the charge of ignorance. The educational

[33]
program of National Socialism is based upon the theory that too much reading, too much familiarity with different

[33]
points of view, fosters criticism, and therewith disrupts the unity with which the nation must face the problem of war. Hitler's

[33]
declaration that he read in order to fortify ideas he already held is, whether true in fact or not (the point has been

[30]
raised by various biographers), highly important because it happens to coincide with a trend in German

[33]
pedagogical thought which, related in a sense to Plato and Fichte, has led to the 'Spartan ' ideal now dominant in

[33]
German higher education and handed down thence to the elementary school. Aurel Kolnai, in his War against the West,

[33]
summarizes the ideas of one spokesman for that trend Professor Alfred Baeumler, latterly Nazi appointee to

[33]
the University of Berlin : 'We set ourselves the task of breeding types, not "individualities." To the ideal

[33]
of universality (many-sidedness) we oppose efficient and disciplined unity; to harmony, force;

[31]
to refinement, greatness and simplicity; to complicated inwardness, an atti- YEARS OF STUDY AND SUFFERING 47

[32]
overlook, if possible, the other, instead of carrying it with them as so much unnecessary ballast. Reading, further-

[32]
more, is not a purpose in itself, but a means to an end. It should serve, first of all, to fill in the frame which Is

[31]
formed by the talents and abilities of the individual; thus reading has to furnish the tools and the building

[34]
material which the individual needs for his profession, no matter whether it serves only the primitive purpose

[33]
of making a living or whether it presents a higher vocation; secondly, reading has to give a general picture

[31]
of the world. In both cases it is necessary that the content of what has been read is registered in the mind, not

[33]
according to the sequence in the book, or according to the sequence in which the books are read, but that, like the small

[33]
pieces of a mosaic, it is put into the place where it belongs, thus tude of steadfastness. The utmost dignity is

[33]
accorded to bodily training, not for reasons of health, but as a direct expression of the preferred "mode of life."

[30]
. . . Amidst a culture that has become too inward, too spiritual, athletics restore the principle of

[33]
"visibleness." Our conditions of life must be simplified; we shall have to resort to the elemental forces in our

[33]
people. 9 Concerning Hitler's own intellectual equipment, the following objective statement made by Professor

[31]
Hans E. Friedrich in 1931 seems readable and interesting today: 'He is an orator, an organizer, a practical

[31]
psychologist; and in addition he possesses physical courage, is unusually able to tap his own

[33]
enthusiasm, and has a fund of glowing personal emotions. But in order to become a leader in the sense that

[32]
Pericles and Napoleon were leaders, he would have to overcome his lack of that which gives a man in supreme

[32]
command personal confidence in himself calmness of analysis (above all where he himself is concerned),

[33]
hardness to the point of rigor, ability to face decisions of importance with an absolutely open mind,

[33]
unemotional seriousness in the act of looking things over, and that measure of inner objectivity that gives

[33]
a man independence and stubborn per' 48 MEIN KAMPF helping to complete the general picture of the world in the mind of

[33]
the reader. Otherwise, the result will be a terrible muddle of things learned, and this is not only of little value,

[34]
but it also makes its unfortunate possessor presumptuous and vain. For now he thinks in all sincerity that he is

[30]
'educated'; he thinks he knows life and has knowledge; whereas in reality, with each new contribution to this

[32]
'education,' he is more and more estranged from the world, till frequently he ends in a sanatorium, or as

[34]
a 'politician' in parliament. Such a person will never succeed in finding, in an hour of need, the right thing in the medley

[33]
of his 'knowledge,' as his mental ballast is not arranged according to the course of life, but in the order in which

[32]
he has read the books and in which their contents are arranged in his mind. If Fate in his daily demands of life were

[33]
always to remind him of the right use of that which he has once read, then it would also have to remind him of each book

[33]
and the page number or else the poor devil in all eternity would never find the right thing. But since it does not do

[33]
this, these extraordinarily wise men are terribly embarrassed at critical moments and seek frantically

[34]
for analogies, and then, of course, they are dead certain to chance upon the wrong recipe. If this were not so, we should

[33]
not be able to understand the political achievements of our learned heroes in the highest government positions,

[30]
unless we decided that they sistence. In addition Hitler seems to lack that elementary knowledge of

[33]
economic and political situations and of history which a leader must have at his command, though he need not

[32]
drag about with him a ballast of information.' (Cf. Die christ- Kche Well, Vol. XLV, nr. 9.) The practical consequences of Hitler's attitude

[32]
towards education will be discussed later on. YEARS OF STUDY AND SUFFERING 49 had pathological inclinations

[33]
instead of infamous villainy. When studying a book, a magazine, or a pamphlet, those who master this art of reading

[33]
will immediately pick out that which in their opinion is suitable for them because it serves their purposes or

[33]
is generally worth knowing and therefore to be remembered forever. As soon as the knowledge so gained finds

[33]
its due place in the one or the other existing picture of this or that thing which imagination has created, it

[33]
will act as a corrective or as a supple- ment, thus enhancing its truth or its clarity. When life suddenly presents

[34]
some question to be examined or an- swered, then this manner of reading will immediately take the already

[33]
existing picture as a standard, and from it it will take all the single contributions to this question which have been

[32]
collected during past decades, and submit them to the intellect for examination and reconsideration till the

[32]
question is clarified or answered. It is only in this fashion that reading is of use and has meaning. A public

[33]
speaker, for instance, who does not in this way supply his intelligence with the necessary support will never, in case

[32]
of contradiction, be able to present his opinion convincingly, no matter whether it may correspond a thousand

[33]
times to truth or reality. His memory will shamefully desert him in all discussions; he will neither find supporting

[32]
arguments for his contentions, nor will he find such with which to confound his adversary. This may be all very well if it

[33]
only concerns a public speaker and only his own personal reputation is involved, but things take a bad turn when

[33]
Fate appoints such a 'know-it-all' who is really a know-nothing, the head of a State. From my early youth I took pains to read

[33]
in the right manner, and in this I was happily assisted by my memory and intellect. And in this light the time I

[32]
spent in Vienna was especially fruitful and useful. The experiences of 50 MEIN KAMPF everyday life gave me the

[33]
stimulus for my renewed study of various problems. As I was thus finally enabled to substantiate theory

[33]
with reality, to examine theory in its relation to reality. I was spared being suffocated in theories and

[32]
from becoming shallow through reality. Apart from the social problem, two other very important questions were also

[33]
experienced in daily life, decisive and stimulating for a thorough theoretical study. Who knows when I might

[33]
have plunged into studying the doctrines and ideas of Marxism if that period had not virtually pushed my nose

[33]
into this problem ! What I knew of Social Democracy during my youth was precious little and mostly wrong. I was secretly

[32]
glad to know that it fought for general suffrage and the secret ballot. My reason already told me that this would lead to the

[33]
weakening of the Habsburg regime which I hated so much. In the conviction that the State on the Danube could never

[32]
be preserved unless the German nationality was sacrificed, and that even paying the price of the gradual

[33]
Slavicizing of the German element Faithful to its internationalist program, Socialism made every effort

[33]
to organize Slav and German workers in a common front. When after the War a constitutional assembly convened

[34]
in Austria, Viktor Adler declared: 'We extend fraternal greetings to our Slavic and Romanic brethren, and are ready

[33]
to unite with the peoples that are our neighbors in a free federation, if they so desire. Otherwise German

[33]
Austria will be compelled to join Germany as a specially constituted state inside the German federation

[30]
of states. The position of the small Austrian National Socialist Party at that time was: it immediately

[33]
repudiated every thought of a common association with the peoples comprising the old Habsburg Empire, and de-

[33]
manded union with Germany. YEARS OF STUDY AND SUFFERING 51 would in no way have guaranteed the survival of the State,

[33]
as it was doubtful if the Slavic nationality could have ac- complished this, I therefore welcomed every

[33]
development which in my opinion would lead to the breakdown of the State which had pronounced the death sentence on ten mil-

[34]
lion German people. The more the linguistic tohuwabohu [Hebrew Genesis 1:2 meaning chaos, confusion, hubbub] ate into

[32]
and tore at the parliament, the sooner would come the hour of doom of this Babylonian realm, and with it, the day of

[33]
freedom for my German-Austrian people. Only in this way could the Anschluss with the old motherland be achieved. I rather

[32]
liked the activity of Social Democracy. The fact that it finally endeavored to raise the standard of

[33]
living of the working class in those days my innocent mind was foolish enough to believe this seemed to speak rather in

[33]
its favor than against it. But what disgusted me most was its hostile attitude towards the fight for the preservation

[33]
of the German nationality, its pitiful courtship of the Slav 'comrades,' who readily accepted this wooing as long

[34]
as it meant practical allowances, but were otherwise arrogantly aloof, thus paying the intruding beggars the wages

[31]
they deserved. At the age of seventeen I had rarely heard the word 'Marxism,' whereas 'Social Democracy' and

[29]
'Socialism' were identical ideas to me. Here, too, the hand of Fate had to open my eyes to this

[33]
unprecedented betrayal of the people. Till then I had known the Social Democratic Party only from a spectator's point

[33]
of view, on the occasion of various mass demonstrations, without having the slightest insight into the mentality of its

[30]
followers or the meaning of its doctrine; but now I suddenly came into contact with the products of its

[33]
education and view of life; I now achieved in a few months what otherwise might have taken decades: 52 MEIN KAMPF

[33]
the realization that it was a pestilential whore covered with the mask of social virtue and brotherly love, and that

[33]
mankind must rid the world of her as soon as possible, or otherwise the world might easily be rid of mankind. While I

[33]
was employed as a building worker, my first encounter with Social Democracy took place. It was not a very enjoyable

[31]
experience from the begin- ning. My clothes were still in good shape, my language was refined, and my manners

[33]
reserved. I still was so preoc- cupied with my own affairs that I did not bother much with my surroundings. I looked for work to

[33]
prevent me from starving, thus hoping to find the possibility for further training, however slow it might be. Perhaps I would

[34]
not have troubled about my new surroundings at all if something had not happened on the third or fourth day which forced me to

[33]
take a stand. I was asked to join the organization. My knowledge of unions was nil at that time. I would not have

[33]
been able to prove the suitability or the uselessness of their existence. When I was told that I had to join,

[33]
I refused. I gave as my reason that I did not understand the whole affair and that, on the whole, I would not let

[33]
myself be forced into anything. The first was perhaps the reason why I was not thrown out immediately. Perhaps they

[32]
hoped that in a few days I would be converted or would give in. In any event, they were thoroughly mis- taken.

[33]
After two weeks 1 was not allowed to wait any longer, even if I had wanted to. During these two weeks I had become

[33]
better acquainted with my surroundings, so that no power on earth could have induced me to join an organization

[33]
whose representatives had meanwhile shown themselves in so unfavorable a light. The first few days I was annoyed.

[33]
At noon some of the men went into the nearest public houses, while others remained on the spot where they in YEARS OF

[33]
STUDY AND SUFFERING 53 most cases ate a very frugal meal. These were the married ones whose wives brought them their

[31]
noonday soup in battered dishes. Their number grew steadily towards the end of the week; why, I knew only later. Now

[31]
politics were discussed. I drank my bottle of milk and ate my piece of bread somewhere on the side,

[32]
cautiously studying my new sur- roundings or pondering over my miserable fate. Yet I heard more than enough ;

[32]
also, more than once it seemed to me as if they approached me intentionally in order to draw me out. In

[33]
any case, what I heard served to annoy me extremely. Everything was rejected: the nation as an in- vention

[33]
of the 'capitalistic' classes how often was I to hear just this word!; the country as the instrument of the bourgeoisie

[33]
for the exploitation of the workers; the authority of the law as a means of suppressing the proletariat; the school

[34]
as an institution for bringing up slaves as well as slave drivers; religion as a means for doping the people destined

[32]
for exploitation; morality as a sign of sheepish patience, and so forth. Nothing remained that was not dragged down

[32]
into the dirt and the filth of the lowest depths. In the beginning I tried to keep silent. But finally I could hold back no

[33]
longer. I began to take part and to contradict. But soon I realized that this was entirely hopeless as long as

[33]
I did not possess at least a certain knowledge of the subjects under argument. Thus I began to look into the sources

[32]
from which the others drew their so-called wis- dom. I studied book after book, pamphlet after pamphlet. On the job the arguments

[33]
often became heated. Being daily better informed about their knowledge than my ad- versaries themselves, I argued

[34]
till finally one day they applied the one means that wins the easiest victory over reason: terror and force. Some of

[32]
the leaders of the other side gave me the choice of either leaving the job at once 54 MEIN KAMPF or of being thrown from the

[32]
scaffold. As I was alone and resistance seemed hopeless, I preferred to follow the former, enriched by

[31]
a new experience. I went away, disgusted, but at the same time I was so stirred that it would have been

[32]
impossible for me to turn my back on the whole affair. No; after my first indignation had passed, my stubbornness

[33]
gained the upper hand. I firmly resolved to return to another construction job. This decision was encouraged by

[33]
Poverty, who, after I had eaten up my small savings in the course of a few weeks, clasped me in her unfeeling arms. Now

[33]
I had to, whether I wanted to or not. The game began again from the beginning, only to end in a similar way

[33]
as it had the first time. My mind was tormented by the question: Are these still human beings, worthy of being part of a great

[33]
nation? A torturing question it was; if answered in the affirma- tive, then the fight for a nation is no longer worth

[30]
the trouble and the sacrifices which the better ones have to make for such outcasts; if the answer is in the

[31]
negative, then our nation is poor in human beings. During these days of pondering and reflection I watched with

[32]
uneasiness the mass of those who could no longer be counted as belonging to the nation grow into a threatening

[32]
legion. How different were my feelings when one day I stared at the endless columns of a mass demonstration of

[32]
Viennese workers, marching by in rows of four! For nearly two hours I stood there and watched with bated breath this terrible

[33]
human dragon creeping slowly along. Depressed and anxious I left the square and walked home. On my way I saw in

[32]
a tobacco shop a copy of the Arbeiterzeitung, the mouthpiece of the old Austrian Social Democracy. It was

[32]
also available in a cheap coffee shop where I sometimes used to go to read the newspapers; but so far

[31]
I had not been able to bring myself to look at this wretched paper YEARS OF STUDY AND SUFFERING 55 for more than two

[32]
minutes, for the effect of its language on me was like that of spiritual vitriol. Under the de- pressing

[33]
influence of the demonstration, an inner voice now urged me to buy the paper for once and to read it thoroughly.

[30]
I did this in the evening, though I sometimes had to fight down the rage rising in me because of this

[32]
concentrated solution of lies. The daily reading of the Social Democratic newspapers enabled me better to

[33]
study the inner meaning of these ideas than all of the theoretic literature put together. What a difference

[32]
between the phrases about liberty, beauty, and dignity, the delusive swaggering which at- tempted to express the

[32]
deepest wisdom, the disgusting and humane morality everything was written with an iron- faced prophetic

[32]
certainty contained in the theoretic literature and this doctrine of salvation of a new mankind in a

[33]
daily press which did not shrink from any baseness whatsoever, and which operated with the most brutal forces of calumny

[33]
and a virtuosity for lying that was out- rageous! The one is intended for the innocent simpletons of the middle,

[32]
and, of course, the upper, classes of the 4 intelligentsia; the other for the masses. For me the concentration on the

[33]
literature and press of this organization and its doctrine was my return to my people. What I first had looked

[34]
upon as an impassable chasm now spurred me on to a greater love for my country than ever before. Aware of

[32]
the terrible workings of this poison, only a fool would condemn the victim. The more independent I be- came in the

[31]
following years, the greater the distance, the wider were my eyes opened to the inner causes of the Social

[33]
Democratic successes. Now I understood the brutal demand to subscribe only to red newspapers, to attend only

[33]
red meetings, to read only red books, and so on. My 56 MEIN KAMPF eyes saw with plastic clarity the enforced result of this doctrine

[33]
of intolerance. The psyche of the great masses is not receptive to half measures or weakness. Like a woman,

[32]
whose psychic feeling is influenced less by abstract reasoning than by an undefinable, sentimental longing for

[33]
complementary strength, who will submit to the strong man rather than dominate the weakling, thus the masses love the ruler

[33]
rather than the suppliant, and inwardly they are far more satisfied by a doctrine which tolerates no rival

[32]
than by the grant of liberal freedom; they often feel at a loss what to do with it, and even easily feel themselves

[31]
deserted. They neither realize the impudence with which they are spiritually terrorized, nor the out-

[33]
rageous curtailment of their human liberties, for in no way does the delusion of this doctrine dawn on them. Thus they see

[32]
only the inconsiderate force, the brutality and the aim of its manifestations to which they finally

[31]
always submit. Social Democracy is confronted by a doctrine of greater truthfulness, carried out with the same

[33]
brutality, then the latter will be victorious, though the struggle may be hard. Before two years had elapsed, the doctrine

[33]
and the technical tools of Social Democracy had become clear to me. I understood the infamous mental terror which

[33]
this movement exercised on the population which could neither morally nor psychically resist such attacks; Social

[33]
De- mocracy, at a given signal, directs a bombardment of lies This statement is of cardinal importance, so that

[33]
an analysis of the underlying thought development is suggested. Hitler, conscious of belonging to a higher social

[33]
caste than his fellow- workers after all, his father had spent a lifetime struggling to rise instinctively retreats

[31]
from the idea of accepting solidarity with them. They persist in their proselyting efforts. YEARS OF STUDY AND

[33]
SUFFERING 57 and calumnies towards the adversary who seemed most dangerous, till finally the nerves of those who had

[32]
been attacked give out and they, for the sake of peace, bow down to the hated enemy. But the fools will not find peace

[33]
after all. The play begins again and is so often repeated till the fear of the mad dog paralyzes them by suggestion.

[33]
As Social Democracy knows, from its own experience, the value of strength, it assaults mostly those in whom it scents a trace

[32]
of that rare material. On the other hand, it praises every weakling of the other side, sometimes cau-

[33]
tiously, sometimes more boldly, according to the mental qualities they appreciate or suspect. It is less

[33]
afraid of a powerless, irresolute genius than of a strong man of even moderate intelligence. Most

[33]
of all it recommends those who are weaklings in mind and power. It knows how to create the appearance as though this were

[32]
the only way in which peace could be maintained; yet relentlessly it conquers one position after another, An

[32]
argument ensues; and appalled by their revolutionary attitudes, he loses his temper. There is a fight.

[33]
Afterward he can only think bitterly of how these large groups of Germans are being weaned away from ardent zeal for

[33]
the expansion of the German nation and made, by persistent regimentation and propaganda, to accept the creed of

[33]
international class warfare. The trend could not, he decided, be halted with reasoning or evidence. Only a group

[32]
still more disciplined, still more ruthless in its methods, would after a bitter struggle be able to suppress such a

[33]
movement. These early reflections colored his later conduct. The Social Democracy of post-War years in Germany

[34]
was not revolutionary but reformist. It was actuated by a deep and intelligent patriotism. But he refused

[33]
to concede that his Vienna impressions needed revision. 56 MEIN KAMPF eyes saw with plastic clarity the enforced result of

[33]
this doctrine of intolerance, <The psyche of the great masses is not receptive to half measures or weakness. Like

[32]
a woman, whose psychic feeling is influenced less by abstract reasoning than by an undefinable, sentimental

[33]
longing for complementary strength, who will submit to the strong man rather than dominate the weakling, thus the masses love the

[33]
ruler rather than the suppliant, and inwardly they are far more satisfied by a doctrine which tolerates no

[31]
rival than by the grant of liberal freedom ; they often feel at a loss what to do with it, and even easily feel

[34]
themselves deserted. They neither realize the impudence with which they are spiritually terrorized, nor the out-

[33]
rageous curtailment of their human liberties, for in no way does the delusion of this doctrine dawn on them. Thus they see

[32]
only the inconsiderate force, the brutality and the aim of its manifestations to which they finally

[31]
always submit. Social Democracy is confronted by a doctrine of greater truthfulness, carried out with the same

[33]
brutality, then the latter will be victorious, though the struggle may be hard. Before two years had elapsed, the doctrine

[33]
and the technical tools of Social Democracy had become clear to me. I understood the infamous mental terror which

[33]
this movement exercised on the population which could neither morally nor psychically resist such attacks; Social

[33]
De- mocracy, at a given signal, directs a bombardment of lies This statement is of cardinal importance, so that

[33]
an analysis of the underlying thought development is suggested. Hitler, conscious of belonging to a higher social

[33]
caste than his fellow- workers after all, his father had spent a lifetime struggling to rise instinctively retreats

[31]
from the idea of accepting solidarity with them. They persist in their proselyting efforts. YEARS OF STUDY AND

[33]
SUFFERING 57 and calumnies towards the adversary who seemed most dangerous, till finally the nerves of those who had

[32]
been attacked give out and they, for the sake of peace, bow down to the hated enemy. But the fools will not find peace

[33]
after all. The play begins again and is so often repeated till the fear of the mad dog paralyzes them by suggestion.

[33]
As Social Democracy knows, from its own experience, the value of strength, it assaults mostly those in whom it scents a trace

[32]
of that rare material. On the other hand, it praises every weakling of the other side, sometimes cau-

[33]
tiously, sometimes more boldly, according to the mental qualities they appreciate or suspect. It is less

[33]
afraid of a powerless, irresolute genius than of a strong man of even moderate intelligence. Most

[33]
of all it recommends those who are weaklings in mind and power. It knows how to create the appearance as though this were

[32]
the only way in which peace could be maintained; yet relentlessly it conquers one position after another, An

[32]
argument ensues; and appalled by their revolutionary attitudes, he loses his temper. There is a fight.

[33]
Afterward he can only think bitterly of how these large groups of Germans are being weaned away from ardent zeal for

[33]
the expansion of the German nation and made, by persistent regimentation and propaganda, to accept the creed of

[33]
international class warfare. The trend could not, he decided, be halted with reasoning or evidence. Only a group

[32]
still more disciplined, still more ruthless in its methods, would after a bitter struggle be able to suppress such a

[33]
movement. These early reflections colored his later conduct. The Social Democracy of post- War yeans in Germany

[34]
was not revolutionary but reformist. It was actuated by a deep and intelligent patriotism. But he refused

[33]
to concede that his Vienna impressions needed revision. 58 MEIN KAMPF either by quiet pressure or by downright robbery

[31]
at mo- ments when public attention is occupied with other things and does not wish to be disturbed or because it

[33]
considers the affair too trifling to be dealt with and does not wish to provoke the adversary anew. These tactics are

[33]
based on an exact calculation of all human weaknesses; their result must lead to success with almost mathematical

[33]
certainty, unless the other side also learns to fight poison gas with poison gas. Weak natures have to be told that it

[32]
simply means 'to be or not to be/ The importance of physical terror against the individual and the masses

[32]
also became clear to me. Here, too, we find exact calculation of the psychological effect. The terror in the

[33]
workshops, in the factory, in the assembly hall, and on occasion of mass demonstrations will always be accompanied by

[33]
success as long as it is not met by an equally great force of terror. Then, of course, the party will cry havoc; scornful

[33]
of State authority it will now call for it, so that in most cases and in the general disorder, it will reach the goal

[31]
that is, it will find some idiot of a higher official who, in the stupid hope of in this way gaining, for the

[33]
future, perhaps the favor of the dreaded enemy, helps to break the adversary of this universal plague. Only

[31]
those who know the soul of a people, not from books but from life, can understand the impression such success makes on the

[34]
sensibilities of the masses of adherents and adversaries as well. While in the ranks of their ad- herents the victory

[32]
gained is looked upon as the triumph of the right in its own cause, the beaten adversary in most cases despairs

[33]
entirely of the success of all further re- sistance. The closer I became acquainted with the methods ofYEARS

[32]
OF STUDY AND SUFFERING 59 physical terror, the more I asked for forgiveness from those hundreds of thousands who

[33]
succumb to it. I owe most of all to that period of suffering that it alone has given my people back to me,

[33]
that I learned to dis- tinguish between victims and seducers. The results of these seductions cannot be called anything

[33]
other than victims. For if I now were to try to draw from life the existence of these 'lowest 1 classes, the picture

[34]
would not be complete without the assurance that in these depths I would also find light in the shape of a rare willing-

[33]
ness to make sacrifices, a faithful comradeship, extreme contentedness, and reserved modesty, especially

[31]
among the older generation of the working class. Though these virtues were lost more and more to the younger

[33]
generation, espe- cially under the general influence of the big city, yet there were many whose sound and

[31]
healthy blood mastered the mean baseness of life. If nevertheless these good-natured, plucky people, in their

[34]
political activity entered the ranks of the deadliest enemy of our nationality, thus helping to close them

[34]
up, the fault was that they did not and could not understand the baseness of the new doctrine, that no- body else took the trouble

[32]
to look after them, and that finally social conditions were perhaps stronger than all the mutual will power present. The

[32]
poverty into which they would fall sooner or later drove them finally into the camp of Social Democracy. As

[33]
innumerable times the bourgeoisie, in the most stupid, but also the most immoral, manner turned against claims which

[32]
were generally and humanly justified, without obtaining any advantages for themselves or expecting

[32]
any, even the most decent worker was driven from trade unionism into political activity. t Millions of

[33]
workers were certainly inwardly enemies of the Social Democratic Party at the beginning, but their resistance

[33]
was overcome in a sometimes idiotic way and 60 MEIN KAMPF manner, because the parties of the bourgeoisie

[31]
turned against all social demands. They foolishly suppressed all attempts to improve working conditions, safety

[34]
devices on machines, abolition of child labor, and protection of the woman at least during those months when she carries

[33]
under her heart the future fellow citizen, thus helping Social Democracy, which gratefully took up every such

[33]
deplorable manifestation to drive the masses into its nets. Never can our political bourgeoisie repair

[32]
the damage it has done. By its resistance to all attempts to remedy social abuses, it sowed seeds of

[32]
hatred and condoned the claims of the arch-enemies of the entire nationality, that the Social Democratic

[30]
Party alone represented the interests of the working classes. Thus it created above all the moral

[32]
justification for the actual existence of trade unions, those organizations which from the beginning

[32]
rendered the greatest touting service to the political party. During my years of apprenticeship in Vienna

[33]
I was forced, whether I wanted or not, to define my attitude regarding the question of unions. As I looked

[33]
upon them as an inseparable part of the Social Democratic Party as a whole, my decision was quick and wrong.

[33]
It was natural that I should reject them flatly. In this enormously important question Fate itself gave me lessons.

[32]
The result was the reversal of my first decision. '' By the time I was twenty I had learned to distinguish between the

[33]
union as a means of defending the general social rights of the employees and of fighting for better living conditions for

[30]
the individual, and the union as a party instrument in the political class war. The fact that Social

[33]
Democracy realized the enormous importance of the union movement secured the instrument YEARS OF STUDY

[32]
AND SUFFERING 61 for it, and with it, success; it cost the bourgeoisie its political position because it did not

[32]
understand this. By an im- pudent rejection it thought that it would be able to put an end to a logical develgpment,

[33]
whereas in reality it only forced it to assume illogical paths. It is nonsense and, furthermore, untrue

[33]
that the union movement in itself is unpatriotic. Quite the contrary is true. If union activity Axes as

[30]
its goal, and carries out, the uplifting of a class which forms part of the basic pillars of the nation, it does not act

[33]
unpatriotically or inimically towards the State, but it is 'national' in the true sense of the word. After

[32]
all, it helps to create the preliminary social conditions without which a general national education is

[33]
unthinkable. It is the highest merit of the union movement that it abolishes deep-seated social evils and that

[33]
it attacks physical and mental infections, thus adding to the general welfare of the national body. The question

[33]
as to its necessity, therefore, is really superfluous. As long as there are amongst the employers people with

[33]
little social understanding or even lacking a sense of justice and fairness, it is not only the right but even

[31]
the duty of their employees, who after all form part of our nationality, to protect the interests of all against the

[32]
avarice and the unreasonableness of the individual; the safeguarding of the faith and loyalty of a

[30]
national body is a concern of the nation, just as is the safeguarding of the health of the people. Both are

[31]
seriously endangered by unworthy employers who do not consider themselves part of the entire national

[33]
community. The ill effects of their avarice and reckless- ness cause grave dangers for the future. To abolish

[33]
the causes of such a development means to deserve well of the nation, and not perhaps the reverse. We cannot say that

[33]
the individual is free to draw the 62 MEIN KAMPF consequences from a real or imagined wrong that has been done to him,

[32]
that means to go [sic]. Oh, no! This would be humbug and must be considered as an attempt at diverting one's attention.

[33]
Either the abolition of evil and unsocial events is in the interest of the nation or it is not. If it is,

[33]
then the battle against it has to be fought with the help of weapons which give hope for success. The individual worker

[31]
is never in a position to maintain his position against the power of big business, because the question

[34]
involved is not that of the victory of the higher right, for with its acknow- ledgment the whole argument, since there would

[33]
be no reasons, would not exist; the question involved is only that of the greater power. On the other hand, the existing

[34]
feel- ing of justice alone would end the quarrel in an honest manner, or, better still, the quarrel would never have started.

[32]
No, if unsocial or unworthy treatment of human beings calls for resistance, and as long as no lawful and judicial

[33]
authorities are created for the abolition of these evils, the struggle can be decided only by the stronger.

[33]
But it is natural that the power of the employer, concentrated into one single person, can be opposed only

[33]
by the masses of employees, united into one single body, as otherwise they would have to renounce aU hope

[31]
for victory at the start. Thus the union organization may lead to a strengthening of a social idea in its

[32]
practical effects on everyday life, and with it help towards the abolition of causes of irritation, which

[33]
again and again bring about dissatisfaction ana complaint. That this is not the fact must for the most part be at- tributed

[33]
to those who knew how to put obstacles in the way of every lawful regulation of social abuses or who have

[33]
prevented it by means of their political influence. In the same measure in which the political bourgeoisie

[32]
did not understand, or rather did not want to understand, YEARS OF STUDY AND SUFFERING 63 the union organization and

[33]
showed resistance against it, Social Democracy embraced the disputed movement. Thus it clear-sightedly created

[33]
a firm basis which has proved itself as a last support in more than one critical hour. Of course, the original

[33]
purposes were abandoned gradually to make room for new goals. Social Democracy never thought of preserving

[33]
the pro- fessional movement it had included as its original task. No, this was not its intention. In the course of

[33]
a few decades, under its skilled hand, ihe means for protecting social and union rights had be- come the instrument for

[33]
the destruction of national economics. The interests of the workers were not to prove the least hindrance. For in

[33]
politics, also, the application of economic means of pressure permits the exercise of ex- tortion, as long

[33]
as there exists a sufficient amount of the necessary recklessness on the one side, and enough stupid, sheepish

[32]
patience on the other. Something which in this case applies to both sides. At the turn of the century the union

[33]
movement had already long since ceased to serve its original purpose. From year to year it had entered more

[32]
and more into the confines of Social Democratic politics, till finally its pur- pose was only that of

[33]
a ram in the class war. By its con- tinued blows it was to bring about the fall of the entire economic body, built up

[33]
with great care, so that the structure of the State, after its economic foundations had been destroyed, would easily meet

[30]
with the same end. The representation of all the economic needs of the workers was receiving less and less

[33]
consideration, till finally po- litical wisdom did not think it desirable to remedy the social or even

[33]
cultural distress of the great masses any more, for once their demands had been satisfied, one would run the risk that they

[33]
could no longer be used as helpless storm troops. 64 MEIN KAMPF So great was the fear that such an ominously perceived development

[31]
had instilled in the leaders of the class war that they at last not only declined, but even opposed, any real

[29]
beneficial social action. They never were at a loss for an explanation for such an apparently

[33]
incomprehensible attitude. By screwing the demands higher and higher, their pos- sible fulfillment seemed so small and

[31]
unimportant that one was able to convince the masses at any time that one had only to deal with the

[30]
devilish attempt to weaken or even paralyze the force of the working class by such a ridiculous

[33]
satisfaction of their holiest claims. Considering the limited thinking power of the masses, the success is not surprising.

[30]
In the camp of the bourgeoisie, the indignation was great at this apparent insincerity of the Social

[31]
Democratic tactics, but without drawing even the slightest deductions for a directive of their own. The Social

[33]
Democrats' very fear of the actual raising of the workers from the depths of their present cultural and social misery

[32]
should have led to the greatest efforts in this direction, so that the instru- ment would gradually have been wrenched from the

[33]
repre- sentatives of the class war. But this was not done. Instead of conquering the position of the enemy by an

[33]
attack of their own, they preferred to be pressed and pushed, till finally the actions which were taken were entirely

[33]
in- adequate because they came too late; as they were too unimportant, it was easy to reject them. Thus in

[32]
reality everything remained as it had been, only the dissatisfaction was greater than before. Like a

[34]
threatening thundercloud, the 'free trades union' hung over the political horizon and the life of the individual.

[34]
It was one of the most terrible instruments of intimida- tion against the security and the independence of

[34]
national economy, the solidity of the State and personal freedom. YEARS OF STUDY AND SUFFERING 65 It was the free

[33]
trades union above all which turned the conception of Democracy into a ridiculous and repellent phrase,

[33]
which profaned liberty and ridiculed fraternity forever with the words ‘ Und willst du nicht Gcnossc sein, so schlagen wir dir

[32]
den Schaedel ein.’ [And if you will not join with us, we’ll crack your skull.] Thus I learned to know this ‘Friend of mankind. 9 My opinion was

[32]
enlarged and deepened in the course of the years, but I had no reason to change it. The more insight I gained

[33]
into the externals of Social Democracy, the greater became my longing to penetrate to the nucleus of its

[32]
doctrine. The official literature of the party, of course, was of little use. As far as economic

[33]
problems are concerned, it is wrong in assertion and proof; as regards the political aims, it lies. In addition, I was

[32]
disgusted with its modern petti- fogging methods and its writing. With an enormous amount of words of unclear content or

[31]
unintelligible meaning it piles up sentences which are supposed to be as ingenious as they are

[33]
meaningless. Only the decadent bohemianism of our big cities may feel at home in this labyrinth of reason, to

[33]
pick up an ‘inner experience 9 from the dung heap of this literary dadaism, supported by the proverbial modesty

[30]
of part of our people, which senses deepest wisdom in the most incomprehensible things. However, by balancing the

[32]
theoretical untruth and the nonsense of this doctrine with the reality of its appearance, I gradually

[33]
gained a clear picture of its inner intention. In such hours I had sad forebodings and was filled with a depressing

[31]
fear, I was faced by a doctrine consisting of egoism and hatred; it could be victorious, following mathe-

[31]
matical laws, but at the same time it could bring about the end of mankind. 66 MEIN KAMPF Meanwhile I had learned to

[32]
understand the connection between this doctrine of destruction and the nature of a race, which hitherto had been

[32]
unknown to me. Understanding Jewry alone is the key to the comprehension of the inner, the real, intention of

[33]
Social Democracy. He who knows this race will raise the veil of false concep- tions, and out of the mist and fog of empty

[33]
social phrases there rises the grinning, ugly face of Marxism. Today I would find it difficult, if not impossible,

[32]
to say when the word 'Jew' gave me cause for special thoughts for the first time. At home, as long as my father lived, I

[32]
cannot remember that I ever heard the word. I am sure that if the old gentleman had mentioned the term in any

[31]
special way, he would probably have been indicating antiquated culture. In the course of his life his

[33]
opinions had been more or less cosmopolitan, which he not only retained despite his strong national feelings, but

[33]
they also had an effect upon me as well. Even in school I found no reason which could cause me to change this accepted

[32]
picture. At the Realschule I became acquainted with a Jewish boy whom we all treated with circumspection, but

[34]
only because experience had taught us not to trust him too much on account of his reticence; neither I nor the others

[33]
had any particular thoughts in the matter. It was only when I was fourteen or fifteen that I came upon the word 'Jew'

[32]
more frequently, partly in connection with political discussions. I felt a slight dislike and could not ward off a

[33]
disagreeable sensation which seized me whenever confessional differences took place in my presence. At that

[33]
time I did not look upon this question from any other point of view. There were only a very few Jews in Linz. In

[32]
the course YEARS OF STUDY AND SUFFERING 67 of the centuries their external appearance had become European and

[34]
human; yes, I even looked upon them as Germans. The nonsense of this notion was not clear to me, since I saw the only

[33]
distinguishing mark in their strange religion. The fact that they had been persecuted on that account (as I believed) turned

[32]
my aversion against un- favorable remarks about them almost into abhorrence. I had no idea at all that

[32]
organized hostility against the Jews existed. And so I arrived in Vienna. Captivated by the mass of

[34]
architectural impressions, depressed by the burden of my fate, I was at first unaware of the classification

[33]
of the population in the huge city. Although Vienna in those years already had two hundred thousand Jews among its

[31]
two million inhabitants, I did not see them. During the first weeks, my eyes and my senses The position of the Jews in

[31]
Austria was far different from what it was in Germany. Census figures for 1890 indicate that there were 17,693,648

[32]
Catholics, and 1,143,305 Jews in the Empire. Other groups Greek Catholics, Protestants, etc. together numbered less than 4,000,000. The only

[33]
really large Jewish settlement in German Austria was in Vienna. Now during the nineteenth century, two sources of

[33]
conflict other than economic class differences arose to plague the Habsburgs rising nationalist sentiment, which

[33]
made every one of the linguistic groups avid for special favors, and growing hostility to the privileges

[31]
accorded the Church. Liberalism, increasing in importance after 1848, had con- siderably strengthened the grip of

[32]
educated Viennese Jews upon the press and literary production. They were then accused by the Catholic

[32]
majority of having fomented antipathy to the Concordat under which the Catholic Church then lived, and more

[34]
generally of spreading liberalistic ideas; and the shifting of responsibility for ill-feeling from one party

[33]
to an- other became in time a normal feature of Austrian intellectual 68 MEIN KAMPF were unable to

[33]
take in the rush of so many new values and ideas. Only after settling down, when the confused pictures began to

[32]
grow clearer, did I look at my new world more attentively, and then I also came upon the Jewish problem. I

[33]
cannot say that I particularly liked the way in which I was to become acquainted with them. I still saw nothing

[30]
but the religion in the Jew, and for reasons of human tolerance I continued to decline fighting on

[33]
religious grounds. In my opinion, therefore, the language of the anti-Semitic Viennese press was unworthy of

[33]
the cultural traditions of a great race. I was depressed by the memory of certain events in the Middle Ages

[33]
which I did not wish to see repeated. Since the newspapers in question had not a high reputation generally for what

[33]
reason I myself did not exactly know I saw in them more the products of envious annoyance rather than the results

[31]
of a fundamental but incorrect opinion. My own opinion was supported by what seemed to me the much more

[33]
dignified manner in which the really great press replied to all these attacks, or, what I thought even more worthy of respect,

[30]
it did not mention them or ignored them completely. I zealously read the so-called world press (Neue Freie and

[32]
journalistic life. The differences might have been ironed out in time if nationalistic sentiment and the

[34]
resultant tendency to look upon Austria-Hungary as a ' state of nations ' had not played its part. The Jews were looked

[32]
upon as a separate 4 nation ' side by side with Germans, Czechs, and others. Consequently, even those Jews who

[30]
became Catholics or Protestants were no longer assimilated. By changing their creed, they separated

[32]
confessionally from a group to which they were nevertheless bound 'nationally.' Theoretically, of course, Jewish

[34]
converts to Catholicism or Protestantism were accepted as equals, but in practice an increasingly large number

[33]
of persons came to look upon such conversions as spurious. YEARS OF STUDY AND SUFFERING 69 Presse, Wiener Tageblatt, etc.) and

[32]
I was astonished at the scope of what it offered its readers in general and at the objectivity of the

[33]
representation in detail. I respected the dignified tone, though the extravagance of its style some- times

[33]
did not quite satisfy me and at times even displeased me. But this was perhaps due to life in the metropolis

[32]
in general. Since at that time I considered Vienna a metropolis, I thought I was justified in letting the

[31]
explanation I had given myself pass for an excuse. What repelled me sometimes, however, was the un-

[31]
dignified manner in which the press wooed the Court. There was hardly any occurrence at the Hofburg which was not

[34]
reported to the reader either in raptures of enthusiasm or in complaining amazement, especially when the 'wisest

[33]
of all monarchs' of all times was concerned, the fuss almost resembled the mating cry of the mountain-cock. To me this seemed

[33]
artificial. In my opinion liberal democracy was blemished by this. To strive for the favor of the Court in

[31]
such an indecent manner signified ridiculing the dignity of the nation. This was the first shadow to cloud my

[33]
spiritual relation- ship with the 'great' Viennese press. In Vienna I continued, as I had done before, to follow

[34]
up all events in Germany with the fieriest enthusiasms, no matter whether political or cultural questions were con-

[31]
cerned. With proud admiration I compared the rise of the Hitler did not, therefore, share the prevailing

[31]
Catholic feeling that Jewish intellectuals and journalists were under- mining the rights of the Church. He was a

[33]
'liberal 9 in the sense that he, though born a Catholic, refused to commit himself seriously to one side of

[31]
a religious discussion. What annoyed him was that the 'liberal' newspapers, to a large extent edited by Jews,

[30]
defended the hated Habsburg House, 70 MEIN KAMPF Reich with the decline of the Austrian State. But while foreign

[33]
political events gave me undivided joy, the less enjoyable domestic affairs often distressed me. At that time

[33]
I did not approve of the fight that was being waged against Wilhelm II. In him I saw not only the German Emperor

[34]
but also the creator of the German navy. The restriction of speech which the Reichstag imposed on the Kaiser annoyed me very

[33]
much for the simple reason that it was issued by that institution which in my opinion had really no authority to

[33]
do so, especially as during one single session these parliamentarian ganders produced more honking nonsense

[31]
than a whole dynasty of emperors, its sorriest weaklings included, could have produced in centuries. I was

[34]
indignant at the fact that in a State where every halfwit not only claimed the right to criticize, but where in

[32]
the Reichstag he was let loose on the nation as a ' legislator/ the bearer of the imperial crown could be given

[34]
'repri- mands' by the greatest babbling institution of all time. It infuriated me even more that the same Viennese

[30]
press which made the deepest curtsy even to the lowest of the Court nags, and which was beside itself with joy at the

[31]
accidental waving of its tail, now with an apparently sorrow- ful mien but, as I thought, with ill-concealed malice

[30]
expressed its objections against the German Kaiser. It was advocated parliamentary government, and

[33]
criticised the all- highest Kaiser Wilhelm II. Here is one reason why he would later on throw German Catholics

[34]
and Marxists into one pot. Both were upon occasion critical of the Prussian znon- archs, and both were dyed-in-the-wool

[33]
advocates of parliamen- tary procedure. In Austria he had no reason to make this identification.

[32]
Because they felt that the Habsburgs had often failed to support the cause of the Church, numerous groups of Catholics had

[34]
waxed critical of the monarchy. YEARS OF STUDY AND SUFFERING 71 farthest from its intentions to interfere with the affairs

[33]
of the German Reich no, God forbid! but by placing a friendly finger on these wounds one fulfilled the duty imposed

[32]
by the mutual alliance, and on the other hand, one's duty to journalistic truth, etc. Now this finger probed

[33]
about in the wound to its heart's content. Such things made the blood rush to my head. It was this that made me look upon the great press

[32]
with increasing caution. I had to admit, however, that one of the anti-Semitic papers, the Deutsche Volkszeitung,

[33]
behaved better on one of these occasions. The disgusting veneration which the press even then expressed for France

[32]
got on my nerves. One had to be ashamed of being a German when seeing these sweetish hymns of praise to the 'great

[32]
culture nation.' More than once this wretched wooing of France made me put down one of these 'world papers.' I

[32]
turned more and more to the Volksblatt, which I considered much smaller but which was also much cleaner than the other

[32]
papers as far as these things were concerned. I did not agree with its sharp anti- Semitic tone, but now and then

[33]
I read explanations which made me stop to think. At any rate and because of this, I gradually learned to know

[33]
the man and the movement who ruled Vienna's destiny: Doktor Karl Lueger and the Christian Socialist Party. Karl Lueger (1844-1910) founded

[33]
the Christian-Social Party (to which Dr. Engelbert Dollf uss and Dr. Kurt von Schuschnigg belonged) on the basis of a program that combined

[33]
a good deal of progressive municipal legislation with a shrewd awareness of the political values latent

[33]
in popular anti-Semitism. He had a Jewish ancestor in his family tree, had numerous Jewish friends, and as Mayor

[33]
ofVienna issued the slogan. 72 MEIN KAMPF When I first came to Vienna I was inimical to both of them. In my opinion,

[33]
the man and the movement were 're- actionary/ f My usual sense of justice made me change this opinion

[33]
as I had the opportunity of getting acquainted with the man and the movement; and slowly my fair judgment turned

[33]
into open admiration. Today more than before I look upon this man as the greatest German mayor of all times.

[32]
How many of my deliberate opinions were thrown over by my change of attitude towards the Christian

[33]
Socialist movement! When because of this my opinions in regard to anti- Semitism also slowly began to change

[33]
in the course of time, it was probably my most serious change. This change caused me most of my severe mental

[31]
strug- 4 1 am the one who decides who is a Jew.' Nevertheless Lueger's newspaper, the Volksblatt read by Hitler, was so

[32]
violently anti- Semitic that the Archbishop of Vienna rebuked it in a Pastoral Letter which denounced

[32]
'heathenish race hatred.' To this Lueger retorted that to his great surprise and sorrow he found that the Archbishop was

[33]
'liberal through and through.' Rome took no definitive stand in the matter, the Papal Nuncio sup- porting the Archbishop

[32]
while Cardinal Rampolla, then Papal Secretary of State, held a protecting hand over Lueger. The Volksblatt is

[33]
indubitably a storehouse of information on the subject of Hitler's development. There one finds used,

[31]
for example, the word voclkisch 'folkish,' i.e., pertaining to one's people, which is both 'race' and 'nation.' Even more

[32]
delectable to Hitler were Lueger's constant brushes with the Emperor. Into this same period of time there

[33]
also falls the origin of statements that the Talmud teaches pernicious ethics, encouraging Jews to gouge their Christian

[33]
neighbors in every possible way. Dr. August Rohling's book, Der Talmud Judt (The Talmud Jew), appeared in 1871, was widely read or

[33]
YEARS OF STUDY AND SUFFERING 73 gles, and only after months of agonizing between reason and feeling, victory began to

[33]
favor reason. Two years later feeling had followed reason, and from now on became its most faithful guard and monitor. In

[32]
the period of this bitter struggle between spiritual education and cold reasoning, the pictures that the streets of

[32]
Vienna showed me rendered me invaluable services. The time came when I no longer walked blindly through the

[32]
mighty city as I had done at first, but, with open eyes, looked at the people as well as the buildings. < One day when

[33]
I was walking through the inner city, I suddenly came upon a being clad in a long caftan, with black curls. Is this also

[32]
a Jew? was my first thought. At Linz they certainly did not look like that. Secretly and cautiously I watched the man, but the

[31]
longer I stared at this strange face and scrutinized one feature after the other, the more my mind

[32]
reshaped the first question into another form : Is this also a German? As was my custom in such cases, I tried to

[33]
remove my doubts by reading. For the first time in my life I bought some anti-Semitic pamphlets for a few pennies.

[33]
They all started with the supposition that the reader already knew the Jewish question in principle or understood it to

[33]
a certain quoted from in subsequent decades, and is still today the source from which all such accusations derive. It

[30]
was debated pro and con at the time, being the object of litigation from which Rohling withdrew. Doubtless Hitler's

[31]
anti-Jewish prejudice derives in part from his reading on this subject. For a Jewish treatment of this matter, cf.

[29]
Erinnerungen aus mcinem Lcben, by Joseph S. Bloch (Vienna, 1922). For a succinct Catholic summary, cf. Zeitalter des

[33]
Individualismus, by L. A. Veit (Freiburg, 193')- 74 MEIN KAMPF degree. Finally, the tone was such that I again had doubts because the

[33]
assertions were supported by such extremely unscientific arguments. I then suffered relapses for weeks, and once

[32]
even for months. The matter seemed so monstrous, the accusations so unbounded that the fear of committing an injustice

[33]
tortured me and made me anxious and uncertain again. However, even I could no longer actually doubt that

[32]
they were not Germans with a special religion, but an entirely different race; since I had begun to think

[33]
about this question, since my attention was drawn to the Jews, I began to see Vienna in a different light from before.

[32]
Wherever I went I saw Jews, and the more I saw of them, the sharper I began to distinguish them from other people. The

[32]
inner city especially and the districts north of the Danube Canal swarmed with a people which through its appearance

[33]
alone had no resemblance to the German people. Even if my doubts had continued, my hesitation was finally

[34]
dispelled by the attitude of part of the Jews them- selves. A great movement amongst them, which was widely represented

[33]
in Vienna, was determined to affirm the na- tional character of Jewry: the Zionists. It appeared as though only part

[33]
of the Jews approved of this attitude and the majority disagreed or even condemned it. The appearance,

[33]
when closely examined, dissolved itself for reasons of expedience into an evil mist of excuses or

[33]
Zionism, as proclaimed and finally established by Theodor Herzl, an Austrian Jewish poet, was undoubtedly the clear- est

[34]
manifesto of the difficulties in which Austrian Jews found themselves. For it accepted a 'national' status for the Jew

[33]
thus barring the route to assimilation and added that such a status led logically to the ideal of separate

[33]
Jewish State. YEARS OF STUDY AND SUFFERING 75 even lies. For the so-called liberal Jews did not deny the Zionists for being

[32]
non-Jewish, but for being Jews whose open acknowledgment of their Jewish nationality was impractical or even

[31]
dangerous. This did not alter their internal solidarity in the least. Soon this apparent fight between Zionists and

[33]
liberal Jews disgusted me; it was unreal throughout, based on lies, and little suited to the generally accepted high

[33]
moral standard and purity of this race. The moral and physical cleanliness of this race was a point in itself. It

[33]
was externally apparent that these were not water-loving people, and unfortunately one could frequently

[32]
tell that even with eyes closed. Later the smell of these caftan wearers often made me ill. Added to this were their

[31]
dirty clothes and their none too heroic appear- ance. Perhaps all this was not very attractive; aside from the

[33]
physical uncleanliness, it was repelling suddenly to discover the moral blemishes of the chosen people. Nothing

[32]
gave me more cause for reflection than the gradually increased insight into the activities of Jews in

[33]
certain fields. Was there any form of filth or profligacy, above all in cultural life, in which at least one Jew

[33]
did not partici- pate? When carefully cutting open such a growth, one could tind a little Jew, blinded by the sudden

[33]
light, like a maggot in a rotting corpse. The Jews' activity in the press, in art, literature, and the theater, as

[31]
I learned to know it, did not add to their credit These criticisms do not reflect actual critical study of the

[33]
literature of the subject, but are echoes of Volksblatt editorials. There were some Jewish scribes of

[31]
an objectionable sort; and they had their gentile bedfellows. To the great poets of 76 MEIN KAMPF in my eyes. All unctuous

[32]
assertions were of little or no avail. It was sufficient to look at the bill-boards, to read the names of those who

[33]
produced these awful works for theaters and movies if one wanted to become hardened for a long time. This was

[33]
pestilence, spiritual pestilence with which the people were infected, worse than the Black Death of former times!

[33]
And in what quantities this poison was produced and distributed! Of course, the lower the spiritual and the moral

[31]
standard of such an art manufac- turer, the greater his fertility, till such a fellow, like a centrifugal

[32]
machine, splashes his dirt into the faces of others. Besides, one must remember their countless num- ber; one must

[33]
remember that for one Goethe, Nature plays a dirty trick upon mankind in producing ten thousand such scribblers who, as

[33]
germ carriers of the worst sort, poison the minds of the world. It could not be overlooked how terrible it was that the Jew above

[32]
all was chosen in so great a number for this disgraceful task. Was this to prove the fact that the Jews were the chosen

[33]
people? Carefully I began to examine the names of those who created these unclean products of artistic

[31]
life. The result had a devastating influence on my previous attitude to-Jewish extraction, Hugo von

[31]
Hoffmansthal or Karl Kraus for example, the nationalists were just as ferociously indifferent as they were to the

[33]
literary efforts of Czechs and Hungarians. This attitude was later on transplanted to Germany. Ques- tioned as

[32]
to German post-War literature, a member of Papen's Cabinet retorted in 1933 that of course none of it could be

[32]
any good. A still more logical sequel was the ' burning of the books f in Nazi Germany. Since then the official

[33]
report on literature written by racially inferior authors is eingestampft i.e., reduced to pulp. YEARS OF

[33]
STUDY AND SUFFERING 77 wards the Jews. No matter how much my feeling resisted, Reason had to draw its own conclusions. The fact was

[33]
not to be denied that ninety per cent of all literary and artistic rubbish and of theatrical humbug was due to

[32]
a race which hardly amounted to one-hundredth of all inhabitants of the country. Yet it was so. Now I also

[32]
began to examine my beloved 'world press' from this point of view. The deeper I probed, the more the subject of my

[32]
former admiration diminished. I could no longer stand its style, I had to reject its contents on account of its

[33]
shallowness, the objectivity of ks presentation seemed untrue rather than honest truth ; the authors, however, were Jews.

[32]
Now I began to notice tj^MA9H"&ihi n &s which previ- ously I had hardly seen^djE^giBBJI^attuierstand others which had

[33]
already ca^ff^Sf^lSS^^^^^, Now I saw the libm-5intiide of th^^^sjain a different light; its dignified lapjS^^^ff 9fiF^$> % tac ^Si or its completely

[31]
ignoring IranK, w^mv^Sedrd twapj a trick as clever as it was m Ww\ he^^riJHpa' thratripfl criticisms always dealt with JewmK rathorel

[32]
dna-ne^ecJold they attack anyone except the GfinXThe sljgtft^ypricks against Wilhelm II proved in mJ^ghsi^^c^J^^methods, and so did the

[32]
commendation of F^tejSaaBrfrore and civilization. The trashy contents of the novel now became obscene, and the

[34]
language contained tones of a foreign race; the general intention was obviously so detrimental to the German

[31]
nationality that it could only have been intentional. But who had an interest in this? Was it all a mere

[33]
accident? Slowly I became uncertain. This development was accelerated by my insight into a series of

[33]
other events. This was the conception of manners and morality as it was openly shown and exercised by a great

[33]
number of Jews. 7t MEIN KAMPF Again the life in the street gave some really evil demon- strations. In no other city ot

[34]
western Europe could the relationship between Jewry and prostitution, and even now the white slave traffic, be studied

[32]
better than in Vienna, with the possible exception of the seaports of Southern France. When walking at night through the streets and

[32]
alleys of the Leopoldsstadt, with every step one could witness things which were unknown to the greater part of the German

[33]
nation until the war gave the soldiers on the Eastern Front an opportunity to see similar things, or rather forced

[31]
them to see them. An icy shudder ran down my spine when seeing for the first time the Jew as a cool, shameless, and

[33]
calculating manager of this shocking vic, the outcome of the scum of the big city. 'L ^f ^ But then my indignation flare'?

[33]
upa Now 1 did not evade the discussidn <$ the Jewish question any longer; no, I sought itou^:. A Cj&rned to look for the Jew

[32]
in every field of our Cultural ajicj^ftistic l^ e > I suddenly bumped against him in a place where I' had

[33]
never suspected. The scales dropped J rom n\y eye^<lvhen I found the Jew as the leader of SociaJ Dejpiocjrac^i This put

[34]
an end to a long internal struggle' v ,, ^_, "' f During my daily contact with my worker comrades, I was struck by the changeability

[33]
with which they demonstrated different attitudes towards one and .the same question, sometimes in the course of

[31]
a few days, sometimes even after a few hours. I could hardly understand how people who expressed sensible

[32]
opinions when talked to individually suddenly changed their minds when influenced by the spell of the masses. It

[33]
often made me despair. After hours of talking I often thought that I had broken the ice or cleared up some nonsense

[33]
and rejoiced at my success, only to find to my dismay on the following day that I had to start all YEARS OF STUDY AND

[32]
SUFFERING 79 over again; everything had been in vain. The madness of their ideas seemed to swing back and forth like a

[32]
pendulum in perpetual motion. I could still understand everything: that they were dissatisfied with their lot and

[32]
cursed Fate for hitting them so hard ; that they hated the employers whom they looked upon as the cruel executives of

[33]
Fate; that they cursed the authorities who in their eyes had no understanding for their situation; that they demonstrated

[33]
against the high cost of living and marched in the streets to make their demands; all this I could understand at least without re- course

[32]
to reason. But what I never understood was their boundless hate towards their own nationality, how they despised their

[33]
national greatness, soiled its history and abused its heroes. The fight against one's own race, against one's own nest

[30]
and homeland, was as senseless as it was incomprehensible. It was unnatural. One could cure them

[33]
temporarily of this vice, but only for days or weeks at the most. If later one met the supposed convert again,

[33]
he had become the same as before. The unnatural had taken hold of him again. < I gradually realized

[33]
that the Social Democratic press was headed primarily by Jews; but I did not attach special importance to this fact,

[33]
as it was the same with the other newspapers. But one thing struck me: there was not one paper that employed Jews which had

[33]
a really national tendency, as I understood it, based on my education and attitude. Now, although I made

[32]
an effort and tried to read these Marxian products of the press, my aversion was intensified ; I tried to get better

[33]
acquainted with the producers of this mass of knavery. 80 MEIN KAMPF They all were Jews from the publishers downwards. I took all

[30]
the Social Democratic pamphlets I could get hold of and traced the names of their authors: they all were Jews. I

[33]
memorized the names of all the leaders; the greater part of them were also members of the 'chosen people'; no matter

[33]
if they were representatives of the Reichsrat or secretaries of the unions, presidents of organizations or

[33]
street agitators. One always found the same uncanny picture. The names Austerlitz, David, Adler, Ellenbogen,

[32]
and so forth, will remain in my memory forever. One thing had become clear to me: the party with whose little

[32]
representatives I had to fight the hardest struggle during many months were almost entirely in the hands of

[33]
a foreign race; it brought me internal happiness to realize definitely that the Jew was no German. Only now

[33]
I learned thoroughly to know the seducers of our people. Only a year of my stay in Vienna had sufficed to con- vince

[33]
me that no worker was so stubborn as not to give in to better knowledge and better arguments. Gradually I be-

[31]
came acquainted with their own doctrine and I used it as a weapon in the battle for my own internal

[32]
conviction. Now success was nearly always on my side. It was possible to save the great masses, but only after the

[31]
greatest sacrifices of time and patience. The theory of preponderant Jewish leadership in Austrian Social

[29]
Democracy is not substantiated by the facts. After the War there were quite a number of Jewish

[30]
intellectuals in dominant positions, yet even then the Party leadership through- out German Austria was

[33]
overwhelmingly Aryan. Moreover the Anschluss, though marked by wholesale arrests, was character- ized by impressive

[33]
leniency towards the former Socialists, who suffered little in comparison with the Legitimists. This would, of course,

[33]
not have been the case had the Socialists been as non-Aryan as Hitler here suggests. YEARS OF STUDY AND SUFFERING 81 But

[33]
it was never possible to free a Jew from his convic- tions. At that time I was still naive enough to try to make clear

[33]
to them the madness of their ideas; in my small circle I talked until my tongue was weary and till my throat was hoarse, and

[33]
I thought I could succeed in convincing them of the destructiveness of their Marxist doctrine of irra- tionality; but

[33]
the result was only the contrary. It seemed as though the increasing realization of the destructive influence of

[32]
Social Democratic theories would serve only to strengthen their determination. The more I argued with them, the more

[33]
I got to know their dialectics. First they counted on the ignorance of their adversary; then, when there was no way out,

[34]
they themselves pretended stupidity. If all this was of no avail, they refused to understand or they changed the subject

[34]
when driven into a corner; they brought up truisms, but they immediately transferred their acceptance to quite different

[33]
subjects, and, if attacked again, they gave way and pretended to know nothing exactly. Wherever one attacked one

[32]
of these prophets, one's hands seized slimy jelly; it slipped through one's fingers only to collect again in the next

[33]
moment. If one smote one of them so thoroughly that, with the bystanders watching, he could but agree, and if one thus

[32]
thought he had advanced at least one step, one was greatly astonished the following day. The Jew did not in the least

[30]
remember the day before, he continued to talk in the same old strain as if nothing had happened, and if

[33]
indignantly confronted, he pretended to be astonished and could not remember anything except that his assertions

[32]
had already been proved true the day before. Often I was stunned. One did not know what to admire more: their

[32]
glibness of tongue or their skill in .lying. I gradually began to hate them. 82 MEIN KAMPF All this had one good side: in the

[33]
measure in which the bearers, or at least the propagators, of Social Democracy caught my attention, my love for my

[33]
own people grew. Knowing the infernal versatility of these seducers, who dared to condemn the unhappy victims?

[34]
How difficult I found it myself to master the dialectical lies of this race! How futile was success with people who

[33]
turned truth into untruth, who denied the word that just has been spoken only to claim it as their own the very next minute!

[33]
No. The better I learned to know the Jew, the more 1 had to forgive the worker. In my eyes the fault was not his but theirs who

[32]
did not consider it worth while to take pity on him, to give the son of the nation what was his due, and to smash the

[33]
seducer and corrupter against the wall. Influenced by the experiences of everyday life, I myself began to

[32]
trace the sources of the Marxist doctrine. Its workings had become clear to me in detail, my observant eye daily

[31]
watched its success, and with a little imagination I was able to picture its consequences. The only

[33]
remaining question was whether its founders imagined the result ot their creation in its ultimate form, or whether they

[33]
them- selves were victims of an error. In my opinion both were possible. On the one hand it was the duty of

[33]
every thinking human being to join the front ranks of the unhappy movement to prevent the worst possible disaster; on

[32]
the other, the instigators of this national illness must have been devils incarnate; only in the brains 'of a

[29]
monster not in the brains of a human being could the plan for an organiza- tion take shape and meaning, an

[31]
organization whose activity must lead to the ultimate collapse of human culture and with it the

[33]
devastation of the world. In this case the only remaining salvation was fight; a fight with all weapons which the human mind,

[33]
reason, and YEARS OF STUDY AND SUFFERING 83 will power are able to grasp, no matter which side will then be favored by

[34]
Fate. Thus I began to make myself acquainted with the found- ers of this doctrine, in order to study the principles

[32]
of the movement. The fact that I reached my goal more quickly than I dared to hope at first was due to the knowledge

[32]
I had gained of the Jewish question, though at that time it had not gone very deep. This alone made possible

[31]
a practical comparison between reality and the theoretical bragging of the apostles who founded Social

[33]
Democracy, as it had taught me to understand the language of the people; they talk in order to conceal or at least to

[33]
veil their thoughts; their real aim cannot be discovered on the lines, but slum- bers well hidden between them. This was the time in which

[32]
the greatest change I was ever to experience took place in me. From a feeble cosmopolite I had turned

[33]
into a fanatical anti-Semite. Only once more it was the last time I was sur- rounded with depressing

[33]
thoughts in my state of deepest despair. While thus examining the working of the Jewish race over long periods of

[33]
history, the anxious question suddenly occurred to me whether perhaps inscrutable Destiny, for reasons unknown to

[33]
us poor mortals, had not unalterably decreed the final victory of this little race? Had this race, which always had

[32]
lived only for this world, been promised the world as a reward? Have we the right to fight objectively for our self-

[33]
preservation, or is this rooted in us only subjectively? While thoroughly studying the Marxist doctrine and by

[33]
looking at the Jewish people's activity with calm clarity, Destiny itself gave me the answer. The Jewish doctrine

[33]
of Marxism rejects the aristocratic principle in nature; instead of the eternal privilege of force 84 MEIN

[31]
KAMPF and strength, it places the mass of numbers and its dead- weight. Thus it denies the value of the individual in man,

[32]
disputes the meaning of nationality and race, depriving mankind of the assumption for its existence and

[33]
culture. As the basis of the universe it would lead up to the end of all order conceivable to man. And as in

[32]
this greatest discernible organism only chaos could be the result of the application of such a law, so on this earth the

[33]
decline of its inhabitants would be the result. If, with the help of the Marxian creed, the Jew conquers the nations of this

[34]
world, his crown will become the funeral wreath of humanity, and once again this planet, empty of mankind, will move through

[33]
the ether as it did thousands of years ago. Eternal Nature inexorably revenges the transgressions of her laws.

[32]
Therefore, I believe today that I am acting in the sense of the Almighty Creator: By warding off the Jews

[32]
I am fighting for the Lord's work. CHAPTER III GENERAL POLITICAL CONSIDERA- TIONS FROM MY TIME IN VIENNA

[33]
I f IT IS my conviction today that a man should not take any active public part in politics before the age

[33]
of thirty, except in cases of outstanding ability. He should not do so because up to that time the formation

[33]
of a general plat- form takes place from which he examines the various political problems and defines his

[30]
own final attitude to- wards them. The man who has now matured at least mentally may or should take part in the

[32]
political guidance of the community only after reaching a fundamental view of life and, with it, a

[33]
stability of his own way of looking at the individual current problems. If this is not the case, he runs the risk

[33]
that some day he will have to change his attitude towards vital questions, or, despite his better knowledge and

[30]
belief, to uphold points of view which reason and conviction have long since rejected. The first case is very

[34]
embarrassing for him, for now personally uncertain, he has no longer the right to expect that his followers have the same

[31]
unshakable belief in him as before ; such a reversal on the part of the leader brings uncertainty to his

[33]
followers and frequently a certain feeling of embarrassment as regards those they have been fighting. But in the second

[33]
case there may happen what 86 MEIN KAMPF we so frequently see today: in the same measure in which the leader no longer

[32]
believes in what he said, his defense will be hollow and shallow, and he will be base in his choice of means. While he

[34]
himself no longer thinks seriously of defending his political revelations (one does not die for something one does

[31]
not believe in), the demands he makes of his followers become greater and more impudent, till finally he

[34]
sacrifices what is left of the leader in order to end up as a 'politician' ; that means that kind of man whose only

[33]
real conviction is to have no conviction, combined with impudent obtrusiveness and the brazen-faced artful- ness

[34]
of lying. If such a fellow, to the misfortune of decent people, be- comes a member of a parliament, it should be known

[33]
from the beginning that the meaning of politics for him is only the heroic struggle for the feeding bottle for himself and

[32]
his family. The closer his wife and children cling to it, the more tenaciously will he stick to his mandate. This

[31]
alone makes all other men with political instincts his enemies; in every new movement he suspects the

[33]
possible beginning of the end, and in every man greater than him- self he scents the probability of a renewed

[32]
danger which threatens him. I will speak of these parliamentary bedbugs in detail later on. A man of thirty will

[34]
also have to learn a lot more in the course of his life, but this will only be the supplement to, and the filling-out

[33]
of, the frame which his view of life places before him. His learning will no longer be a re- learning in principle, but

[33]
an adding to what he has learned, and his followers will not have to swallow the oppressing feeling that so far he has taught

[32]
them the wrong ideas; on the contrary: the visible organic growth of the leader will give them satisfaction, as his

[34]
learning means only the deepening of their own doctrine. This is, in their eyes, POLITICAL CONSIDERATIONS IN VIENNA 87 the proof

[33]
for the truth of the opinions they have held so fan The leader who has to give up the platform of his general view of

[30]
life because he found that it was wrong only acts with decency if he is ready to face the ultimate

[33]
consequences from the realization that his previous views have been wrong. In such a case he must for all future times

[32]
renounce at least all public political activity. As he has been already once the victim of a basic

[33]
error, the possibility exists that this may happen a second time. On no account is he entitled to continue

[33]
to utilize, or even demand, the confidence of his fellow citizens. The general profligacy of the cads

[32]
who today consider themselves authorized to 'make' politics hardly lives up to his standard of decency.

[33]
Hardly one of them is predestined for this task. I restrained myself from appearing in public, though I believe that

[33]
I have occupied myself with politics more than many others. I talked of what occupied my mind or attracted

[33]
me only in the narrowest circle. This speaking within the most limited frame had many advantages; I learned less

[32]
to 'speak' than to gain an insight into the un- believably primitive opinions and arguments of the people. Thus

[33]
I trained myself for my own further education with- out losing time or ignoring opportunities. Nowhere in

[33]
Germany was the opportunity for this so favorable as in Vienna at that time. <The general political

[33]
thinking in the old Danubian monarchy was wider and more comprehensive in scope than in the old Germany,

[34]
except for parts of Prussia, Hamburg, and the North Sea coast at that period. By 'Austria 1 I mean, in this case, that part of the great

[31]
Habs- burg realm which, in consequence of its German coloniza- 88 MEIN KAMPF don, not only gave in every respect the

[34]
original conditions for the formation of this State as a whole, but the popula- tion of which showed that force that

[31]
exclusively for many centuries was able to give the inner cultural life to this artificial

[32]
formation. The more time advanced, the more the existence and the future of this State depended on the

[31]
maintenance of this germ cell of the realm. While the old hereditary lands represented the heart of the realm which

[33]
continuously pumped fresh blood into the circulatory system of its political and cultural life, Vienna

[33]
combined its brains and will power. Even the outward appearance of this city revealed the force it required to

[32]
rule as the uniting queen over this conglomerate of nations, so that the splendor of her beauty made one

[34]
forget the signs of approaching age of the whole. No matter how much the interior of the realm might twitch during the bloody

[34]
struggles of the various nationali- ties, the countries abroad, especially Germany, saw only the lovely picture of

[33]
that city. The delusion was the greater as Vienna in those days seemed to rise, perhaps for the last time, visibly

[33]
and higher than before. Under the rule of a really ingenious mayor the venerable imperial residence

[32]
of the emperors of the old realm once more awoke to a wonderfully young life. Officially, the last great

[33]
German whom the ranks of the colonizing people of the Ostmark brought forth was not counted among the so-called 'states' men' ; but

[33]
while Doktor Lueger, as mayor of the 'capital and the imperial residential city' of Vienna, produced as if by

[31]
magic one amazing achievement after the other in nearly all domains of economic and cultural

[33]
politics, he strengthened the heart of the entire realm, and in this roundabout fashion he became a statesman greater

[29]
than all the so-called 'diplomats' of that period put together. If nevertheless the conglomeration of the

[32]
nationalities called 'Austria 9 perished in the end, this does not speak
POLITICAL CONSIDERATIONS IN VIENNA 89

[33]
unfavorably in the least of the political ability of the German nationality in the old Ostmark, for

[33]
it was the in- evitable result of the impossibility of trying to safeguard permanently with the help of ten

[33]
million people a State of fifty million people of various nationalities, unless definite suppositions were

[32]
established in time. The German-Austrian thought in more than large terms, He was always accustomed to living

[33]
within the frame of a great realm, and he never lost his understanding for the tasks connected with it. He was the only one

[32]
in this State who saw, beyond the boundaries of the narrow crownland, the frontiers of the Reich ; even when Destiny finally

[30]
sepa- rated him from the common motherland, he still tried to master the enormous task and to guard for the German

[32]
nationality what his forefathers once had wrested from the East in never-ending struggles. Whereby one should

[32]
remember that this could only be done with divided energy ; for the hearts and the memories of the best men never

[33]
ceased to feel sympathy for the common motherland, and only the rest remained to the homeland. The German-Austrian's

[32]
general horizon already was comparatively wide. His economic relations frequently included

[32]
almost the entire many-sided realm. Nearly all great enterprises were in his hands, he supplied the greater part of the

[34]
leading technical experts and officials. But he was also the representative of the foreign trade, as far as the Jew

[31]
had not laid his hands upon this domain which had been his of old. As regards politics the German alone held the State

[33]
together. Even the period of the military service in the army thrust him far across the narrow borders of

[33]
the homeland. Though the German-Austrian recruit might enlist in a German regiment, it might as possibly be stationed

[32]
in Herzegovina as in Vienna or Galicia. The officers' corps was still German and so was predominantly the

[33]
body of officials. Finally, art and science were German. 90 MEIN KAMPF Apart from the trash of the modern development of

[33]
art, which might just as well have been produced by a Negro race, the German was the sole owner and propagator of

[29]
a truly artistic mind. In music, architecture, sculpture, and painting, Vienna was the fountain which in

[34]
inexhaustible profusion supplied the entire dual monarchy without ever visibly drying up. Finally, the German

[31]
nation was also the pillar of the entire field of foreign politics, if one excepted a small number of

[33]
Hungarians. Yet every attempt at preserving the realm was in vain, since the essentials were missing. In the Austrian State

[32]
of nationalities there was but one way by which it could conquer the centrifugal forces of its various nations.

[30]
Either the State was governed from the center and organized in the same way internally, or it was

[32]
altogether unthinkable. This knowledge dawned on the Very highest 1 authority in various enlightened

[32]
moments, but in most cases it was soon forgotten or put aside as being too difficult to be carried out. Every

[33]
idea of giving the realm a more feder- alistic form was bound to fail in consequence of the absence of a strong

[33]
germ cell of superior force in the State. To this was added the various other internal conditions of the Austrian

[33]
State which in principle differed from those of the German Reich of Bismarck. In Germany, the main problem was only to

[34]
overcome political tradition, as there always had been a common cultural basis. But the Reich, with the exception

[33]
of a few foreign splinters, possessed only members of one race. In Austria the situation was the reverse.

[34]
Here the political memory of the various nations' own greatness, except for Hungary, was either entirely lacking,

[31]
or it had been wiped out by the sponge of time, or at least was blurred and indistinct. To make up for this, in the

[31]
POLITICAL CONSIDERATIONS IN VIENNA 91 period of the development of the principle of nationalities, the

[34]
various countries began to develop popular forces; the conquering of these forces became the more difficult

[33]
as nation-States began to form themselves on the border of the monarchy whose people were either similar or

[33]
racially related to the individual Austrian national splinters and they were now able to exercise a

[33]
greater force of attraction than that possible to the German -Austrian. Even Vienna was not able to keep up this fight

[33]
in the long run. With Budapest's development into a capital, Vienna was for the first time faced with a rival whose

[33]
task was no longer the concentration of the entire monarchy, but rather the strengthening of one of its parts. After

[32]
a short time Prague was to follow this example, then came Lemberg, Laibach, etc. With the rise of these one-time

[32]
provincial towns to national capitals of the individual countries, there were now also formed centers for

[33]
a growing independ- ent cultural life. It was only through this that the national political instincts now received

[31]
their spiritual foundation and depth. Thus the time was bound to come when the driving forces of the individual

[33]
nationalities became more powerful than the force of their combined interests, and then Austria would be done

[32]
for. Since the death of Joseph II, the course of this develop- ment could be distinctly traced. Its speed depended on

[33]
a series of factors which were partly rooted in the monarchy itself, but which were, on the other hand, the results of

[33]
the position of the realm in foreign politics. If the struggle for the preservation of the State was to be taken up

[30]
seriously and fought to a finish, a ruthless and persistent centralization alone could lead to the goal. But the

[32]
homogeneity was to be stressed by the establishment in principle of a uniform State language, while the

[32]
admin- istration was to be given the technical instrument without 92 MEIN KAMPF which such a State simply cannot exist.

[33]
Only then could permanent uniform State consciousness be cultivated through schools and education. This could not be achieved

[30]
in the course of ten or twenty years; one had to count on centuries, as in all questions of colonization

[34]
persistency plays a more important rdle than the energy of the moment. That the administration and the political

[34]
guidance have then to be carried out in strict uniformity is obvious. It is now very enlightening for me to

[32]
establish why this did not happen, or rather, why it had not been done. Only he who was guilty of this omission was

[33]
also guilty of the collapse of the realm. Old Austria, more than any other State, depended on the greatness of

[33]
its leaders. Here the foundation of the national State was missing, which always possesses a power of preservation

[33]
in its national basis, no matter how weak the leaders may be. The uniformly national State, thanks to the inherent

[33]
indolence of its inhabitants and the powers of resistance connected with it, can sometime sustain itself

[33]
for astoundingly long periods of incompetent administration or government, without thereby destroying its internal

[34]
existence. Often it seems as though there were no more life in such a body, as though it were dead and done for,

[29]
till suddenly the supposedly dead rises again and gives the rest of mankind astonishing proofs of its

[31]
imperishable force of life. It is different, however, with a realm which is not com- posed of similar

[31]
nationalities and which is not kept to- gether by common blood but by a common fist. Here every weakness of the

[32]
leadership will not cause the State to hibernate, but it will cause an awakening of all individual

[32]
instincts which are present by virtue of blood and race, but which have no chance of developing in times of pre-

[33]
dominating will power. Only centuries of common educa- tion, common tradition, common interests, etc.. can miti-

[33]
POLITICAL CONSIDERATIONS IN VIENNA 93 gate this danger. Therefore such State formations, the younger they are the

[33]
more will they depend on the compe- tence of the leadership; even if they are the works of men of overwhelming force

[33]
and of spiritual heroes, they will fall to pieces after the death of their one great founder. But even after centuries

[33]
these dangers cannot be regarded as overcome; they merely slumber, and often awake quite suddenly as

[34]
soon as the weakness of the common leader- ship, the force of education, and the sublimity of all tradi- tions are no

[34]
longer able to overcome the sweep of the in- dividual vital instinct of the various tribes. The failure to

[32]
understand this is perhaps the tragic guilt of the House of Habsburg. For only one of them did Fate uphold the torch

[33]
over the future of his country, then it was extinguished forever. Joseph II, Roman Emperor of the German

[32]
Nation, saw with trembling fear that his house, pushed toward the most remote corner of the realm, was bound to disappear in the

[31]
maelstrom of a Babylon of nationalities unless the shortcomings of his forefathers were made good in the

[33]
eleventh hour. This 'friend of man' opposed with super- human force the neglect of his ancestors and tried to recover, in

[34]
the course of a decade, what centuries had let Joseph II (1765-1790) was actuated by a desire to strengthen the power

[30]
of Austria, and believed the means to be adopted were a strong central government and a policy of

[32]
Germaniza- tion. The official language was to be German; the Church was to be subordinated to the State, its

[34]
servants being treated as dependent on the government in the normal sense of the civil service; and the universities

[33]
were to teach, in the German lan- guage, whatever would serve to produce a well-trained official. These policies

[32]
embroiled Austria in cultural strife of so serious an import that most of Joseph's laws were abrogated

[32]
before his death. 94 MEIN KAMPF slip by. Had he been granted forty years for his work, and had only two generations continued

[33]
after him to carry out what he had begun, then the miracle would probably have been achieved. But when he died after

[33]
a reign of hardly ten years, worn out in body and soul, his work was en- tombed with him never to be awakened again and

[33]
went to sleep in the crypt of the Capucins forever. His followers were unequal to the task, either in spirit or in

[33]
will power. When the first revolutionary flashes of lightning of a new era flamed through Europe, Austria also

[31]
began gradu- ally to catch fire. But when at last the fire broke out, it was fanned not so much by social or

[34]
general political causes, but rather by impulsive forces of national origin. The revolution of the year

[32]
1848 may have been a class war everywhere else, but in Austria it was the beginning of a new race struggle. The

[31]
German, forgetting or not ac- knowledging his origin, sealed his own doom by entering into the service of the

[33]
revolutionary movement. He helped in awakening the spirit of Western Democracy which after a short time

[31]
deprived him of the foundation of his own existence. The foundation stone for the end of the German nation-

[30]
ality's domination in the monarchy was laid by the forma- tion of a parliamentary body of

[33]
representatives without the establishment and the solidification of a common State language. But from this

[33]
moment on the State itself was doomed. Everything that now followed was only the historical liquidation of

[33]
a realm. It was as shocking as it was instructive to trace this dissolution. This execution of an historical

[33]
sentence was carried out in thousands and thousands of individual forms. That the gods willed the destruction of Austria

[30]
was proved by the fact that a goodly part of the people marched blindly through the signs of decline. POLITICAL

[33]
CONSIDERATIONS IN VIENNA 95 I do not wish to lose myself in details, as that is not the purpose of this book. I want

[33]
to include in the circle of closer observation only those events which are the constant causes of the decline

[34]
of nations and States and which possess significance for our era as well, and which finally helped to guard the principles

[32]
of my political thought. Among the institutions which might have revealed the disintegration of the Austrian

[32]
monarchy, to the bourgeoisie who were not blessed with very sharp eyes, was one which should have chosen strength as its

[32]
greatest quality the parliament, or, as it is called in Austria, the Reichsrat. Obviously, the example for this

[32]
body was situated in England, the country of classical 'Democracy. 1 The entire blissful arrangement was

[33]
transplanted from that country to Vienna with as little change as possible. The English two-chamber system celebrated its

[33]
resur- rection in the Abgeordnetenhaus and the Herrenhaus. Only the 'houses' themselves were somewhat different. When

[33]
Barry's Houses of Parliament reared themselves out of the waters of the Thames, he thrust his hand into the history

[32]
of the British Empire and drew from it the decora- tions for the twelve hundred niches, consoles, and pillars of this

[33]
magnificent building. Thus in sculpture and paint- ing the House of Lords and the Commons became the temple of the nation's

[34]
glory. This was the first difficulty Vienna encountered. When the Danish Hansen had completed the last pinnacle on the marble

[31]
building of the new diet, he had no choice but to borrow decorations from the ancient Greeks and Ro- mans. Roman and Greek

[33]
statesmen and philosophers now embellish this theater building of 'Western Democracy,' and on top of the two houses, in

[32]
symbolical irony, the quadrigae [sic] pull away from each other towards the four 96 MEIN KAMPF corners of the globe, thus

[30]
giving the truest external expres- sion of what was then going on internally. The 'nationalities' considered the

[34]
glorification of Austrian history in this work an insult and a provocation, just as in the Reich proper one did

[32]
not dare to consecrate Wallot's building, the Reichstag, to the German people until the thunder of the World War's battles

[33]
roared. I was not quite twenty years old when I went for the first time into the magnificent building on the Franzenring,

[34]
in order to attend a meeting of the House of Deputies as a spectator and auditor, and I was filled with the most

[32]
contradictory feelings. I had always hated the parliament, yet not at all as an institution in itself. On the

[32]
contrary, as a liberal thinking man I could not imagine any other possible form of govern- ment, for my

[32]
attitude towards the House of Habsburg being what it was, I would have considered any kind of dictatorship

[33]
a crime against all liberty and reason. In consequence of my thorough reading of newspapers in my youth, I had been

[33]
inoculated with a certain admira- tion for the English parliament, although I probably did not suspect it, and

[34]
this fact, which I was not able to give up so easily, contributed not a little to my attitude. The dignity

[32]
with which there the House of Commons devoted itself to its task our press know how to describe it so nicely made

[32]
a great impression on me. Was there a more dignified form of self-government of a nation any- where? For this

[33]
very reason, however, I was an enemy of the Austrian parliament. In my opinion the entire form of its

[31]
behavior was unworthy of its great prototype. But now the following was added : The fate of the German

[33]
nationality in the Austrian State was dependent on its position in the Reichsrat. Up to the introduction of

[31]
general suffrage and the secret ballot, a POLITICAL CONSIDERATIONS IN VIENNA 97 German majority

[33]
existed in parliament, insignificant though it was. But this condition was precarious, for Social De- mocracy, with its

[33]
unreliable attitude, always turned against the German interests so as not to estrange the followers of

[33]
the individual foreign nationalities whenever critical questions concerning the German nationality were

[33]
in- volved. Social Democracy could not be considered a German party even at that time. With the introduction

[32]
of general suffrage, the German numerical superiority ceased to exist. Now the last obstacle to the

[32]
de-Germanization of the State was removed. For this reason my national instinct of self-preservation did not

[33]
inspire me with any love, for a representation of the people by which the German nationality was never

[32]
'represented' but always 'betrayed.' But like so many other things, these were faults that were not due to the matter

[31]
itself, but were to be attributed to the Austrian State. In those days, I still believed that with the re-

[33]
establishment of the German majority in the representative bodies I would no longer have any reason

[33]
for objections on general principles, as long as the old State continued to exist. With all this in mind, I entered

[33]
for the first time the sacred and much-disputed rooms. For me, however, they were only sacred because of the sublime

[33]
beauty of the magnificent building. It was a Hellenic miracle on German soil. But how indignant I was, even

[33]
after a short time, when seeing the miserable comedy that was going on before my eyes. t Several hundred of these

[33]
representatives of the people were present who at that moment had to decide about a question of important

[33]
economic significance. The first day sufficed to give me food for thought for many weeks. The spiritual content

[34]
of what was said was on a truly 98 MEIN KAMPF depressing 'high level/ as far as the talk was at all intel- ligible; for some of

[32]
the gentlemen did not speak German, but their Slavic mother tongue or rather dialects. What I had only known from reading the

[32]
papers, I now had an opportunity of hearing with my own ears. It was a gesticu- lating mass, shrieking in all keys,

[31]
wildly stirred, presided over by a good-natured old uncle who, by the sweat of his brow, tried to re-establish the

[33]
dignity of the House by violently ringing a bell and by alternately kind and earnest remonstrances. I could

[33]
not help laughing. A few weeks later I was again in the House. The picture had changed, it was hardly recognizable.

[33]
The hall was empty. Down below everybody was sleeping. Some of the deputies were in their seats and yawned at each

[33]
other, one of them 'spoke.' A vice-president of the House was present, looking around the hall, visibly bored. My

[34]
first doubts arose. Now, whenever time permitted, I went there repeatedly, and quietly and attentively watched

[32]
the scene of the moment, listened to the speeches as far as they were intelligible, studied the more or less

[33]
intelligent faces of those elect of the nations of this de- plorable State and gradually I formed my own

[32]
opinions. One year of this quiet observation sufficed to change, or to wipe out entirely, my former

[33]
opinion of the nature of this institution. Now my mind no longer objected to this misshapen form which this idea

[32]
had assumed in Austria; no, now indeed I was no longer able to accept parliament as such. So far I had seen the

[32]
misfortune of the Austrian parliament in the absence of a German majority, but now I saw its doom in the

[33]
makeup and nature of this institution altogether. Quite a number of questions occurred to me at that time.

[32]
I began to familiarize myself with the democratic prin- ciple of decision by a majority as the

[32]
basis of this entire POLITICAL CONSIDERATIONS IN VIENNA 99 institution, but I paid no less attention to the

[33]
spiritual and moral values of the gentlemen, who, chosen by the nation, were supposed to serve this purpose.

[33]
Thus I learned to know the institution, and at the same time, its representatives. In "the course of a few years,

[33]
therefore, my knowledge and realization created the type of the most dignified representative of modern

[33]
times with plastic clarity: the parliamentarian. He began to make an impression on me in a form which never

[32]
again underwent a fundamental change. This time, also, practical reality with its object lessons had guarded me

[34]
against suffocating in a theory which at first sight appears so tempting to many people, but which nevertheless must be counted

[32]
among the symptoms of the decay of mankind. < Democracy of the West today is the forerunner of Marxism, which would be

[33]
inconceivable without it. It is democracy alone which furnishes this universal plague with the soil in which

[33]
it spreads. In parliamentarianism, its outward form of expression, democracy created a 'monstrosity of filth and fire'

[34]
(Spottgeburt aus Dreck und Feuer) in which, to my regret, the 'fire' seems to have burned out for the moment. I have to be more

[33]
than thankful to Fate that it also made me examine this question while I was still in Vienna, for I feel that had

[33]
I been in Germany I would have found the answer too easily. Had I become acquainted with this ridiculous

[32]
institution called 'parliament' for the first time in Berlin, I probably would have gone to the opposite

[33]
extreme and would have joined the side of those who see the salvation of the nation and the Reich in the exclusive

[34]
promotion of the Imperial power alone, and who thus blindly and incomprehensibly confront mankind and the times.

[33]
In Austria this was impossible. 100 MEIN KAMPF Here it was not so easy to fall from one mistake into another.

[30]
If parliament was worth nothing, the Habsburgs were worth still less, certainly no more. Here the rejec- tion of 4

[33]
parliamentarianism ' alone would not do ; for then the question, 'What now?' still remained. The rejection and abolition

[33]
of the Reichsrat would have left the House of Habsburg as the sole governmental power, and this idea was especially

[34]
unbearable to me. The difficulty of this special case led me to a more thorough consideration of the problem

[34]
as a whole than would otherwise have taken place at such an early age. First and most of all that which gave me food

[32]
for thought was the visible lack of responsibility on the part of any single individual. Parliament

[33]
makes a decision the consequences of which may be ever so devastating nobody is responsible for Hitler's

[33]
argument is: the Germans of 1848 were led to water the principles which had guided their absolutistic leaders with 'western

[33]
democracy/ The essence of this democracy is (he holds) the grant of the right of franchise and representation to

[33]
all citizens, with the result that an outlet is provided for the hitherto suppressed cravings of the masses. These want,

[33]
how- ever, constantly to improve their lot, and so demand from rather than give to the State. Marxism is the theory which

[31]
most effectively and audaciously sponsors the needs of the largest and most destitute group, and therefore the

[34]
movement which exacts most from the State. In Austria the Socialists were particularly reprehensible because their

[33]
relentless champion- ing of the class struggle obliterated ' national ' boundaries and therewith weakened the position

[33]
of the Empire's rightful rulers, the Germans. In Germany the strength of democracy, symbol- ized by the Reichstag, was far

[33]
less impressive. This Reichstag had some rights of importance, but waged a continuous struggle to exercise them

[34]
as a matter of fact. If Hitler had been in Berlin, therefore, he might possibly have been content with the POLITICAL

[28]
CONSIDERATIONS IN VIENNA 101 it, nobody can ever be called to account. For, does it mean assuming

[33]
responsibility if, after an unheard-of collapse, the guilty government resigns? Or if the coalition changes, or

[32]
even if parliament dissolves itself? Is it at all possible to make a wavering majority of people

[34]
ever responsible? Is not the very idea of all responsibility closely connected with the individual?

[33]
Is it practically possible to make the leading person of a government liable for actions, the development

[33]
and execu- tion of which are to be laid exclusively to the account of the will and the inclination of a large

[33]
number of men? Or must not the task of the leading statesman be seen in the birth of a creative idea or plan in itself,

[33]
rather than in the ability to make the ingenuity of his plans understand taken by the Conservatives and

[33]
as a consequence never have seen that salvation can come only from a dictatorship. Compare his statement

[33]
at the Niirnberg Party Conference of 1935 : 'To build up the public service and the army in accord- ance with the law

[34]
of personal responsibility and at the same time to fashion the general political direction of the State

[33]
according to the principles of parliamentary democracy that is, of irresponsibility is bound to prove

[32]
impossible. The democratic state, in its insecurity, proved helpless against the onslaughts of Bolshevistic

[33]
Judaism. Confronted with this danger, monarchy was found to be equally ineffectual. So were the Christian confessions.'

[33]
Elaborate theories of totalitarianism have since been devel- oped in number by German professors

[33]
and writers. It may be doubted, however, whether they have more than an academic significance. On the other

[33]
hand, Hitler's criticism of democracy as powerless to ward off Bolshevism had a profound effect upon the thinking of

[33]
the middle classes. It is clear from the German newspapers of 1931 that many had begun to think that the only choice remaining

[33]
to them was one between 102 MEIN KAMPF standable to a flock of sheep and empty-heads for the pur- pose of begging for their gracious

[32]
consent? fls this the criterion of a statesman that he masters the art of persuasion to the same extent as that of the

[33]
diplomatic shrewdness in the choice of great lines of direc- tion or decision? Is the inability of a leader

[33]
proved by the fact that he does not succeed in winning the majority of a crowd of people for a certain idea, dumped

[33]
together by more or less fine accidents? Has this crowd ever been able to grasp an idea before its success was

[32]
proclaimed by its greatness? Is not every ingenious deed in this world the visible protest of genius against the

[33]
inertia of the masses? But what is the statesman to do who does not succeed in winning, by flattery, the favor of this

[33]
crowd for his plans? Is he to buy it? Or is he now, considering the stupidity of his fellow citizens, to give up

[33]
the carrying-out of the tasks he recog- nizes as of vital importance, or is he to retire, or should he still remain?

[32]
Does not, in such a case, a real character find himself in an inextricable dilemma between knowledge and de-

[31]
cency, or rather honest conviction? Where is the border that separates duty towards the community from the

[34]
obligations of personal honor? Must not every real leader refuse to be degraded in such a way to the level

[32]
of a political profiteer? And must not, on the other hand, every profiteer feel Mussolini and Stalin. This

[33]
feeling grew until the carefully planned Reichstag fire (both Centrist ex-Chancellors, Dr. Wirth and Dr Brtining, declared in public

[32]
addresses a few days after the event that it had been carefully planned) of 1933 made large groups of voters feel that

[33]
Communism was upon them. POLITICAL CONSIDERATIONS IN VIENNA 103 himself called on to 'make 1 politics, as it is

[30]
not he who bears the ultimate responsibility, but rather some incom- prehensible crowd? Must not our

[32]
parliamentary principle of the majority lead to the demolition of the idea of leadership as a

[33]
whole? Or does one believe that the progress of the world has originated in the brains of majorities and not in

[30]
the head of an individual? Or are we of the opinion that in the future we can do without this

[33]
preliminary presumption of human culture? Does it not, on the contrary, appear more necessary today than

[33]
ever before? << The parliamentary principle of decision by majority, by denying the authority of

[32]
the person and placing in its stead the number of the crowd in question, sins against the aristocratic basic idea of

[31]
Nature, whose opinion of aristocracy, however, need in no way be represented by the present-day

[33]
decadence of our Upper Ten Thousand. The reader of Jewish newspapers can hardly imagine the devastation which

[32]
results from this institution of modern democratic parliamentary rule, unless he has learned to think and

[33]
examine for himself. It is above all the cause of the terrible flooding of the entire political life

[33]
with the most inferior products of our time. No matter how far the true leader withdraws from political activity,

[34]
which to a great extent does not consist of creative work and achievement, but rather of bargaining and haggling for the favor

[34]
of a majority, this very activity, however, will agree with and attract the people of low mentality. The more

[33]
dwarfish the mentality and the abilities of such a present-day leather merchant are, the more clearly his knowledge

[32]
makes him conscious of the wretchedness of his actual appearance, the more will he praise a system that does not

[33]
demand of him the strength and the genius of a giant, but rather which calls for the cunning of a 104 MEIN KAMPF village chief or

[29]
which even prefers this kind of wisdom to that of a Pericles. Such a simpleton need never worry about the

[33]
responsibility of his actions. He is relieved of this care for the reason that he knows, no matter what the result

[34]
of his 'statesmanlike' bungling may be, that his end has long been predicted by the stars; some day he will have to make room

[32]
for another, an equally great mind. It is, among other things, a symptom of such a decline that the number of great

[31]
statesmen increases in the meas- ure in which the competence of the individual one de- creases. With

[34]
increasing dependence on parliamentary majorities, he is bound to shrink, for great minds will refuse to serve as

[33]
bailiff for stupid good-for-nothings and babblers, and on the other hand, the representatives of the majority, that is,

[32]
of stupidity, hate nothing more ardently than a superior mind. For such an assembly of wise men of

[32]
Gotham, it is always a comforting feeling to know that they are headed by a leader whose wisdom corresponds to the

[31]
mentality of the assembly; for, is it not pleasant to let one's intellect flash forth from time to time, and

[32]
finally, if Smith can be master, why not Jones also? This invention of democracy most closely conforms to a

[31]
quality which lately has developed into a crying shame, that is, the cowardice of a great part of our

[33]
so-called 'leaders.' How fortunate to be able to hide, whenever decisions of importance are involved,

[32]
behind the coat-tails of a so-called majority! One has only to watch such a political footpad to see how he

[32]
anxiously begs for the consent of the majority for every action so that he may secure the necessary

[32]
accom- plices, so as to be able to cast off responsibility at any time. But this is one of the chief

[30]
reasons why such political activity is loathsome and hateful to a really decent, and therefore

[33]
courageous, man, while it is attractive to all POLITICAL CONSIDERATIONS IN VIENNA 105 wretched characters and

[31]
he who is not willing personally to assume the responsibility for his acts, but looks for cover, is a

[34]
cowardly wretch. As soon as the leaders of a nation consist of such wretched fellows, vengeance will follow soon after. One will

[29]
no longer be able to manifest the courage for decisive action; one would undergo any

[33]
humiliating dishonor rather than make up one's mind ; be- cause there is nobody who is ready to risk his

[32]
person and his head for the carrying-out of a ruthless decision. One thing we must and may never forget: here, too, a

[32]
majority can never replace the Man. It is not only always a representative of stupidity, but

[34]
also of cowardice. Just as a hundred fools do not make one wise man, an heroic decision is not likely to

[32]
come from a hundred cowards. The easier the responsibility of the individual leader is, the more will the

[33]
number of those grow who, even with the most wretched dimensions, will feel called upon to put their immortal energies at

[32]
the disposal of the nation. Yes, they can hardly await their turn; lined up in a long queue, they count the number of those

[33]
waiting ahead of them with sorrowful regret, and they figure out the hour when in all human probability their turn will

[31]
come. Therefore, they long for every change in the office they aspire to, and are grateful for

[32]
every scandal that thins out the ranks ahead of them. But if one of them refuses to vacate the place he has

[33]
taken, they almost consider it a breach of the sacred agreement of mutual solidarity. Then they become vin-

[32]
dictive, and do not rest till the impudent fellow, finally overthrown, puts his warm place at the disposition of the

[33]
community. He will not regain his place quite so soon. For as soon as one of these creatures has been forced to

[33]
give up his post, he will again try to push himself into the rows of the 'waiting,' provided he is not prevented from doing

[33]
so by the outcry and the abuse of the others. The result of all this is the terrifyingly rapid change in 106 MEIN KAMPF

[33]
the most important positions and offices in such a State entity, a result which is unfavorable in any

[33]
case, but which sometimes is even catastrophic. But now not only the stupid and inefficient will be victims to

[33]
this custom, but even more so the true leader, provided Fate is able at al! to place him in that position. Once

[33]
this has been realized, a united front of defense will be formed, especially if such a head, not originating

[31]
from the ranks, nevertheless tries to force his way into this sublime society. They want to be by themselves on

[31]
general principles, and hate a head, which could turn out to be number one among all these naughts, as a common

[33]
enemy. In this direction the instinct is the sharper, no matter how much it may lack in other respects. Thus the consequence

[34]
will be an ever-increasing intel- lectual impoverishment of the leading classes. Anyone can judge what the results

[33]
will be for the nation and the State if he does not personally belong to this kind of 'leaders.' fOld Austria already

[33]
had parliamentary government in its purest breeding. Of course, it was the emperor and king who appointed the prime

[33]
minister, but this appointing was nothing but the carrying-out of the parliamentary will. The bargaining and trading for

[32]
the individual ministers' offices, however, was Western Democracy of the purest water. The results, of

[33]
course, were in keeping with the principles applied. The change of personalities especially took place in even

[31]
shorter periods of time, till finally it would become a regular chase. Also, the intellectual

[34]
dimensions of the occasional 'states- men' shrank more and more, till finally there remained only that small type of

[30]
parliamentary profiteers whose value as statesmen was measured and acknowledged ac- cording to the

[32]
ability with which they succeeded in pasting together the coalition of the moment ; that means carrying out the smallest

[33]
political trading transactions which alone POLITICAL CONSIDERATIONS IN VIENNA 107 are able to justify

[32]
the suitability of these representatives for practical action. Thus the Viennese school rendered the best

[32]
insight in these fields. I was attracted no less by the comparison between the abilities and knowledge of these

[34]
people's representatives and the tasks awaiting them. Whether one wanted to or not, one had to inspect more closely

[33]
the intellectual horizon of these elected ones of the nations, whereby one could not avoid also paying

[33]
the attention necessary to those events which led to the discovery of these magnificent specimens of our

[33]
public life. Also the way and the manner in which the real abilities of these gentlemen were applied and put in

[33]
the service of the fatherland, which is the technical side of their ac- tivities, was worthy of being examined and

[33]
closely scruti- nized. The entire picture of parliamentary life became the more miserable

[32]
the more one decided to penetrate into these internal situations and to study basic facts with

[33]
ruthless and sharp objectivity. Indeed, one may apply this method towards an institution which leads one to point, by

[32]
its supports, to this very 'objectivity 1 as the only justified basis for examination and defining of

[33]
attitude. Therefore, one had better examine these gentlemen and the laws of their bitter existence,

[29]
and the result will be surprising. There is no principle looked at objectively that is as wrong as the

[30]
parliamentary principle. Here we must also disregard entirely the manner in which the people's

[34]
representatives are elected, and how as a whole, they attain their offices and their new ranks. That only the smallest

[34]
fraction of the common will or need is fulfilled here must be apparent to anyone who realizes that the political

[33]
understanding of the great masses is not sufficiently developed for them to arrive at certain general 108 MEIN KAMPF

[33]
political opinions by themselves and to select suitable persons. <What we mean by the word 'public opinion 1 depends

[33]
only to the smallest extent on the individual's own ex- periences or knowledge, and largely on an image,

[30]
frequently created by a penetrating and persistent sort of so-called 1 enlightenment.' Just as confessional

[33]
orientation is the result of education, and religious need, as such, slumbers in the mind of man, so the political

[32]
opinion of the masses represents only the final result of a sometimes unbelievably tough and thor- ough

[32]
belaboring of soul and mind. By far the greatest bulk of the political 'education,' which in this case one may

[33]
rightly define with the word 1 propaganda,' is the work of the press. It is the press above all else that carries out this

[33]
'work of enlightenment,' thus forming a sort of school for adults. This instruction, how- ever, does not rest in the hand of the State,

[30]
but partly in the claws of very inferior forces. As a very young man in Vienna, I had the very best

[33]
opportunity of becoming really acquainted with the owners and spiritual producers of this machine for

[33]
educating the masses. At the beginning I was astonished how short a time it took this most evil of all the great

[34]
powers in the State to create a certain opinion, even if this involved complete falsification of the wishes

[32]
or opinions in the minds of the public. In the course of a few days a ridiculous trifle was turned into an

[31]
affair of State, whereas, at the same time, problems of vital importance were dropped into general

[32]
oblivion, or rather f were stolen from the minds and the memory of the masses. So they succeeded, in the course of

[34]
a few weeks, in con- juring up some names out of nothing and attaching incred- ible hopes to them on the part of the great

[31]
public, in even giving them a popularity which the really important man may never attain during his whole

[33]
lifetime; names which. POLITICAL CONSIDERATIONS IN VIENNA 109 in addition, nobody had even heard of only

[32]
a month before, whereas at the same time old and trustworthy representa- tives of public or political

[32]
life, though in the bloom of health, simply died in the minds of their contemporaries, or they were showered with such wretched

[31]
abuses that soon their names were in danger of becoming the symbol of villainy and rascality. It is

[32]
necessary to study this infa- mous Jewish method with which they simultaneously and from all directions, as at

[33]
a given magic word, pour bucket- fuls of the basest calumnies and defamation over the clean garb of honest people, in

[33]
order to appreciate the entire danger of these rascals of the press. Then, too, there is hardly anything which

[33]
does not suit the purposes of such an intellectual robber baron in order to reach his end. Then he spys into the most

[33]
secret family affairs and does not rest till his truffle-searching instinct finds some trifling event destined to bring about

[32]
the unfortunate victim's fall. But even if the most thorough nosing about does not stir up anything at all in his

[31]
victim's public or private life, then such a fellow will turn to calumny with the firm conviction that not only

[33]
something of it will stick to his victim, despite thousandfold refutation, but that, in consequence of the hundredfold

[30]
repetition of the calum- nies by all his accomplices, the victim is in most cases \ The propagandistic

[33]
usefulness of snooping around in the private lives of opponents was recognized early by anti- clericals

[31]
in Austria, and the lesson has not been lost on the Nazis. The Volkischer Beobachter (Hitler's official daily) and its

[33]
immediate predecessors, Dietrich Eckart's Auf gut Deutsch, reveled in stories purporting to be based on the private

[32]
lives of wealthier Jews. The terrain was later extended to take in the secret orgies of the Republic's officials, the

[34]
Nacktbatt (dance in the nude) being a specialty. Gradually Julius Streicher's 110 MEIN KAMPF unable to fight it; the motives

[33]
of these scoundrels are never those which would be comprehensible or credible to others. God forbid! Such a rascal,

[33]
by attacking the rest of his dear contemporary world in such an infamous fashion, wraps himself, like a cuttlefish, in

[33]
a cloud of decency and unctuous phrases; he talks of 'journalistic' duty and simi- lar mendacious stuff; he even goes so

[32]
far that during ses- sions and congresses occasions when one sees this plague assembled in greater numbers he twaddles of

[32]
a special, that is, journalistic, "honor/ of which the assembled rascals bumptiously assure one another. This

[32]
rabble, however, manufactures more than two- thirds of the so-called 'public' opinion, and out of its foam rises the

[33]
parliamentary Aphrodite. One would have to write volumes to describe this pro- cedure correctly

[30]
in its entire mendacity and untruthful- ness. However, if one leaves this out of account, and Sturmer

[33]
outdistanced all rivals, becoming the world's champion illustration in pornographic defamation. More important, no

[33]
doubt, was the use to which records taken from Catholic dio- cesan and monastic archives were put after 1934. Hundreds

[32]
of trials for 'immorality' brought priests, religious, and lay- folk to court. Many were declared guilty; and even the

[33]
inno- cent found themselves under a permanent cloud by reason of the difficulty with which such charges can be refuted.

[31]
One amusing instance of how such stories were spread concerns Walther Rathenau, Foreign Minister in the Wirth

[31]
Cabinet. He gave a dinner one evening for eighteen diplomats; and the next morning a very correct and

[31]
honorable official came to call on the Chancellor. 'I regret having to warn Your Excellency against Heir

[33]
Rathenau/ he said. 'But it is shocking last night he dined with eighteen naked ladies.' 4 I know all about it,' Dr. Wirth replied, 'I was

[33]
there myself. But come into the next room and meet some of the ladies.' The surprised official was then introduced

[31]
to half a dozen diplomats. POLITICAL CONSIDERATIONS IN VIENNA 111 looking only at the resulting product

[32]
together with its activity, it should suffice that the objective lunacy of this institution would dawn on

[34]
even the most orthodox mind. It will be easiest to understand this absurd and danger- ous human error if one compares

[32]
the democratic parliamen- tarianism with true Germanic democracy. The characteristic of the first is that

[33]
a number of say five hundred, men and recently also women, are elected, who are entrusted with the final

[33]
decision on everything. They alone practically represent the government, for though they elect the cabinet which

[34]
to all outward appear- ances seems to take on the guidance of the State's affairs, this is nevertheless mere pretense.

[30]
In reality, this so-called government cannot take one step without having first These passages reflect

[33]
dissatisfaction with parliamentary in- stitutions as the foes of the Republic saw them after 1918. The German Reichstag

[33]
was during these years probably the intellectual and moral equal of any parliament in the world. Yet, apart

[33]
from the difficulties with which it was steadily con- fronted and which naturally added little to its popularity,

[33]
it was handicapped by the fact that, when compared with the gentry and nobility who had ruled before the War, its

[33]
spokes- men and ministers were 'little people.' Even Ernst Trdltsch, a great scholar and in his way a democrat, could not avoid that

[33]
feeling. Newspapers loyal to the Republic could jest that there was hardly a man in the government who knew how to enter- tain

[34]
at dinner. Nothing worse could be said about Matthias Erzberger, who signed the armistice and then became Minister

[33]
of Finance, than that he had been 'only a school-teacher'; and few were honestly proud that Friedrich Ebert had once worked

[33]
as a saddler. The result was that many honest parlia- mentarians especially among the Social Democrats suf- fered

[34]
from what is often termed an inferiority complex. After the depression of 1929 set in, these feelings were intensified

[31]
and 112 MEIN KAMPF obtained the consent of the general assembly. Therefore, it cannot be held responsible for

[30]
anything at all, as it is not the government which has the ultimate decision, but the majority of

[32]
parliament. In all cases, therefore, the government is only the executive of the will of the major-

[33]
ity. We could judge its political ability only by the skill it shows either in adapting itself to the will

[32]
of the majority, or in winning it over. But then it sinks from the height of a real government to that of a beggar

[33]
appealing to the majority. Its most important task now consists of securing either the favor of the majority,

[33]
from case to case, or of taking upon itself the formation of a more gracious new majority. If it succeeds in

[34]
this, then it may continue to 'rule' for a short time longer, but if it does not, it must go. Whether its intentions are right

[32]
or not is of no consequence. mixed with hatred. The petty sums received by the 'little men ' as delegates to the

[34]
Reichstag were magnified into fabulous salaries; and many were afraid to go to the theater lest they be accused

[32]
of undue prodigality. But after the Nazis came to power, all was different. During 1937, Dr. Goebbels authorized

[32]
a film showing his beautiful new villa and its lawns. The re- ception was so bad that the picture had to be withdrawn.

[32]
Thereupon Der Angriff, Goebbels's newspaper, denounced all those who ' muttered around ' that the Nazis were now strutting

[32]
about in the top hats they had found so reprehensible on the heads of their predecessors. 'These critics forget/ the com-

[33]
mentator wrote, ' that those we once stigmatized were skunks . . . while those who now represent the State are men

[34]
who have achieved a great deal in four years. An American delegation cannot be asked to dine on sausage and

[31]
sauerkraut by people going around in their shirtsleeves. They must be entertained as they are accustomed to being

[31]
entertained, for we expect them to put in a good word for us when they return home. That is why we wear top hats and

[28]
cutaways. That is also why we build villas/ POLITICAL CONSIDERATIONS IN VIENNA 113 fBut with this all

[30]
responsibility is practically excluded. To what consequences this now leads follows from a quite simple

[32]
consideration : The internal composition of a group of these five hundred representatives, measured

[33]
according to profession or abil- ities of the individual, gives a picture that is as confused as it

[31]
is pitiful. For one cannot expect that these elected ones of the nation are also the elect of

[32]
intellect or even of common sense! And I hope that one does not think that from the ballots cast by a body of

[33]
voters which is anything but clever, the statesmen will come forth by hundreds! On the whole, one cannot contradict too

[34]
sharply the absurd opinion that men of genius are born out of general elections. First, there is only one real

[32]
' statesman ' once in a blue moon in one nation and not a hundred or more at a time; and second, the masses'

[34]
aversion to every superior genius is an instinctive one. It is easier for a camel to go through the eye

[32]
of a needle than that a great man is 'dis- covered ' in an election. What really stands out of the norm of the great masses

[33]
generally personally announces its arrival in world history. So that it is five hundred men of more than

[33]
modest com- petence who vote on the most important concerns of the nation; they appoint governments which, in turn, in each single

[31]
case and in each special question, have to obtain the consent of the illustrious assembly, and thus politics are

[33]
actually made by five hundred men. And it usually looks like it, too. Even when not speaking of the genius

[33]
of these people's representatives, one should consider the different kind of problems awaiting solution and how

[32]
widely spread the fields are in which solutions and decisions are to be made, and one will well understand how

[33]
unfit this form of govern- ment must be for this task which puts the right of final decisions into the hands of a mass assembly

[33]
of people, of 114 MEIN KAMPF whom only a small portion has the knowledge and experi- ence required by the affairs under

[31]
consideration. Thus the most important economic measures are brought before a forum, while only

[31]
one-tenth of its members can evidence any economic training. This means nothing short of plac- ing the final

[33]
decision of affairs into the hands of men who entirely lack all qualification for this task. This is also the case

[33]
with all other questions. They will always be decided by a majority of ignoramuses and incompetents, since the

[32]
composition of this institution re- mains unchanged, while the problems to be dealt with extend to nearly all fields of

[33]
public life, and therefore would require a continuous change of the deputies who have to judge and to

[33]
decide them. It is indeed impossible to permit affairs of transportation to be passed upon by the same people

[33]
who deal with a question, let us say, of high foreign politics. Indeed, they would all have to be universal gen- iuses,

[31]
such hardly as come forth once in centuries. Un- fortunately, in most cases they are not at all ' heads, ' but

[32]
narrow-minded, vainglorious, and arrogant amateurs, an intellectual demi-monde of the worst kind. From this there

[33]
often results the inconceivable carelessness with which these gentlemen discuss and decide on affairs which would give

[33]
even the greatest minds cause for careful reflection. Measures of the gravest importance for the future of an

[33]
entire State, even of a nation, are taken, as though a hand of Schqffkopf [a game of cards especially popular

[34]
in Southern Germany] or taroc, which would certainly suit them better, were before them on the table and not the fate of

[33]
a race. But it would certainly be unjust to believe that each of the deputies of such a parliament was always

[29]
endowed with so slight a feeling of responsibility. No, not at all. But because this system forces the

[33]
individual to define his attitude towards questions for which he may not be POLITICAL CONSIDERATIONS

[31]
IN VIENNA 115 suited, it gradually spoils the character. None of them would have enough courage to declare:

[33]
'Gentlemen, I think we don't understand anything about this question. At least I can say that with certainty as far as I am

[33]
con- cerned. 1 (Besides, this would hardly make any difference, for such honesty would certainly not be understood, and

[33]
they would hardly permit the game to be spoiled by such an honest ass.) Those who know human beings will under- stand that in such

[33]
an illustrious society nobody likes to be the most stupid, and in certain circles, honesty is synony- mous

[33]
with stupidity. Thus a representative, at first still honest, is forced into the path of general mendacity

[32]
and deceit. The very con- viction that the individual's non-participation would not alter the matter in the least

[33]
stifles any honest impulse which perhaps may rise in one or the other deputy. Finally, he will persuade

[32]
himself that he is not the worst by far among the others and that his participation might perhaps even prevent greater

[32]
evil. Of course, one will now raise the objection that the indi- vidual deputy has actually but little

[29]
understanding for the one or the other matter; that in coming to a decision he is advised by the

[33]
parliamentary faction as the leader of the policies of the gentlemen in question ; that this faction always has its

[33]
special committees which are more than amply advised by experts. At first sight this seems to be correct. Then the question would

[31]
still be: Why does one elect five hundred if only a few of them have sufficient wisdom to define their

[32]
attitudes towards the most important matters? This, then, was the gist of the matter! [Ja, darinliegt eben des Pudels Kern.

[31]
A paraphrase of a line in Goethe's Faust.} ' It is not the object of our present-day democratic parlia-

[32]
mentarianism to form an assembly of wise men, but rather 116 MEIN KAMPF to gather a crowd of mentally dependent

[30]
ciphers which may be more easily led in certain directions, the more lim- ited the intelligence of the

[32]
individual. Only thus can parties make politics in the worse sense of the word today. Only thus is it

[33]
also possible that the actual wirepuller is able to remain cautiously in the background without ever being

[32]
personally called to account. Because no decision, no matter how detrimental it is to the nation, can now be

[33]
charged to the account of a rascal who is in the public eye, but it is dumped on the shoulders of an entire faction.

[33]
With this, however, all responsibility is practically re- moved, because it can only be the duty of an

[33]
individual and never that of a parliamentary assembly of babblers. This institution can be pleasing and

[32]
valuable only to the most mendacious sneaks who carefully shun the light of day, whereas it must be loathsome to

[33]
every honest and straightforward fellow who is ready to assume personal responsibility. Therefore, this

[33]
kind of democracy has become the instru- ment of that race which shuns the sunlight because of its internal aims, now

[33]
and for all time. Only the Jew can praise an institution that is as dirty and false as he is himself. 'This system

[33]
is opposed by the true Germanic democracy of the free choice of a leader with the latter's obligation to take

[33]
over fully all responsibility for what he does or does The legend of the 'freely chosen German leader' was proba-

[33]
bly born in the fertile brain of Houston Stewart Chamberlain, a Britisher who became an uncompromising Pan-German

[33]
dur- ing the years preceding 1914 and who buttressed this contention with a theory of race superiority derived in part

[33]
from Count Arthur de Gobineau, author of books which attributed the success of the 'supermen' of the Renaissance to

[32]
their 'Aryan' POLITICAL CONSIDERATIONS IN VIENNA 117 not do. There will be no voting by a majority on single

[33]
questions, but only the decision of the individual who backs it with his life and all he has. If the objection were

[34]
raised that under such circum- stances no one could be found ready to devote himself to such a hazardous task, there can

[33]
be one reply: God be thanked, this is just the meaning of Germanic democracy, that no unworthy climber or moral

[33]
shirker can come in the back way to rule his fellow citizens, but that the greatness of the position to be assumed

[33]
will discourage incompetents and weaklings. But should, nevertheless, such a fellow try to sneak in, then he will be easily

[32]
found out and ruthlessly rebuffed: Out with you, cowardly wretch ! Step back, you are soiling blood. It has since become a

[31]
favorite topic of conversation. Not a few Nazi authors have attempted to unearth instances of such

[33]
leadership. Favorite candidates from early Germanic history are Arminius, Widukind the Saxon King,

[31]
and Genseric the Vandal chieftain. In Nazi usage the word Fuhrer (leader) has a very special connotation,

[33]
difficult for an outsider to understand. The Fdhrcr is a man who gives expression to the divinity that is enshrined

[33]
in his people a 'Traumlaller' (one who speaks oracularly in his dreams), in George Schott's phrase. Gottfried Feder, author of

[33]
the Party program, once described the Fiihrer as follows : ' He must have a somnambu- listic feeling of certainty.

[32]
... In the pursuit of his goal, he must not shrink from bloodshed or war even/ For many, perhaps for himself, Hitler is the German

[32]
Messiah, whose kingdom is to last thousands of years, even as has that of Christ. Hitler, too, began with a small number of

[33]
disciples the first group was of the mystic number seven one or the other of whom proved unfaithful. Addressing Nazi

[33]
congresses, he has fre- quently stressed his ability to wait until 'what is in the folk- sour dictates the course he is

[34]
to pursue. That is why he con- tinuously needs assurance that the folk is actually one in spirit 118 MEIN KAMPF the steps;

[32]
the front stairs leading to the Pantheon of History is not for sneaks but for heroes! 1 had come to this opinion after an

[33]
internal struggle dur- ing the two years in which I visited the Viennese parlia- ment. Thereafter I never went again.

[34]
The parliamentary r6gime had a great share in the progressive weakening of the old Habsburg State during the past

[33]
few years. The more the superiority of the German nationality was broken up through its efforts, the more recourse

[33]
was taken to a system of playing off the various nationalities against one another. In the Reichsrat this always was

[32]
done at the expense of the Germans and so, in the last instance, at the expense of the realm; for at the turn of the

[31]
century even the most simple-minded had to realize that the monarchy's power of attraction was no with him. The

[32]
various plebiscites serve much the same pur- pose as would a mesmerist's look round to see whether the members of

[33]
a group are joining hands. Hitler believes that ninety-nine per cent of the German people support him, and refuses

[32]
to weigh evidence to the contrary. Accordingly any German who resists him is a pariah, a blasphemer

[33]
against the decree of the German providence. Dr. Schuschnigg, who under- stood these things not at all who fully believed that if

[32]
the Nazis gained Austria he could resume his law practice has been kept in confinement since March, 1938, for having

[34]
sinned against the light. Hitler's anti-Semitism must likewise be weighed on this scale. It was out of gratitude to

[32]
the German God for the successes of 1938 that he decreed the pogrom of November 9. He said earlier: ' I believe today that

[33]
I am acting in the sense of the Almighty Creator: By warding off the Jew' I om fighting for the Lord's work' POLITICAL

[33]
CONSIDERATIONS IN VIENNA 119 longer able to counteract the individual countries' en- deavors towards separation.

[33]
On the contrary. The poorer the means became which the State had at its disposal for its preservation, the higher rose

[34]
the general contempt for it. Not in Hungary alone, but also in the individual Slav provinces, the people felt

[33]
themselves so little identified with the common monarchy that its weak- ness was not looked upon as their own disgrace.

[32]
They rather rejoiced over the signs of approaching old age; because they hoped more for its death than for its con-

[32]
valescence. In parliament, the complete collapse was further pre- vented by an undignified submission and

[32]
fulfillment of all and every extortion, for which the Germans then had to pay; in the realm this was done by a clever

[31]
playing-off of the individual nations against one another. But the gen- eral line of development was

[33]
directed against the Germans. Especially since his succession to the throne began to give some influence to

[33]
the Archduke Franz Ferdinand, order and organization were brought into the Czechization car- ried out from above.

[30]
With all possible means this future ruler of the dual monarchy tried to facilitate and to pro- mote

[32]
personally, or at least to shield, the de-Germanization of the realm. Thus purely German places were slowly but

[31]
steadily pushed into the danger zone of mixed languages by roundabout official means. Even in Lower

[33]
Austria this process began to progress rapidly, and many Czechs already considered Vienna as their biggest city.

[33]
The leading idea of this Habsburg, whose family spoke only Czech (his wife, a former Czech countess, had married the prince

[33]
morganatically; she came from circles in which the anti-German attitude was traditional) was gradually

[32]
to form a Slav State in Central Europe to be founded on a strictly Catholic basis, as a protection against

[33]
Orthodox 120 MEIN KAMPF Russia. In this manner, as the Habsburgs had done previ- ously on several occasions, religion

[33]
once more was placed in the service of a purely political idea, above all at least from the German

[34]
point of view of an unfortunate idea. The result was more than deplorable in many respects. Neither the House of

[32]
Habsburg nor the Catholic Church received the expected reward. Habsburg lost the throne, Rome a great State. By using

[33]
religious forces for political purposes, the crown awakened a spirit which it had not at first thought possible.

[31]
The attempt to extinguish Germanism in the old mon- archy by all possible means was answered by the Pan- German

[31]
movement in Austria. fin the eighties, Manchester Liberalism, with a basic Jewish tendency, had reached or

[32]
already passed its climax in the monarchy. Reaction against it came, as was the case with everything in old

[33]
Austria, not primarily from social, but from national, points of view. Its instinct of self-preservation forced Germanism

[33]
to offer the sharpest possible resistance. Only in the second instance economic considerations began

[34]
to gain a decisive influence. Thus out of the general political muddle emerged two party forma- tions, the one

[33]
with a more national, the other with a more social, tendency, but both extremely interesting and in- structive

[34]
for the future. After the depressing end of the war of 1866, the House of Habsburg harbored the idea of a revenge on

[30]
the battle- field. Only the death of Emperor Max [sic] of Mexico, whose unfortunate expedition was

[30]
attributed primarily to Napoleon III, and whose abandonment by the French roused general

[34]
indignation, prevented a closer co-operation with France. Yet Habsburg was on the watch. Had the war of 1870-71 not become such

[33]
a uniquely victorious cam- paign, the Court of Vienna would probably have risked the bloody game of a revenge

[32]
for Sadowa. But when the first POLITICAL CONSIDERATIONS IN VIENNA 121 amazing and incredible heroic tales

[33]
arrived from the battle- fields, yet true, then the 'wisest' of all monarchs recognized that the hour was inconvenient, and ho had

[34]
to grin and bear it as best he could. But the heroic fight of these two years had achieved a still greater miracle ; for the Habsburgs

[32]
a changed attitude never corresponded to an impulse of the heart, but to the pressure of circumstances. The

[33]
German people in the old Ostmark were carried away by the victorious ecstasy of the Reich, and, deeply moved, saw
[31]
the dreams of the fore- fathers resurrected to glorious reality. For let there be no mistake : the really

[33]
German-minded Austrian had recognized at Koeniggraetz the tragic though necessary condition for the resurrection

[33]
of a realm which should not be, and which actually was not, afflicted with the foul marasmus of the old union. He thoroughly

[32]
learned to understand, by his own experience, that the House of Habsburg had now finally ended its historical

[33]
mission, and that the new realm was to elect as emperor only one who, through his heroic character, could offer a worthy

[33]
head to the 'Crown of the Rhine/ How much more was Fate to be praised because it carried out this investiture on

[33]
a member of a House which in the person of Frederick the Great had in times past given to the nation a brilliant

[30]
symbol for the rise of the nation forever. <When after the Great War the House of Habsburg started with utmost

[34]
determination to root out, slowly but steadily, the dangerous Germanism of the dual monarchy (about whose inner

[32]
conviction there could be no doubt) for this would mean the end of the policy of Slavization the resistance of this

[33]
doomed people broke out in a way that the German history of modern times had never known. For the first time men with

[33]
national and patriotic feel- ings became rebels. Rebels, not against the nation, not against the State as 122 MEIN KAMPF such, but

[34]
against a form of government which in their opinion was bound to lead their own nationality to its doom. For the first time in

[33]
modern German history, traditional dynastic patriotism separated from national love for country and people.

[32]
It was the merit of the Pan-German movement in Austria, during the nineties, that it clearly demonstrated beyond

[33]
a doubt that a State authority can only demand respect and protection as long as it corresponds to the desires

[33]
of a nationality and at least does not harm it. There can be no State authority as a means in itself, as in

[34]
that case all tyranny on earth would be unassailable and sacred. If a people is led to destruction by the instrument

[32]
of governmental power, then the rebellion on the part of each and every member of such a nation is not only

[33]
a right but a duty. The question, however, when such a case arises, is not decided by theoretical treatises

[33]
but by force and suc- cess. As every governmental power naturally claims the right of preserving the authority

[32]
of the State, no matter how inferior it is or that it has betrayed the concerns of the nation a thousand times, the f

[34]
olkish instinct of self-preserva- tion, when subduing such a power in order to gain freedom or independence, will have to

[33]
use the same weapons with which the adversary is trying to hold his own. The struggle will be carried on with ' legal ' means as

[32]
long as the power to be overthrown uses such means; but one will not hesitate to use illegal weapons if the

[33]
oppressor also uses them. But in general it should never be forgotten that not the preservation of a State or

[33]
a government is the highest aim of human existence, but the preservation of its kind. But once the latter itself

[31]
is in danger of being oppressed POLITICAL CONSIDERATIONS IN VIENNA 123 or abolished, then the question of

[33]
legality plays only a subordinate r6le. Then it may be that the ruling power may use a thousand so-called

[33]
'legal' means, yet the in- stinct of self-preservation of the oppressed then is always the most sublime justification for

[31]
their fighting with all weapons. Only by acknowledging the above principle were the wars of rebellion, against

[32]
enslavement from within and without, carried on in such great historical examples. Human rights break State rights. But if

[32]
a nation succumbs in its struggle for the rights of mankind, then it was probably found weighing too lightly in the scales of

[33]
destiny to justify its good fortune of being allowed to continue on this mortal globe. For if a man is not

[32]
ready or able to fight for his existence, righteous Provi- dence has already decreed his doom. The world is not

[33]
intended for cowardly nations. fBut how easy it is for a tyranny to drape itself with the mantle of so-called

[33]
'legality' is again shown most clearly and definitely by Austria's example. The legal State authority

[33]
of that period was rooted in the anti-German soil of parliament with its non-German majorities and also in

[33]
the ruling anti-German dynasty. The entire State authority was incorporated in these two factors. To

[31]
attempt to change the fate of the German- Austrian people from this point was nonsense. In the opin- ion of our

[33]
admirers of the only possible 4 legal ' way and of the State authority itself, all resistance would have had

[33]
to be relinquished because it could not be carried out by legal means. But this would have meant the end of the German people

[33]
within the monarchy in a very short time. As a matter of fact the German nation was only saved from such a fate

[33]
by the collapse of this State. 124 MEIN KAMPF The bespectacled theorist, however, would rather die ior his doctrine than for

[34]
his people. Because it is men who first make the laws, he thinks that they afterwards exist for these laws. To have thoroughly

[33]
swept out this nonsense, much to the alarm of all theoretical dogmatists and other govern- mental insular fetishists,

[31]
was the merit of the Pan-German movement in Austria at that time. As the Habsburgs tried to attack the German

[33]
nationality with all possible means, this party in turn now attacked the 'exalted ' ruling house itself in the most

[33]
ruthless manner. For the first time it probed into this foul State and opened the eyes of hundreds of thousands. It is to

[31]
the credit of the party that it freed the glorious idea of patriotism from the embrace of this deplorable

[31]
dynasty. At the time of its first appearance, the number of its fol- lowers was so enormous that it even

[34]
threatened to develop into a very avalanche. But the success did not last. When I came to Vienna, the movement

[33]
had long been overshad- owed, and had even been almost reduced to insignificance, by the Christian Socialist Party

[32]
which had come into power in the meantime. <The entire process of the rise and decline of the Pan- German

[34]
movement, on the one hand, and of the unheard-of rise of the Christian Socialist Party, on the other, was to gain the greatest

[32]
importance for me as a classical object for study. When I came to Vienna, my sympathies were fully and

[30]
wholly on the side of the Pan-German movement. That one had the courage in parliament to shout 'Heil

[32]
Hohenzollern ' impressed me as much as it infinitely pleased me; that one considered oneself only

[31]
temporarily separated from the Reich, and that no occasion was overlooked to manifest this publicly,

[30]
awakened joyous confidence in me ; the fact that one openly demonstrated one's opinion in all

[33]
POLITICAL CONSIDERATIONS IN VIENNA 125 questions concerning German nationality and that one never yielded to

[33]
compromises seemed to me the only way still open for the salvation of our people; but that the movement, after its

[32]
first glorious rise, had sunk so deeply, this I could not understand. I could understand far less that at the same time the

[33]
Christian Socialist Party was able to rise to such enormous power. It had just reached the zenith of its glory at that

[31]
time. When I tried to compare the two movements, Fate, ac- celerated by my otherwise miserable

[33]
situation, here also gave me the best instruction for the understanding of the causes of this riddle. I begin

[32]
my reflections at first with the two men who may be looked upon as the leaders and the founders of the two parties : Georg von

[32]
Schoenerer and Doktor Karl Lueger. From the purely human point of view they stand out, the one as well as the other, far

[33]
above the frame and the dimensions of the so-called parliamentarian types. In the George von Schoenerer (1824-1921) was

[31]
the mouthpiece of a pan-Germanistic hatred of the Jews which found expression in violent speeches. The beer hall was a

[32]
favorite Schoenerer assembly room. But though his diction was crude, his followers were recruited from the upper

[32]
middle classes and blended hatred of the Habsburgs and the Catholic Church with anti-Semitism. Nevertheless he had not

[33]
a few sympathizers even among the clergy. Funds to support the movement were supplied by extremist Protestant groups

[33]
in Germany, and Schoenerer him- self became a Protestant in a wave of secession from the Catholic Church that was

[34]
the greatest Austria had known since the Reformation. The principal tenet of his political doctrine was that the Jews

[33]
had undermined the national economy and therewith created the social problem, which in turn was costing much money.

[34]
Close to Schoenerer was the Ostara group, the publication sponsored by whom is an important source of more modern

[33]
anti-Semitic propaganda. 126 MEIN KAMPF swamp of general political corruption, their entire lives remained pure

[32]
and unimpeachable. Nevertheless, at first my personal sympathy was more with the Pan-German Schoenerer, and then

[32]
gradually turned to the Christian Socialist leader. Comparing their abilities, Schoenerer seemed to me even then the

[32]
better and more thorough thinker in fundamental problems. He recognized more clearly and more correctly than

[33]
anyone else the inevitable end of the Austrian State. Had one listened more attentively to

[31]
his warnings, espe- cially in the Reich, about the Habsburg monarchy, then the misfortune of the World War which placed

[33]
Germany against all Europe would never have come. But if Schoenerer recognized the internal nature of

[33]
the problems, he was wrong as regards the people. That was again the strength of Doktor Lueger. He was a rare judge of human

[32]
nature, especially on his guard against believing that men were better than they were. Therefore, he took more

[33]
into account the real possi- bilities of life, while Schoenerer showed little understanding for this. Everything

[33]
the Pan-German thought was correct from the theoretical point of view; but while the force and the understanding were lacking

[33]
with which to transmit the theoretical knowledge to the masses that means to bring it into a form which was in keeping with their

[33]
per- ceptive ability, which is and will always be limited all knowledge was only prophetic wisdom and had no

[33]
chance ever to become reality. This lack of an actual knowledge of human nature, however, led later

[33]
on to an error in the evaluation of the forces of entire movements as well as of age-old institu-

[34]
tions. But Schoenerer finally had recognized that the questions involved were those of various views of life, but he had

[32]
not understood that above all only the great masses of a people POLITICAL CONSIDERATIONS IN VIENNA 127 are

[33]
suited to be the bearers of such almost religious con- victions. Unfortunately, he understood only to a very

[33]
small degree the extreme limitation of the will to fight in the so- called 4 bourgeois ' circles, in consequence of their

[32]
economic situation which makes the individual fear to lose too much and therefore holds him back. And yet,

[33]
a view of life may in general only hope for victory if the broad masses, as the bearers of the new doc- trine,

[31]
declare themselves ready to take upon themselves the necessary fight. From this lack of understanding of the

[32]
importance of the lower classes there resulted also a totally insufficient conception of the social

[33]
question. In all this Doktor Lueger was the reverse of Schoenerer. His thorough knowledge of human nature made him

[33]
The phrase 'religious faith' would seem to reflect Georges Sorel's theory of the revolutionary myth as expounded in his

[33]
Reflexions sur la violence. It is improbable, however, that Hitler ever saw the book, and in addition there are

[33]
important differences between Sorel's conception and Hitler's. Nor is the affinity with Friedrich Nietzsche, often taken

[33]
for granted, in any sense real. It may well be that Sorel and Nietzsche induced many German intellectuals to join

[33]
the Nazi movement, but the reasoning was clearly erroneous. Hitler subscribes to no doctrine of the superman.

[33]
His strength and originality lie in the fact that he identifies himself with the masses in so far as these want to

[32]
arm for national aggrandizement. It does not matter how much the individual component man or woman in these

[33]
masses knows or what he or she is, so long as willingness is present to be subordinate to the instinct of common 'self-

[33]
preservation' i.e., organization for the conquest of whatever is necessary to extend the sway of the folk as

[33]
a whole. The leader is he who most strongly senses the needs and desires of the unified nation, and not he who as Nietzsche

[31]
and Stefan 128 MEIN KAMPF estimate the possible forces just as correctly, as he was also prevented by this from

[33]
underestimating existing institu- tions, and perhaps for this very reason he learned to use them as instruments

[32]
in attaining his aims. He also understood only too well that in our time the up- per bourgeoisie's energy for

[34]
a political fight was only limited and not sufficient to help a great movement to victory. Therefore, he put

[33]
the weight of his political activity on win- ning over those classes the existence of which was threat- ened, and

[33]
this, therefore, became a stimulant rather than an impediment of the will to fight. In the same way he was in-

[33]
clined to use all the instruments of power already existing, and to gain the favor of influential institutions,

[32]
in order to be able to draw the greatest possible advantage for his own movement from such old-established

[33]
sources of power. So he based his party primarily on the middle classes which were threatened with extinction, and

[33]
so assured him- self a group of followers almost impossible to unnerve, filled with a readiness for sacrifice

[33]
as well as with a tough fighting strength. His infinitely clever policy towards the Catholic Church won for him in a short

[33]
time the younger clergy to such an extent that the old Clerical Party was either forced to leave the battlefield or,

[33]
more wisely still, to join the new party in order thus slowly to regain one po- sition after the other. If one

[33]
were to consider this the sole characteristic of his George believed makes use of the ' slaves ' in order

[32]
to assure the triumph and happiness of a more regal aristocracy than the world has known. In short, for all his

[33]
elements of patriotic mysticism, Hitler is no Platonist, but a Spartan in the simplest sense. That is why Germans

[33]
have found it so difficult to resist him. As one of them has put it, ' He flatters us all into acqui- escence.' It

[30]
may be added that when Hitler says that the 'psyche of the masses is feminine/ he is echoing Gustav Le Bon.

[32]
POLITICAL CONSIDERATIONS IN VIENNA 129 nature, one would do him a grave injustice. For to the clever

[33]
tactician were added the qualities of a really great and ingenious reformer. Also here, of course, his

[30]
actions were limited by the exact knowledge of already existing pos- sibilities and also by the

[32]
abilities of his own person. It was an infinitely practical goal which this really im- portant man had set for

[32]
himself. He wanted to conquer Vienna. Vienna was the heart of the monarchy, and it was from this city that the last bit of

[32]
vitality went out into the ailing and aging body of the decaying realm. The healthier the heart should become, the more

[33]
freshly would the rest of the body revive. A fundamentally correct idea, which, how- ever, was applicable only

[33]
for a prescribed and limited time. And therein lay the weakness of this man. What he achieved, as mayor of the city of

[32]
Vienna, is im- mortal in the best sense of the word ; however, he was not able to save the monarchy, it was too

[31]
late. This his adversary Schoenerer had realized more clearly. Doktor Lueger succeeded in everything he

[33]
attacked prac- tically ; the result he had hoped for did not come. Schoenerer did not succeed in what he wanted, but what

[33]
he feared occurred in an only too terrible manner. Thus neither man achieved his broader goal. Lueger was no longer

[32]
able to save Austria, and Schoenerer could not save the German people from decline. Now, it is infinitely

[33]
instructive for our time to study the causes of this failure of both parties. This is especially use- ful for

[32]
my friends, as in many points circumstances are to- day similar to those of that period, and thus mistakes may be

[34]
avoided which had already brought about the end of the first movement and the frustration of the second. In my eyes there were

[31]
three causes for the collapse of the Pan-German movement in Austria : 130 MEIN KAMPF First, the confused conception of the

[33]
importance of social problems for a new party, the inner nature of which was revolutionary. Inasmuch as

[32]
Schoenerer primarily turned to the bour- geois classes, the result could only be a very weak and tame one. The

[32]
German bourgeoisie in its higher circles, though the individual is not aware of this, is pacifistic to the

[33]
degree of self-denial, where the domestic affairs of the nation or of the State are concerned. In good times

[34]
that means in times under a good government such an attitude is a reason for the extreme value which these classes

[33]
have for the State; in times of bad government, however, it has a really de- vastating effect. In order to make

[33]
the carrying-out of a really serious struggle possible at all, the Pan-German move- ment should have devoted itself

[33]
to winning over the masses. The fact that it did not do so took from it at the beginning the elementary impetus

[32]
that such a wave requires if it is not to ebb after even a short time. But as soon as this principle is not

[33]
observed and carried out from the beginning, the new party loses all chances to This passage gains in interest when one

[31]
compares it with the tactic adopted by the Nazis after their political victory of September, 1930. They now

[32]
entered the Reichstag in hitherto unparalleled numbers; but from the beginning they refused to accept any

[30]
responsibility for what was being done and con- tinuously disrupted and hampered the proceedings. Some

[32]
individual members were willing to share the burden of legisla- tive activity, but they were not

[32]
permitted to have their way. Initially the 107 elected parliamentarians had marched into the Reichstag clad in brown

[33]
uniforms. Outside the building, groups of partisans demonstrated, and when police detachments ap- peared they marched off

[31]
to the Leipzigerstrasse and smashed the windows of Jewish shops. Later disturbances were even POLITICAL

[33]
CONSIDERATIONS IN VIENNA 131 make up later for what it had neglected. For now, with the admission of extremely great

[33]
and moderate bourgeois elements, the internal attitude of the movement will always shape itself towards

[34]
these, and thus it will lose all hope of ever winning any worth-while forces from the great masses of the population.

[33]
What is more such a movement will not get over the stage of pale [sic] grumbling and criticizing. The more or less

[33]
almost religious belief, combined with a similar readiness for sacrifice, will never be found again; whereas

[30]
it might probably be replaced by the endeavor to polish gradually the harsh sides of the struggle by '

[32]
positive' co-operation; that means, in this case, by recognition of given facts, so that finally one will

[33]
arrive at a foul peace. So it also happened to the Pan-German movement, be- cause it had not laid enough stress

[33]
on winning its followers from the circles of the great masses at the start. It achieved a ' bourgeois dignity, mutedly

[31]
radical/ From this mistake resulted the second cause of its rapid decline. The German nationality's

[33]
situation in Austria was al- ready desperate at the time when the Pan-German move- ment appeared. From year

[30]
to year parliament had become an instrument for the gradual destruction of the German people. Only the

[34]
abolition of this institution could promise more grotesque. But with Hindenburg's re-election in 1931 the prestige of

[33]
the Nazi Party began to fade, only to be revived again when Chancellor Brtining was dismissed and the govern-

[32]
ment entrusted to Franz von Papen against the will of the Reichstag. Papen thereupon systematically undermined the

[33]
Republic, so that it was virtually defenseless when in 1933 Hitler was entrusted with the government. Had it not been for

[32]
this sudden change in the German leadership, Hitler might eventually have been compelled to seek a status as

[32]
a normal political leader and try his hand at the parliamentarian game. 132 MEIN KAMPF moderate success in

[33]
any attempted salvation in the elev- enth hour. fWith this the movement was approached by a question that was important

[33]
in principle. In order to destroy parliament, was one to go into it and ' to hollow it out from within/ as one

[33]
was accustomed to ex- press it, or was one to lead this fight from the outside by attacking the institution as such?

[33]
One went in and came out beaten. Of course, one had to go in. To carry out the fight against such an institution

[30]
from the outside means to arm oneself with unshakable courage, and also to be ready for unheard-of

[32]
sacrifices. This means to seize the bull by the horns and to receive many blows, to fall to the ground sometimes, and

[33]
perhaps to rise again with broken bones, and only after the hardest struggle will vic- tory turn to the courageous

[32]
aggressor. Only the greatness of the sacrifices will win new fighters for the cause, till per- severance finally

[32]
receives the reward of success. But for this one needs the children from the great masses of the nation. They alone are

[33]
determined and tough enough to fight this struggle to the bloody end. But the Pan-German movement did not possess these broad

[33]
masses; thus it had no other choice but to go into parliament. It would be wrong to believe that this decision had

[29]
been the result of long mental agonies or even reflections; no, one did not think of anything else. The

[33]
participation in this nonsense was only the sediment of general and confused conceptions of the importance

[33]
and the effect of participa- tion in an institution which had already been recognized as being fundamentally

[33]
wrong. In general, one probably hoped for relief in the work of the enlightenment of the great masses, because now

[33]
one had an opportunity to speak POLITICAL CONSIDERATIONS IN VIENNA 133 before the 'forum of the entire

[33]
nation/ Further, it seemed evident that it was more successful to attack the evil at the root than from the outside.

[31]
By protection through im- munity one believed the security of the individual protago- nist would be

[33]
strengthened, so that the force of the attack could only be increased thereby. But in reality things came about quite

[33]
differently. <The forum before which the Pan-German deputies spoke had not become greater but rather smaller; for

[33]
everybody speaks only before the audience that is able to hear him, or that receives a description of

[31]
what has been said through the reports of the press. But the greatest direct audience is not represented by the hall of

[33]
parliament, but by the great public meeting. For there, there will be thousands of people who have only come to hear

[33]
what the speaker has to say, whereas in the session hall of the House of Deputies there are only a few hundred, whose

[32]
chief reason for coming is only to re- ceive their remuneration and not to let themselves be en- lightened by the

[34]
wisdom of the one or the other of the ' peo- ple's representative.' But above all : It is always the same public

[33]
which will never add to its knowledge, not only because it lacks the brains for this, but also the necessary, though modest,

[33]
will power. Never will one of these deputies willingly do better [$ic] truth the honor of entering its service.

[33]
No, not one of them will do that, except he hopes to save or to regain his mandate for a further session. For as

[32]
soon as it is in the air that the existing party will not do very well in a coming election, only then will these

[33]
ornaments of manliness set out to see how they can gain the other, prob- ably winning party or direction, whereby this

[33]
change of po- sition takes place under a cloudburst of moral motivations. Therefore, whenever an existing

[33]
party seems to be out of 134 MEIN KAMPF the people's favor to the extent that an annihilating defeat is threatened, a great

[33]
migration begins: the parliamentary rats leave the party ship. This has nothing to do with greater knowledge or will

[32]
power, but with that clairvoyant ability which warns such a parliamentary bedbug just in time, so that it can let

[33]
itself drop on another warm party bed. To speak before such a 4 forum' means really to cast pearls before certain well-known

[31]
animals. This is really not worth while. The result cannot be other than naught. This, then, was actually the case. The

[32]
Pan-German deputies could talk on till their throats were hoarse; the effect was naught. The press, however, passed over it in

[31]
silence or mutilated the speeches in a way that every connection, even often their meaning, was lost or

[33]
distorted, so that public opinion was given only a very poor picture of the intentions of the new movement.

[33]
It was of no importance whatsoever what the individual gentlemen now said; the importance rested in what one

[33]
read of them. But this was only an abstract of their speeches, which, in its tattered condition, was nothing but nonsense and so

[33]
it was intended. But the only forum before which they actually spoke consisted of barely five hundred

[32]
parliamentarians, and that says enough. But the worst was the following: The Pan-German movement could hope for success

[33]
only if it realized from the very first day that the question in- volved was not that of a new party but that of a new

[33]
view of life. The latter alone was able to summon the internal strength to fight out this gigantic struggle. But for this

[34]
only the best and the most courageous characters are suited to act as leaders. If the fight for a new view of life is

[33]
not led by heroes will- ing to sacrifice themselves, then no more will death-defying fighters be found. He who in such a case

[32]
fights for his POLITICAL CONSIDERATIONS IN VIENNA 135 own existence cannot have much consideration left for the

[33]
community. fBut in order to preserve this assumption, it is necessary for everybody to know that the new

[29]
movement has nothing to offer to the present except the honor and the fame of posterity. The more

[32]
easily-to-be-won positions such a movement has to offer, the greater will be the onrush of in- ferior stuff, till

[32]
finally these political jobbers overcrowd a successful political party in such numbers that the honest

[33]
fighter of an earlier time no longer recognizes the old move- ment, so that the newcomers themselves decidedly

[31]
reject him as an unwelcome ' intruder/ With this the ' mission ' of such a movement is finished. From the moment the

[32]
Pan-German movement sold itself to parliament, it gained 'parliamentarians' instead of lead- ers and fighters. Thus it

[32]
deteriorated to the level of ordinary political parties of the day and lost the force to oppose

[31]
a catastrophic destiny with the defiance of martyrdom. Instead. of fight- ing, it now learned to 'speak' and to

[31]
'negotiate.' The new parliamentarian considered it, within a short time, a nicer duty, because it

[33]
involved less risk, to fight for the new view of life with the ' intellectual ' weapons of parliamentary elo- quence

[33]
than to throw himself into a fight, and possibly risking his own life, whose end was uncertain and in any case did

[33]
not promise any gain. But as now the party was in parliament, the followers out- side began to hope and to

[33]
wait for miracles, which, of course, never happened and never could happen. Therefore, they became impatient within

[32]
a short time; for also what one heard of one's own deputies in no way corresponded with the expectations of the

[31]
voters. This was only too natural, as the hostile press took heed not to report a true-to-life picture of the

[32]
Pan-German representative to the people. But the more the new deputies began to find palatable 136 MEIN KAMPF the

[33]
rather mild form of 'revolutionary' fight in parliament and the diet, the less were they ready to return to the more

[33]
dangerous work of enlightening the nation's great masses. Therefore, the mass meeting, being direct and personal, and which was

[34]
the only way of exercising a really effective influence and which, therefore, alone could enable the win-

[33]
ning of great parts of the nation, was pushed more and more into the background. Once the beer table of the meeting hall was

[32]
exchanged for the platform of parliament, so that from this exalted forum speeches could be poured into the heads of the

[32]
so-called 'elected representatives' instead of into the people, the Pan-German movement ceased to be a

[31]
people's movement and gradually sank into a club for academic discussion, to be taken more or less

[33]
seriously. Now also the bad impression that the press had rendered was in no way repaired by the personal assembly

[34]
activity of the various gentlemen, so that finally the word 4 Pan-German' had a very bad sound in the ears of the great

[33]
public. For let it be said to all knights of the pen and to all the political dandies, especially of today : the greatest

[33]
changes in this world have never yet been brought about by a goose-quill! No, the pen has always been reserved to motivate

[32]
these changes theoretically. But the power which set the greatest historical avalanches of political and

[33]
religious nature sliding was, from the begin- ning of time, the magic force of the spoken word alone. The great

[34]
masses of a nation will always and only suc- cumb to the force of the spoken word. But all great move- ments are movements

[32]
of the people, are volcanic eruptions of human passions and spiritual sensations, stirred either by the cruel

[33]
Goddess of Misery or by the torch of the word thrown into the masses, and are not the lemonade-like out- pourings

[33]
of aestheticizing literati and drawing-room heroes. POLITICAL CONSIDERATIONS IN VIENNA 137 Only a storm of

[33]
burning passion can turn people's des- tinies, but only he who harbors passion in himself can arouse passion. Passion alone

[33]
will give to him, who is chosen by her, the words that, like beats of a hammer, are able to open the doors to the heart

[33]
of a people. He to whom passion is denied and whose mouth remains closed is not chosen by Heaven as the prophet of its

[31]
will. Therefore, may every writer remain by his inkwell in order to work 'theoretically' if his brains and

[31]
ability are sufficient for this ; such writers are neither born nor chosen to become leaders. Every

[32]
movement with great aims has anxiously to watch that it may not lose connection with the great masses. It has to examine

[33]
every question primarily from this point of view and to make decisions in this direction. Further, it has to avoid

[30]
everything that could diminish or even weaken its ability to influence the masses; perhaps not for

[33]
'demagogic' reasons, no, but because of the simple realization that without the enormous power of the masses of

[32]
a people no great idea, no matter how sublime and lofty it may appear, is realizable. Hard reality alone

[33]
conditions the way that leads to every goal; shunning disagreeable ways means, in this world, only too often to renounce the

[32]
goal; one may wish this or not. As soon as the Pan-German movement, because of its parliamentary position,

[34]
began to place the weight of its ac- tivity upon parliament instead of upon the people, it lost its future and

[32]
won cheap successes of the moment. It chose the easier fight, and therewith it was no longer worthy of the ultimate

[33]
victory. Already in Vienna I had thought most thoroughly about just this question, and in its non-recognition I saw one

[32]
of the causes for the decline of the movement whose mission. 138 MEIN KAMPF in my eyes, was to take the leadership of

[32]
Germanity into its hands. The first two mistakes which made the Pan-German movement fail were related to each

[33]
other. The lack of knowledge of the internal driving forces of great changes led to an insufficient evaluation

[32]
of the importance of the great masses of the people ; from this resulted the scanty in- terest in the social question, the

[31]
deficient and insufficient courting of the soul of the nation's lower classes, but also the attitude towards

[33]
parliament that favored this condi- tion. If one had recognized the tremendous power which at all times is due

[33]
to the masses as the bearer of revolutionary resistance, one would certainly have applied a different

[33]
policy as regards social and propagandistic directions. Then the center of weight of this movement would not have been

[33]
removed to the parliament, but stressed in the workshops and streets. But the third mistake also bears the ultimate germ

[30]
in the non-recognition of the value of the masses, which, like a fly-wheel, gives impetus and uniform

[32]
continuance to the force of the attack, once they have been set in motion in one certain direction by

[33]
superior minds. < The serious struggle that the Pan-German movement had to fight out with the Catholic Church can be explained

[32]
only by the insufficient understanding which one had for the spiritual disposition of the people. The new

[32]
party's violent attacks against Rome were caused by the following: As soon as the House of Habsburg had reached the

[33]
final determination to transform Austria into a Slavic State, it took up every means that seemed suitable

[33]
in this direction. Religious institutions also were dishonestly taken into the service of the neW 'idea

[32]
of State' by the most unscrupulous of all dynasties. POLITICAL CONSIDERATIONS IN VIENNA 139 The use of Czech

[33]
pastorates and their spiritual pastors was only one of the many means to reach the goal of Aus- tria's general

[32]
Slavization. The procedure involved was about the following: In purely German parishes Czech pastors were

[32]
appointed who slowly but steadily began to put the interests of the Czech nation above those of the Church, thus

[32]
becoming germ cells of the process of de-Germanization. Unfortunately, the German clergy almost failed com-

[33]
pletely in the face of such a procedure. Not only that the clergy themselves were entirely unfit for

[34]
a similar struggle from the German point of view ; they were not able to meet the attacks of the other with the necessary

[33]
resistance. Thus, by way of religious abuse on the one hand, the German na- tion was not well enough defended on

[34]
the other hand, and was being pushed back slowly but incessantly. If this happened in small matters, unfortunately the sit-

[30]
uation in general was not very different. Here, too, the anti-German attempts of the Habsburgs did not meet the

[33]
necessary resistance, especially on the part of the higher clergy, while the representation of the German

[31]
interests was pushed completely into the back- ground. The general impression could but be that this was a bru- tal

[33]
infringement on German rights by the Catholic clergy as such. With this, however, the Church did not seem to feel with the German

[33]
people, but seemed unjustly to take sides with its enemies. The root of the evil was, especially in Schoener- er's

[32]
opinion, that the head of the Catholic Church was not in Germany, a fact which accounted for the hostility to- wards the

[33]
concerns of our nationality. The so-called cultural problems were almost completely pushed into the background,

[33]
as was the case with nearly everything in Austria at that time Decisive for the atti- 140 MEIN KAMPF tude of

[33]
the Pan-German movement towards the Catholic Church was far less the Church's attitude against, perhaps, science, etc., than, what is

[31]
more, its insufficient representa- tion of German rights, and, on the other hand, its continued advancement of

[33]
especially Slavic arrogance and greed. Now, George Schoenerer was not the man to do things by halves. He took up the fight

[32]
against the Church with the conviction that only thus could the German people perhaps still be saved. The ' Los-von-Rom 9 movement

[31]
seemed the most powerful, but also the most difficult, procedure of at- tack destined to smash the fortress of the

[34]
enemy. If it was successful, then the unfortunate schism of the Church in Germany was overcome, and the internal

[33]
strength of the Reich and the German nation could not fail to gain enor- mously by such a victory. But neither the assumption nor

[34]
the conclusion of this fight was correct. In all questions concerning the German nationality, the national resistance of

[30]
the Catholic clergy of German na- tionality was undoubtedly weaker than that of their non- German brethren,

[33]
especially the Czechs. Also, only an ignoramus could fail to see that the Ger- man clergy never so much as thought of an

[33]
active represen- tation of German interests. Also, everyone who was not blind had to admit that this was due first

[33]
of all to a circumstance from which we Ger- mans all have to suffer severely; it is the objectivity of our

[31]
attitude towards our nationality as well as towards anything else. Just as the Czech clergyman has an

[33]
attitude that is sub- jective towards his people and only objective towards the Church, thus the German clergyman

[34]
was subjective to- wards the Church and objective towards the nation. It was a fact which we may unfortunately observe

[33]
in thou- sands of other cases. POLITICAL CONSIDERATIONS IN VIENNA 141 This is in no way a special hereditary

[30]
feature of Cathol- icism, but in our country it eats into almost any, especially governmental or

[32]
idealistic institutions. Compare the attitude which our officials show towards the attempts of a national

[34]
rebirth with that which in such a case the officials of another nation would show. Or does one believe that the officers'

[33]
corps of the rest of the world would in a similar way place the concerns of their nation in the background with the phrase of 'State

[32]
authority/ as has been our custom for these past five years, a fact that is even looked upon as especially

[33]
meritorious? Do not both reli- gions today, for instance, take an attitude towards the Jewish question that neither

[33]
answers the concerns of the nation nor the real needs of religion? Compare the attitude of a Jewish rabbi towards

[33]
all questions, even of only minor importance for Judaism as a race, with that of the far greater part of our clergy,

[31]
but, if you please, of both reli- gions! We find this symptom whenever the representation of an abstract idea is

[33]
involved. 'State authority/ 'democracy/ 'pacifism/ 'international solidarity/ etc., are all conceptions

[34]
which in our country nearly always turn into stiff, purely doctrinary notions, so that every judgment of the general

[33]
national necessities of life originates exclusively from their point of view. This unfortunate way of

[33]
looking at all concerns from the angle of a previously accepted idea kills all ability to think subjectively

[32]
of a thing that is objectively contradictory to one's own doctrine, and eventually it leads to a

[33]
complete reversal of means and end. Then one will turn against every attempt at a national rising if this could take

[33]
place only after first doing away with an inefficient, destructive regime, as this would mean an offense against

[32]
'State au- thority/ but since 'State authority' is not a means to an end, but in the eyes of such an 'objective'

[33]
fanatic it repre- 142 MEIN KAMPF sents the end itself, that is sufficient to fill out his entire miserable life. Then one

[33]
will indignantly resist an at- tempted dictatorship, even if it were Frederick the Great, and if the State artists

[34]
of a parliamentary majority were only inefficient dwarfs or even inferior scoundrels, because to

[32]
such a stickler for principles the law of democracy seems more sacred than the welfare of a nation. The one,

[33]
there- fore, will protect the worst tyranny that ruins a people, as for the moment it represents the 'State authority/

[33]
while the other rejects even the most blessed government, as long as it does not represent his idea of 'democracy.'

[33]
In exactly the same way our German pacifist will pass over in silence the most bloody rape of the nation, it

[34]
may come from even the fiercest military powers, if a change of At no time was German pacifism more highly

[33]
developed than pacifism was in any other country subscribing to the principles of civilization. But it is

[33]
true that the Social Democrats had taught international worker solidarity more ardently than had some other

[32]
Socialist groups, though they too barring a few leaders succumbed to the enthusiasm of 1914. Later on, when doubts concerning the War

[31]
began to arise, some of the older feeling returned and the dissident leaders were able to muster

[33]
considerable strength. Christian pacifism, on the other hand, was after the War given a powerful impetus by the Peace

[33]
Encyclicals of the Pope, which made an impression on Catho- lics and Protestants alike. The coming of Hitler to

[31]
power naturally spelled the end of such efforts. All members of pacifist organizations which did not question the

[34]
legitimacy of national defense in a just war were penalized. A number of professors were dismissed

[31]
from the universities, and State employees were thrown out of office whenever the label of pacifist could be

[32]
affixed to them. The most sensational instance was the trial of Professor Friedrich Dessauer in 1933, when the Center

[31]
Party statesman was subjected to imprisonment and loss of property for alleged pacifist activity.

[33]
POLITICAL CONSIDERATIONS IN VIENNA 143 this lot could be brought about only by resistance, that means force, for this would

[33]
be contrary to the spirit of his peace league. But the international German socialist may be robbed conjointly

[33]
by the other world; he accepts it with fraternal affection and does not think oij^m^a^pr even mere protest, because he is

[33]
a Ger This may be deplorable, but to means first to understand it. The same is the case with the] concerns by a part of

[31]
the clergy. | This is neither wicked nor ma caused by orders from, let us sa) national determination in which a

[32]
defective education for GermanisnT well as a complete submission to the i an idol. Education for

[33]
democracy, for international socialism, for pacifism, etc., is such a stiff and exclusive one and so purely

[33]
subjective from these various points of view, that therefore the whole picture of the remaining part of the world

[33]
is also influenced by this principal conception, while from childhood on the attitude towards the German nation has

[33]
been merely objective. Thus the pacifist, by giving him- self subjectively and entirely to his idea, in

[32]
face of any threat to his people no matter how unjust and serious it may be (as long as he is a German), will

[31]
always look first for the objective right and he never will join the ranks and fight with his flock out of pure instinct for

[31]
self-preservation. How far this is true for the various denominations as well, the following shows: Protestantism

[34]
represents the concerns of the German na- This point was to prove of the greatest importance. Lutheran teaching on the subject

[33]
of baptism -- which is regarded as the greatest sacrament is that through baptism equality of 144 MEIN KAMPF tion in a better way,

[33]
so far as this is already rooted in its birth and later tradition; but it breaks down in the moment when the defense of

[33]
these national interests take place in a field which is not included in the general line of its ideal world

[33]
and traditional development, or which perhaps is rejected for some reason or other. Thus Protestantism will always

[32]
interest itself in the pro- motion of all things Gertnan as such, whenever it is a mat- ter of inner purity or

[33]
increasing national sentiment, the de- fense of German^ life, the German language and German liberty, as all this

[33]
is also rooted firmly in Protestantism; status before God and in the Church is conferred on men. Difference of

[33]
race and endowment may and do subsist, but they are not of essential importance. Moreover, the sacred ministry

[32]
is open to all who have been baptized and are called. Therewith Lutheranism denies the priority of

[33]
race. When Hitler came to power, he immediately tried to place the governance of the Lutheran Church in

[33]
the hands of men who were willing to alter the traditional teaching. A large group of 'German Christians' who subscribed to

[33]
Hitler's views were recruited, and their representative Pastor Ludwig M tiller was named Archbishop at the command of

[33]
the government. The majority of German theologians refused, however, to accept so drastic a tampering with

[33]
their creed. Gradually they formed the Confessional Synod, and this has until now despite all pressure and suffering

[33]
clung resolutely to the orthodox point of view. The best-known spokesman for this point of view is Pastor Martin Niemoller,

[33]
who was imprisoned by command of Hitler and is still held in virtually solitary confinement; but there are

[33]
hundreds of clergymen who have learned to know the meaning of opposition. More than twelve hundred of their number have

[32]
gone to prison; some are dead. The crisis through which Lutherism is passing is unquestion- ably the gravest in its

[32]
history. Cf. Der Kampfder cvangelischen Kircke in Deutschland. by Arthur Frey (Zollikon, 1937). POLITICAL CONSIDERATIONS IN

[32]
VIENNA 145 but it will immediately and sharply fight every attempt at saving the nation from the grip of its most

[33]
deadly enemy, as its attitude towards Judaism is fixed more or less by dogma. But this involves a question

[33]
without the solution of which all attempts at a German renaissance or a national revival are and will remain

[34]
absurd and impossible, f During my time at Vienna I had enough leisure and op- portunity to examine this

[31]
question also without prejudice, and in daily contacts I was able to determine the direction of this

[33]
opinion in a thousand ways. In this focus of the various nationalities, it was shown most clearly that only the German

[33]
pacifist tries to look ob- jectively at the concerns of his own nation, but the Jew, for instance, will never do the same

[33]
with those of the Jewish people; that only the German socialist is ' international' in a sense that forbids him to

[33]
ask for justice for his people other than by whining and moaning before his international comrades, but never

[33]
the Czech or the Pole, etc. ; in short, I recognized even then that the misfortune is to be sought only partly in those

[32]
doctrines, but, for the other part, in our entirely insufficient education for our own nationality as

[32]
a whole, and, conditioned by this, in a weakened devo- tion to the latter. This eliminated the first purely

[31]
theoretical motivation of the fight of the Pan-German movement against Cathol- icism in itself. One should

[32]
educate the German people, from childhood These words seem to define Hitler's point of view at the time this book was

[32]
written, and doubtless reflects the situation in which he found himself in the Bavaria of 1923. The statements here made

[33]
aroused the ire of General Ludendorff, already then a violent opponent of Rome and the Jesuits, and were

[33]
dealt with in magazine articles in which the General accused Hitler of having 'sold out' to Rome. The Fuhrer was

[33]
at the time un' 146 MEIN KAMPF on, to the exclusive acknowledgment of the right of their own nationality, and one should

[33]
not poison the children's hearts with the curse of our 'objectivity/ also in matters of the preservation of the ego,

[33]
so that after a short time it will be seen (provided there exists also a radical national gov- ernment) that, as

[33]
in Ireland, Poland, or France, in Germany also a Catholic will always be a German. The most convincing proof for

[30]
this was offered at a time when for the last time our people were summoned, for the protection of its

[32]
existence, before the tribunal of History for its struggle for life or death. As long as the leadership from

[33]
above did not fail, the peo- ple fulfilled their duty in the most overwhelming manner. Whether they were Protestant or

[31]
Catholic clergy, they both had an immensely large share in preserving for so long a time our force of

[33]
resistance not only at the front but even certain of what the future might bring, and is known to have interviewed

[31]
leaders of the Bavarian People's Party (Catholic) concerning the terms under which he might be admitted to that

[32]
organization. Heiden puts the matter somewhat differently, suggesting that Hitler had merely been trying to get

[33]
permission to reorganize the Nazi Party. In addition one of the best friends the Nazis had in the Bavarian

[33]
regular army was General Franz von Epp, a Catholic who would have frowned on any- thing smacking of religious

[33]
warfare. Perhaps it is not possible as yet to substantiate the state- ment in full the change in Hitler's personal

[33]
attitude is attributable primarily to the conversion of Cardinal Faulhaber, Archbishop of Munich, from

[32]
monarchist restorationism to democracy and pacifism. The Cardinal proclaimed this new attitude in a

[34]
sensational open letter which implied criticism of the Nazis. In addition Hitler had come more under the influence

[32]
of Alfred Rosenberg, whose ideas on racialism and religion have since become standard Party fare. At

[33]
any rate, the Catholic Church took up in earnest the fight against POLITICAL CONSIDERATIONS IN VIENNA 147 more so

[34]
at home. During these years, especially during the first flare-up, there existed for both camps only one single and

[34]
sacred German Reich, and everyone turned to his own heaven for its existence and future. There is one question

[33]
which the Pan-German movement in Austria ought to have asked itself: Is the preservation of the German nation in

[31]
Austria possible under a Catholic faith? If it is possible, then the political party had no right to

[30]
occupy itself with religious or even denominational af- fairs; if not, however, then a religious

[32]
reformation had to set in, and not a political party. He who believes he may arrive at a religious

[33]
reformation by the roundabout way of a political organization only shows that he really has not the slightest

[34]
idea of the way in which religious conceptions or even dogmas originate and their effect upon the Church. the Nazi

[33]
creed after the triumphant elections of 1930. A number of pastoral letters denounced the errors contained in the Party

[33]
program and in the books of important leaders; and late in 1930 the Ordinary of the diocese of Mayence refused

[33]
to grant Catholic burial to a Nazi. After Hitler came to powei , all this was changed. The Bishops revised their

[31]
attitude; a Concordat was signed with the Holy See. Even more re- cently some Catholic leaders have

[33]
professed to believe that a modus vivendi with Hitler might be reached. We possess authentic records of Chancellor

[32]
Hitler's private views of the religious situation. One of these may be cited in part: 'Hitler said concerning

[32]
Catholic opposition, especially in Bavaria, that its fomentors were wasting their time. They might as well stop

[33]
pipe-dreaming. He would not follow the example of Bismarck. He was a Catholic. Providence had arranged that. Bismarck

[31]
had failed because he had been a Protestant and Protestants have no conception of what the Catholic Church is. The

[34]
important thing was to sense what 148 MEIN KAMPF Here one really cannot serve two masters. In this, I con- sider the foundation

[33]
or the destruction of a religion essen- tially more important than the foundation or destruction of a State, let

[32]
alone a party. But one must not say that this was only the warding- off of attacks from the other side! It is

[33]
certain that at all times unscrupulous people did not shrink from making religion a tool of their political business

[33]
affairs (for this is almost exclusively and nearly always the main object of such fellows) ; and it is equally certain

[33]
that it would be wrong to hold religion or a denomination responsible for a number of scoundrels who abuse it

[32]
just as surely as they would very probably abuse anything else placed into the service of their base

[33]
instincts. Nothing would suit such a parliamentary good-for- people felt in religious matters and what endeared the Church

[33]
to them. If the clerical caste would not disappear voluntarily, he would direct propaganda against the Church until

[34]
people would be unable to hide their disgust when the word ' Church ' was mentioned. Why, it was necessary only to make Church

[33]
history popular. He would have films made. Looking at them the German people would see how the clergy had exploited them,

[32]
lived off them. How they had sucked the money out of the country. How they had worked hand in glove with the Jews, how they had

[33]
practiced immoral vice, how they had spread lies. These films would be so interesting that everybody would itch to see

[33]
them. He would make the clergy ridiculous. He would expose all the tangled mass of corruption, selfishness and deceit of

[31]
which they had been guilty. Let the bourgeoisie tear its hair. He would have the youth and the people on his side. He would

[33]
guarantee that if he set his mind to it, he could destroy the Church in a few years. The whole institution was just a hollow

[33]
shell. One good kick, and it would tumble together in a heap.' POLITICAL CONSIDERATIONS IN VIENNA 149 nothing and sluggard

[32]
better than if he were offered an op- portunity, at least later, of having some justification for his

[31]
political wirepulling. For, as soon as religion or a denomination is made re- sponsible for his

[32]
personal wickedness and is attacked for this reason, such a mendacious fellow will clamor aloud and call the world to

[33]
witness how justified his actions were, and that the salvation of religion and church is due to him and to his eloquence

[34]
alone. His fellow citizens, as stupid as they are forgetful, will not recognize the real orginator of the en-

[34]
tire dispute, merely because of the great noise he makes, or they will no longer remember him, and so the scoundrel

[33]
has actually achieved his goal. Such a sly fox knows only too well that this has nothing whatsoever to do with religion,

[33]
and he will therefore laugh up his sleeve, while his honest and less skilled adversary loses the game, so that some

[33]
day, despairing of faith and loyalty in mankind, he will withdraw from everything. But also in another direction it would

[33]
be unjust to make religion as such or even the Church responsible for the mis- takes of various individuals.

[34]
One should compare the visi- ble greatness of the organization which one has before one- self with the average

[33]
faultiness of men in general, and one will have to admit that the proportion between good and bad is here perhaps

[32]
better than anywhere else. Even among the priests there are certainly such to whom their sacred office is

[33]
only the instrument for the gratification of their political ambition, and who, in the political fight, forget

[33]
in a more than deplorable manner that they should be the guardians of a higher truth and not the promoters of lies and

[32]
calumnies but such an unworthy individual is out- weighed, on the other hand, by a thousand and more honest

[33]
pastors, most faithfully devoted to their mission, who stand out like little islands in a communal swamp in our menda- cious and

[32]
demoralized time. 150 MEIN KAMPF However little I condemn the Church as such, or may, if perhaps a demoralized

[34]
villain in a priest's frock offends morality in an unclean fashion, just as little may I condemn another among the many

[33]
who befouls and betrays his na- tionality in times when this is almost a daily practice any- how. Especially

[34]
today one should not forget that for one such an Ephialtes there are thousands who with bleeding hearts sympathize with

[33]
the misfortune of their people and who, just like the best of our nation, long for the hour when at last Heaven will smile on

[33]
us again. But to him who now answers that the problems involved are not everyday trifles but questions of essential

[34]
truth or dogmatic content, one can only give the necessary reply by another question : If you believe yourself

[32]
to be chosen by Destiny to an- nounce the truth, then do so; but then have the courage to do so not by way of

[31]
a political party for this is also wire- pulling but instead of the present 'worse' place your 'better' of

[33]
tomorrow! But if you lack the courage to do so, or if you are uncertain about your 'better,' then keep your hands off; in

[33]
any case do not try to do by roundabout sneaking through a political movement what you would not dare to do with

[32]
your visor open. < Political parties have nothing to do with religious prob- lems, as long as these are not

[33]
hostile to the nation and do not undermine the ethics and morality of their own race; just as religion is

[33]
not to be combined with the absurdity of politi- cal parties. Whenever ecclesiastical dignitaries make

[33]
use of religious institutions or doctrines in order to harm their nationality, one should not follow them and

[33]
fight them with the same weapons. To the political leader the religious doctrines and institutions of his people should

[33]
always be inviolable, or else he ought not to POLITICAL CONSIDERATIONS IN VIENNA 151 be a politician

[32]
but should become a reformer, provided he is made of the right stuff I Any other attitude would lead to

[33]
a catastrophe, especially in Germany. While studying the Pan-German movement and its fight against Rome, at that

[33]
time and especially in the course of the following years, I came to the following conclusion: The party of that

[32]
time, through its limited understanding of the importance of social problems, lost the masses of the people that were

[34]
really fit to fight; joining parliament de- prived it of its enormous impetus and burdened it with all the weaknesses

[31]
of that institution ; it made itself impossible in numerous small and medium circles through its fight against the

[33]
Catholic Church, thus robbing itself of innumer- able of the best elements which the nation can call its own. The practical

[33]
result of the Austrian Kulturkampf was equal to nil. t However, one succeeded in tearing away from the Church almost

[34]
one hundred thousand members, but she did not suf- fer any particular loss because of this. She really did not have to

[33]
shed any tears for the lost 'lambs'; for the Church lost only what for a long time had not fully belonged to her internally.

[33]
This was the difference between the new refor- mation and the old one : that once many of the best of the Church turned

[31]
away from it because of their inner religious conviction, while now only those went who were not only

[34]
lukewarm, but for 'considerations' of a political nature. But even from the political point of view the result

[32]
was just as ridiculous and yet again saddening. Once more a political movement, promising success and

[33]
salvation to the German nation, had perished, because it had not been led with the necessary ruthless sobriety,

[33]
but lost itself in directions that were bound to lead to disunion. For one thing is certainly true: 152 MEIN KAMPF The Pan-German

[34]
movement would probably never have made this mistake if it had not possessed too little under- standing for the psyche

[32]
of the great masses. If its leaders had known that, in order to achieve any success, one must not present, for purely

[33]
psychological reasons, two enemies to the masses, because this would lead to a complete split-up of the fighting strength,

[32]
then for this reason alone the direc- tion of the blows of the Pan-German movement would have been aimed against one

[29]
adversary alone. Nothing is more dangerous for a political party than to be led by those

[32]
jacks-of-all-trades who want to do everything without ever attaining the least thing. No matter how much one had to

[34]
criticize an individual denomination, the political party must not for a moment lose sight of the fact

[32]
that, according to all previous experience of history, a purely political party, in a similar

[33]
situation, has never succeeded in bringing about a religious refor-mation. But one does not study history

[32]
in order to for- get its doctrines when they are to be applied in practice, or to believe that things are now

[33]
different that is, that the eternal truth of history is now no longer applicable; but from history one learns just

[32]
the practical application for the present. But he who is not able to do this must not imagine that he is a

[33]
political 'leader' ; he is in reality a shallow, and also frequently a very vainglorious, simpleton, and no

[34]
amount of good-will excuses his practical inability. As a whole, and at all times, the efficiency of the trulv

[32]
national leader consists primarily in preventing the division of the attention of a people, and always in

[33]
concentrating it on a single enemy. The more uniformly the fighting will of a people is put into action,

[33]
the greater will be the magnetic force of the movement and the more powerful the impetus of the blow. It is part

[32]
of the genius of a great leader to make adversaries of different fields appear as always belonging to one

[33]
category only, because to weak and unstable characters POLITICAL CONSIDERATIONS IN VIENNA 153 the knowledge

[33]
that there are various enemies will lead only too easily to incipient doubts as to their own cause. As soon as

[33]
the wavering masses find themselves con- fronting too many enemies, objectivity at once steps in, and the question

[32]
is raised whether actually all the others are wrong and their own nation or their own movement alone is right.

[32]
Also with this comes the first paralysis of their own strength. Therefore, a number of essentially different in-

[32]
ternal enemies must always be regarded as one in such a way that in the opinion of the mass of one's own

[32]
adherents the war is being waged against one enemy alone. This strengthens the belief in one's own cause and

[33]
increases one's bitterness against the attacker. It cost the former Pan-German movement its success be- cause it did

[32]
not comprehend this. Its goal was rightly viewed, its will was pure, but the way it chose was wrong. It was like a mountain

[31]
climber who fixes the peak that he is to climb well and correctly with his eyes and who sets out on his way with the greatest

[32]
determination and energy, but who, paying no attention to the way, always fixing his eye on the goal, neither sees nor

[33]
examines the condition of the ascent thus finally failing. The situation seemed to be the reverse with its

[32]
great competitor, the Christian Socialist Party. The way on which it set out was intelligently and rightly chosen, but it

[33]
lacked the clear knowledge of the goal. < In nearly all matters in which the Pan-German move- ment failed, the attitude of

[33]
the Christian Socialist Party was correct and carefully planned. It had the necessary understanding of the importance

[33]
of the masses and it secured at least part of them by apparent stress on its social character from the very first day. By

[33]
aiming essentially at the winning of the small and lower middle class and the craftsmen classes, it gained a body of 154 MEIN

[31]
KAMPF followers that was as faithful as it was enduring, ready for sacrifice. It avoided all fights against a

[33]
religious institu- tion, thus securing the support of such a mighty organiza- tion as the Church represents. Thus it had

[32]
only one really great chief adversary. It recognized the value of large-scale propaganda and it was

[33]
a virtuoso in influencing the spiritual instincts of the great masses of its followers. The fact that, nevertheless, it

[33]
was unable to reach the desired goal of Austria's salvation was due to two faults of its way and to the obscurity

[32]
of the goal itself. The new movement's anti-Semitism was built up on religious imagination instead of racial

[33]
knowledge. The reason for making this mistake was the same as that which caused the second error as well. If the Christian

[34]
Socialist Party was to save Austria, then in the opinion of its founders it was not to approach the question from the racial

[31]
principle, as otherwise and after a short time the general dissolution of the State would set in. But the

[31]
situation in Vienna especially re- quired, in the opinion of the party leaders, the greatest possible

[33]
elimination of all disrupting circumstances and in its place a stress on all unifying points of view. Vienna, at that

[33]
time, was already so heavily interspersed with Czech elements that only the greatest tolerance with respect to

[32]
all racial problems was able to keep them in a party that was not anti-German at the start. If one wanted to save

[33]
Austria, one could not renounce them. So, one tried to win the small Czech tradesmen, especially numerous in Vienna, for

[31]
the fight against the liberal Manchester move- ment, and thereby believed that one had found a slogan against

[33]
Judaism on a religious basis, overshadowing all of the racial differences of old Austria. It is obvious that

[32]
a fight on such a basis gave Jewry but limited cause for worry. If the worse came to the worst, a splash of

[32]
baptismal POLITICAL CONSIDERATIONS IN VIENNA 155 water would always save the business and Judaism at the same

[33]
time. With so superficial a motivation one never arrived at a serious and scientific treatment of the whole

[33]
problem, and therefore only too many people, who could not understand this kind of anti-Semitism, were repelled

[29]
altogether. The attractive force of the idea was therefore almost exclusively tied to

[32]
intellectually limited circles, if one wanted to arrive at a real knowledge, by means of a purely

[33]
senti- mental feeling. The intelligentsia, as a matter of principle, turned aside. Thus the matter was given

[33]
more and more the appearance as though the question involved was only the attempt at a new conversion of the Jews

[33]
or even the expression of a "certain competitive envy. But with this the fight lost the character of an inner and

[33]
higher consecra- Traditional anti-Semitism had in Germany always been based on confessional differences.

[33]
Any other motivation was forbidden by the Church ; and in all the pogroms of the Middle Ages, Jews were able to

[31]
escape the rigor of the persecution by accepting baptism. Surprisingly few availed themselves of that

[33]
opportunity; and on the Christian side Saint Bernard had pointed out that the worst possible way to attempt conversions was

[32]
to inflict torture and death on the recalcitrant. Therefore racial anti-Semitism as an integral part of

[32]
a program of political action remains Hitler's 'Copernican discovery. 1 For now there is no escape for the

[33]
victim no escape even for his Jewish grandmother, by reason of whom he is a pariah under the Nazi laws. It

[33]
must be conceded that however numerous the sources from which Hitler's anti-Semitism derives may be, his proposed

[32]
solution for the 'Jewish problem 1 is original. Probably there were few among the older Nazi leaders who

[33]
accepted it. Goer- ing, Strasser, Roehm and the rest envisaged certain Jews of whom they wished to rid Germany. Jealousy of

[33]
Jewish business rivals or professional competitors ; popular views of Jewish meth- 156 MEIN KAMPF tion, and thus it appeared

[33]
to many, and not the worst, as immoral and objectionable. The conviction was lacking that this was a question of vital

[33]
importance to the whole of mankind and that on its solution the fate of all non-Jewish people depended. Through these

[31]
half-measures the value of the Christian Socialist Party's anti-Semitic attitude was destroyed. It was a sham

[33]
anti-Semitism that was worse than no anti-Semitism at all; because one was thus lulled into security;

[32]
one thought that one had caught the enemy by the ears, whereas in reality one was being led about by one's own

[32]
nose. The Jew, however, after a short time had so accustomed ods of investing capital; age-old, almost

[33]
atavistic sentiment handed down from the days when Jews lived in ghettos; soldierly hatred of Jewish pacifists: all these

[32]
things played their part, but there exists overwhelming evidence from the years 1933 and 1934 to show that even inside the Party the

[33]
general view was that the anti- Jewish campaign would be kept within certain limits. Only Hitler has refused to budge.

[34]
It was he who rode down all opposition and ordered the pogrom of November 9. As originally planned, the outbreak

[33]
was to coincide with the opening of the 'Eternal Jew' exposition in Berlin, it being assumed that the Government

[32]
could claim that the people' had been so 'impressed' by the material displayed there that a 'spontaneous uprising' was

[32]
unavoidable. The murder of Ernst von Rath, a German diplomat in Paris, by a young Jewish refugee, provided

[33]
a far better excuse. More than 70,000 Jews were arrested, and those among the victim? who had money were ordered

[33]
to leave the country within a specified time. Many thousands more were ejected from their homes, made to walk

[32]
the streets all night, and virtually suffered to starve. In Vienna and Innsbruck the spectacle was so fright- ful that even

[34]
hardened Nazis are known to have protested. Yet from the point of view of ruthless politics such steps are POLITICAL

[34]
CONSIDERATIONS IN VIENNA 157 himself to this kind of anti-Semitism that he would cer- tainly have missed its absence more

[33]
than its presence hindered him. As one had to make heavy sacrifices to the State of nationalities, one

[33]
had to do so even more in the case of the representation of the German nationality itself. One could

[34]
not be 'nationalistic' if one did not want to lose the ground under one's feet, even in Vienna. By gentle evasion

[33]
of this question, one hoped to save the Habsburg State, while in reality one drove it towards its doom by this

[32]
very attitude. But with this the movement lost its enormous source of power which in the long run alone is

[32]
able to replenish a political party with its internal force. Only through this the Christian Socialist movement

[34]
became a party like all the others. In those days I closely observed both movements, the one out of the beat

[33]
of my heart, the other by being carried away with admiration for the rare man who even then appeared to me to be the

[34]
bitter symbol of the whole German nationality in Austria. When the impressive funeral procession of the dead

[34]
mayor left the Rathaus and turned towards the Ring- strasse, I, too, was among the many hundreds of thousands who watched the tragedy.

[33]
My feelings told me with undeniably clever. For in view of the world-wide economic depression, the arrival of

[32]
Jewish refugees in any number creates for the country harboring them a variety of difficult problems. First,

[32]
giving them jobs will be resented by the unemployed; and establishing them in business or a profession will add to the

[30]
pressure of competition. The total effect upon the national economy may be negligible, but the

[33]
psychological effect may, owing to the fact that discussion of the refugee problem is constantly in the foreground,

[33]
be very considerable. 158 MEIN KAMPF internal emotion that the work of this man too was bound to be in vain because of

[34]
the fate that would lead this State to its inevitable doom. Had Doktor Karl Lueger lived in Germany, he would have been

[34]
placed in the ranks of the great figures of our nation ; that he had labored in this impos- sible State was the misfortune

[33]
of his work as well as his own. When he died, the little flames in the Balkans leaped up more greedily from month to month, so

[33]
that Fate graciously spared him the sight of that which he still thought he would have been able to prevent. I, however, tried to

[32]
find the causes of the ill success of the one movement and the failure of the second, and I came to the firm

[31]
conclusion that, apart from the impossi- bility of ever reaching a consolidation of the State in old

[32]
Austria, the mistakes of both parties were the following: The Pan-German movement was right on the whole in its

[29]
fundamental opinion about a German rebirth, but it was unlucky in the choice of its way. It was

[32]
nationalistic, but unfortunately not social enough to win the masses. Its anti-Semitism was based on the

[32]
correct realization of the importance of the race problem and not on the im- possibility of religious

[33]
ideas. Its fight against a certain denomination, however, was wrong both in fact and tactics. The Christian Socialist movement

[33]
had an unclear con- ception as to the goal of a German renaissance, but it showed sense and was lucky in seeking its

[32]
way as a party. It understood the social question's importance, but it was wrong in its fight against Judaism and had no

[33]
idea of the power of the national idea. tHad the Christian Socialist Party, in addition to its clever knowledge of

[33]
the great masses, also had the right conception of the importance of the race problem as the Pan-German movement had

[33]
comprehended it, or if it had finally become nationalistic, or if the Pan-German move- ment had accepted,

[33]
in addition to the correct realization of POLITICAL CONSIDERATIONS IN VIENNA 159 the goal, of the Jewish question

[31]
and the importance of the national idea, also the practical cleverness of the Christian Socialist Party, but

[33]
especially the latter's attitude towards socialism, then this would have even then created that movement which in my

[33]
opinion could have intervened suc- cessfully in the fate of the German nation. That this was not the case was due

[32]
for the most part to the nature of the Austrian State. As I did not see this conviction of mine realized in

[32]
any other party, I could not make up my mind in the days that followed to join or even to fight with one of the

[33]
existing organizations. Even then I thought that all the political movements had failed and were incompetent,

[30]
that a na- tional renaissance of the German people on a larger and not really superficial scale was

[33]
impossible. My inner aversion to the Habsburg State grew more and more during that time. The more I began

[33]
to occupy myself especially with the question of foreign politics, the more my opinion grew and the firmer it

[32]
took root that this State formation was bound to become the misfortune of the German nationality. Finally,

[33]
I saw more and more clearly that the fate of the German nation would not be decided from this place, but in the Reich

[33]
proper. This was not only true of all general political questions, but no less for all manifestations of the entire

[31]
cultural life. Here, too, the Austrian State also showed all symptoms of debility or at least of its

[33]
unimportance for the German nation in the domain of purely cultural or artistic affairs. This was true most of

[33]
all in the field of architecture. The new architecture could not be successful in Austria for the reason that since

[31]
the completion of the Ringstrasse the commissions were unimportant, at least as far as Vienna was concerned, as

[33]
compared with the increasing plans of Germany. 160 MEIN KAMPF Thus I began more and more to lead a double life: reason

[33]
and reality forced me to go through a school in Austria that was as bitter as it was blissful, but the heart dwelt somewhere

[34]
else.-^ At that time an oppressive feeling of dissatisfaction seized me; the more I recognized the internal

[32]
hollowness of this State and the impossibility of saving it, the more I felt with certainty that in all and

[33]
everything it only repre- sented the misfortune of the German people. I was convinced that this State was bound

[33]
to oppress and to handicap every really great German, as, on the other hand, it promoted everything non-German.

[32]
I detested the conglomerate of races that the realm's capital manifested ; all this racial mixture of Czechs,

[33]
Poles, Hungarians, Ruthenians, Serbs, and Croats, etc., and among them all, like the eternal fission-fungus [sic] of mankind Jews

[32]
and more Jews. To me the big city appeared as the personification of incest. The German language of my

[32]
childhood was the dialect that was spoken also in Lower Bavaria; I was neither able to forget it nor to learn the

[32]
Viennese jargon. The longer I stayed in this city, the more my hatred increased against the mixture of foreign

[33]
nations that began to eat up this site of old German culture. The idea that this State could still be maintained even

[33]
then seemed ridiculous to me. Austria was at that time like an old mosaic; the cement which held the single little

[31]
stones together had become old and brittle; as long as the masterpiece is untouched, it can still pretend to be

[33]
existent, but as soon as it is given a blow, it breaks into a thousand fragments. The question, therefore, was only when

[32]
the blow would come. Since my heart had never beaten for an Austrian mon- archy but only for a German Reich, I could

[32]
only look upon POLITICAL CONSIDERATIONS IN VIENNA 161 the hour of the ruin of this State as the beginning of the

[33]
salvation of the German nation. For all these reasons the longing grew stronger to go there where since my early youth

[33]
I had been drawn by secret wishes and secret love. I hoped to make a name for myself in the future as an

[32]
architect, and thus, be it in a narrow or a wide frame that Fate was to bestow upon me, to devote my

[33]
honest services to the nation. But finally I wanted to share the happiness of being allowed to work on that spot

[32]
from which the most ardent wish of my heart was bound to be fulfilled: the union of my own beloved country with the common

[33]
fatherland, the German Reich. There are many who even today will not be able to understand the intensity of

[32]
such a longing, but now I appeal to those to whom Fate either has denied this hap- piness or from whom it has again

[33]
cruelly taken it; I appeal to all those who, severed from the motherland, have to fight for the holy treasure of

[31]
their language, those who, because of their faithful adherence to the fatherland, are being persecuted and

[32]
tortured and who now in painful emotion long for the hour that will allow them to return to the arms of the beloved

[33]
mother; I appeal to all those and I know they will understand me. Only he who through his own experience knows what it means

[33]
to be a German without being allowed to belong to the dear fatherland will be able to comprehend the deep longing that

[33]
burns at all times in the hearts of the children who are separated from the motherland. This longing tortures those it

[33]
has seized and denies them contentedness and happiness until the doors of the father's house open and the common blood finds

[32]
peace and quiet again in the common Reich. But Vienna was and remained for me the hardest, but 162 MEIN KAMPF also the most

[33]
thorough, school of my life. I had once entered this city when still half a boy and I left it as a man who had become

[33]
quiet and serious. In that city I received the basis of a view of life in general and a political way

[32]
of looking at things in particular which later on I had only to supplement in single instances, but which never

[34]
again deserted me. But it is only today that I am able to ap- preciate fully the real value of those years

[33]
of learning. This is the reason why I have dealt with this period more fully, as it gave me the first object lessons

[31]
in those very questions which formed part of the fundamental principles of the party which, rising from the smallest

[33]
beginnings, is in the course of hardly five years on the way to develop into a great mass movement. I do not know

[34]
what my attitude towards Judaism, Social Democracy, or better Marxism, social problems, etc., would be today if the basic

[33]
stock of personal opinions had not been formed at so early a time under the pressure of fate and of my own

[31]
learning. For, though the fatherland's misfortune may stimulate thousands upon thousands of people to thinking about the

[33]
internal causes of this collapse, this can never lead to that thoroughness and deeper insight which is opened to him who

[33]
only after years of struggle becomes master of his fate. CHAPTER IV MUNICH IN THE spring of 1912 I came to Munich for

[33]
good, t The town itself was as familiar to me as if I had lived inside its walls for years. The reason for this was that

[33]
my studies, step by step, directed me towards this metro- polis of German art. One has not only not seen Germany if

[33]
one does not know Munich no, above all else, one does not know German art if one has not seen Munich. At any

[33]
rate, this period before the War was the happiest and most satisfying time of my life. Although my income was

[30]
still very meager, I did not live in order to be able to paint, but I painted in order to secure the

[33]
possibility of my existence, or rather in order in this way to permit my-self further study. I harbored

[33]
the conviction that, never- theless and finally, I would reach the goal that I had set before myself. And this alone made

[33]
me bear all other little troubles of my daily life easily and indifferently. But to this was added the inner

[33]
love that seized me, almost from the first hour of my stay, for this town more than any other place known to me.<- A German

[33]
town! What a difference as compared with Vienna! It made me sick only to think back to this racial Babylon. What is

[33]
more, the dialect here was much closer to me, and especially the contact with the Lower Bavarians reminded me of

[33]
the 164 MEIN KAMPF days of my youth. There must have been thousands of things that were, that became, dear to me. But most of all I was

[34]
attracted by the amazing union of inherent strength and delicate, artistic atmosphere, this unique line from

[33]
the Hofbrauhaus to the Odeon, from the Oktoberfest to the Pinakothek, etc. That today I feel more attached to this

[33]
town than to any other place in the world is probably ex- plained by the fact that it is inseparably connected

[33]
with the development of my own life, and will remain so; but that I even then attained the happiness of a really

[32]
inner contentedness was attributable only to the charm that this beautiful residence of the Wittelsbachs

[29]
exercises on every human being who is blessed not only with calculating rea- son but also with

[32]
appreciative feeling, f Apart from my professional work, what attracted me most was again the study of current

[32]
political events, among them especially those of foreign politics. I arrived at the latter by way of the

[33]
German coalition policy, which I had regarded as both wrong and erroneous ever since my time in Austria.

[33]
However, when I was still in Vienna, the full extent of this self-deception of the Reich had not yet be- come fully clear to

[32]
me. In those days I was inclined to assume (or perhaps I only tried to tell myself this as an excuse) that

[33]
possibly Berlin already knew how weak and unreliable the ally would be in reality, but that for more or less

[33]
mysterious reasons they were withholding this know- ledge, in order to support the coalition politics which Bismarck himself

[33]
once had founded, for a sudden break was not desirable for fear one might arouse the foreign countries which were on

[33]
the lookout, and alarm the phi- listines at home. However, contact with the people themselves especially very soon

[31]
made me realize to my great horror that this belief was wrong. To my astonishment I ascertained that ~ven in

[34]
well-informed circles everywhere one had not the MUNICH 165 slightest idea of the internal structure of the Habsburg

[32]
monarchy. The people especially were ensnared with the delusion that one could look upon the ally as a

[33]
serious power that in the hour of distress would certainly be up to the mark. The masses still considered the monarchy

[34]
as a ' German ' State and believed that one could count on this. The opinion was prevalent that its force might be measured

[34]
by millions, as perhaps in Germany itself, and completely forgot that, in the first place, Austria had long since ceased

[32]
to be a German State-entity; that, in the second place, the internal conditions of this realm were constantly

[32]
pressing towards dissolution. I had known this State formation better than these so- called official 'diplomats,' who,

[32]
nearly blind as always, were swaying towards disaster; because the sentiments of the people were only and always the

[33]
outflow of that which was poured into public opinion from above. But up above one worshiped this 'ally' like

[33]
the golden calf. Perhaps one hoped to replace the sincerity which was lacking by ami- ability. In this one

[33]
always accepted words instead of true values. It was already in Vienna that I was seized with fury when I looked at

[31]
the difference between the speeches of the official statesmen and the contents of the Viennese press that was so

[31]
apparent from time to time. Nevertheless, Vienna was still a German city, at least by appearance. But how

[33]
different things were when, leaving Vienna or rather German- Austria behind, one came into the Slavic provinces

[32]
of the realm ! One only had to pick up the news- papers published in Prague if one wanted to know how the sublime

[33]
jugglery of the Triple Alliance was judged there. Nothing was left for this 'statesmanlike' masterpiece but cruel

[33]
taunts and sneers. With absolute peace reigning, and the two emperors exchanging kisses of friendship, no secret was made of

[34]
the opinion that this alliance would collapse 166 MEIN KAMPF the very day an attempt was made to lead it out of the glamor

[32]
of the Nibelungen ideal into practical reality. How excited one got a few years later when, as the hour

[33]
finally had come in which the alliances were to prove themselves, Italy jumped out of the Triple Alliance

[33]
and let its two allies go their own way, and she herself finally be- came an enemy in the end! Only those who were

[33]
not stricken with diplomatic blindness could not understand that people had even dared to believe for a single minute

[32]
in the possibility of such a miracle, namely, that Italy would fight hand in hand with Austria. Even in

[34]
Austria things did not differ by a hair's breadth. <' In Austria, the only bearers of the idea of the alliance were the Habsburgs

[33]
and the Germans. The Habsburgs out of calculation and compulsion, the Germans out of good faith and political stupidity.

[33]
Out of good faith because they thought that through the Triple Alliance they rendered a good service to the German Reich, that

[32]
they helped to strengthen and to protect it: out of political stupidity, however, because neither was the first

[32]
opinion right, but, on the contrary, they helped thus to shackle the Reich to a State carcass that was bound to pull them both

[30]
into an abyss, but above all because through this alliance they themselves fell more and more to

[34]
de-Germanization. For by the alliance with the Reich the Habsburgs were, and unfortunately could be, sure against

[32]
an interference from this side; they were able to carry out more easily and with less risk their internal

[33]
policy of the slow removal of Ger- manism. Not only that with the notorious 'objectivity' one no longer

[33]
had to fear any objection on the part of the Reich's government, but by pointing at the alliance one was able to

[33]
silence the German-Austrian voices that might be raised, from the German side, against Slavization in too infamous

[33]
a fashion. Furthermore, what was the German in Austria to do if MUNICH 167 the Germans in the Reich proper expressed their

[32]
esteem and confidence in the Habsburg regime? Was he to offer resistance, so that in the entire German

[33]
public opinion he would be branded a traitor towards his own nationality? He who for centuries had made the most

[31]
unheard-of sacri- fices for his nationality! But what was the value of this alliance, once the German

[31]
nationality had been rooted out of the Habsburg monarchy? Did not the value of the Triple Alliance for

[32]
Germany really depend on the preservation of the German superiority in Austria? Or did one really

[33]
believe that one could still live in an alliance with a Slavic Habsburg realm? The attitude of official German

[30]
diplomacy, but also that of the entire public opinion, towards the Austrian internal problem of

[31]
nationalities was no longer stupid, no, it was absolutely insane. They trusted in an alliance,

[32]
adjusted the safety of a people of seventy million to it and watched the partner systematically and

[32]
relentlessly destroy the only foundation of this alliance from year to year. One day a ' treaty ' with the Viennese

[32]
diplomacy would remain, but the allied assistance of a realm would be lost. This had been the case with Italy from the

[32]
very begin- ning. If one had studied history a little more clearly in Ger- many, and if one had applied

[33]
a little racial psychology, one would not have believed for even one hour that the Quirinal in Rome and

[32]
the Hofburg in Vienna would ever stand side by side in a common battle front. Italy would rather have become

[31]
a volcano before any government could have dared to place even one single Italian on the

[33]
battlefield of the so fanatically hated Habsburg State, except as an enemy. In Vienna I saw the passionate

[32]
contempt and the bottom- less hatred flare up more than once with which the Italian was 'devoted 1 to the Austrian

[33]
State. The damage that the House of Habsburg had done to Italian liberty and in- 168 MEIN KAMPF dependence for

[33]
centuries was too great to have been for- gotten, even if the will to do so had been present. But it was not at all present;

[33]
neither among the people nor with the Italian government. For Italy, therefore, there existed only two

[32]
possibilities for living together with Austria; either alliance or war. By choosing the first, one was able

[32]
quietly to prepare for the second. The German policy of alliance was as absurd as it was dangerous,

[33]
especially since Austria's relation to Russia was drifting more and more towards a bellicose settle- ment. It

[32]
was a classical case in which the lack of any great and correct line of thought was lacking. Why, then, did one form an

[33]
alliance at all? Certainly only in order to be able to guard the future of the Reich better than Germany,

[34]
standing alone, would have been able to do. But the future of the Reich was nothing but the question of guarding the German

[33]
people's possibility of existence. Therefore, the question could only be formulated thus: Along what lines

[31]
should the life of the German nation develop in the near future, and how can one give this de- velopment the

[33]
necessary foundations and the required security, within the frame of the general European rela- tions of

[32]
power? When considering clearly the suppositions for German statesmanship's activity in foreign politics, one

[32]
necessarily came to the following conclusion : Germany has an annual increase in population of

[33]
almost 900,000 souls. The difficulty of feeding this army of new citizens would become greater with every year, and was bound

[31]
some day to end in a catastrophe, provided ways and means were not found to avert this impending danger of

[33]
hunger-pauperization in time. MUNICH 169 jThere were four ways in which to avoid such a terrible future: (i) One

[32]
could, following the French example, arti- ficially restrict the increase of births and thus avoid over- population.

[33]
Nature herself, in times of great distress or bad climatic conditions, or where the yields of the soil are poor, steps in

[33]
by restricting the population of certain countries or races; this, however, is a method that is as wise as it is

[33]
ruthless. She does not restrict the procreative faculty as such, but the conservation of the propagated, by subjecting

[32]
them to such severe trials and deprivations that all less strong and healthy are forced to return to the bosom of the

[33]
eternally Unknown. What she allows to endure beyond the inclemency of existence is tested in a thousand ways,

[33]
hard and well suited to continue to procreate, so that the This is one of the most important and frequently misunder-

[33]
stood passages in the book. Oddly enough it has been looked upon as substantiating the 'healthy outlook' of the Third Reich. It

[33]
is true, of course, the chronic artificial limitation of the population increase leads to highly deplorable

[32]
social con- sequences: the age structure of the nation may change, so that the burden of age is abnormally

[33]
heavy; normal economic markets, dependent upon the birth of children and the supply- ing of things children need, may dry up;

[33]
and the inner structure of the family may be adversely affected. Hitler's argument is, however, derived

[33]
from the racialistic materialists who, in the balmy days before the World War, predicted that the German population

[31]
structure guaranteed success in the coming conflict. Their statement that the survival of the fittest assures that the

[33]
begetters of new generations will be stronger and therefore more martial is an un verifiable assumption; and

[33]
the view that nature is an infallible selector can easily be tested by the history of savage races

[33]
now under observation. More significant, however, is the view that a people can hold 170 MEIN KAMPF thoroughgoing selection

[32]
may start again from the beginning. Thus, by acting brutally against the individual and calling him back to herself the

[33]
moment he is not equal to weather the storms of life, she conserves the strength of the race and species itself and even

[33]
spurs it towards the highest achievements. Her diminishing of the number is a strengthening of the individual, thus

[32]
finally a strengthening of the species. But it is different if man decides to carry out the re- striction of his

[33]
numbers. He is not cut out of the same wood as Nature, but is 'human. 1 He knows better than this cruel Queen of all Wisdom.

[33]
He does not restrict the continued existence of the individual, but rather propaga- tion itself. This seems to him,

[29]
who always sees only him- self and never the race, more human and more justified than the reverse.

[31]
Unfortunately, the consequences are also now the reverse: While Nature, by giving free rein to

[34]
propagation but its place in the world only if it produces sufficient excess popula- tion to assure victory

[32]
in wars of conquest. There is hardly another statement which has so profoundly disturbed com- fortable visions of the

[33]
terrestial future. For many years it has underlain prophecies concerning the eventual war between 'races'; and it

[33]
has now for some time been a factor in the re- armament of Europe. All the dictatorships Russia, Italy,

[32]
and Germany refer to their reservoirs of man-power as a warning to the weak and the small. In no other case, how-

[32]
ever, has the campaign to increase the population because soldiers are needed been so dramatic as in Get

[33]
many. The most eloquent summary of results to date is Hitler's Reichstag address of February, 1.938. He contended that

[33]
there had been a notable increase in the number of children born. But when the figures advanced are set against

[33]
the population curve, it becomes exceedingly doubtful whether the birth-rate per thousand married women is higher

[32]
than it was previously. MUNICH 171 subjecting the conservation of life to the severest trials, and by choosing, from a

[33]
surplus number of individuals, those who are most worthy of living, thus preserving them alone and now making

[33]
them the bearers of the preservation of the species, man restricts propagation, but on the other hand he makes efforts to

[33]
keep alive, at any price, every human being once it is born. This correction of the divine will seems to him

[33]
to be as wise as it is human, and he is glad that he has outwitted Nature once more in such a matter, and

[33]
that he even has given proof of her shortcomings. But, of course, the Lord's dear little monkey does not at all like to see or

[32]
to hear that in reality, although the number has certainly been restricted, the value of the individual has been

[33]
diminished. Because, once propagation as such has been limited and the number of births reduced, the natural

[33]
struggle for existence, that allows only the very strongest and healthiest to survive, is replaced by the natural

[33]
urge to 'save' at any price also the weakest and even sickest, thus planting the germ for a succession that is bound

[33]
to become more and more miserable the longer this derision of Nature and of her will is continued. But

[32]
the result will be that one day existence in this world will be denied such a people; because man may certainly

[33]
defy the eternal law of the will to continue, but nevertheless revenge will come, sooner or later. A stronger

[33]
generation will drive out the weaklings, because in its ulti- mate form the urge to live will again and again

[33]
break the ridiculous fetters of a so-called ' humanity' of the indi- vidual, so that its place will be taken

[33]
by the 'humanity' of Nature which destroys weakness in order to give its place to strength. He who, therefore, would

[33]
secure the German people's existence by way of a self-restriction of its increase robs it of its future. 172 . MEIN

[31]
KAMPF (2) A second way would be the one that is being sug- gested and eulogized more and more frequently today;

[33]
domestic colonization. This is a suggestion which is well intended by as many as it is generally badly

[31]
understood by most, so that it causes the greatest imaginable damage. The productivity of the soil can

[33]
undoubtedly be in- creased to a certain limit. But of course only to a certain limit, and not continuously

[33]
without end. Therefore, one could be able to balance the increase of the German people by the increased yield

[33]
of our soil for some time, without having to think immediately of hunger. But this is con- fronted by the fact that,

[33]
generally, the demands upon life increase faster than the number of the population. Men's demands with regard to

[31]
food and clothes increase from year to year, and even now they are no longer in proportion When Hitler wrote these

[32]
passages, they meant more than they do now. Prior to the War, Germany had depended to a considerable extent

[33]
upon the exchange of manufactured goods for foodstuffs. Afterward, instructed by the blockade and handicapped by

[33]
a lack of foreign exchange, she began to encourage more intensive farming. The results were a steady rise

[33]
in crop production, aided by rigidly controlled markets. As a matter of fact, the government was able to take grain

[32]
from Russia and resell it at a profit through Amsterdam. The argument now arose as to whether the attempt to

[33]
supply sufficient grain ought not to be abandoned in favor of more specialized farming the production of poultry,

[33]
eggs, milk. This could be realized if the eastern section of the country were broken up into small farms. Advocates of such

[34]
resettlement program, modest beginnings in carrying out which had been made, insisted that it would also stop the overcrowding

[32]
of cities and place a cordon of dependable men along the Polish border. In an official statement issued

[33]
during March, 1930, the Nazis also expressed their approval of the idea, and some of their fading spokesmen promised to

[32]
carry it out efficiently if they MUNICH 173 ro the needs of our forefathers of about a hundred years ago. It is,

[33]
therefore, erroneous to believe that each increase in production creates the presupposition for an increase

[33]
of the population: no; this is true only to a certain degree, for at least part of the surplus yield of the soil is used

[32]
to satisfy the increased demands of men. But even with greatest economy on the one hand, and with the utmost

[33]
industry on the other, here, also, though postponed for some time, a limit will become apparent one day,

[33]
prescribed by the soil itself. Famine will return from time to time in periods of poor harvests, etc. This will occur

[33]
more and more often with the increasing number of the population, and finally will fail to appear only at such

[33]
rare times when years of plenty will have filled the granaries. But finally the time comes when it will no longer

[33]
be possible to satisfy the needs, and famine will have become the eternal companion of such a people. Now

[33]
Nature has to help again and to choose among those she has selected to live, or man will again help himself; that

[34]
means, he turns to artificial restriction with all the grave consequences for race and species alluded to. Now, one may

[33]
object that this future will threaten entire mankind in this way or the other, and that thus the individual peoples

[32]
will not be able to escape this fate. At first sight this is certainly correct. Yet here one has to consider the

[34]
following: Certainly the time will come, in consequence of the impossibility of adapting the fertility

[32]
of the soil to the number of the increasing population, when the whole of came to power. But when the Republic

[32]
attempted in 1931 to carry out an inner colonization program in dead earnest, it was dismissed by President von

[33]
Hindenburg, now himself the owner of an East Prussian estate. Since that time, no real ef- fort has been made to tackle

[32]
the problem. 174 MEIN KAMPF mankind will be forced to stop the increase of the human race and either let Nature decide

[33]
again or to create the necessary balance by self-help, if possible, but then in a better way than that of today.

[34]
But this would hit all na- tions, whereas today only those races are stricken by such distress which no longer have sufficient

[33]
energy and strength to secure for themselves the soil they need in this world. For even today things are such that there is

[33]
still soil on this earth in enormous extent that is unused and only awaits its cultivator. But it is also correct

[32]
that Nature did not reserve this soil in itself for a certain nation or race as re- served territory for the

[34]
future, but it is land and soil for that people which has the energy to take it and the in- dustry to cultivate it.

[31]
Nature does not know political frontiers. She first puts the living beings on this globe and watches the free game of

[33]
energies. He who is strongest in courage and industry receives, as her favorite child, the right to be the master

[33]
of existence. If a people limits itself to domestic colonization, at a time when other races cling to

[32]
greater and greater surfaces of the earth's soil, it will be forced to exercise self-restriction even while other

[32]
nations will continue to increase. For some day this case will occur, and it will arrive the earlier the smaller the

[33]
living space is that a people has at its dis- posal. As, unfortunately only too frequently, the best nations, or,

[33]
better still, the really unique cultured races, the pillars of all human progress, in their pacifistic blindness decide

[31]
to renounce the acquisition of new soil in order to content themselves with 'domestic' colonization, while

[33]
inferior nations know full well how to secure enormous areas on this earth for themselves, this would lead to the following

[33]
result: The culturally superior, but less ruthless, races would have to limit, in consequence of their limited

[34]
soil, their MUNICH 175 increase even at a time when the culturally inferior, but more brutal and more natural,

[33]
people, in consequence of their greater living areas, would be able to increase them- selves without limit. In other

[32]
words: the world will, there- fore, some day come into the hands of a mankind that is inferior in culture but

[33]
superior in energy and activity. For then there will be only two possibilities in the no matter how

[33]
distant future: either the world will be ruled according to the ideas of our modern democracy, and then the stress of

[34]
every decision falls on the races which are stronger in numbers, or the world will be dominated ac- cording to the law

[33]
of the natural order of energy, and then the people of brute strength will be victorious, and again, therefore,

[31]
not the nations of self-restriction. But one may well believe that this world will still be subject to the fiercest fights for the

[33]
existence of mankind. In the end, only the urge for self-preservation will eternally succeed. Under its pressure

[33]
so-called 'humanity,' as the expression of a mixture of stupidity, cowardice, and an imaginary

[33]
superior intelligence, will melt like snow under the March sun. Mankind has grown strong in eternal struggles and it will

[33]
only perish through eternal peace. For us Germans, however, the watchword 'domestic colonization' is unfortunate

[33]
for the reason that with us it The 'Programme der N.S.D.A.P.' drawn up by Feder, stipu- lated that the government would insist upon

[33]
a 'land reform consonant with our national needs, passage of a law to provide for the confiscation, without payment,

[31]
of ground needed for communal purposes, abolition of interest on land, and preven- tion of every kind of

[31]
speculation in land.' This passage created a good deal of bad blood, and on April 13, 1928, Hitler pub- lished an official

[33]
correction stating that since the Party believed in private property, this clause could only mean that land ac- quired

[32]
in unlawful or immoral ways by Jewish speculators. 176 MEIN KAMPF at once enhances, from the pacifistic outlook, the

[33]
opinion that we have found a means which allows us to 'work out' an existence in twilight sleep. Once this doctrine will

[33]
have been taken seriously with us, it would mean the end of every effort to secure in this world the place that

[33]
is ours. Once the average German gained the conviction that he might secure his life and his future in such

[32]
a way, every attempt at an active and fruitful representation of the German necessities of life would be

[33]
eliminated. By such an attitude on the part of the nation all really useful foreign politics, and, with it,

[30]
the future of the German people on the whole, could be looked upon as dead and buried. In realizing these

[31]
consequences it is not by accident that primarily the Jew always tries, and knows how, to implant such deadly and

[33]
dangerous thoughts in our people. He knows his customers only too well not to know that they gratefully fall victims to any

[33]
Spanish treasure swindler who tries to make them believe that a means has now been found to play a trick on Nature, to make

[32]
the hard and in- exorable struggle for life superfluous, so that in its place, be it by work or sometimes

[32]
also by merely doing nothing, just 'as the case may be/ one can rise to be master of the planets. It cannot be

[31]
emphasized sharply enough that all German domestic colonization has to serve, primarily, only to

[32]
abolish social abuses, but above all to withdraw the soil from general speculation, and that it can never

[32]
suffice to secure the future of the nation without new land and soil. If this is not done, then, after a short

[30]
time, we will not Expropriation of property owned by Jews or political enemies has been fairly

[34]
continuous, but reached new heights during 1938. In Austria Jewish cultural centers and Jewish homes alike were taken

[33]
away, without any legal formality other than registration. MUNICH 177 only have arrived at the limit of

[32]
our soil, but also at the end of our strength. But finally, the following must also be established : The restriction to

[33]
a certain small surface of soil, as con- ditioned by domestic colonization, and the same final result which is

[33]
achieved by limitation of propagation, lead to an extremely unfavorable military political

[32]
situation of the nation involved. The size of a people's living area includes an essential factor for the

[33]
determination of its outward security. The greater the amount of room a people has at its disposal, the greater

[33]
is also its natural protection; because military victories over nations crowded in small territories have

[33]
always been reached more quickly and more easily, espe- cially more effectively and more completely,

[33]
than in the cases of States which are territorially greater in size. The size of the State territory,

[32]
therefore, gives a certain pro- tection against frivolous attacks, as success may be gained only after long and

[32]
severe fighting and, therefore, the risk of an impertinent surprise attack, except for quite unusual

[31]
reasons, will appear too great. In the greatness of the State territory, therefore, lies a reason for the easier

[32]
preservation of a nation's liberty and independence, whereas, in the reverse case, the smallness of such a

[33]
formation simply in- vites seizure. The two first-mentioned possibilities for the creation of a balance between

[31]
the rising numbers of population and the unchanging territory were indeed rejected by the so- called

[31]
national circles of the Reich. The reasons for this attitude were of course different from those mentioned

[32]
above: towards birth control one primarily showed a nega- tive attitude because of a certain

[34]
moral feeling; domestic colonization was indignantly rejected, as in it one scented an attack against the great

[32]
landowners, and with it the beginning of a general fight against private property aa 178 MEIN KAMPF such. The form in which the

[32]
latter doctrine of salvation especially was recommended justified this assumption. In general, however, the

[33]
defense against the great masses was not very skillful and did not meet the nucleus of the problem. Thus, there remained but

[32]
two ways to assure work and bread to the increasing number of people. (3) One could either acquire new soil in order

[31]
annually to send off the superfluous millions, and thus conserve the na- tion further on on the basis of a

[33]
self-sustainment, or one could set about, (4) through industry and trade, to produce for foreign consumption and to live on

[33]
the proceeds. <? That means: either territorial policy, or colonial and trade policy. Both ways were examined,

[33]
investigated, recommended, and fought, till finally the second one was carried out. The healthier of the two, of course,

[31]
was the first. The acquisition of new land and soil for the settling of the superfluous population has no end of

[32]
advantages, especially when turning away from the present towards the future. The very possibility of

[33]
preserving a healthy peasant class as the basis of the entire nation can never be sufficiently valued. To a great

[32]
extent many of our present sufferings are only the consequences of the unhealthy proportion be- tween town and

[33]
country population. A solid stock of small and medium peasants was at all times the best protection against social ills

[33]
as we have them today. This is also the only solution that allows a nation to find its daily bread in the inner

[33]
circle of its domestic economy. Industry and trade step back from their unwholesome leading positions into

[34]
the general frame of a national economy of balanced demand and supply. Both are then no longer the basis

[33]
of a nation's subsistence, but a means to it. Inasmuch as now they have a balance between their supply and demand

[33]
in all MUNICH 179 fields, they make the entire support of the nation inde- pendent of foreign countries, thus helping to secure

[33]
the lib- erty of the State and the independence of the nation, especially in times of distress. Obviously, such

[33]
a territorial policy, howe^ its fulfillment in the Cameroons, for exclusively only in Europe. One

[32]
must i accept the point of view that it certainly/ intention to give fifty times as much earth to one nation as

[33]
compared with ai! political frontiers must not keep us awaj of eternal right. If this earth really has : to live in, then

[32]
one should give us the spa? for living. One will certainly not like to do this. Then, however, the Here Hitler,

[31]
following Rosenberg and some other theorists, professes disinterestedness in what has since become a

[33]
familiar Nazi demand. The two greatest apostles of colonial acquisition in Africa and elsewhere have

[34]
been Dr. Heinrich Schnee and Dr. Hjalmar Schacht. The first, who was a prominent Ger- man colonial officer before the War, has led the fight

[33]
to revise the Treaty of Versailles to permit restoration to Germany of her former colonies. But the influence

[33]
of Dr. Schacht has been far greater. In the memoirs of President Friedrich Ebert, one reads that Schacht, then a little known official whose

[32]
affiliation with the Democratic Party had brought him good Jewish con- nections, had proposed a scheme whereby

[30]
Germany was to purchase with American money the Portuguese colony of Angola. After 1933 Schacht

[33]
intensified his drive, with the result that the point of view taken in Mein Kampf appeared to have been revised. It is

[31]
probable, however, that recent agita- tion has been directed in the main towards getting possession of Southwest

[33]
Africa and possibly indirect control of the whole of South Africa, where a great deal of money has been spent on

[32]
propaganda and where the party is relatively strong. For a 180 MEIN KAMPF right of self-preservation comes into

[32]
effect; and what has been denied to kindness will have to be taken with the fist. Had our forefathers once made their

[32]
decisions dependent on the same pacifistic nonsense as that of our present time, we should own altogether

[32]
only one third of our present terri- tory; but in that case a German people would not have any cause for

[33]
uneasiness in Europe. No. To their natural de- termination to fight for their own existence we owe the two

[32]
Ostmarks of the Reich and with it that internal strength of the greatness of our State and national territory that alone

[32]
enabled us to exist to this day. This solution would have been the right one for another reason also: Many

[31]
European States today are comparable to pyramids standing on their points. Their European territory is

[31]
ridicu- lously small as compared with their burden of colonies, for- eign trade, etc. One may say, the point is in

[33]
Europe, the base in the whole world ; in comparison with the American Union, which still has its bases in its own

[33]
continent and touches the remaining part of the world only with its points. From this results, however, the unheard-of internal

[34]
strength of this State and the weakness of most of the European colonial powers. Even England is no proof to the contrary,

[33]
for because of the British Empire, one only too easily forgets the Anglo- Saxon world as such. England cannot

[33]
be compared with any other State in Europe, if only because of her linguistic and cultural communion

[33]
with the American Union. time it seemed as if the British were willing to make a deal, but more recently

[32]
their ardor has cooled perceptibly. At the close of 1938 'colonial schools' in Germany were training young people for

[33]
colonial administration. Some also feel that the Ger- man government would also not be averse to dividing

[33]
the French colonies in Africa with the Italians. MUNICH 181 For Germany, therefore, the only possibility

[33]
of carrying out a sound territorial policy was to be found in the acquisi- tion of new soil in Europe proper.

[32]
Colonies cannot serve this purpose, since they do not appear suitable for settle- ment with Europeans on a large

[32]
scale. But in the nine- teenth century it was no longer possible to gain such colo- nial territories in a

[34]
peaceful way. Such a colonial policy could only have been carried out by means of a hard struggle which would have been

[33]
fought out more suitably, not for territories outside Europe, but rather for land in the home continent itself.

[31]
Such a decision, however, requires undivided devotion. It doesn't do to set out half-heartedly or even

[33]
hesitatingly on a task, the execution of which seems possible only with the exertion of the utmost energy.

[31]
Then also the entire The theory that Germany can expand at the expense of Russia has very complex

[33]
origins and possibly an equally com- plicated future. A large section of the Nazi Party has always been

[33]
skeptical of this idea; and after 1919 the dominant point of view among German nationalists was that Russia must be made

[32]
an ally, with whose help the war of revenge might be waged against the Western Powers. Even Count Ernst zu Reventlow,

[31]
a Nazi but with a nuance all his own, once conferred with Karl Radek on the possibility of such an

[33]
alliance. From time to time since 1933 army officers in the two countries have discussed the thing anew. It is

[34]
usually thought that the ' crisis ' which Stalin solved by ordering the execution of many high officials in the Soviet

[33]
government and army was the product of one such conversation. It is therefore not at all improbable that this

[33]
policy may triumph ultimately despite all that has been said to the contrary. Hitler's attitude as stated

[30]
here seems in the main derivative from two sources: first, the speculations of Alfred Rosenberg, and the views

[31]
entertained by Generals Ludendorff and Max Hoffman on the Treaty of Brest-Li tovsk, signed with Bolshevist 181 MEIN KAMPF

[33]
political authority of the Reich would have had to serve this exclusive purpose; never should any step have

[33]
been taken from considerations other than the realization of this task and its conditions. One had to make it clear

[30]
to oneself that this goal could be reached only through fighting, and quietly to face the passage at arms. All the

[33]
alliances should have been examined exclusively from this point of view and evaluated according to their

[32]
suitability. If one wanted land and soil in Europe, then by and large this could only have been done at

[31]
Russia's ex- pense, and then the new Reich would again have to start marching along the road of the knights of the orders

[33]
[Ordensritter: it is possible that the author meant to use the word Ritterorden, i.e., crusaders] of former times

[34]
to give, Russia in 1918. Rosenberg was born in Reval and educated in Moscow. Following the triumph of Lenin, he came

[32]
to Germany and settled in Munich, where he met Hitler and became the 'philosopher' of the Nazi Party. His

[33]
obscure racial origins he is certainly partly of Tartar blood and may even have Jewish ancestors his cloudy

[30]
intellectual background, and his advo- cacy of a Germanic religion are familiar topics of

[31]
conversation in all circles where Germany is discussed. He once drew from Dr. Brtlning, speaking before the Reichstag, the

[33]
following fa- mous rebuke: 'I have been accused of a dearth of affection for my country by a gentleman who, while

[32]
I was fighting for the fatherland, had not yet made up his mind if he had a father- land. 1 It is quite probable that

[33]
Rosenberg was initiated in the out- look of the 'Black Hundred,' as a rightist secret organization which kept the Czarist

[33]
police on their toes before the War was called. This ultra-nationalistic and violently anti-Semitic group may,

[32]
indeed, have transmitted to Hitler, through Rosen- berg, the deeper bases of his doctrine. Careful study of the pos-

[34]
sible sources of this man's views is badly needed. At any rate, Rosenberg: argued that just as a Bolshevist Russia had

[32]
once MUNICH 183 with the help of the German sword, the soil to the plow and the daily bread to the nation. For such a policy,

[33]
however, there was only one single ally in Europe: England. With England alone, one's back being covered,

[33]
could one begin the new Germanic invasion. Our right to do this would not have been less than that of our forefathers. None

[33]
of our pacifists refuses to eat the bread of the East, although the first plow was once called ' sword ' ! To gain England's favor, no

[34]
sacrifice should have been too great. Then one would have had to renounce colonies and sea power, but to spare British

[33]
industry our compe- tition. Only an unconditionally clear attitude could lead to such a goal: renouncing world trade

[34]
and colonies; renouncing a almost seized Germany, so in turn a Nazi Germany might seize Russia. The coveted

[34]
territory is sometimes held to be Ac Ukraine which Ludendorff and Hoffman set up as an independent State in

[32]
1918. This is a 'wheat granary' and much else besides. Assuming that the Ukrainians are dissatisfied with Soviet

[31]
rule, the plan would be to foment a revolution there, set up an independent State, and exercise a

[34]
protectorate over it. But in 1918 Poland objected bitterly to the cession of the Province of Cholm to the Ukraine,

[31]
and without Cholm a united Ukraine is incon- ceivable. The effect of a new step in this direction during 1938

[32]
immediately caused the Polish government to foster better relations with Russia. Moreover, it is not dear

[32]
whether, sup- posing that all obstacles were surmounted and an independent Ukraine were set up, Germany could

[33]
exploit the region as the theorists assume. As for Russia, it cannot give up without a struggle a region upon

[32]
which it depends for bread and inside which some of its major industrial plants are situated. Accordingly the

[33]
arguments in favor of assuming that the German future lies where Hitler said it did in 1925 must be set 184 MEIN KAMPF German

[32]
war fleet. Concentration of the State's entire means of power in the land army. The result would certainly have been

[33]
a momentary re- striction, but a great and powerful future. There was a time when England would have permitted

[33]
herself to engage in discussions such as these. She under- stood quite well that Germany, in consequence of her in-

[33]
crease in population, had to look for some way out, and would find this either with England's co-operation in Europe,

[33]
or without England in the world. It was attributable, probably, to this idea that at the turn of the century London

[30]
herself tried to approach Germany. In those days there appeared for the first time that which we have had an

[31]
opportunity of observing in a really terrify- ing manner in these times. One was unpleasantly

[33]
affected off against arguments that stress the difficulties in the way. Equally important as a factor is the growing

[32]
similarity between the Russian and the German regimes, now often pointed out. During 1920, a Social Democratic

[33]
commission went from Ger- many to study the actual achievements of the Soviet system. The report then issued by one

[32]
of its members, Wilhelm Ditt- mann, corresponds strikingly with any of the number of reports on the Nazi system now being

[33]
written by observers of the same school. Rosenberg and others have been convinced that British sup- port could be gained for

[32]
any serious attempt to undermine the Russian system and therewith stamp out the Third Interna- tional as a

[33]
fomenter of world revolution. Two reasons for this conviction are usually advanced. The first is the support re-

[32]
ceived by White Russian revolutionists from English sources, which support has occasionally been deflected to

[32]
Hitler. The second is the feud long since in progress between certain British financiers and the Soviet system. Sir Henry

[33]
Deterding, the oil magnate, was themost manifest of the partisans of Germany ; and MUNICH 185 by the idea that now one

[32]
would have to 'pull the chestnuts out of the fire ' for England ; as if an alliance were at all con- ceivable on

[32]
a basis other than that of mutual business transactions! Such a business could very well have been done with

[31]
England. British diplomacy was still clever enough to know that, without reciprocal service, no service could be

[33]
expected. Imagine that a clever German foreign policy assumed Japan's r61e in 1904, and one can hardly realize

[33]
what conse- quences this would have had for Germany. It would never have come to a 'World War.' The blood of the year 1904 would have

[31]
saved the tenfold amount of the years 1914 till 1918. But what position would Germany have in the world today? To be sure, the

[33]
alliance with Austria was an absurdity in that case. Because this mummy of a State did not unite with

[31]
Ger- many in order to fight a war, but rather for the conserva- tion of eternal peace, which then could have been

[33]
cleverly used for the slow but certain extinction of the German nation in the monarchy. This alliance, however,

[33]
was an impossibility, for the rea- son that one could not expect official representation of national German

[34]
interests on the part of a State, so long as it had not even the power and the determination to make the reader

[33]
can surmise the existence of other connections if he studies Ourselves and Germany, by Lord Londonderry, Doubt-

[31]
less a more important factor has been the British endeavor to deflect a war if there must be war from western

[33]
Europe. Yet, however willing London might be to let Germany become entangled in the East, the chances have grown

[32]
less and less im- pressive that any support for such a maneuver would be forth- coming. 116 MEIN KAMPF an end to the process of

[33]
de-Germanization outside its imme- diate frontier. If Germany did not possess enough national consciousness and

[33]
also ruthlessness to tear the disposition of the fate of the ten million tribesmen from the hands of this impossible

[34]
Habsburg State, then one could hardly expect that it would ever offer its help to such farseeing and daring plans. The attitude

[33]
of the old Reich towards the Austrian question was the touchstone for its attitude in the entire nation's fateful

[33]
struggle. IH any event, one should not have looked on idly while the German nation was being pushed back from year to

[31]
year, as Austria's value as an ally was determined exclu- sively by the preservation of the German

[34]
element. However, one did not go this way at all. One feared nothing more than a fight, so that finally in the least

[33]
favorable hour one was nevertheless forced into it. One tried to escape Fate and was overtaken by

[33]
it. One dreamed of the preservation of world peace and landed in the World War. For this was the most important reason why

[33]
one never considered this third way of the formation of a German future. One knew that the acquisition of

[33]
new soil was to be These passages imply not only a critique of Germany's pre- War policy, but also indeed,

[33]
primarily a negation of the views then prevalent in the Alldeutscher Verband (Pan-German League). Its leaders, Heinrich Class

[32]
in particular, had looked upon a war with the western powers as inevitable, had there- fore cherished the

[34]
alliance with Austria, and had counseled rapprochement with Russia. After the War generals who had sponsored the Treaty

[33]
of Brest-Litovsk professed to believe that the opposite point of view had been theirs all along; and to their analysis

[33]
Hitler added his contempt for the Habsburg State. It is still far too early to predict that the plan sponsored in Mein Kampf will

[34]
be rigidly adhered to. MUNICH 187 attained only in the East, and one saw the necessary fight, and yet one wanted

[33]
peace at any price; for the watchword of German foreign politics had long ceased to be, preserva- tion of the German

[33]
nation by all means, but rather, preser- vation of the world peace by all available means. It is well known how this succeeded.

[32]
I will come back to this point in particular. Thus there remained still the fourth possibility: industry and world

[32]
trade, sea power and colonies. Such a development, in the first instance, could be reached more easily and more

[33]
quickly. The settlement of land and soil is a slow process that often takes centuries; in this its inner strength may be sought that

[32]
it does not mean a sudden flaring-up, but a slow but thorough and continued growing, as compared with the industrial

[32]
development which can be blown up in the course of a few years, which then, however, resembles a soap bubble more than

[33]
genuine strength. Of course, a fleet can be built more quickly than the establishment of farms and settling them with farmers, a tough

[33]
struggle; but it can also be destroyed more quickly. If Germany, nevertheless, chose this way, then one had at least to

[32]
recognize clearly that this development also would some day end in fighting. Only children could be- lieve that, through

[33]
friendly and civilized behavior and con- tinued emphasis on a friendly disposition, could they gather their ' bananas'

[32]
in a 'peaceful competition of na- tions/ as one so nicely and unctuously chattered, without ever being

[32]
forced to take up arms. No; if we went this way, then England would some day become our enemy. It was more than

[33]
absurd to get indig- nant at this, but it was in keeping with our own harmless- ness that England took the liberty of some day

[33]
meeting our peaceful activity with the brutality of the violent egoist. We, I regret to say, would never have

[33]
done this. If European territorial policy could be carried out against 188 MEIN KAMPF Russia only with England as an

[33]
ally, then, on the other hand, colonial and world trade policy was conceivable only against England with the help

[33]
of Russia. But then one would here also have had to accept the consequences ruth- lessly and above all one

[33]
would have to drop Austria immediately. Looked at from any direction, this alliance was genuine madness as

[33]
early as the turn of the century. However, one did not at all think of forming an alliance with Russia against

[33]
England, nor with England against Russia, for in both cases the end would have been war, and to prevent this one decided

[32]
in favor of a trade and indus- trial policy. With the 'peaceful economic' conquest of the world one had

[33]
a formula which was supposed to break the neck of the former policy of force once and for all. But sometimes

[34]
one was not quite sure of this, especially when from time to time quite unintelligible threats came over

[33]
from England; therefore, one decided to build a fleet, but again not for attack or for the destruction of England, but

[33]
for the 'defense' of the already mentioned 'world peace' and of the 'peaceful conquest' of the world. Therefore, it was

[34]
kept a little more modestly in all and everything, not only in number, but also in tonnage of the single ships

[34]
as well as in armament, so that finally one could manifest 'peaceful' intentions after all. The talk of the 'peaceful

[33]
economic conquest' of the world was certainly the greatest folly that was ever made the leading principle of a State

[32]
policy. This nonsense was still further increased by the fact that one did not shy off from calling England as the crown

[32]
witness for the possibility of such an achievement. What sins the historical doctrine and conception of our

[32]
professors helped on thereby can hardly be remedied, and it is only a striking proof of the manner in which people

[31]
today 'learn' history without understanding or even grasping it. Precisely in England MUNICH 189 one should have

[32]
realized the striking refutation of this theory: no nation has more carefully prepared its economic

[32]
conquest with the sword with greater brutality and de- fended it later on more ruthlessly than the British. Is it not

[33]
a characteristic of British statesmanship to draw economic conquests from political force and at once to

[33]
mold every economic strengthening into political power? But what a mistake to believe that England was

[34]
perhaps personally too ' cowardly ' to shed her own blood in defense of her economic policy! The fact that the English

[33]
people had no 'national army' in no way proved the contrary; for it is not the mili- tary form of the defensive

[33]
power of the moment that counts, but rather the will and the determination to risk what is at hand. England always possessed

[33]
the armament that she needed. She always fought with the weapons that were required for success. She fought with mercenaries as

[31]
long as mercenaries sufficed; but she also dipped into the most valuable blood of the entire nation

[32]
whenever such a sacrifice alone was able to bring about victory; but the determina- tion to fight and the

[33]
tenacity and unflinching conduct always remained the same. In Germany, however, by way of school, press, and comic

[33]
papers, one gradually created an image of the character of the Englishman and even more of his realm that

[32]
led to one of the most catastrophic self-deceptions; because everything was gradually infected by this

[33]
folly, and its consequence was an underestimation that took its most bitter revenge. This deception went so deep and

[33]
was so great that one was This is doubtless intended for the consumption of the ' English cousins.' In 1914 Germany was not misled

[33]
by a few cartoons into thinking that the English were gulls; it jumped, by reason of the British government's non-committal

[33]
statements, to the belief that it would find England neutral . . . long enough, at any rate, to permit Moltke to defeat France.

[31]
190 MEIN KAMPF convinced that one saw in the Englishman a merchant as crafty as he was personally incredibly

[31]
cowardly. That an empire of the size of the British had not been brought to- gether by sneaking and swindling never

[33]
occurred to our sublime teachers of professorial wisdom. The few who uttered warnings were not listened to

[34]
or were passed by in silence. I well remember the astonished faces of my com- rades, when in Flanders we faced

[33]
the Tommies personally. After the first few days of battle the conviction dawned on everyone that these Scots did not

[33]
quite correspond to those one had thought fit to describe to us in comic papers and newspaper dispatches. In those

[33]
days I formed my first reflections about the use- fulness of the form of propaganda. But this falsification had one

[32]
good side for those who spread it; by this example, although it was wrong, one was able to demonstrate the fact that the

[33]
economic conquest of the world was correct. We, too, could succeed where the Englishman had succeeded, where by our greater

[34]
honesty the lack of that specific English 'perfidy' could be looked upon as a special asset. For in this one hoped

[31]
to win the sympathy of the smaller nations especially as well as the confidence of the greater ones more

[33]
easily. For the reason alone that we believed all this quite seri- ously, we did not see that our honesty was

[33]
an abomination in the eyes of the others, while the rest of the world consid- ered this behavior as the expression

[32]
of an especially sly mendacity, till at last, to the greatest astonishment of all, the revolution gave a

[33]
deeper insight into the unlimited stupidity of our 'honest' conviction. But from the nonsense of this 'peaceful

[33]
economic con- quest 9 of the world the absurdity of the Triple Alliance was at once clear and understandable.

[32]
With what other State, then, could we form an alliance? Together with Austria one could really not set out on a ' martial '

[33]
conquest, let us say, MUNICH 191 even in Europe. In this very fact lay the inner weakness of this alliance from the first

[33]
day. A Bismarck was allowed to take this emergency measure, but not any bungling suc- cessor, and least of all at

[34]
a time when the essential supposi- tions for Bismarck's alliance had long ceased to exist; for Bismarck still believed he had

[33]
a German State in Austria. With the gradual introduction of general suffrage, however, this country had come

[31]
down to the level of a parliamentar- ily ruled, un-German medley. Then, too, the alliance with Austria was

[33]
disastrous from the point of view of a racial policy. One tolerated the rising of a new Slavic great power at

[33]
the frontier of the Reich which sooner or later would take an attitude towards Ger- many quite different from that of,

[32]
for example, Russia. But the alliance itself, therefore, was bound to become weaker from year to year and more

[31]
hollow internally in the same proportion in which the only supporters of this idea lost their influence in the

[33]
monarchy and were crowded out of the most authoritative posts. At the turn of the century the alliance with

[32]
Austria had entered into exactly the same state as Austria's alliance with Italy. IJere, too, there

[33]
existed only two possibilities: either one was in alliance with the Habsburg monarchy, or one had to

[30]
protest against the suppression of the German nationality. Once one starts a thing like that, the end is

[34]
usually open battle. The value of the Triple Alliance was psychologically mod- est, as the stability

[33]
of an alliance increases in the measure in which the individual contracting parties hope to attain cer-

[32]
tain seizable, expansive goals through it. On the other hand, an alliance will be the weaker the more it restricts

[33]
itself to the preservation of an existing condition as such. Here also, as everywhere, the strength lies not in

[33]
defense but in attack. 192 MEIN KAMPF This was already recognized in those days by various sides, unfortunately

[33]
not by those who were the so-called 'chosen/ Especially Ludendorff, then Colonel in the Great Army Staff, pointed to

[33]
these weaknesses in a memorandum of the year 1912. But on the part of the 'statesmen,' of course, no value or importance

[33]
was attributed to the mat- ter; for, on the whole, clear common sense becomes appar- ent only through common mortals, but

[31]
is not necessary where 'diplomats' are concerned. It was indeed fortunate for Germany that the war

[33]
finally broke out in 1914 by way of Austria, so that the Habsburgs were forced to join; had it been the other way round, Ger-

[33]
many would have stood alone. Never would the Habsburg State have been able or willing to join in a fight that had been

[33]
caused by Germany. What later one judged so severely about Italy would have happened even earlier

[32]
with Austria; one would have remained 'neutral/ so as to save the State from a revolution at the very

[31]
beginning. The Austrian Slavic nationalities would have smashed the mon- archy in 1914 rather than have helped

[34]
Germany. But only very few were able to realize how great the dangers and difficulties were which the alliance

[32]
with the Danubian monarchy involved. First of all, Austria had too many enemies who hoped to inherit from the

[30]
decaying State, so that a certain hatred was bound to break out against Germany in the course of time, as one

[33]
considered Germany the cause preventing the decline of the monarchy, hoped for and longed for from all sides.

[32]
One arrived at the conviction that Vienna was only to be reached by way of Berlin. But with this Germany lost,

[33]
secondly, the best and most hopeful possibilities for an alliance. It was replaced by an ever-increasing

[31]
tension with Russia and even Italy. In Rome especially the general mood was as pro-German as it was

[34]
anti-Austrian in the heart of even the most humble Italian, sometimes flaring up vividly. MUNICH 193 t Now, since one

[33]
had taken up a commercial and industrial policy, there was no longer even the slightest cause for a war against

[30]
Russia. Only the enemies of both nations could still have a lively interest in that. Indeed, it was

[33]
primarily only Jews and socialists who stirred and fanned public opinion towards a war between these two States

[33]
with all possible means. Finally, and thirdly, this alliance must needs harbor an unlimited danger for Germany for

[31]
the reason that a great power that was hostile to the Reich of Bismarck could easily succeed at any time in

[33]
mobilizing quite a number of States against Germany, as one was able to promise enrichment for each of

[33]
them at the expense of Austria's ally. One had to stir up the entire East of Europe against the Danubian

[33]
monarchy, especially Russia and Italy. Never would the world coalition have come together that began to form

[32]
itself with King Edward's initiating activity, had not Austria, as Germany's ally, represented a too tempting

[33]
legacy. Only thus did it become possible to bring States, which otherwise had such heterogeneous wishes

[33]
and aims, into one single front. With a general advance against Germany, every one of them could hope to

[33]
receive enrichment at the expense of Austria. The danger was increased exceed- ingly by the fact that now Turkey

[33]
also seemed to be a silent partner of this unfortunate alliance. But international Jewish world finance

[30]
needed this bait in order to carry out the longed-for plan of a destruction of 4 International Jewry' as the

[31]
instigator of war was one of divers concoctions made to soothe the patriotic ache. It is served up

[33]
constantly in anti-Semitic brochures and periodicals of the post-War period. A favorite name was that

[33]
of Mr. J. P. Morgan, who was endowed with Hebrew blood. The theory is a kind of extreme Rightist counterpart to the Marxist view that

[34]
the drift to war is inherent in the capitalist system. 194 MEIN KAMPF Germany, which did not yet submit herself to the general

[34]
super-State control of finance and economics. Only with this was one able to forge a coalition, made strong

[34]
and cour- ageous by the armies numbering millions now on the march, ready to attack the horned Siegfried at last. The alliance

[34]
with the Habsburg monarchy, which had filled me with discontent while I was still in Austria, now began to become the cause

[33]
of long internal trials which in the interval merely strengthened the opinion I had previ- ously made.-' Even

[33]
in those days, in the small circles which I fre- quented, I did not conceal my opinion that this unfortunate treaty with

[33]
a State destined to destruction would also lead to a catastrophic collapse of Germany, unless one knew how

[33]
to break away in time, I never wavered even for a moment in my firm conviction, even when the storm of the World

[34]
War seemed to have excluded all reasonable thinking and the ecstasy of enthusiasm had even seized those for

[34]
whom there should have existed the coldest consideration of real- ity. When I was at the front, whenever these problems

[32]
were discussed, I upheld my opinion that the alliance should be broken, the sooner the better for the German

[33]
nation, and that the price of the abandonment of the Austrian monarchy would be no sacrifice at all, if by this

[32]
Germany could gain a lessening in the number of her enemies; because it was not for the preservation of a

[33]
dissolute dynasty that mil- lions had put on the steel helmet, but for the salvation of the German nation. A few times

[32]
before the War it seemed as though at least in one camp there had appeared a slight doubt about the cor- rectness of the

[32]
policy of alliance. German conservative cir- cles from time to time began to warn against too great a

[33]
confidence, but this was thrown to the wind, as was done with all that was sensible. One was convinced that one was on

[30]
the right way to a 'conquest' of the world, the success of MUNICH 195 which would be enormous, the sacrifices for which would be

[32]
negligible. Once more the only choice of the notorious 'un-chosen' was to watch in silence why and how the

[33]
'chosen' marched straight towards destruction, drawing the innocent people behind them like the piper of Hamelin. The deeper

[31]
causes of the possibility of presenting, and even of making understandable, the absurdity of an

[33]
'economic conquest' as a practical political way, the preservation of 'world peace' as a political goal, to

[33]
an entire people was found in the general indisposition of our entire political thinking as a whole.

[33]
With the victorious march of German technical skill and industry, with the rising successes of German trade, the knowledge

[32]
was gradually lost that all this was only possible on the basis of a strong State. On the contrary, in many

[32]
circles one went so far as to have the opinion that the State itself owed its existence only to these

[32]
developments, that the State itself represented only an economic institution, that it was to be ruled

[33]
according to economic rules, and that therefore it depended in its makeup on economics, a condi- tion

[33]
which was then looked upon and praised as by far the soundest and most natural. But the State has nothing whatsoever to do

[33]
with a definite conception of economics or development of eco- nomics. The State is not an assembly

[33]
of commercial parties in a certain prescribed space for the fulfillment of economic tasks, but the organization

[34]
of a community of physically and mentally equal human beings for the better possibility of the furtherance

[33]
of their species as well as for the fulfill- ment of the goal of their existence assigned to them by Providence. This, and

[33]
nothing else, is the purpose and the 196 MEIN KAMPF meaning of a State. Economy is, therefore, only one of

[32]
the many auxiliary means necessary for reaching this goal. But it is never the cause or the purpose of

[33]
a State, provided the latter is not based from the start on a foundation that is wrong because it is unnatural.

[33]
Only thus can it be explained that the State, as such, need not even have a territorial limitation as its

[33]
assumption. This will be necessary only with those nations which for their own part want to secure the maintenance of

[33]
their fellow men; that means that they are ready to fight the struggle for existence by their own work. Nations which are able

[33]
to sneak their way into the rest of mankind like drones, in order to make them work for them under all kinds of pretexts, are

[33]
able to form States without any certain limited living area of their own. This may be said primarily of that people

[33]
under the parasitism of which, especially today, the entire honest mankind has to suffer: the Jews. The Jewish State

[32]
was never spatially limited in itself; it was universally unlimited in respect to space, but it was

[33]
restricted to the collectivity of a race. This is the reason why this people always forms a State within other

[32]
States. It was one of the most ingenious tricks that was ever in- vented to let this State sail under the flag of

[30]
'religion/ thus securing for it the tolerance that the Aryan is always ready to grant to a religious

[33]
denomination. Actually the Mosaic religion is nothing but a doctrine of the preservation of the Jewish

[33]
race. Therefore, it comprises also nearly all The Old Testament conceived of as a volume written to ex-

[33]
pound the nationalistic philosophy of the Jewish race is now a favorite item on the Nazi cultural

[31]
menu. Rosenberg writes in Mythus des 2on Jahrhunderts (Myth of the 2Oth Century): 4 As a book of religion, the Old

[33]
Testament must be done away with once and for all. That will end the unsuccessful attempt of 1500 years to turn us mentally

[33]
into Jews, with the result, MUNICH 197 sociological, political, and economic fields of knowledge which could ever

[33]
come into question. fThe instinct of preserving the species is the first cause of the formation of human communities.

[33]
But the State is a folk organism and not an economic organization. A difference that is as great as it

[33]
remains incomprehensible to the so-called 'statesmen/ especially of today. They believe, therefore, that they

[32]
can build up the State by economy, whereas in reality it is always the result of the activity of those

[33]
qualities which lie in line with the will to preserve the species and the race. But these are always heroic virtues

[29]
and never commercial egoism, since the pre- servation of the existence of a species presupposes the

[32]
individual's willingness to sacrifice itself. This is the very among other things, that we are at present

[32]
materially depend- ent upon Jews.' For him as for his assistants in Nazi educa- tional effort (J. Von Leers, for

[31]
instance), the Old Testament is nothing but a collection of stories about prostitutes and cattle- traders. By

[33]
comparison the Germanic legends and the German mystics teach heroism, soldierly conduct, and purity. The endeavors of

[34]
the Christian Churches to defend the Sacred Books against the official propagandists are reflected in the answers to the Mythits

[33]
written by Catholic and Protestant scholars. Of especial importance are the Advent sermons preached by Cardinal

[31]
Faulhaber, of Munich, on the sub- ject. These are reprinted in Judaism, Christianity and Ger- many. A recent

[32]
pamphleteer puts this more succinctly: 'Our people in arms is no longer an army. It has become the youthful fight- ing

[31]
nation. The army, the police, the armed organizations of our youth, can now be used for greater national

[32]
purposes. Producers of foodstuffs, members of the teaching profession, and all other groups in the community are now

[33]
prepared to work for the good of the nation as a whole when emergency 198 MEIN KAMPF meaning of the poet's words ' Und setzet ihr

[31]
nicht das Leben tin, nie wird Euch das Leben gewonnen sein' [Unless you stake your life, never will life be won], that the

[34]
sacrifice of the personal existence is necessary in order to guarantee the preservation of the species.

[33]
Thus the most essential sup- position for the formation and preservation of a State is the presence of a certain

[33]
feeling of homogeneity on the basis of the same entity and the same species, as well as the readiness to

[32]
risk one's life for this with all means, something that will lead nations on their own soil to the creation of heroic virtues, but

[30]
parasites to mendacious hypocrisy and malicious cruelty; that is, these qualities must be present as the

[34]
supposition for their existence which varies in the various State forms. But the formation of a State will always be brought

[33]
about by at least originally risking these qualities, whereby in the struggle of self-preservation those people

[33]
will be defeated that means be subject to enslave- ment and thus, sooner or later, die out who, in the mutual battle, call

[32]
the smallest share of heroic virtues their own, or which are not adequate to the mendacious ruse of the hostile

[29]
parasite. But in this case also this is due not so much to a lack of cleverness as to a lack of

[33]
determination and danger arise.' Cf. Der ideak Stoat (The Ideal State), by Hanz Hartmann. Another writes: 'A people which

[33]
seeks above all else to safeguard its national existence will endeavor to strengthen and increase its power.

[31]
A weak state is always a temptation to neighboring states to expand their possessions at its expense. As a

[32]
consequence there can be no peace in Europe until Germany is the equal in power and prestige of the

[32]
other states. Frederick the Great's maxim that peace is best guaranteed in the shadow of bayonets is still true today. A

[32]
people's will to live and its military strength are one and the same.' Cf . Deutschland, Deutschland, nichts als Deutschland (Germany,

[33]
Germany, Nothing but Germany), by Walter Wallowitz. MUNICH 199 and courage that tries to conceal itself under the cloak of

[31]
a humanitarian attitude. However, how little the qualities forming and preserving a State are

[34]
connected with economy is shown most clearly by the fact that the inner strength of a State coincides only in the very

[32]
rarest cases with the so-called economic zenith, but that this usually announces in so many examples the

[33]
already approaching decay of the State. If one had to ascribe the formation of human communities first of

[34]
all to economic forces or impulses, then the highest economic development should at the same time indicate

[34]
the greatest strength of the State, and not vice versa. The belief in the force of economy to form or preserve States

[33]
seems especially unintelligible when it is predominant in a country which in each and every thing shows clearly

[30]
and impressively the historical reverse. Particularly in Prussia it is shown with wonderful

[33]
acuteness that not material qualities but idealistic virtues alone make possible the formation of

[31]
a State. Only under their protection is economy able to flourish, but with the collapse of the purely

[33]
State-forming abilities, economy also breaks down again; an event that we are able to observe just now

[33]
in so terribly a saddening manner. Man's material interests are able to thrive best as long as they remain

[34]
in the shadow of heroic virtues; but as soon as they try to enter the first circle of existence, they destroy the conditions

[33]
of their own ex- istence. -'? Whenever in Germany an upswing of political power took place, economy also

[31]
began to rise; but thereafter, whenever economy was made the sole content of our people's life, thus

[33]
suffocating the ideal virtues, the State collapsed again, and after a certain time it pulled economy down

[32]
with it into the grave. But if one asks oneself the question what the force' forming or otherwise preserving

[34]
a State are in reality, it 200 MEIN KAMPF can be summed up with one single characterization: the individual's

[33]
ability and willingness to sacrifice himself for the community. But that these virtues have really nothing

[33]
whatsoever to do with economics is shown by the simple realization that man never sacrifices himself for them; that

[33]
means : one does not die for business, but for ideals. Nothing proved the Englishman's psychological superiority

[33]
in knowledge of the people's psyche better than the motivation with which he cloaked his fight. While we fought for bread, England

[33]
fought for 'liberty,' and not even for her own, no, for that of the smaller nations. We laughed at this impu- dence or we were

[33]
annoyed by it, thus only proving how thoughtless and stupid Germany's so-called statesmanship had become even before

[31]
the War. Not the slightest idea was left concerning the nature of the force that leads men to death out of free will and

[32]
resolution. As long as in 1914 the German people was still able to fight for ideals, it resisted; but as soon as it was

[31]
allowed to fight only for its daily bread, it preferred to give up the game. But our wise 'statesmen' were

[31]
astonished at this change of attitude. It never became clear to them, from the mo- ment a man fights for an

[32]
economic interest he tries to avoid death, as this would rob him forever of the enjoyment of the reward of his

[33]
fighting. The anxiety for the rescue of her own child turns even the most weak mother into a heroine, and only the fight

[33]
for the preservation of the species and the hearth or the State that protected them, drove men at all times towards the spears

[32]
of the enemy. The following sentence may be established as an eternally valid truth: Never was a State

[33]
founded by peaceful economy, but always only by the instincts of preserving the species, no matter whether they are

[32]
found in the field of heroic virtues or sly cunning; the one results then in Aryan States of MUNICH 801 work and culture, the

[32]
other in Jewish colonies of parasites. But as soon as in a people or in a State, economy as such

[32]
begins to choke these instincts, economy itself becomes the enticing cause for subjection and suppression. The

[33]
belief of pre-War times, that by a trade or colonial policy the world could be opened or even conquered

[33]
for the German people in a peaceful way, was a classical symptom of the loss of the virtues that really form and preserve

[33]
a State and of all insight, will power, and active determina- tion resulting from them; the result of this was, by law

[33]
of nature, the World War and its consequences. For one who did not make deeper researches, however, this attitude

[32]
of the German nation for it was really almost general could only represent an insoluble riddle; was not just

[33]
Germany a really wonderful example of a realm that had grown from fundamentals that were purely politi- cal

[31]
from the point of view of power? Prussia, the germ cell of the Reich, was created by resplendent heroism and not by financial

[31]
operations or commercial affairs, and the Reich itself was in turn only the most glorious reward of political

[32]
leadership and military death-defying courage. How could just the German people's political instincts be- come so

[33]
morbid? For the question involved here was not that of a single symptom, but instances of decay which flared up now in

[33]
legion like delusive lights brushing up and down the national body, or which like poisonous ulcers ate into

[32]
the nation now here, now there. It seemed as though a continuous flow of poison was driven into the farthest blood

[31]
vessels of this one-time heroic body by a mysterious power, so as to lead to ever more severe

[33]
paralysis of sound reason and of the simple instinct of self-preservation. By letting these questions pass through my mind in-

[30]
numerable times, conditioned by my attitude towards the German policy of alliance and

[33]
economy in the years 1912 to 1914, there remained more and more for the solution of 202 MEIN KAMPF the riddle that power that

[33]
I had become acquainted with previously in Vienna, determined from quite different points of view: the Marxian

[33]
doctrine and view of life and its ultimate organizatory effects. For the second time in my life I

[33]
dug into this doctrine of destruction this time, of course, no longer led by the influences and effects of my daily

[32]
surroundings, but directed by the observation of general events of political life. As I had recently

[32]
begun to plunge into the theoretical literature of this new world and had tried to make clear to myself its

[33]
possible effects, I compared these with the daily symptoms and events of its effect in political, cultural, and

[32]
economic life. But now for the first time I also turned my attention to the attempts at mastering this world

[33]
plague. I studied Bismarck's exemption laws as to their intention, struggle, and success. But gradually I gained a truly

[33]
granite foundation for my own conviction, so that from that time on I was never forced to make a change in my

[32]
internal attitude towards the matter. Also, the relation- ship between Marxism and Judaism was subjected to a

[33]
further thorough examination. If formerly in Vienna, Germany had above all else ap- peared to me as an

[34]
unshakable colossus, now, however, anxious doubts sometimes began to rise in my mind. With myself and in the small

[31]
circles of my acquaintances, I was wrathful at German foreign politics, and also at what seemed to me an

[34]
unbelievably frivolous manner with which one faced the most important problem that confronted Germany in those days:

[33]
Marxism. I really could not understand how one was able to stagger blindly towards a danger the ultimate effects

[33]
of which, corresponding to its own intentions, were one day bound to be monstrous. In those days I warned those around

[33]
me, as I am doing today on a larger scale, against the fervent prayer of all cowardly MUNICH 803 wretches: 'Nothing can happen

[32]
to us!' Was not Germany subject to exactly the same laws as all other human communities? In the years 1913 and 1914, in

[33]
various circles, some of which today stand faithfully by the movement, I expressed for the first time the conviction that

[32]
the question of the future of the German nation is the question of the destruc- tion of Marxism. In the fatal German

[33]
policy of alliances I saw only one of the after-effects that were caused by the destructive working

[33]
of this doctrine; for the terrible thing was just the fact that this poison almost invisibly destroyed all the foundations of

[32]
a sound conception of State and economics, frequently preventing those who were attacked by it even from

[32]
guessing how far their activity and intentions already were the results of this otherwise most decidedly

[32]
objection- able view of life. The internal decline of the German nation had begun long before, but, as so

[31]
frequently in life, without the people seeing clearly who the destroyer of their existence was. Sometimes one

[33]
doctored about with the disease, but one confused the forms of the symptoms with the cause. As one did not know, or

[33]
did not want to know, this, the fight against Marxism had only the value of prattling quackery CHAPTER V THE WORLD WAR DURING the years

[33]
of my unruly youth nothing had grieved me more than having been born at a time when temples of glory were only

[33]
erected to mer- chants or State officials. The waves of historical events seemed to have calmed down to such an

[32]
extent that the future appeared really to belong to the 'peaceful compe- tition of nations/ that means a quiet

[32]
mutual cheating, ex- cluding forceful measures. The individual States began more and more to resemble

[33]
enterprises which cut the ground from under each other, stole each other's customers and orders, and tried to cheat each'other by

[32]
every means, setting this in a scene which was as noisy as it was harmless. This development, however, not only

[32]
seemed to endure, but it was intended to transform the world (with general ap- proval) into one big department

[34]
store, in the lobbies of which the busts of the most cunning profiteers and the most harmless administration officials were to

[33]
be stored for eter- nity. The business men were to be supplied by the English, the administration officials by

[33]
the Germans; the Jews, how- ever, would have to sacrifice themselves to being propri- etors, because, as they themselves

[34]
admitted, they never earn anything but only 'pay/ and, besides, they speak most of the languages. THE WORLD WAR 205 Why could one not

[33]
have been born a hundred years earlier? For instance, at the time of the Wars of Liberation when a man really was worth

[32]
something, even without 'business'?! 1 1 was often filled with annoying thoughts because, as it appeared, of the belated

[33]
entrance of my journey into this world, and I looked upon this period of 'quiet and order' that awaited me as

[33]
an unmerited mean trick of Fate. Even as a boy I was not a 'pacifist,' and all attempts at an educa- tion in

[33]
this direction came to naught. The Boer War appeared to me like summer lightning. Every day I was on the lookout for

[33]
the newspapers; I devoured dispatches and reports, and I was happy that 1 was being allowed to witness this heroic struggle,

[34]
if only from afar. The Russo-Japanese War already found me much more mature and also more attentive.

[33]
At that time I had taken sides more for national reasons, and when settling my opinions I had at once taken

[31]
the side of the Japanese. In the defeat of the Russians I saw also a defeat of the Austrian Slavic

[32]
nationalities. Many years since had passed, and what then appeared to me a foul and lingering illness when I was

[32]
a boy, I now considered as the calm before the storm. Already during my Viennese time there hovered

[32]
over the Balkans that fallow sultriness which usually announces a hurricane, but at times a brighter light

[33]
flashed up only to return immedi- ately into the uncanny darkness. But then came the Bal- kan War, and with it

[32]
the first gust of wind swept over a Europe which had grown nervous. The time that followed, however, weighed heavily

[32]
upon the people like a nightmare, brooding like the feverish heat of the tropics, so that in consequence of the

[33]
continued anxiety, the feeling of the impending catastrophe finally turned into longing; might Heaven at last let

[34]
Destiny, no longer to be restrained, take 206 MEIN KAMPF its full course! The first powerful lightning flashed upon the earth; the storm

[33]
broke out, and the thunder of the heavens mingled with the roaring of the batteries of the World War. <When the news of the murder

[33]
of Archduke Franz Ferdi- nand reached Munich (I was in the house and heard only vague details of the event), I was at

[33]
first worried that the bullets might perhaps have come from the pistols of Ger- man students, who, because of their indignation

[31]
at the continued Slavization activities of the Heir Presumptive, wished to free the German nation from this

[33]
internal enemy. One could imagine well what the consequences would have been in that case: a new wave of

[32]
persecutions which would now have been 'justified' and 'motivated' in the face of the whole world. When, however, soon

[31]
after I heard the names of the suspected murderers, and read that their nationality had been established as

[33]
Serbian, a slight horror began to creep over me because of this revenge of inscrutable Destiny. The greatest

[31]
friend of the Slavs had been felled by the bullets of Slav fanatics. Those who had had an opportunity to observe

[33]
continu- ously the relations between Austria and Serbia during the last few years could not doubt for even a moment that

[31]
the stone had been set rolling on a course that could no longer be checked. One does the Viennese government an

[32]
injustice when today one showers it with reproaches regarding the form and the contents of the ultimatum it

[33]
issued. No other power on earth would have been able to act differently in a similar situation and under

[33]
the same circumstances. On the south- east bordfer of her realm Austria had an inexorable and mortal enemy who

[34]
challenged the monarchy at shorter and shorter intervals, and who would not have given in til! finally the favorable

[32]
moment for the destruction of the THE WORLD WAR 207 realm had actually come. One had reason to fear that this event would

[33]
happen not later than with the death of the old emperor; but then perhaps the monarchy would no longer be in a position

[32]
to render any serious resistance. The entire State, during these last years, was represented to such an

[32]
extent by the person of Franz Joseph that from the beginning, the death of this aged personification of the realm was

[31]
looked upon by the great masses as the death of the realm itself. It was indeed the most cunning artfulness of the Slav

[33]
policy to create the impression as though the Austrian State owed its existence to the really wonderful and

[30]
unique skill of this monarch; a flattery which was the more favorably received in the Hofburg as it

[33]
corresponded least of all to the actual merits of the emperor. One was not able to discover the sting tkat was

[33]
hidden in this praise. One did not see, or perhaps one did not want to see, that the more the monarchy was based on

[33]
the superior ruling skill of, as one used to say, this 'wisest of all monarchs' of all times, the more desperate

[33]
was the situation bound to be- come when some day here too Destiny would knock at the door to collect its tribute.

[32]
Would then the old Austria be conceivable without the old emperor? Would not the tragedy, which once had met Maria

[33]
Theresa, immediately repeat itself? No, one really does an injustice to Viennese government circles

[32]
if they are reproached with the fact that now they were driving towards a war which perhaps would have been avoidable

[34]
after all. It was no longer avoidable, but it could have been postponed for only one or two more years at the most.

[33]
But this was the very curse of the German as well as of the Austrian diplomacy that it had always tried to post- pone

[33]
the unavoidable settlement till at last it was forced to strike at an unfavorable hour. One can be certain

[33]
that a renewed attempt at preserving the peace would have SOB MEIN KAMPF brought on the war in spite of this at an even

[31]
less favorable time. No, those who did not want this war would have had to summon the courage to assume the

[33]
consequences. These, however, could have only consisted in the sacrificing of Austria. But even then the war

[32]
would have come, though perhaps not in the form of a fight against all, but in the form of a dismemberment of the Habsburg

[33]
monarchy. But there one would have had to decide whether one wanted to join or whether one wanted to watch,

[32]
with empty hands, Fate take its course. It is just those who today curse most and pronounce the wisest opinions

[30]
about the beginning of the war, who helped most catastrophically to steer towards war. For decades Social

[33]
Democracy had carried on the most The question of responsibility for the War is still a moot one, but Hitler is

[33]
not discussing it here in the sense in which it is usually propounded. He is taking his stand on the platform of

[32]
Ludendorff, Graefe, Class and other Pan-Germans for whom the issue was never whether a war was coming or whether it could be

[30]
avoided, but whether Germany would choose the right moment to strike and whether it would possess the requisite

[33]
military strength. This group was bitterly antagon- istic to Bethmann-Hollweg for having desired to keep the peace and

[34]
for having refused to endorse certain items proposed for inclusion in the military budget of 1913. That the 'people'

[30]
were with them they have never doubted, and still do not doubt. The whole blame falls, they maintain, on Bethmann- Hollweg.

[33]
Accordingly one readies this interesting conclusion: it seems impossible to hold the German government of 1914 solely

[33]
responsible for the declaration of war, but the head of the German government of 1938 has gone on record in this book as

[33]
wishing that his predecessor had assumed that responsibility. Hitler has promised to guarantee that the next time

[33]
there be no such blunders. On November 28, 1934, Mr. Winston THE WORLD WAR 209 villainous war propaganda against Russia, but the Center

[33]
Party, for religious reasons, had made the Austrian State most of all the center and turning-point of German poli-

[32]
tics. Now one had to bear the consequences of this mad- ness. What now came had to come, and it was unavoidable

[32]
under any circumstances. The German government's fault therein was that, in order to preserve peace, it again and

[33]
again missed the favorable hour for striking; that it got entangled in the alliance for the preservation of world

[31]
peace, thus finally falling victim to a world coalition which opposed the very preservation of peace with the

[32]
determi- nation of a world war. If at that time the Viennese government had given the ultimatum another,

[33]
milder wording, this would not have changed anything in the situation except perhaps the fact that the government itself

[32]
would have been swept away by the indignation of the people. Because, in the eyes of the great masses, the tone of the

[33]
ultimatum was much too con- Churchill addressed the House of Commons on the subject of Germany's program of rearmament.

[33]
Referring to the air force, he said: 'On the same basis, that is to say, both sides con- tinuing with their existing program

[33]
as at present arranged, by the end of 1936 that is, one year farther on, and two years from now the German military air force

[33]
will be nearly 50 per cent stronger, and in 1937 nearly double. ... So much for the comparison of what may be called the first line air

[33]
forces of the two countries/ Replying on behalf of the government, Stanley Baldwin said: 'I say there is no ground at this moment

[33]
for undue alarm and much less for panic. There is no imme- diate danger confronting us or anyone else in

[32]
Europe at this moment. But we must look ahead, and there is ground for grave anxiety, and that is why we have been

[33]
watching the situation for months past, are watching it now, and shall continue to watch it.' S10 MEIN KAMPF siderate and in no

[33]
way too brutal or even too far-reaching. Those who today try to deny this are either forgetful empty- heads or quite

[33]
deliberately cheats and liars. The fight of the year 1914 was certainly not forced upon the masses, good God! but desired

[33]
by the entire people itself. One wanted at last to make an end to the general uncer- tainty. Only thus is

[31]
it understandable that for this most serious of all struggles more than two million German men and boys joined the flag

[34]
voluntarily, ready to protect it with their last drop of blood. To me personally those hours appeared like the redemp-

[33]
tion from the annoying moods of my youth. Therefore I am not ashamed today to say that, overwhelmed by impas- sionate

[32]
enthusiasm, I had fallen on my knees and thanked Heaven out of my overflowing heart that it had granted me the good

[32]
fortune of being allowed to live in these times. A struggle for freedom had broken out, greater than the world had

[33]
ever seen before; because, once Fate had begun its course, the conviction began to dawn on the great masses that

[32]
this time the question involved was not Serbia's or Austria's fate, but the existence or non-existence of the

[33]
German nation. For the last time in many years, the German nation had become clairvoyant about its own future. Thus, at

[33]
the very beginning of the enormous struggle the intoxication of the exuberant enthusiasm was mixed with

[34]
the necessary serious undertone; for this realization alone made the national ris- ing become something

[33]
greater than a mere bonfire. But this was only too necessary; even then one had no idea of the possible

[31]
length and duration of the struggle now beginning. One dreamt of being home again in winter to continue work in

[33]
renewed peace. THE WORLD WAR 211 What man desires, he hopes and believes. The over- whelming majority of the nation

[33]
had long been tired of the eternally uncertain state of things; thus one could only too readily understand that one

[33]
no longer believed in a peaceful adjustment of the Austro-Serbian conflict, but hoped for the final settlement.

[30]
I, too, belonged to these millions. Hardly had the news of the assassination spread in Munich, when two ideas

[34]
immediately entered my head: first, that war would now at last be unavoidable, and further, that the Habsburg State would

[33]
be forced to keep the alliance; for what I had always feared most was the possibility that one day Germany

[33]
herself, perhaps just in consequence of this alliance, would be entangled in a con- flict without Austria being the direct

[31]
cause for this, but that in such a case the Austrian State, for domestic political reasons, would not summon the

[33]
energy to decide to stand by its ally. The Slav majority would certainly immediately have begun

[33]
to sabotage such an intention by the State itself, and would certainly have preferred to smash the entire State

[34]
into bits rather than to give the required help to the ally. This danger, however, was now averted. The old State had

[33]
to fight whether it wanted to or not. My own attitude towards the conflict was very clear and simple to me : in my eyes

[32]
it was not Austria fighting for some Serbian satisfaction, but Germany fighting for her exist- ence, the German

[32]
nation for its being or non-being, for freedom and future. Bismarck's work now had to fight; what the fathers once had gained by

[33]
fighting with their heroic blood in the battles from Weissenburg to Sedan and Paris, now young Germany had to earn again. If this

[33]
fight would be carried through victoriously, then our nation would also have returned to the circle of ,'the nations which arc great

[33]
in external power, and only then could the German Reich prove a powerful shield of peace without being forced to reduce

[33]
its children's daily bread for the sake of this peace. 212 MEIN KAMPF As a boy and a young man I had often formed the wish that at

[33]
least once I might be allowed to prove by deeds that my national enthusiasm was not an empty delusion. Often

[32]
I considered it a sin to shout 'hurrah' without per- haps having the inner right to do so; for who may use this cry

[33]
without having proved himself there where all play is at an end and where the inexorable hand of the Goddess of

[34]
Fate begins to weigh nations and men according to the truth and the durability of their convictions? Thus my heart, like that

[33]
of a million others, was overflowing with proud happiness that at last I was able to free myself from this paralyzing

[32]
feeling. So many times had I sung 'Deutsch- land uber dies' and shouted with full voice 'Heil,' that I considered it almost

[33]
a belated favor that I was now allowed to appear as a witness before the tribunal of the Eternal Judge

[33]
in order to proclaim the truth and the sincerity of my convictions. From the first hour I was certain that in the event of

[33]
war (which appeared unavoidable to me), I would abandon my books in one way or the other. But I knew just the same

[32]
that my place would be there where my inner voice directed me to go. I had left Austria primarily for

[32]
political reasons: but what was more natural that now that the fight had begun that I had to act according to this

[33]
conviction? I did not want to fight for the Habsburg State, but I was ready to die ^t any time for my people and the Reich

[33]
it constituted. On August 3 I submitted a direct petition to His Majesty King Ludwig III with the request

[32]
that I be permitted to serve in a Bavarian regiment. The cabinet office was cer- tainly more than

[33]
busy in those days; my joy was the greater when on the following day I received the reply to my re- quest. My joy and

[33]
my gratitude knew no end when I had opened the letter with trembling hands and read that my request had been granted and that

[33]
I was summoned to report to a Bavarian regiment. A few days later I wore THE WORLD WAR 213 the uniform which

[31]
I waa not to take off again for six years. Thus, as probably for every German, there began for me the most

[32]
unforgettable and the greatest period of my mortal life. In the face of the events of this mighty struggle the

[33]
entire past fell back into shallow oblivion. It is now ten years since this mighty event happened, and with proud sadness

[33]
I think back to those weeks of the beginning of the heroic fight of our people which Fate had graciously per- mitted me to

[33]
share. f As if it were yesterday, one picture after the other passes before my eyes: I see myself donning

[34]
the uniform in the circle of my dear comrades, turning out for the first time, drilling, etc., till finally the day came when

[34]
we marched. There was only one thing that worried me at that time, like so many others also: that was whether we would

[30]
not arrive at the front too late. This alone disturbed my peace again and again. Thus in every

[31]
jubilation over a new heroic deed there seemed to be a hidden drop of bitterness as with every new

[33]
victory the danger of our being delayed seemed to increase. Finally, the day came when we left Munich in order to

[33]
start fulfilling our duty. Now for the first time I saw the Rhine as we were riding towards the west along its quiet

[33]
waters, the German river of all rivers, in order to protect it against the greed of the old enemy. When through the deli-

[33]
cate veil of the dawn's mist the mild rays of the early sun set the Niederwalddenkmal shimmering before our eyes, the 'Watch on

[33]
the Rhine' roared up to the morning sky from the interminably long transport train and I had a feeling as though my chest would

[34]
burst. Then at last came a damp, cold night in Flanders through which we marched silently, and when the day began to emerge from the fog,

[33]
suddenly an iron salute came whizzing over our heads towards us and with a sharp report the 214 MEIN KAMPF small bullets struck

[33]
between our rows, whipping up the wet earth; but before the small cloud had dispersed, out of two hundred throats the first hurrah roared

[33]
a welcome to the first messenger of death. But then it began to crackle and roar, to sing and howl, and with feverish eyes each

[33]
one of us was drawn forward faster and faster over turnip fields and hedges till suddenly the fight began, the fight of man

[31]
against man. But from the distance the sounds of a song met our ears, coming nearer and nearer, passing from com- pany to

[33]
company, and then, while Death busily plunged his hand into our rows, the song reached also us, and now we passed it on

[31]
:‘ De utschland, DeutscUand uber alles, Uber dttes inderWeltl’ After four days we came back. Even our step had be- come

[31]
different. Boys of seventeen now resembled men. The volunteers of the regiment had perhaps not yet learned to fight

[33]
properly, but they knew how to die like old soldiers. This was the beginning. <’Thus it continued year after year; but the romance

[31]
of Hitler here set the example for what would later prove to be a deluge of war tales. Concerning his

[33]
military record, the fol- lowing facts are known ; that he served as a messenger between regimental headquarters and

[33]
the front; that he was a good soldier who refused to the very end to join in criticism of the way things were being run; that

[33]
his temperament made his commanding officer doubt the wisdom of promoting him to any sort of non-commissioned

[31]
rank above that of corporal, and that he occupies a modest but honorable place in the history of the

[31]
Regiment List, to which he belonged. The particular ex- ploit for which he received the Iron Cross is shrouded in

[33]
secrecy, but most biographers agree that there was no reason why it should not have been awarded. Hitler, by Rudolf

[32]
Olden, at- tempts a critical evaluation of the legend that had grown up round Hitler's war experience. THE WORLD WAR 215 the

[33]
battles had turned into horror. The enthusiasm gradu- ally cooled down and the exuberant joy was suffocated

[32]
by the fear of death. The time came when everyone had to fight between the instinct of self-preservation and the ad-

[31]
monition of duty. I, too, was not spared this inner struggle. Whenever death was on the hunt, an undefinable

[31]
something tried to revolt, tried to present itself to the weak body in the form of reason and was really nothing but

[33]
cowardice which in this disguise tried to ensnare the individual. A strong pulling and warning set in and only

[34]
the last remain- ing spark of conscience made the decision. But the more this voice tried to warn me to take heed, the louder

[33]
and the more urgently it lured, the sharper was my resistance, till finally after a long inner struggle my sense

[33]
of duty tri- umphed. This struggle had already been decided for me during the winter of 1915-16. My will had finally become

[33]
master. Whereas during the first days I was able to join exuberantly and laughingly in the storm, now I was quiet and

[32]
determined. This was the most enduring. Only now could Fate set out for the last tests without tearing my nerves or my

[34]
reason giving out. The young volunteer had become an old soldier. But this change had taken place in the entire army.

[33]
It had become old and hard through perpetual fighting, and those who were not able to resist the storm were broken

[33]
by it. But only now could one judge this army. Now, after two or three years during which it had been thrown from one battle

[32]
into the other, constantly fighting against a force superior in number and weapons, suffering hunger and en-

[32]
during deprivations, now was the time to prove the quality of this unique army. Thousands of years may pass, but

[33]
never will one be allowed to talk about or mention heroism without remem- bering the German army of the World War.

[33]
Then, out of the veil of the past, the iron front of the gray steel helmet 816 MEIN KAMPF will become visible, not wavering and not

[33]
retreating, a mon- ument to immortality. As long as Germans live they will remember that these were the sons of

[32]
their nation, f At that time I was a soldier and did not want to discuss politics. It really was not the time for it.

[33]
I am still con- vinced today that even the most humble carter had done his fatherland more valuable services

[33]
than the first, let us say, 'parliamentarian.' I never hated these prattlers more than just at that time, when every

[33]
regular fellow who had to say something shouted it into the enemy's face, or, more appropriately, left

[34]
his mouth at home and silently did his duty in some place. Yes, in those days I hated all these 'politicians,

[33]
1 and if I had had anything to say, a parlia- mentarian spade battalion would have been formed at once; then they

[33]
would have been able to babble among themselves to their hearts 1 content if they had to, and they would not have been able to

[31]
annoy or even to harm the decent and honest part of mankind. ^ At that time, therefore, I did not want to hear

[31]
anything about politics, but I could not help defining my attitude towards certain manifestations which

[34]
concerned, after all, the entire nation, but most of all us soldiers, f There were two things which in those days annoyed me and

[32]
which I considered detrimental. Soon after the news of the first victories, a certain press Not a few of the Reichstag

[33]
delegates served at the front; some were killed in action. Most of the others were beyond military age, and

[33]
some of these served on difficult and danger- ous missions. More interesting is the unrestrained endorse- ment

[33]
of LudendorfFa military totalitarianism the absolute disavowal of political action in

[31]
time of war. The wicked ones are those who believed that peace might be reached, after years of destructive

[31]
warfare, on a basis of compromise and who felt that Germany, by giving guarantees not to violate the

[32]
integrity of Belgium, might divide her foes. THE WORLD WAR 217 began slowly, and at first perhaps unrecognizably to

[30]
many, to pour drops of wormwood into the general enthusiasm. This was done under the mask of a certain

[33]
benevolence and well-meaning, even of a certain anxiety. One harbored doubts about too great an exuberance

[33]
in celebrating the victories. One feared that in this form it was unworthy and did not correspond to the dignity

[33]
of such a great nation. The bravery and the heroic courage of the German soldier were really a matter of course,

[33]
and one should not be carried away too much by thoughtless outbursts of joy, especially for the sake of public opinion

[34]
abroad which would certainly be more impressed by a quiet and dignified form of joy than by excessive exultation,

[34]
etc. Finally we Germans were not to forget even now that the war had not been our intention, and that therefore we should

[33]
not be ashamed to admit, openly and like men, that we were ready to contribute, at any time, our share

[33]
towards the reconciliation of mankind. Therefore it would not be wise to blacken the purity of the army's

[32]
deeds with too much shouting, as the rest of the world would show but little understanding for such behav- ior. One admired

[31]
nothing more than the modesty with which a genuine hero quietly and silently forgets his deeds; for this was

[33]
supposed to be the essence of the whole affair. But now, instead of taking such a fellow by his long ears and leading

[33]
him to, and pulling him up on, a high pole with a rope, so that the celebrating nation would no longer be able to

[32]
insult the aesthetic feeling of this knight of the ink, one actually began to protest this 'unseemly' manner of

[32]
jubilating over victories. One had not the faintest idea, however, that this enthu- siasm, once it has been

[33]
broken, cannot be reawakened at will. It is an intoxication and it is best to keep it in this condition. But how

[33]
was one to endure in a fight without this power, a fight which in all human probability made the 211 MEIN KAMPF most

[33]
enormous demands on the spiritual qualities of the nation? I knew the psyche of the great masses only too well not

[33]
to know that one would not be able to stoke the fire neces- sary to keep this iron hot with ‘aesthetic 9 elation.

[32]
In my eyes one was mad because nothing was done to increase this boiling heat of passion; but I simply could not

[33]
understand that one even curtailed that which fortunately was present. The second thing that annoyed me was the way and

[32]
the manner in which one thought fit to face Marxism. In my eyes, this only proved that one really had not the slightest

[33]
idea of this pestilence. One seemed to believe, in all seri- ousness, that by the assurance that one no

[33]
longer knew parties, one thought one had brought Marxism to reason and restraint. That here one has to deal not with a party

[33]
but with a doctrine which must of necessity lead to the destruction of entire mankind, this one understood the less

[33]
as one did not hear it in the Jew-infested universities, and as otherwise only too many of our higher

[34]
officials, particularly, out of idiotic conceit, inculcated in them by education, did not think it worth the trouble

[33]
to pick up a book and to learn something which did not belong in the curriculum of their high school. The most important changes

[34]
pass by these ‘heads’ without leaving a trace, and therefore the State institutions nearly always lag behind the private

[33]
ones. God knows that to them, most of all, the popular proverb applies: 'Was der Bauer nicht kennt, das frisst er nicht 9 [a peasant does not

[33]
eat what he does not know]. It was an unequaled absurdity to identify the German worker with Marxism in the days

[32]
of August, 1914. In those hours the German worker had disentangled himself from the embrace of this poisonous plague, as

[32]
otherwise he would never have been able to start this fight. But one was stupid enough to think that Marxism had now

[32]
perhaps THE WORLD WAR 219 become ' national ' ; a flash of genius which only shows that during these long years none of these

[32]
official State leaders had thought it worth the trouble to study the nature of this doctrine, for otherwise such

[33]
insanity would hardly have occurred.-^ Marxism, the ultimate aim of which was and will always be the destruction of

[34]
all non-Jewish national States, to its dismay saw during July, 1914, the German working class, which it had ensnared, awake to

[32]
enlist in the service of the country more and more quickly from hour to hour. In a few days the whole show of this

[31]
infamous deception of the nation had frittered away, and the Jewish rabble leaders stood there lonely and

[33]
abandoned, as though not a trace of the idiocy and lunacy which it had infiltered into the masses for

[33]
sixty years remained. It was a bad moment for the deceivers of the German nation 's working class. But immediately the

[31]
leaders recognized the danger which threatened them, they at once pulled the magic cap of lies over their ears and

[32]
impudently joined in aping the national rising. But now the time should have arrived for proceeding against the

[33]
entire fraudulent company of these Jewish poisonmongers of the nation. Now one should have dealt summarily

[33]
with them without the slightest consideration for the clamor that would probably arise, or, what would have been still better,

[33]
without pity for all their lamenta- tions. In August of the year 1914, the Jewish haggling of international solidarity

[32]
had disappeared at one stroke from the heads of the German working class, and instead, after a few weeks, American

[32]
shrapnel began to pour down the blessings of fraternity on the helmets of the marching col- umns. It was the duty of a

[32]
prudent government, now that the German laborer had found his way back to his nation- ality, to root out without pity the

[32]
instigators against this nationality. 220 MEIN KAMPF If the best were killed on the front, then one could at least destroy the

[33]
vermin at home. But instead of this, His Majesty the Kaiser in person extended his hand towards the old criminals, thus

[34]
showing the cunning murderers of the nation forbearance and giving them the chance to set their minds at ease, f Now the serpent

[34]
had a chance to continue its work, more carefully than before but also more dangerously. While the honest

[33]
ones were dreaming of peace within the castle walls, the perjured criminals organized the revolution. It made

[33]
me discontented in my mind that at that time one had decided on such terrible half measures; but that its end would

[33]
be such a terrible one even I would not have thought possible. But what was to be done now? To put the leaders of

[32]
the whole movement behind lock and bar, to put them on trial and deliver the nation of them. To apply ruthlessly the

[32]
entire military means in order to root out this pestilence. The parties had to be dissolved, the Reichstag, if

[33]
necessary, to be brought to reason at the point of the bayonet, but, better still, to adjourn it immediately. Just as

[33]
today the Republic is allowed to dissolve parties, one would have had more reason to apply similar means

[32]
in those days. The ex- istence or non-existence of an entire nation was at stake ! But then, of course, a

[32]
question arose: Can spiritual ideas be extinguished by the sword? Can one fight ‘views of life 1 by applying brute

[33]
force? Even then I asked myself this question more than once. When thinking over analogous cases to be found in

[31]
his- tory, particularly on a religious basis, the following funda- mental realization is the result:

[34]
Conceptions and ideas, as well as movements with a cer- tain spiritual foundation, may these be right or wrong, can be broken

[33]
at a certain point of their development with technical means of power only if these physical weapons are THE WORLD

[33]
WAR 221 at the same time the supporters of a new kindling thought, an idea or view of life. Use of force alone,

[33]
without the driving forces of a spir- itual basic idea as presupposition, can never lead to the destruction of

[33]
an idea and its spreading, except in the form of a thorough eradication of even the last representative and

[33]
the destruction of the last tradition. This, however, means the disappearance of such a State body for endless times,

[33]
sometimes forever, from the circle of political and powerful importance, as such a sacrifice in blood,

[33]
as shown by experience, often hits the best part of a nationality, be- cause every persecution that takes

[32]
place without being based on a spiritual presupposition does not seem justified from the moral point of view, thus

[31]
instigating just the more valuable parts of a nation to voice a protest which then expresses itself in the

[34]
acquisition of the spiritual contents of the unjustly persecuted movement. This happens with many merely out

[33]
of the feeling of opposition against the attempt at throttling an idea by brute force. With this, however, the number

[33]
of the internal adher- ents grows in the measure in which the persecution grows. Therefore, the complete extinction

[31]
of a new doctrine can be carried out only by way of an eradication which is thorough and so constantly

[33]
increasing that by this all the really val- uable blood is withdrawn from the nation or the State involved. But this will take

[34]
its revenge, because there now can take place a so-called 'inner' purification, this, however, at the expense

[32]
of a general weakness. But from the very beginning such procedure will be in vain if the doctrine tc be fought has

[33]
already stepped outside of a certain small circle. As with all growth, here, too, the early period of child- hood offers

[33]
the best possibility for such extinction, for with the growing years the force of resistance increases, till finally

[33]
with approaching age it again gives way to the 222 MEIN KAMPF weakness of youth, though in a different form and for other reasons.

[33]
It is a fact that all attempts at the extinction of a doc- trine and its organizatory effects by force without

[33]
a spir- itual foundation lead to failures and frequently even end contrary to that desired, for the following

[31]
reason: The very first condition for such a manner of fight with the weapons of pure force is, and will always be,

[33]
persever- ance. That means that only the continued and regular use of the methods applied for suppressing a doctrine

[34]
permits of the possibility of success. But as soon as intermittent force alternates with indulgence, the doctrine

[32]
to be sup- pressed will not only recover again and again, but it will be able to draw new values from every

[33]
persecution, for after the ebbing of such a wave of pressure, the indignation at the misery suffered leads

[33]
new followers to the old doctrine, but those who are already present will with sharper spite and deeper hatred than

[33]
before adhere to it, and even those who have fallen off will try to return to their old attitude after

[31]
the danger has been averted. Only in the eternally regular use of force lies the preliminary

[32]
condition for success. This perseverance is only and always the result of a certain spiritual conviction

[32]
alone. All force which does not spring from a firm spiritual foundation will be hesitat- ing and uncertain. It lacks the

[34]
stability which can only rest in a fanatical view of life. It is the outcome of the energy of the moment

[33]
and the brutal determination of a single individual, but therefore it is subjected to the change of

[34]
the personality and its nature and strength. But to this something else must be added : -<' Every view of life, be it

[33]
more of a political or of a religious nature (sometimes the borderline between them can be as-

[33]
certained only with difficulty), fights less for the negative destruction of the adversary's world of ideas, and more

[32]
for the positive carrying-out of its own doctrine. Therefore, its THE WORLD WAR 223 fight is less a defense than an

[33]
attack. Even as regards the definiteness of its goal, it has an advantage, as this goal represents the victory

[33]
of its own idea, while the other way round it is difficult to decide when the negative aim of the destruction

[33]
of the enemy's doctrine may be considered as completed and assured. For this reason alone the attack on

[31]
a view of life will be more carefully planned and also more powerful than the defense of such a

[30]
doctrine; as here, too, the decision is due to the attack and not to the defense. But the fight against a

[34]
spiritual power by means of force is only a defense as long as the sword itself does not appear as the supporter,

[33]
propagator, and announcer of a new spir- itual doctrine. Thus, summing up, one can say the following: Every

[33]
attempt at fighting a view of life by means of force will finally fail, unless the fight against it represents the form of

[33]
an attack for the sake of a new spiritual direction. Only in the struggle of two views of life with each other

[33]
can the weapon of brute force, used continuously and ruth- lessly, bring about the decision in favor of the side

[31]
it sup- ports. It was on this account that the fight against Marxism had failed so far. This was also the reason why Bismarck's

[34]
anti-socialist laws finally failed and were bound to fail, despite all efforts. The platform of a new view of life was

[33]
lacking for the rise of which the fight could have been fought. Only the pro- verbial wisdom of ministerial high officials could

[31]
produce the opinion that the trash about the so-called 'State author- ity' and 'peace and order' could be a

[30]
suitable basis for the spiritual impetus of a struggle for life and death. fBut because a really

[33]
spiritual foundation of this fight was lacking, Bismarck was forced to hand the carrying-out of his anti-socialist laws to

[34]
the judgment and the volition of those institutions which themselves were already the 2S4 MEIN KAMPF product of the Marxian

[31]
way of thinking. Thus the Iron Chancellor, by handing over the responsibility for his fight against Marxism to the

[32]
benevolence of the bourgeois democracy, set the wolf to mind the sheep. But all this was only the necessary

[33]
result of the lack of a fundamentally new view of life opposed to Marxism, with an impetuous will to conquer.

[33]
Thus the result of Bismarck's fight was only a severe dis- appointment. But were circumstances different during or at

[33]
the begin- ning of the World War? Unfortunately not. The more I occupied myself in those days with the idea of

[31]
a necessary change in the attitude of State governments towards Social Democracy as the present

[33]
personification of Marxism, the more I recognized the lack of a suitable sub- stitute for this doctrine.

[33]
What, then, did one want to give to the masses, if one were to suppose that Social Democracy would be broken?

[33]
There was not one movement of which one could have assumed that it would have succeeded in drawing under its

[30]
spell the more or less leaderless great masses of workers. It is absurd and more than stupid to assume that the

[32]
international fanatic who has left the class party would now immediately join a bourgeois party; that means

[32]
a new class organization. No matter how disagree- able this may be for several organizations, it cannot be

[33]
denied that to the bourgeois politician the separation of classes appears absolutely natural as long

[31]
as the political effects are not unfavorable to him. The denial of these facts proves not only the

[32]
impudence but also the stupidity of the liars, i On the whole, one should guard against believing the great

[31]
masses to be more stupid than they actually are. In political matters feeling often decides more

[31]
accurately than reason. The opinion, however, that the masses 9 stupid international attitude is

[31]
sufficient proof of the incorrectness THE WORLD WAR 225 of their feeling can be refuted thoroughly at once by the simple

[33]
argument that the pacifistic democracy is not less insane, but that its supporters come almost exclusively

[33]
from the bourgeois camp. As long as millions of citizens ardently worship the Jewish democratic press every morn- ing,

[33]
it would not do for the masters to make jokes about the stupidity of the 'comrade' who, after all, devours only

[31]
the same rubbish though in a different makeup. In both cases the manufacturer is one and the same Jew.

[33]
Therefore, one should guard well against refuting things which actually exist. The fact that the class question is not at all

[32]
one of spiritual problems as one would like to make us believe, especially before elections,

[33]
cannot be denied. The class pride of a great part of our people, just like the low esteem of the hand laborer, is, above

[30]
all, a symptom which does not come from the imagination of one who is moon- struck. But apart from this, it shows the

[32]
inferior thinking ability of our so-called intelligentsia when just in those circles one does not

[32]
understand that a condition which was not able to prevent the rise of a pestilence, such as Marxism, will far less be

[30]
able to regain that which is lost. The ' bourgeois ' parties, as they call themselves, will never be able to draw the 4

[33]
proletarian ' masses into their camp, as here two worlds face each other, separated partly naturally, partly

[34]
artificially, and their attitude towards each other can only be a fighting one. But here the younger one will

[33]
succeed and this would be Marxism. ^ In fact, a fight against Social Democracy in 1914 was conceivable, but it was doubtful how long

[32]
this condition could have lasted because of the lack of every practical sub- stitute. There was a great gap.

[31]
I was of this opinion long before the War, and therefore I could not make up my mind to join one of the

[31]
existing 226 MEIN KAMPF parties. This opinion was enhanced in the course of the events of the World War by the obvious

[33]
impossibility of fighting ruthlessly against Social Democracy because of the absence of a movement

[34]
which had to be more than a ' par- liamentarian' party. I talked openly about this to my more intimate friends.

[32]
What is more, I now had for the first time the idea of occupying myself politically later on. And this was the

[32]
particular reason that made me assure my small circle of friends that after the War I would be active as an

[34]
orator along with my profession. I think that I meant this very seriously. CHAPTER VI WAR PROPAGANDA AT THE time of

[31]
my attentive following of all political events, the activities of propaganda had always been of

[31]
extremely great interest to me. In it I saw an instrument which just the Socialist-Marxist organiza- tions

[33]
mastered and knew how to apply with expert skill. I learned very soon that the right use of propaganda repre- sents an

[32]
art which was and remained almost entirely un- known to the bourgeois parties. Only the Christian-Social- ist movement,

[32]
especially during Lueger's time, acquired a certain virtuosity with this instrument and it owed much of its

[31]
success to it. But it was shown only during the War to what enor- mously important results a suitably applied

[33]
propaganda may lead. Unfortunately, everything has to be studied on the other side; for the activity

[33]
on our side was more than modest in this respect. However, the very failure of the en- tire enlightenment on

[33]
the side of the Germans a fact which was bound to stare in the face of every soldier now caused me to occupy

[30]
myself still more thoroughly with this question. There was often more than enough time for thinking, but it was

[33]
unfortunately the enemy who gave us only too good an object lesson. 228 MEIN KAMPF For what we failed to do in

[32]
this direction was made up by the enemy with really unheard-of skill and ingenious deliberation. I learned

[33]
infinitely much more from the enemy's war propaganda. But time marched on without leaving an impression on

[33]
the brains of those who most of all should have taken this as a lesson; partly because they deemed themselves too clever

[33]
to take lessons from others, and partly because the honest will to do so was lacking. Was there any propaganda

[33]
at all on our side? To my regret, I can only answer no. Everything that was actually undertaken in this

[32]
direction was so incomplete and wrong from the very first moment that it not only did not help, tnit sometimes did

[34]
considerable harm. Insufficient in form its nature was psychologically wrong : this was necessarily the result

[34]
of a careful examination of the German war propaganda. It seemed that one was not quite clear about the first

[34]
question, namely: Is war propaganda a means or an end? It is a means, and therefore it has to be judged from the point

[31]
of view of the end. But its form has to be properly adapted to the aim which it serves. But it is also clear that the

[32]
importance of its aim can be a different one according to the point of view of the general demand and that

[34]
there- fore propaganda is also defined differently according to its inner value. But the aim for which the War

[32]
was fought was the most sublime and the most overpowering which man is able to imagine: it was the freedom and

[32]
independence of our nation, the assurance of subsistence for the future, and the honor of the nation;

[33]
something that, despite all opinions to the contrary, is still present today or rather ought to be present, as nations

[31]
without honor usually lose their freedom and independence, which, in turn, cor- responds only to a higher

[33]
justice, as generations of scoun- drels without honor do not deserve freedom. But he who wants to be a cowardly slave

[32]
must not and cannot have WAR PROPAGANDA 2S9 any honor, as thus honor would become subject to general disdain

[33]
within the shortest time. It was for the struggle for its human existence that the German people fought, and to support this

[33]
si purpose of the war propaganda; the aim it to victory. But if nations fight for their existenc that means if they are

[33]
approached by of ' to be or not to be ' all reflections ity or aesthetics resolve themselves to n^ eluded; because

[33]
all these ideas are not flodKnc^atout in they^v world ether, but come from the imaginat' are connected with him. His

[33]
departure from dissolves these ideas into insubstantial non-< Nature does not know them. But in mankind, too, they are

[34]
characteristics of only a few people or rather races accord- ing to the measure in which they originate from

[34]
their feel- ings. Humanity and aesthetics would even disappear from a world inhabited by men as soon as it lost the races

[33]
which are the creators and bearers of these ideas. Where a people's fight for existence in this world is con- cerned, all

[33]
these ideas are of subordinate importance; they even have no bearing on the form of this struggle at all

[33]
as soon as they might bring on a paralysis of the struggling nation's force of self-preservation. But in this case this is

[34]
always the only visible result. As regards the question of humanity, Moltke once ex- pressed himself to the effect

[33]
that in case of war humanity always resides in the brevity of the procedure, so that the sharpest kind of

[33]
fight is most suitable for it. However, if one were now to try to bring up the drivel of aesthetics, etc., where these

[31]
considerations are concerned, there can be really only one answer to it: questions of des- tiny, as

[31]
important as a people's struggle for existence, elim- inate all obligation towards beauty. The least

[33]
beauti- 230 MEIN KAMPF ful that can exist in human life is and remains the yoke of slavery. Or does this Schwdbing decadence

[33]
perhaps per- ceive tne present-day fate of the German nation as 'aes- thetic 1 ? There is certainly no need to discuss this

[32]
with the Jews, the modern inventors of this culture perfume. Their entire existence is a protest incarnate

[33]
against the aesthetics of the Lord's image. But once these^, points of view of humanity and beauty are beside

[32]
the point where the struggle is concerned, they cannot be applied as a means to measure propaganda. During the War

[32]
propaganda was a means to an end, but this in turn was the German people's fight for existence; thus propaganda could

[33]
therefore be looked upon only from the principles proper to it. Then the most cruel weapons were humane if they

[33]
conditioned the quicker victory, and beautiful were only those methods which helped the nation to secure the

[32]
dignity of its freedom. This was the only possible attitude towards the question of war propaganda in such

[33]
a fight for life or death. Had the so-called responsible authorities made this clear to themselves, the uncertainty

[32]
about the form and the ap- plication of this weapon would never have originated; for this is also only a

[34]
weapon, though a frightful one, in the hand of the expert. fThe second question of actually decisive importance was

[33]
the following: To whom has propaganda to appeal? To the scientific intelligentsia or to the less educated

[33]
masses? It has to appeal forever and only to the masses! : Propaganda is not for the intelligentsia or for

[33]
those who unfortunately call themselves by that name today, but scientific teaching. But propaganda is in its

[34]
contents as far from being science as perhaps a poster is art in its presentation as such. A poster's art lies in the designer's

[32]
ability to catch the masses' attention by outline and color. The poster for an art exhibition has to point

[34]
only to the art WAR PROPAGANDA 231 of the exhibition; the more it succeeds in this, the greater therefore is the art

[31]
of the poster itself. Further, the poster is to give to the masses an idea of the importance of the ex-

[33]
hibition, but it is in no way to be a substitute for the art represented by the exhibition. Therefore,

[33]
he who wants to occupy himself with art itself has really to study more than the poster; yes, for him it is by far not

[29]
sufficient merely to 'walk through' the exhibition. It may be expected of him that he bury himself in the

[32]
individual works by thoroughly looking them over so that then he may gradually form a just opinion for himself. The

[32]
situation is a similar one with what today we call propaganda. The task of propaganda lies not in a

[33]
scientific training of the individual, but rather in directing the masses towards certain facts, events, necessities,

[33]
etc., the purpose being to move their importance into the masses' field of vision. The art now is exclusively to

[32]
attack this so skillfully that a general conviction of the reality of a fact, of the necessity Hitler says he

[33]
awakened during the War to the importance of propaganda, discovered that German methods were too high-brow

[33]
and too little adapted to drum up popular emotion, and learned that the first rule of the propagandist must be to

[33]
find out what will affect the masses. In view of the fact that propaganda became a fundamental concern of the Nazi

[33]
r6gime, some attention to Hitler's contributions to this science is called for. There is a convenient analysis

[33]
in Propaganda Analysis, Vol. I (New York, 1938). This essay, prepared by experts, reveals very clearly how the various

[32]
weapons of the militant propagandist e.g., calling names have been employed. It relegates to a position of

[33]
minor importance, an aspect of the matter on which Hitler lays great stress that the propa- gandist who is trying to wage war

[32]
must eliminate the 'esthetic' and concentrate on stirring up hatred. Therefore this may be emphasized

[32]
here. Many are convinced (and base this convic- 232 MEIN KAMPF of an event, that something; that is necessary is

[32]
also right, etc., is created. But as it is not and cannot be science in it- self, as its task consists of catching the masses 9

[33]
attention, just like that of the poster, and not in teaching one who is already scientifically experienced or

[34]
is striving towards education and knowledge, its effect has always to be directed more and more towards the feeling,

[32]
and only to a certain extent to so-called reason." All propaganda has to be popular and has to adapt its

[32]
spiritual level to the perception of the least intelligent of those towards whom it intends to direct itself.

[32]
Therefore its spiritual level has to be screwed the lower, the greater the mass of people which one wants to

[33]
attract. But if the prob- lem involved, like the propaganda for carrying on a war, is to include an entire people

[33]
in its field of action, the caution tion on long personal experience) that the most effective in- strument in the Nazi

[33]
propagandist's hands has been the spectacle of cruelty. When masses of men have been repressed for a long time by adverse

[32]
social, political and economic con- ditions, they seem to accept the open expression above all the open

[30]
demonstration of hatred with deep satisfaction. Almost every war is followed by strange manias of

[33]
persecution which affect the civilian population more than they do the returning soldier, unless that soldier deems

[33]
himself a victim of ingratitude. Thus after 1918 the United States witnessed the spread of the Ku Klux Klan, a crusade

[32]
against the 'Reds/ and several anti-negro riots in major cities. In France hostility to American and

[32]
other foreign troops was so marked that cantonments had to be evacuated more speedily than had been planned. In

[33]
Germany, at all events, one principal reason why the Rightist revolt against the Republic succeeded was the progres-

[33]
sive emphasis upon hatred in action. The bloody repression which marked the end of the short-lived 'Soviet' state in

[33]
Bavaria did not arouse sentiments of pity in all the citizens of WAR PROPAGANDA 233 in avoiding too high

[30]
spiritual assumptions cannot be too great. The more modest, then, its scientific ballast is, and the more it

[33]
exclusively considers the feelings of the masses, the more striking will be its success. This, however, is the best proof

[33]
whether a particular piece of propaganda is right or wrong, and not the successful satisfaction of a few scholars

[33]
or ' aesthetic ' languishing monkeys. This is just the art of propaganda that it, understanding the great masses' world of ideas

[33]
and feelings, finds, by a correct psychological form, the way to the attention, and further to the heart, of the great masses. That

[33]
our super- clever heads never understand this proves only their mental inertia or their conceit. But if one understands

[33]
the necessity of the attitude of Munich. The Hitler putsch of 1923 made the Party more popular in the city

[33]
than it had been before. When the Nazis drove dissenters or imaginary dissenters from their meet- ings with cudgels, their

[33]
audiences grew larger. Few people in Germany were at bottom anti-Semitic, but the joy large num- bers felt in

[32]
promises of blood-curdling treatment to be meted out to the helpless minority made them responsive to the sug-

[33]
gestion. Smashing windows and street fighting were relied upon to win the crowd. The propagandists encouraged them all. ' We shall

[33]
reach our goal,' declared Goebbels, ' when we have the courage to laugh as we destroy, as we smash, whatever was sacred to us

[33]
as tradition, as education, as friendship and as human affection.' In the Vienna of March, 1938, ordinary citizens who

[34]
had hitherto gone about peacefully, confessed to a strange delight in the sufferings visited upon the Jewish

[33]
group. After a while that craving subsides in the great majority, to be followed by widespread loathing of what is

[32]
termed ‘barbarism. 9 The pogrom of 1938, for example, elicited widespread open criticism. With such lapses of fervor the

[34]
agents of propaganda must deal. 234 MEIN KAMPF the attracting skill of propaganda towards the great masses, the following rule then

[32]
results: It is wrong to wish to give propaganda the versatility of perhaps scientific teaching. The great masses 9

[32]
receptive ability is only very limited, their understanding is small, but their forgetfulness is great. As

[33]
a consequence of these facts, all effective propa- ganda has to limit itself only to a very few points and

[32]
to use them like slogans until even the very last man is able to imagine what is intended by such

[33]
a word. As soon as one sacrifices this basic principle and tries to become versatile, the effect will fritter

[33]
away, as the masses are neither able to digest the material offered nor to retain it. Thus the re- sult is

[34]
weakened and finally eliminated. The greater the line of its representation has to be, the more correctly

[33]
from the psychological point of view will its tactics have to be outlined. For example, it was completely wrong to

[31]
ridicule the ad- versary as was done in Austrian and German propaganda in comic papers. It was

[31]
basically wrong for the reason that when a man met the adversary in reality he was bound to re- ceive an

[32]
entirely different impression; something that took its most terrible revenge; for now the German soldier, under the

[34]
direct impression of the resistance of the enemy, felt himself deceived by those who so far were responsible

[33]
for his enlightenment, and instead of strengthening his fight- ing spirit or even his firmness, quite the contrary occurred.

[33]
The man despaired. Compared with this, the war propaganda of the British and the Americans was psychologically

[34]
right. By introduc- ing the German as a barbarian and a Hun to its own people, it thus prepared the individual

[32]
soldier for the terrors of war and helped guard him against disappointment. The most terrible weapon which was now being used

[33]
against him then appeared to him only as the proof of the enlightenment al- WAR PROPAGANDA 835 ready bestowed upon

[33]
him, thus strengthening his belief that his government's assertions were right, and on the other hand it increased his fury and

[33]
hatred against the atrocious enemy. For the cruel effect of the weapon of his enemy which he learned to know by his

[32]
own experience appeared to him gradually as the proof of the already proclaimed 'Hunnish' brutality of the

[32]
barbaric enemy, without, how- ever, making him think for even a moment that his own weapons could have, perhaps, or

[34]
even probably, a still more terrible effect. Thus the English soldier could not even for a moment have the impression

[33]
that his country had taught him the wrong facts, something which was unfortunately the case to such an extent with the German

[32]
soldier that he finally rejected everything that came from this side as 'swindle' and 'bunk' (Krampf). All these things were

[33]
consequences of the fact that they believed they had a right to assign to propaganda just any idiot (or even

[33]
'otherwise' clever peo- ple) instead of understanding that sometimes even the most outstanding judges of the human

[31]
soul are barely good enough for this purpose. Thus the German war propaganda offered an incom- Allied

[33]
propaganda as such had no lasting effect upon soldiers at the Front; and we may be sure that Hitler was thinking rather

[32]
of what could be done to keep enthusiasm alive among civilians. By 1917 French soldiers doubted every word that their

[33]
papers printed; and yet those papers were no longer en- couraging waves of hatred but were stressing lofty ideals

[31]
such as religious resignation and the beauty of a difficult task patiently done. ' I do not believe that the

[33]
veteran soldier can thrive on hatred,' said an able writer at the time. And the greatest triumph British propaganda

[32]
ever achieved was the promulgation of what later on became Mr. Wilson's ' Fourteen Points.' 236 MEIN KAMPF parable lesson for

[33]
teaching and instruction for an 'enlight- enment' that worked in just the reverse direction, in con- sequence of a complete

[32]
lack of all psychologically suitable consideration. The enemy, however, offered no end of study

[33]
material for one who, with open eyes and a feeling that had not yet become calcified, pondered over the flood

[31]
wave of the enemy's propaganda which had stormed upon him during four and a half years. But least of all did one

[30]
understand the very primary con- dition for all propagandistic activity as a whole: namely, the

[33]
subjectively biased attitude of propaganda towards the questions to be dealt with. In this field one sinned

[33]
from above in such a manner, and from the very beginning of the War, that one was entitled to doubt whether so much

[33]
non- sense could actually only be ascribed to stupidity. What would one say about a poster, for instance,

[32]
which was to advertise a new soap, and which nevertheless de- scribes other soaps as also being 'good'? At this one would

[33]
certainly shake one's head. Exactly the same is the case with political advertising. Propaganda's task is,

[33]
for instance, not to evaluate the various rights, but far more to stress exclusively the one that is to

[33]
be represented by it. It has not to search into truth as far as this is favorable to others, in order to present

[33]
it then to the masses with doctrinary honesty, but it has rather to serve its own truth uninterruptedly. It was

[33]
fundamentally wrong to discuss the war guilt from the point of view that not Germany alone could be made responsible

[33]
for the outbreak of this catastrophe, but it would have been far better to burden the enemy entirely with this guilt,

[33]
even if this had not been in accordance with the real facts, as was indeed the case. What, now, was the consequence of these

[31]
half measures? The great mass of a people is not composed of diplomats WAR PROPAGANDA 237 or even teachers of

[32]
political law, nor even of purely reason' able individuals who are able to pass judgment, but of

[33]
human beings who are as undecided as they are inclined to- wards doubts and uncertainty. As soon as by one's own

[33]
propaganda even a glimpse of right on the other side is ad- mitted, the cause for doubting one's own right is laid.

[34]
The masses are not in a position to distinguish where the wrong of the others ends and their own begins. In this case they

[33]
become uncertain and mistrusting, especially if the enemy does not produce the same nonsense, but, in turn,

[32]
burdens their enemy with all and the whole guilt. What is more easily explained than that finally one's own people

[32]
believe more in the enemy's propaganda, which proceeds more completely and more uniformly, than in

[32]
one's own? This, however, may be said most easily of a people which suffers so severely from the mania of

[32]
objectivity as the German people does. For now they will take pains not to do an in- justice to the enemy,

[32]
even at the risk of the severest strain on, or destruction of, his own nation and State. But the masses do not at all

[30]
realize that this is not the in- tention of the responsible authorities. The people, in an overwhelming

[30]
majority, are so feminine in their nature and attitude that their activities and thoughts are

[30]
motivated less by sober consideration than by feeling and sentiment. This sentiment, however, is not

[34]
complicated but very simple and complete. There are not many differentiations, but rather a positive or

[32]
a negative; love or hate, right or wrong, truth or lie; but never half this and half that, or partially, etc. The English

[31]
propaganda understood and considered all this in the most ingenious manner. There were really no half

[33]
measures which perhaps might have given cause for doubt. The proof of this brilliant knowledge of the primitiveness 238 MEIN

[32]
KAMPF of feeling of the great masses was to be found in the atrocity propaganda that had been adapted to this, thus

[33]
ruthlessly and ingeniously securing moral steadfastness at the front, even during the greatest defeats, and further in

[30]
the just as striking pinning down of the German enemy as the only party guilty of the War's outbreak; a lie, the

[33]
unsurpassed, impudent, and biased stubbornness of which and how it was brought forth took into account the sentimental and

[31]
extreme attitude of this great people and therefore gained credence. fBut how effective this kind of

[33]
propaganda is is shown most strikingly by the fact that after four years it was not only able to make the enemy

[33]
hold his own, but it even be- gan to eat into our own people. We must not be surprised, however, that our propaganda

[33]
was not rewarded with this success. Its inner ambiguity included the germ of failure. But finally, in consequence

[33]
of its contents, it was hardly probable that it would make the necessary impression on the masses. Only our brainless

[33]
'statesmen' were able to hope that with this stale pacifistic dishwater one could succeed in arousing men to

[32]
die volun- tarily. Thus this miserable stuff was useless, even harmful. Nevertheless, all geniality in the

[29]
makeup of propaganda will not lead to success unless a fundamental principle is considered with

[32]
continually sharp attention : it has to con- fine itself to little and to repeat this eternally. Here, too,

[33]
persistency, as in so many other things in this world, is the first and the most important condition for success. In the field

[33]
of propaganda particularly one must never be guided by aestheticists or blast persons; not by the first, because

[33]
otherwise propaganda's form and expression would after a short time, instead of being suitable for the masses, only

[33]
have an attraction for literary tea parties; but against the second one ought to guard oneself carefully for

[34]
the rea- WAR PROPAGANDA 239 son that their shortage of fresh sentiments of their own is always looking for new stimulants. These people

[31]
tire of everything after a short time; they want a change and they will never understand or be able to

[32]
imagine the needs of their fellow citizens who are not yet so hard-boiled. They are always the first critics of

[33]
propaganda, or rather of its content, which appears to them to be too old, too hack- neyed, then again too out-of-date, etc. They

[34]
always want something new, they look for changes, thus becoming mor- tal enemies of any effective winning of the masses.

[33]
For as soon as the organization and the content of a propaganda begin to orientate themselves after their

[30]
needs, it will lose all complexity and will completely fritter itself away in- stead. Now the purpose of

[31]
propaganda is not continually to produce interesting changes for a few blast little masters, but to

[33]
convince; that means, to convince the masses. The masses, however, with their inertia, always need a certain time before

[33]
they are ready even to notice a thing, and they will lend their memories only to the thousandfold repetition of

[33]
the most simple ideas. < A change must never alter the content of what is being brought forth by propaganda, but in the end it

[33]
always has to say the same. Thus the slogan has to be illuminated from various sides, but the end of every

[32]
reflection has al- ways and again to be the slogan itself. Only thus can and will propaganda have uniform and

[32]
complete effect. This great line alone, which one must never leave, brings the final success to maturity by

[32]
continually regular and consistent emphasis. But then one will be able to deter- This is very true and

[32]
Hitler has demonstrated it. From 1920 to 1933 he permitted himself few variations. His was always the same pose, the same

[31]
gestures (fists clutched and shaken in front of his face, right arm stretched above his head with the 240 MEIN KAMPF mine with

[32]
astonishment to what enormous and hardly un- derstandable results such perseverance will lead. All advertising,

[30]
whether it lies in the field of business or of politics, will carry success by continuity and regular

[32]
uniformity of application. Here, too, the enemy's war propaganda set a typical ex- ample. It was

[32]
limited to a few points of view, calculated exclusively for the masses, and it was carried out with un- tiring

[33]
persistency. Basic ideas and forms of execution which had once been recognized as being right were em- ployed throughout

[33]
the entire War, and never did one make even the slightest change. At the beginning it was appar- ently crazy

[33]
in the impudence of its assertions, later it be- came disagreeable, and finally it was believed. After

[30]
four and a half years a revolution broke out in Germany the slogan of which came from the enemy's war

[33]
propaganda. In England, however, one understood one thing more: that for this spiritual weapon the possible

[33]
success lies only in the mass of its application, but that success amply covers all expenses. There, propaganda was

[33]
considered a weapon of the first order, whereas with us it was the last bread of the politician without office,

[33]
and a pot-boiler for the modest hero. All in all, its effect was just nil. index finger pointing toward the heavens), the same

[32]
theme. The rhythm of the National-Socialist march is unmistakable; the conventions which surround official meetings are

[31]
never dispensed with. There is always music of an approved military variety. The propaganda

[33]
intended for consumption in foreign coun- tries has been carefully adjusted to meet the requirements. Every country

[31]
has its quota of agents, to whom money, ma- terials and instructions are freely supplied. Ernst Wilhelro Bohle,

[34]
manager of the Foreign Organization WAR PROPAGANDA 241 isation) of the Party has associated with him the heads

[31]
of a number of other groups also working in their way to inter- nationalize the doctrines of National

[30]
Socialism. The two most effective weapons are these: the contention that Hitler is the bulwark of Western

[33]
civilization against the revolutionary machinations of Moscow; and the doctrine that Jewry is the root of

[31]
all evil. There are many people in this world who fear the Bolshevists; there are equally many who can be

[32]
persuaded to dislike the Jew. Whenever violent nationalism is in the ascendancy, as is the case at

[33]
present, both Jew and believing Christian necessarily suffer, but the first is at an especial dis- advantage because he

[32]
can be stigmatized as a member of an alien race. Yet there are other things, too, which the propa- ganda

[33]
attempts to stress the debt of civilization to the 'Nordic'; the sins inherent in the democratic system of gov- ernment;

[32]
and the blessings of totalitarianism. Throughout the Balkans, where there are in every country important

[33]
Jewish minorities, this propaganda falls on welcome ears, particularly since a great number of peasants now for

[31]
the most part in economic straits have long since been anti-Semitic. In Slovakia and northern Hungary, the

[33]
disarray attendant upon the Munich settlement seems to have encouraged a kind of belief that Hitler is the Grand

[32]
Mogul. Roumania, Jugoslavia, and other States are torn between 'Fascist' and 'anti-Fascist 1 propaganda. A

[33]
particularly interesting example is Greece, whence young ladies and gentlemen have traveled to Germany

[31]
at Nazi expense, then to set their experiences down in books and brochures. The government of the country being a

[33]
dictatorship, there seems to be considerable official willingness to foster sympathy for Hitler. In Switzerland

[34]
a determined government found it necessary during 1938 to ferret out a whole group of Nazi agents and spies. Some of

[32]
these lived in fashionable hotels, adorning their rooms with photographs of Hitler and Goebbels and dispensing hospi-

[34]
tality on a lavish scale. The Swiss government unearthed a scheme for settling all the German nationals in the Canton

[33]
of St. Gallen, dose to the Austrian border. The Basle police ar- rested a ring of agents who had been active in

[33]
Alsace-Lorraine 42 MEIN KAMPF Holland and Belgium, too, are under considerable Nazi pres- sure, but in both countries

[33]
the vigorous stand taken by the Catholic hierarchy has presented a formidable obstacle. France has witnessed,

[33]
primarily as a result of the ' new deal ' sponsored by L6on Blum, a recrudescence of anti-Semitism, but this has

[31]
little to do, in all probability, with Nazi influence. There are some French propagandists for Nazism,

[33]
notable Alphonse de Chateaubriant and Darquier de Pellepoix. Nazi aid was granted to General Franco in Spain,

[33]
and as a result a vast amount of Nazi propaganda is spread throughout insurgent territory. The United States

[33]
has had to deal with Nazi agents on nu- merous occasions. The Dickstein Committee and the Dies Committee have heard reams of

[33]
testimony, usually of a some- what confused kind, concerning among other things the Deutscher Volksbund (German Folk

[33]
Association) and other or- ganizations friendly to Hitler. During 1938 a federal grand jury indicted, tried, and found

[29]
guilty a number of persons in- volved in a plot to obtain military secrets. A number of ' Fas- cist'

[33]
organizations throughout the country receive literature directly from German sources, the most important of which

[32]
are the Fichtc-Bund and World Service. Naturalized Germans resident in the country are expected to fill out

[33]
formulae indi- cating their ancestry and their present political convictions. Subtler methods of exercising influence

[33]
are analyzed in The German Reich and Americans of German Origin, which lists many ties binding citizens of

[32]
this country to the Third Reich. Cf. also The Nazi International (London, Friends of Europe Publications, Nr. 69). CHAPTER VII THE

[32]
REVOLUTION fiN THE year 1915 the enemy's propaganda had started I on our side ; in 1 9 1 6 it became more and more

[32]
intensive, till finally, at the beginning of the year 1918, it swelled to a very flood. Now one could recognize the

[33]
results of this fishing for souls on all sides. The army gradually learned to think the way the enemy wished it to.

[33]
The German counter-action failed completely. The army, by virtue of the spirit and will power of its leader at that

[32]
time, certainly had the intention and de- termination to take up the battle in this field also, but it lacked the

[32]
instrument which would have been necessary to do so. From the psychological point of view also it was wrong that this

[33]
enlightenment be carried out by the troops themselves. If it was to be effective, it had to come from home. Only

[34]
then could one expect to be successful with men who, in the end, had performed immortal deeds of heroism and sacrifice for

[34]
their home country for almost four years. But what did come from home? Was this failure stupidity or criminal? In the height

[31]
of the summer of 1918, after the southern banks of the Marne had been cleared, the German press, above all. behaved so

[33]
miserably and clumsily, nay crim- 244 MEIN KAMPF inally stupidly, that with my daily growing wrath the ques- tion arose in

[33]
my mind whether there was really nobody at all who would put an end to this waste of the army's spirit- ual heroism?

[31]
What happened in France, when in the year 1914 we rushed into that country in an unheard-of victorious storm? What did

[32]
Italy do in the days of the collapse of its front on the Isonzo? What again did France do in the spring of 1918 when the

[32]
stormy assaults of the German divisions seemed to unhinge its positions and when the far-reaching arm of the heavy

[32]
long-distance batteries began to knock at the doors of Paris? How had the fever heat of national passion been whipped

[32]
into the faces of the hastily retreating regiments! How did propaganda and ingenious influence work on the

[33]
masses in order to hammer the faith in a final victory into the hearts of the broken fronts ! But what was done on our

[33]
side? Nothing, or even worse than that. At that time I often felt fury and indignation rise in me whenever

[33]
we received the latest papers which enabled us to read of this psychological mass-murder which was being carried out. But

[33]
more than once I was tormented by the thought that, if Destiny had put me in the place of these incapable or

[33]
criminal scamps or incompetents of our propagand a serv- ice, a different kind of battle would have been announced

[34]
to Destiny. In those months, for the first time, I felt fully the whims of fortune which kept me at the front in a place where

[33]
any lucky move on the part of a negro could shoot me down, while somewhere else I would have been able to

[34]
render a different service to my country. For I was bold enough to believe even then that I would have succeeded

[32]
in thuu THE REVOLUTION 245 However. I was one without a name, one among eight millions! Therefore it was

[33]
better to keep my mouth shut and to do my duty as best I could. In the summer of 191 j the enemy's first leaflets fell into our

[33]
hands. Despite some changes in form, their contents were nearly always the same, namely: that distress in Germany was

[31]
growing more and more; that the duration of the war would be endless, while the hope of winning it was dwin- dling

[34]
gradually; that the people at home were longing for peace for this reason, but that 'militarism' as well as the 'Kaiser'

[33]
would not permit this; that the entire world (which was very well aware of this) therefore did not fight against the German

[33]
people, but rather exclusively against the sole culprit, the Kaiser; that this fight would not end unless this enemy of

[31]
peaceful mankind should be eliminated ; that after the end of the War, the liberal and democratic nations,

[31]
however, would accept Germany into the league of eternal world peace which would be assured from the hour when '

[33]
Prussian ' militarism was destroyed. For the better illustration of what was thus presented 'letters from home' were not

[31]
infrequently reprinted, the contents of which seemed to corroborate these statements. But in those days one

[33]
generally merely laughed at these attempts. The leaflets were read, then passed on to the rear to the higher army

[33]
staffs, then they were usually for- gotten till the wind forwarded a new shipment into the trenches from above; for it

[33]
was mostly airplanes which served for bringing over these leaflets. In the nature of this propaganda, one point was

[31]
bound to attract attention, that is, that in every section of the trenches where there were Bavarians, it

[33]
persistently made 246 MEIN KAMPF front against Prussia by asserting not only that the latter was the real culprit and solely

[33]
responsible for the entire War, but that there was not the slightest hostility against Bavaria; however, one

[33]
would not be able to help her as long as she assisted in serving Prussian militarism, by pull- ing its chestnuts out of

[34]
the fire. As early as the year 1915 this sort of persuasion actually began to have definite effects. Among the troops

[32]
the feeling against Prussia grew quite visibly but the authorities did not even once interfere. This was

[33]
even worse than a sin of omission, for sooner or later it was bound to take a most unfortunate revenge,

[33]
not only on the 'Prussians' but on the German people, and to this the Bavarians themselves last but not least belong. In this

[31]
direction the hostile propaganda began to show decided success as early as the year 1916. In the same way, the

[31]
lamenting letters from home had long since begun to have an effect. Now it was no longer necessary for the

[33]
enemy to forward these letters to the front in the form of leaflets, etc. Also nothing was done against this except for

[32]
some indescribably stupid 'warn- ings' from the 'side of the government.' Now, as before, the front was flooded with this

[31]
poison, manufactured by thoughtless women at home, without their guessing, how- ever, that this was the means to strengthen

[33]
enormously the enemy's belief in his victory, thus prolonging and in- creasing the sufferings of their own people on

[33]
the battle front. The German women's silly letters in the time that followed cost hundreds of thousands of men their lives. Thus

[32]
it was already in 1916 that various symptoms be- came apparent which would better not have been present. At the front one

[32]
abused and 'grumbled/ one was already discontented with many things and sometimes justly so. While the front

[31]
suffered hunger and deprivations, while the families at home were in distress, there was abundance THE

[33]
REVOLUTION 247 and revelry in other places. Nay, even on the battle front itself, not everything was as it should have

[33]
been in this respect. Even then there was a slight crisis; however, these were still 'domestic' affairs. The same man who

[33]
at first had cursed and grumbled, a few minutes later performed si- lently his duty as though this were a matter of

[32]
course. The same company, which at first was discontented, clung to the section of the trenches it had to protect as though

[33]
Germany's destiny depended upon these hundred meters of mud holes. It was still the front of the old and glorious

[32]
army of heroes! I was to learn the difference between home and the army in a drastic change. At the end of

[33]
September, 1916, my division joined in the Somme battle. For us this was the first of these enormous material battles,

[33]
and it was only too difficult to describe our impressions. This really seemed to resemble hell rather than war. During

[33]
weeks of a whirlwind of drum fire the German front stood its ground, pushed back a little at times, then pushing ahead again, but

[32]
never retreating. On October 7, 1916, I was wounded. I was luckily brought to the rear and was to be sent to Germany with

[33]
a transport. Two years now had passed since I had seen home, an almost endless time under these circumstances. I was

[32]
hardly able to imagine what Germans who were not clad in uniforms looked like. When I was lying in the field

[33]
hospi- tal at Hermies, I almost jumped from the shock when I suddenly heard the voice of a German woman she was a nurse

[33]
speak to one of the men lying next to me. For the first time, a sound like that after two years! But the nearer the train which was

[33]
to bring us home ap- oroached the border, the more restless each one of us be- 248 MEIN KAMPF came. All the places passed

[34]
by through which we had marched two years before as young soldiers: Brussels, Louvain, Lige, and finally we thought that we recognized

[32]
the first German house by its high gable and its beautiful shutters. The fatherland! In October, 1914, we burned with wild

[31]
enthusiasm when we passed the frontier; now quiet and emotion prevailed. Each one was happy that Destiny

[31]
allowed him once more to see what he had to protect so earnestly with his life; and each one was almost

[33]
ashamed to look the other in the eye. It was almost on the anniversary of the day of my march- ing out that I was

[33]
brought into the hospital at Beelitz near Berlin. What a change! From the mud of the Somme battle into the white beds of

[33]
this building of marvels! At the begin- ning one hardly dared to lie down properly. Only slowly was one able to

[34]
become accustomed again to this new world. Unfortunately, this world was new in still another direc- tion. The spirit

[33]
of the army on the front seemed no longer to be a guest here. I heard here for the first time something that was still

[33]
unknown at the front: bragging about one's own cowardice! For, no matter how much one heard cursing and 'grousing 1 at the front,

[32]
it was never an invita- tion to shirk duty or even a glorification of the coward. No. The coward was still

[33]
considered a coward, and no more; and the contempt he met with was still general, ex- actly as the admiration paid

[33]
the real hero. But here in the hospital it was already the reverse: the unprincipled agita- tors had the word

[30]
and tried with all the means of their mis- erable eloquence to picture the idea of the honest soldier as

[33]
ridiculous and the coward's lack of character as an exam- ple to be followed. A few wretched fellows, above all,

[33]
set THE REVOLUTION 249 the fashion. One of them bragged about having pulled his own hand through the barbed-wire fence so

[33]
that he could come to the hospital; despite this ridiculous accident, he seemed to have been here an endless

[33]
time, just as he had come in the transport to Germany by swindle. But this poisonous fellow actually went so far

[33]
as to describe, with impudent cheek, his own cowardice as the result of a brav- ery higher than the heroic death of

[33]
the honest soldier. Many listened in silence, others went out, but still others agreed with him. 1 felt disgust rise in my

[33]
throat, but the instigator was quietly tolerated in the hospital. What was to be done? The authorities must have

[33]
known, and did know who and what he was. Yet nothing was done. When I was able to walk again, I was given permission to go

[31]
to Berlin. It was apparent that distress was very great everywhere. The city of millions suffered hunger.

[31]
Discontent was great. In various homes, however, where soldiers visited, the feeling was similar to that of the

[33]
hospital. The general impression was as though these fellows intentionally sought out such places in order to air their

[33]
opinions. But how much worse were conditions in Munich! When, after being cured, I was dismissed from the hos- pital and

[31]
turned over to the reserve battalion, I thought I The winter of 1916 was a difficult one in all armies. War

[30]
weariness, privation, and dissatisfaction with inevitable gov- ernmental inefficiency were rife

[32]
everywhere. What Hitler says here concerning the feeling in Germany could be matched with reports from France and

[33]
England. But in Munich and in- deed throughout most of Bavaria the situation was in a measure different. Ancient

[32]
Bavarian particularism now made a scapegoat of Prussia, attributing to it the militarism that had

[33]
plunged the Empire into war. Separatism was openly advo- 250 MEIN KAMPF hardly recognized the town again. Anger,

[33]
grumbling, and cursing met me on all sides. In the reserve battalion the feeling was beyond all criticism. The clumsy manner

[33]
in which the soldiers from the front were treated by the old instruction officers, who had not been at the front for even an hour

[32]
and who, for this reason alone, were able only par- tially to establish good relations with the old soldiers, con-

[33]
tributed to this. The returning soldiers could not help but show certain peculiarities which were explicable by their

[32]
service at the front, but which were and remained entirely incomprehensible to the leaders of the reserve

[34]
units, while the officer who had also been at the front could understand them. Finally, the latter was respected by the men

[33]
in quite a different way from the commanders from the rear. But quite apart from this, the general mood was more than bad

[33]
; shirking of duty was looked upon almost as a sign of higher wisdom, but faithful endurance as a sign of inner

[33]
weakness and narrow-mindedness. But the offices of the authorities cated. By 1918, newspapers in northern Bavaria were

[33]
counsel- ing sabotage of the War; and in alarm Crown Prince Rupprecht urged upon the High Command the necessity for

[33]
making the speediest possible peace. Hitler's subsequent course was dic- tated in a measure by these phenomena.

[32]
After the War Bavaria was a place of refuge for all nationalist agitators who were pursued by the

[33]
Republic, but it was also the custodian of the monarchical and particularist doctrines. Its government was

[34]
motivated by a desire to put Rupprecht on the throne, and to regulate the affairs of Bavaria more or

[31]
less independently of those of Germany as a whole. This could not be Hitler's pur- pose, since he was a

[34]
Pan-German. Accordingly he tried to force the issue and to compel the Bavarian government to participate in

[32]
a march on Berlin by staging the putsch of 1923. In a measure he was abetted by the fact that Rupprecht was averse to

[33]
accepting the crown of Bavaria unless monarchical restoration took place throughout Germany. THE REVOLUTION

[34]
851 were occupied by Jews. Almost every clerk a Jew and every Jew a clerk. I was amazed by this multitude of

[31]
fighters of the Chosen People and could not help comparing them with the few representatives they had on the front. In the

[32]
business world things were even worse. Here the Jewish people had really become 'indispensable/ fThe spider

[33]
began slowly to suck the people's blood out of its pores. By way of the war societies one had found the instru- ment with which

[33]
to put an end, bit by bit, to a national and free economy. Now one stressed the necessity of a limitless

[33]
centraliza- tion. As early as in the year 1916-17 almost the entire pro- duction was indeed under the control of the Jewry

[33]
of high finance. But against whom did the people's hatred direct itself? At that time I saw with horror a fate approach

[33]
which, if it was not warded off in the eleventh hour, was bound to lead us to destruction. Jewish citizens of Germany at

[34]
the time the War broke out numbered about 550,000. Of these 100,000 were in uniform, and of these four-fifths saw duty at the front.

[33]
There were 12,000 casualties, BO that the ratio was virtually the same as that for the population as a whole; 35,000 Jews

[33]
were decorated for bravery; 23,000 were promoted; and 2000 received com- missions a remarkable fact seeing that prior to

[33]
the War the Prussian army had barred Jewish officers. There were 165 Jew- ish aviators, a fifth of whom were killed

[32]
in action. These fig- ures are based on official German war records. The first asser- tion that Jews had shirked their

[32]
duty in war-time was made by General Ernest von Wrisberg. (Cf. his Erinnerungen.) Jewish veterans formed an

[31]
organization of their own. General von Linsingen, a distinguished commander on the eastern front, applied for

[32]
admission to this organization during 1933, on the ground that he had a Jewish grandmother. 252 MEIN KAMPF While the Jew robbed the

[33]
entire nation and pressed it under his rule, people agitated against the ‘Prussians/ Exactly as on the front,

[33]
at home nothing was done by the authorities against this poison propaganda. It seemed that one did not guess that

[33]
Prussia’s breakdown would not mean the rise for Bavaria, but that, on the contrary, the downfall of the one was also bound

[33]
to hurl the other hope- lessly into the abyss. At that time I felt infinitely sorry because of this. In

[33]
these things I could only see the most ingenious trick of the Jew to divert general attention from himself and draw it to

[33]
others. While now the Bavarian and the Prussian quar- reled, the Jew pulled away their means of existence from under

[33]
the very nose of both ; while abusing the Prussian, the Jew organized the revolution and smashed Prussia as

[32]
well as Bavaria at the same time. I could not stand this cursed feud between the German tribes, and I was glad to

[33]
return to the front for which I registered immediately after my arrival at Munich. During the War commerce

[33]
in produce was regulated by the government, through the so-called Kriegsgesellschaften. Officials regulated prices,

[33]
distributed ration cards, and supervised the stocks of materials needed for the conduct of the War. During 1914 and 1915, Walther

[33]
Rathenau was director of the war ma- terials section of this organization. He was a Jewish industrial- ist and

[33]
author of treatises on social problems, who later on became Foreign Minister in the Wirth Cabinet and whose mur-

[32]
der by a band of Rightist assassins in 1922 almost precipitated another civil war. Doubtless the major reason for the

[33]
hatred which nationalists of the kind to whom Hitler appealed felt for Rathenau was nothing more serious than a remark

[32]
once ated from his writings by General Ludendorff. The charge that Rathenau could have used his office to

[33]
further Jewish financial interests is a fabrication. THE REVOLUTION 253 At the beginning of March, 1917, I was again with

[33]
my regiment. Towards the end of the year 1917 it seemed as though the depth of the army's despair had passed. After the Russian

[33]
breakdown the entire army now breathed new hope and fresh courage. The conviction that the fight would yet end with a German

[32]
victory began to take hold of the troops more and more. Now one could hear them sing again, and the croakers became

[33]
fewer in number. Once more one be- lieved in the fatherland's future. Especially the Italian breakdown of

[34]
the fall of 1917 had exercised the most wonderful influence; for one saw in this victory the proof of the possibility

[33]
that one would be able to break through the front at a place distant from the Rus- sian battlefield. Now again a marvelous

[33]
faith filled the hearts of the millions and made them look forward to the spring of 1918 with revived confidence. The enemy, how-

[32]
ever, was visibly depressed. In this winter he remained a little more quiet than at other times. The calm

[33]
before the storm had set in. While now the front undertook the ultimate preparations for the final termination

[32]
of the eternal struggle, while end- less transports of men and material rolled towards the Western Front and the troops were

[33]
given their final train- ing for the great attack, the worst piece of villainy of the entire War, up to that time, took place

[33]
in Germany. Germany was not to be victorious; thus in the last hour, when victory already threatened to fasten

[33]
itself to the Ger- man flags, one had seized means which seemed suitable to nip in the bud at one blow the German attack

[33]
of that spring and to make victory impossible. The munitions strike was organized. !f it succeeded, then the German

[33]
front was bound to S54 MEIN KAMPF break down, and the wish of the Vorwaerts, that this victory was not to entwine itself with the German flags,

[33]
would be fulfilled. With the shortage of munitions the front must necessarily be pierced in the course of a few weeks,

[33]
the attack was thus prevented, the Entente was saved, but international capital was made Germany's master; for

[32]
this was the inner aim of the Marxist betrayal of the people. The smashing of the national economy in favor of the

[33]
establishment of the rule of international capital; some- thing in which these gentlemen now succeeded, thanks to

[31]
the stupidity and the credulity of the one and the bottom- less cowardice of the other. < However, the

[33]
munitions strike had not the ultimately desired success as far as starving the front of weapons was concerned; it

[32]
broke down too early to allow the shortage of munitions as such to sentence the army to doom, such as the plan

[34]
presented itself. But how much more terrible was the moral damage which now had been done! First, for what, now, did the army

[32]
continue to fight, if home itself no longer wanted victory? For whom the The Munitions Strike was declared in

[29]
Berlin and some other cities during February, 1918. It was an effort to secure amelio- rations,

[32]
particularly of the food ration; but it was also used by some of its sponsors as an act of protest against the

[33]
continuance of the War. Leaders of the Socialist Party had entered the strike committee specifically in

[33]
order to see to it that the move- ment did not sponsor sabotage. General Ludendorff placed Berlin under martial

[33]
law, mass arrests were made, and large numbers of workers were sent to the front. This broke the strike before any

[33]
military damage was done, but the psycho- logical effect on the workers was bad. They felt that their just demands had

[32]
been answered with nothing but brutal repression. For their part the generals felt that German morale had been seriously

[33]
undermined. (Cf . Die 14 Jahre, by Friedrich Stamp- fer.) THE REVOLUTION 255 enormous sacrifices and deprivations? The soldier was

[33]
to fight for victory and at home they were striking against it! But what was, secondly, the effect on the enemy? In

[33]
the winter of 1917-18 dark douds rose for the first time over the horizon of the Allied world. For almost four years now one had

[33]
attacked the German giant and could not bring him to fall; but in addition, it was only the arm holding the shield which was free

[33]
to defend himself, while he had to raise the sword for striking now in the East, now in the South. Now, at last, the giant was free

[33]
in the back. Streams of blood had flown till he succeeded in finally striking down one of the enemies. Now in the West the sword

[33]
was to help the shield, and had the enemy not succeeded so far in breaking the defense, now he was to be hit by attack.

[32]
Vorwaerts, the Berlin Social Democratic daily, had demanded a peace of understanding rather than a peace of

[33]
victory. But the sentence here quoted from an editorial of October 20, 1918, is taken out of its context, as will

[33]
be evident when the passage as a whole is cited: 'We stand against overwhelming odds. We will not win this war. We will

[32]
not fight a moment longer than we must fight, and we are fighting not for victory but for peace in which there will not be

[32]
present the germ of another war. Germany shall that is our firm decision as Socialists furl its battle flags forever

[33]
without having brought them home in victory the last time. That is a heavy moral burden for every people, and those

[32]
who wish to make that burden heavier than it can be borne take a great measure of responsibility upon

[33]
themselves. No peace can make us unable to defend ourselves. Even the victor can obtain security only

[34]
from a peace that dis- arms all and makes friends of enemies. But a peace is a danger for him too, if it be a peace which

[32]
sends a people home to read in the bloody history of the past that the vanquished of today are the victors of

[33]
tomorrow.' It is, of course, perfectly obvious that this editorial written after the armistice parleys had

[34]
be- gun was only a plea for a just treaty of peace. 256 MEIN KAMPF fOne feared him and one was worried about the victory.

[34]
In London and Paris one conference chased the other, but on the front a sleepy silence prevailed. The gentlemen

[33]
had suddenly lost their impudence. Even the hostile propa- ganda had hard work now; it was no longer so easy to

[33]
prove the hopelessness of the German victory. But this was true also as regards the Allied troops on the fronts themselves.

[34]
Now also an uncanny realization began to dawn gradually upon them. Their inner attitude towards the German

[31]
soldier had changed now. Up till now he might be looked upon as a fool who was nevertheless destined to doom; now,

[33]
however, they were confronted by the conqueror of the Russian ally. The limitations of the German attacks in

[32]
the East, born of necessity, now seemed ingenious tactics. For three years now these Germans had stormed Russia, at the

[33]
beginning without even the slight- est seeming success. One almost laughed at this senseless enterprise; because, by

[33]
the overwhelming number of his men, the Russian giant was finally sure to remain the victor, Germany, however,

[33]
would collapse after having bled herself out. Reality seemed to confirm this hope. Since September, 1914, when for the first time

[33]
the end- less masses of Russian prisoners from the Tannenberg battle began to roll towards Germany on roads and rail- ways,

[31]
this stream hardly ever came to an end; but for every beaten and destroyed army, a new one arose. In-

[32]
exhaustibly the gigantic realm continued to give the Czar new soldiers and the war new victims. How long would Germany be

[32]
able to hold her own in this race? Was not the day to arrive when, after the last German victory, still not the last

[33]
Russian armies would march up for the very last battle? And what then? In all human probability, a Russian victory

[34]
could well be postponed, but it was bound to come. Now all these hopes were at an end; the ally who had THE REVOLUTION

[33]
257 laid down the greatest sacrifice in blood on the altar of common interests was at the end of his strength and was lying prostrate

[33]
on the ground before the inexorable aggres- sor. Fear and horror crept into the hearts of the soldiers who hitherto had

[34]
trusted blindly. One feared the coming spring. For, if so far one had not succeeded in breaking the German even though he was

[32]
able to present himself only in part on the Western Front, how could one still count on a victory now that the entire

[34]
power of this un- canny State of heroes seemed to concentrate itself for an attack of its own? The shadows of the South

[33]
Tyrolean mountains cast gloom on the imagination : as far as into the fogs of Flanders the beaten armies of Cadorna

[33]
conjured up dreary faces, and the confidence in the victory gave way before the fear of the coming defeat.

[32]
There, when out of the cool nights one thought one already heard the monotonous rolling of advancing storm units of the

[33]
German army, and when one started with oppressing fear at the coming judgment, suddenly a fierce red light flashed up in

[33]
Germany and threw its rays as far as into the remotest shell hole of the enemy's front ;< at the moment when the German

[33]
divisions received their last instructions for the great attack, the general strike broke out in Germany. At first the world

[33]
was speechless. But then the hostile propaganda threw itself with sighs of relief upon this aid in the eleventh hour. Now at

[33]
one blow the means was found with which one was able to raise the sinking confi- dence of the Allied soldiers, to make the

[34]
probability of victory appear realizable again, and to turn the gloomy This is part of the famous 'stab in the back'

[32]
theory of why Germany lost the War. A statement concerning this theory is appended to this chapter. S58 MEIN KAMPF fear of the

[33]
coming events into determined confidence. Now the conviction that the decision about the end of this war would not

[32]
be due to the daring of the German storm, but to their endurance in warding it off, could be given to the regiments,

[32]
expecting the German attack, on their way to the greatest battle of all times. One could let the Germans win as many

[32]
victories as they might want to; Revolution awaited its entry into their country and not the victorious army. Now

[30]
British, French, and American papers began to plant again this belief into the hearts of their readers, while an

[31]
infinitely skillful propaganda whipped up the troops on the front. 'Germany on the eve of Revolution.

[32]
Victory of the Allies inevitable/ This was the best medicine in order to set the wavering poilu or

[32]
Tommy on his feet once more. Now rifles and machine guns could be made to fire once more, and a rushing

[33]
away in panicky flight was replaced by hopeful resistance. This was the result of the munitions strike. It strength-

[33]
ened the hostile nation's confidence in victory and elimi- nated the paralyzing despair of the Allied

[32]
front. But in the time that followed, thousands of German soldiers had to pay for this with their blood. The originators of the

[33]
villainous act were the aspirants to the highest State posi- tions of revolutionary Germany. On the German

[33]
side one was at first certainly able appar- ently to overcome the most visible reaction to this act, but on

[32]
the side of the enemy the consequences soon became apparent. The resistance had lost the aimlessness of

[32]
any army that considered everything as lost, and in its stead appeared the exasperation of a fight for

[33]
victory. For in all human probability, victory was now bound to come if the Western Front resisted the German

[33]
attack for only a few months. In the parliaments of the Entente, THE REVOLUTION 259 however, one recognized

[33]
the possibilities of the future, and one granted unheard-of funds for the continuation of the propaganda

[33]
for Germany's destruction. I had the good fortune to be able to join in the first two attacks and in the last one. These

[33]
have become the most enormous impressions of my life; enormous for the reason that now for the last time, as in

[33]
1914, the fight lost its character of defense and assumed that of attack. A breath of relief passed along the trenches and posts

[33]
of the German army, when finally, after more than three years of perseverance in the hostile inferno, the day

[32]
of revenge approached. Once more the victorious battalions jubilated, and the last wreaths of immortal On March 21, 1918, the

[32]
Germans launched an attack on the British Fifth Army along the Picardy front. The onslaught waa heaviest at the point where the

[32]
English and French forces joined, and for some days it seemed as if the Fifth Army would be destroyed. But French reinforcements

[33]
arrived in time to stem the tide. In April the Germans struck another blow farther to the north, and in the battle of

[33]
Armentiftres imperiled Calais and other Channel ports. British losses were heavy, but Ludendorff failed to reach his

[33]
objective. Thereupon, during the months of May and June, three attacks were made in the hope of encircling Paris.

[33]
The Germans succeeded in crossing the Marne at Chateau-Thierry, but the Rheims salient held and therewith the German thrust

[33]
had failed. On July 18, Marshal Foch began the series of successful counter-attacks that ended the War. There can be no doubt

[33]
that Ludendorff 's offensives consti- tute one of the most brilliant and most futile military opera- tions

[33]
in history. A magnificent German army, sure that it could end the conflict and cheered by the elimination of

[32]
Russia, struck with a vigor that will forever honor its history. But the 260 MEIN KAMPF laurel hung themselves on the flags

[32]
around which victory waved. Once more the songs of the fatherland roared up to the sky along the endless marching

[31]
columns and for the last time the Lord's grace smiled down on his ungrate- ful children. ' In the height of the summer of 1918

[33]
oppressive sultriness hovered over the front. At home one quarreled. What about? Many stories were told in

[32]
the various units of the field army. Now the War was hopeless, and only fools were still able to believe in

[33]
victory. The people no longer had an interest in holding out any further, but only Capital and the monarchy

[33]
this news came from home and was also discussed on the front. At first it reacted only very moderately to this.

[32]
What had we to do with universal suffrage? Was it perhaps for this that we had fought for four years? It was a mean act of

[33]
banditry to steal in this way the aim of the War from the heroes dead in their graves. Not with the call, ' Long live universal

[33]
suffrage and the secret ballot,' had the young regiments once marched towards death in Flanders, but with the cry, 'Deutschland uber

[32]
dttes inder Welt.' A small but not quite unimportant difference. But those who called for the right to vote had for the

[33]
greater part not been there where now they wanted to fight for this. The front did not know the whole pack of political parties.

[32]
One saw only a fraction of the 'parliamentarian' gentlemen there wisdom of LudendorfFs strategy in these

[33]
battles von Hin- denburg was little more than a moral force has been doubted by the best German students of military

[33]
science. He had staked the future of Germany on a desperate gamble, using all available man-power and

[32]
destroying every hope of reaching a peace by negotiation. THE REVOLUTION 261 where decent Germans stayed at that

[33]
time, provided their limbs were only straight. The front in its old makeup was therefore only little susceptible to

[33]
these new war aims of the Messrs. Ebert, Scheidemann, Earth, Liebknecht, etc. Also, one did not at all understand why these shirkers

[33]
should now suddenly have the right to assume control of the State by going over the heads of the army. My personal

[33]
attitude towards this was fixed from the beginning: I whole-heartedly hated the entire Jot of these wretched

[32]
party rascals who betrayed the people. Long since I had clearly seen the fact that this gang were really not concerned with the

[33]
welfare of the nation, but rather with filling their own empty pockets. But that even now they were ready to sacrifice

[33]
the entire people to this pur- Hitler, as Heiden points out in a brilliant passage, is here describing what may have

[31]
been the experience which shaped his own future. He did not question the right fulness of the kind of leadership then

[31]
directing the destinies of Germany. The hard-headed tenacity with which Ludendorff clung to a war of conquest, the

[33]
declaration of U-boat warfare in spite of the United States, the harshness of the Treaty of Brest-Litovsk, the march

[32]
through Belgium, the sacrifice of all moral prestige in the world all these things and more he was wholly willing to

[33]
accept because they meant the extension of German power. But he saw that this military government and the caste which

[33]
had supported it had failed to catch the ear of the people. Even the instruments of propaganda which the nationalists

[34]
devised among them the Vatcrlandspartei (Fatherland Party) and its orators who accused every moderate German

[33]
of high treason failed abysmally to do the necessary work. Personal contact with other soldiers had brought Hitler as

[32]
little success as had his relations with Viennese workingmen. The rest avoided him, looked upon his formalistic

[31]
fidelity to military routine as 'bootlicking;/ and laughed at his patriotic 262 MEIN KAMPF pose, and, if

[33]
necessary, to let Germany go to the dogs, this, in my eyes, made them ripe for the rope. To consider their wishes

[33]
would mean to sacrifice the interests of the working classes in favor of a number of sluggards; but one could fulfill

[32]
them only if one was ready to give up Germany. These were still the thoughts of by far the majority of the

[31]
fighting army. Only the reinforcements coming from home now rapidly became worse and worse, so that their

[33]
arrival did not mean a strengthening, but rather a weaken- ing, of the fighting forces. The young reinforcements especially

[33]
were for the greater part worthless. Often one could believe only with difficulty that these were supposed to

[32]
be the sons of the same nation which once had sent its youth into the battle ofYpres. During August and September the

[33]
symptoms of decay increased rapidly, although the effects of the enemy at- tacks could not be compared with the horrors

[34]
of our defensive battles of some time ago. Compared with them, speeches. The reason was, he decided, that these men

[33]
had been misled by 'democratic' propaganda. They really believed that the War was being fought for the sake of the nobles

[33]
and the rich. To them electoral reform did mean something, and their labor organizations were matters of great import

[29]
to them. No- body had made them realize that alj^uch things were of minor consequence compared with the

[33]
aggrandizement of Germany. For that aggrandizement would mean the nation's enrichment and therewith prosperity and

[31]
prestige. In Hitler's mind there ripened the decision to supply the missing contact between Pan-Germanism and

[32]
democracy. He would talk to the people in their own language, but he would persuade them to adopt the Pan-German

[32]
outlook. Now his ad- miration for Lueger, and his respect for Allied statesmen like Wilson and Lloyd George, bred in him the

[34]
conviction that he would give Germany the benefit of a similar methodology. THE REVOLUTION 263 the Somme and

[33]
Flanders battles were ghastly memories of the past. At the end of September my division for the third time came to

[32]
those positions we once, as young volunteer regi- ments, had attacked. What a memory! t There, in October and

[33]
November, 1914, we had received our baptism of fire. With the love for the fatherland in our hearts and with songs on our lips, our

[32]
young regiment had marched into battle as to a dance. The most valuable blood gave itself up joyfully in the

[33]
belief that it would guard the fatherland's independence and freedom. In July, 1917, we stepped for the second time on the soil

[33]
that was sacred to us. For under it there slumbered the best comrades, almost children still, who once with beaming eyes had

[33]
run into the arms of death for the only and dear fatherland ! Now we old ones, who once had marched out with the regiment,

[31]
stood in reverential emotion on the soil of the oath for 'loyalty and obedience unto death/ This soil which our

[31]
regiment had conquered by storm three years before, it had now to guard in a difficult de- fensive battle. With

[33]
continuous drum fire for three weeks, the British prepared the great attack of Flanders. There the spirits of the dead seemed

[32]
to come to life again ; the regiment clutched the dirty mud and fastened its grip into the individual

[34]
holes and craters and did not give way and did not waver, and thus, as once before in this place, it became smaller

[34]
and thinner in number, till finally on July 31, 1917, the English attack broke out. In the first days of August we were relieved.

[34]
The regiment had been reduced to a few companies; these now made their way back, stumbling and encrusted with mud, more like

[34]
ghosts than human beings. But apart 264 MEIN KAMPF from a few hundred meters of shell holes, the English had only gained death. << Now, in the fall

[32]
of 1918, we stood for the third time on the soil of the storms of 1914. Our one-time resting place, Comines, had now become the

[33]
battlefield. However, even though the battlefield was the same, the men had changed; now one also 'discussed polities'

[32]
among the troops. The poison from home, as everywhere else, began to show its effect here also. The younger

[33]
reinforcements, however, failed completely, they came from home. In the night from October 13 to October 14 the English

[33]
began to throw gas on the southern front ofYpres; yellow- cross gas was being used, the effects of which were unknown to us so

[34]
far as personal experience was concerned. I was to get to know it personally in this very night. On the eve of

[33]
October 13, on a hill south of Wervick, we had come under a drum fire of gas shells, lasting several hours, which continued

[33]
more or less violently throughout the entire night. Towards midnight a part of us passed out, some of our comrades

[32]
forever. Towards morning I, too, was seized with pains which grew worse with every quarter hour, and at seven o'clock in the

[33]
morning I stumbled and tottered rearwards with burning eyes, but taking with me my last report in the War. Already a few hours

[32]
later the eyes had turned into burning coals; it had become dark around me. Thus I was brought into the hospital at

[33]
Pasevalk in Pomerania and there I was to experience the greatest villainy of the century. Something

[33]
uncertain and disgusting had hovered in the air for a long time. People told each other that during the coming weeks it

[33]
would 'go off, 9 but I was not able to imagine what was to be understood by this. First of all THE REVOLUTION 265 I thought

[34]
of a strike, similar to that of spring. Unfavorable rumors continued to come from the navy which was said to be in

[33]
ferment. But also this appeared to me more a product of the imagination of various fellows than some' thing that

[32]
concerned the masses. In the hospital, however, everybody hoped that the end of the War might come soon, but

[31]
nobody counted on an 'immediately.' However, I was not able to read newspapers. During November the

[32]
general tension increased. There one day suddenly and without warning the disaster came upon us. Sailors

[32]
arrived on trucks and called out for the Revolution; a few Jew boys, however, were the 'leaders' in the fight that now

[33]
started also here, the fight for 'free- dom/ 'beauty/ and 'dignity' of our people's existence. None of them had been at

[33]
the front. By way of a so-called 'gonorrhoea-hospital 1 these three Orientals had been sent home from the base behind

[33]
the front. Now they pulled up the red rag here. I had been somewhat better lately. The boring pain in the sockets of my

[33]
eyes had diminished; gradually I suc- ceeded in learning to distinguish my surroundings in rough outlines; I could hope

[33]
to regain my eyesight at least enough that later I would be able to take up some profession ; how- ever, I could no

[31]
longer hope that I would ever again be able to draw; nevertheless I was on the way to improve- ment when the

[32]
iponstrous event happened. My first hope was still that the high treason was nothing but a more or less local affair.

[31]
I also tried to convince some of my comrades to that effect. Especially my Bava- rian comrades in the

[32]
hospital were more than receptive to this. The mood was anything but ‘ revolutionary.’ Further, I could not

[33]
imagine that the lunacy would break out in Munich also. The loyalty towards the honorable House of Wittelsbach

[34]
seemed to me to be stronger than the will of a few Jews. Thus I could but believe that this was only a 266 MEIN KAMPF putsch on the part

[31]
of the navy which would be suppressed in the following days. The following days came, and with them the most ter- rible

[33]
certainty of my life. The rumors became more and more depressing. What I had taken to be a local affair

[31]
was now to be a general revolution. To this was added the shameful news from the front. One intended to

[33]
capitulate. Why was something of that kind really possible? On November 10 the pastor came into the hospital

[33]
for a short address; now we knew everything. In utmost excitement, I, too, was present during the short speech: The dignified

[33]
old gentleman seemed to tremble very much when he told us that now the House of Hohenzollern was no longer allowed

[34]
to wear the German imperial crown, that the country had now become a ‘re- public/ and that now one should ask the Almighty

[33]
not to deny His blessings upon this change and not to abandon our people in the time to come. He certainly could

[33]
not help it, but in a few words he had to remember the Royal House, he wanted to praise its merits in Pomerania,

[31]
in Prussia, even in the entire country and there he began to weep silently; but in the small hall deepest

[33]
depression seized all hearts, and I believe that not one eye was able to hold back the tears. But then as the old gentleman

[33]
tried to continue and began to tell us that now we had to end the long war, that even our fatherland would now be sub- mitted

[34]
to severe oppressions in the future, that now the War was lost and that we had to surrender to the mercy of the victors

[32]
. . , that the armistice should be accepted with confidence in the generosity of our previous enemies . . . there

[32]
I could stand it no more. It was impossible for me to stay any longer. While everything began to go black

[33]
again before my eyes, stumbling, I groped my way back to the dormitory, threw myself on my cot and buried my burning

[31]
head in the covers and pillows. THb REVOLUTION 267 I had not wept since the day I had stood at the grave of my mother.

[32]
Whenever during my youth Fate handled me roughly, my stubbornness grew; when thereafter, dur- ing the long years of the War, Death

[33]
called more than one of my dear comrades or friends from our ranks, to me it would have seemed almost a sin to complain.

[32]
They died for Germany! And even when, during the last days of the terrible struggle, the creeping gas attacked me too and

[33]
began to eat into my eyes, and when, under the impact of the shock of fear of becoming blind forever, I was about to

[32]
despair for a moment, the voice of Conscience thundered at me: Miserable wretch, you want to cry while thousands are

[33]
a hundred times worse off than you; then I bore my fate apathetically and silently. But now I could not help

[32]
it any longer, only now I saw how completely all personal grief disappears in the face of the fatherland's

[33]
disaster. Now all had been in vain. In vain all the sacrifices and deprivations, in vain the hunger and thirst of endless months,

[33]
in vain the hours during which, gripped by the fear of death, we nevertheless did our duty, and in vain the death of two millions who

[33]
died thereby. Would not the graves of all the hundreds of thousands open up, the graves of those who once had marched out

[33]
with faith in the fatherland, never to return? Would they not open up and send the silent heroes, covered with mud and blood, home

[33]
as spirits of revenge, to the country that had so mockingly cheated them of the highest sacrifice which in this world man

[32]
is able to bring to his people? Was it for this that they had died, the soldiers of August and Sep- tember, 1914, was it for this that the

[33]
regiments of volun- teers followed the old comrades in the fall of the same year? Was it for this that boys of seventeen

[34]
sank into Flanders Fields? Was that the meaning of the sacrifice which the German mother brought to the fatherland when in those days,

[32]
with an aching heart, she let her most b'- 268 MEIN KAMPF loved boys go away, never to aee them again? Was it all for this that now

[33]
a handful of miserable criminals was allowed to lay hands on the fatherland? Was it for this that the German soldier

[33]
had persevered in burning sun and in snowstorms, suffering hunger, thirst, and cold, tired by sleepless nights and endless marches? Was

[32]
it for this that he had lain in the hell of drum fire and in the fever of gas attacks, without receding, always his sole

[31]
duty in mind, to guard the fatherland against the distress from the enemy? Truly, these heroes too deserve a

[32]
memorial : 'Wanderer, ye who come to Germany, announce to the homeland that we are lying here, loyal to the

[31]
fatherland and faithful to duty/ And the homeland? Was it only our own sacrifice which we had to throw into the

[33]
balance? Was the Germany of the past worthless? Was there not also an obligation towards our own history? Were we

[31]
still worthy of applying the fame of the past to us also? How was this deed to be submitted to the future for

[33]
justification? Wretched and miserable criminals! The more I tried to clarify this terrible event in that hour,

[32]
the stronger burned the shame of indignation and dishonor on my forehead. What was now all the pain of my eyes as

[33]
compared with this misery? What now followed were terrible days and even worse nights. Now I knew that everything

[33]
was lost. Only fools or liars and criminals were able to hope for the mercy of the enemy. In those nights my

[33]
hatred arose, the hatred against the originators of this deed. In days that followed, I became aware of

[33]
my own destiny. Now I had to laugh at the thought of my own future, which until recently had worried me so much. Was it

[33]
not ridicu- lous to wish to build houses on such ground? Finally it THE REVOLUTION 269 also became clear to me that what

[33]
happened was only what I had feared so long, and which my feelings had not been able to believe. Kaiser Wilhelm II

[32]
was the first German Emperor who extended his hand to the leaders of Marxism without guess- ing that scoundrels are without

[33]
honor. While they were still holding the imperial hand in their own, the other was feeling for the dagger. With the Jews there

[33]
is no bargaining, but only the hard either or. I, however, resolved now to become a politician. It is

[32]
important to note that Hitler's hatred was not directed primarily at the Treaty of Versailles. That was a mere

[33]
minor detail a peace similar to what Germany would have dic- tated had it been victorious. National life is

[32]
the expression of the law of the survival of the fittest; only fools like Kurt Eisner would have it otherwise. The

[31]
horrible, the detestable, thing was that Germany had lost the War. Lost it, so ran the ex- planation, because of

[31]
sabotage from within. Therewith the notion that Germany had been stabbed in the back became of primary

[33]
political importance. Some time after the War, General Sir Neill Malcolm was dining with Ludendorff in Berlin,

[33]
listening to Ludendorff main- tain that he had failed to win the War because of lack of sup- port from the government. ' Do you

[34]
mean you were stabbed in the back?' the Englishman asked. 'Yes,' was the eager reply, 'stabbed in the back! 1 This version of the affair

[31]
was then offered by von Hindenburg when he appeared before the Com- mittee of Enquiry which the Reichstag had

[33]
appointed to find out why the War was lost. Speaking on November 18, 1919, the Marshal declared that the Revolution had only been

[33]
the Mast straw' in a systematic process of undermining the army and that it had been on the testimony of British

[30]
generals 'stabbed in the back.' (Cf. The Wooden Titan, by John W. Wheeler-Bennett.) The appointment of this committee had been

[30]
necessitated bv 870 MEIN KAMPF debates which had deeply stirred the German Constitutional Assembly at Weimar.

[33]
Nationalists, led by Karl Helfferich (war-time Minister of Finance), had denounced Matthias Erzberger, who signed

[33]
the armistice, as a traitor to his country. Erzberger replied in bitter speeches which for the first time tore the mask

[32]
from the methods employed by the High Command during the War. He accused Ludendorff of having undermined every

[33]
effort to reach a peace by compromise, and in particulai of having looked upon the entry of the United

[33]
States into the conflict as a mere bagatelle. Had not Helfferich said that Wil- son was just in time to pay the bills

[33]
Germany had run up for military supplies? The effect of Erzberger's speeches was tre- mendous. Delegates screamed and

[34]
wept aloud as the fiery or- ator attacked Pan-Germanism as the cause of national dis- aster. Thereafter the issue

[33]
became one of central importance in the nation's political life. Immediately a campaign to ruin

[34]
Erzberger was started by Helfferich, and as a result he was compelled to retire from public life. Neither the Centrists

[33]
nor the Social Democrats realized at the time how great a blow the Republican cause had suffered ; and even when

[33]
Erzberger was assassinated by a group of fanatics, the import of what had happened was clear only to a few. Soon

[33]
the charge that every member of the Republican government was a 'November criminal' was being made in a great

[31]
variety of nationalist journals or pamphlets; and a wave of political murders swept over the country. The

[31]
Commission of Enquiry heard a great deal of testimony, which is enshrined in many volumes, but reached few

[30]
conclusions. The prestige of the generals was still so great that few were in a position to challenge their

[31]
authority. Perhaps the major result was that a vigorous critique of General Ludendorff s military

[33]
policy in 1918 was read into the record, Professor Hans Delbrueck con- tending that every canon of the soldier's science had

[32]
been violated. It was proved that when the offensives of that year were begun, the army had been in excellent

[32]
condition, and that the supply of matirid de guerre was more than adequate. But on August 8 it had suffered

[33]
a defeat described by Ludendorff as THE REVOLUTION 271 the 'black day in German history. 9 A few days later, the Kaiser

[34]
discussed the situation with his generals and concluded : 1 1 see, we must add up accounts. We have arrived at the limit

[31]
of our energies. The War must be stopped.' But on August 13 Ludendorff insisted to the Chancellor, Count von Hertling, that

[32]
Germany could accept no peace that did not conserve German rights in Belgium and Poland ; and on the next day, at a Crown

[33]
Council in Spa, he stated that the proper moment to sue for peace would have arrived as soon as he had won another

[33]
victory on the western front. By the middle of September, however, the Austrians were suing for peace and the Mace-

[31]
donian front had collapsed. On the 2ist of the same month, Ludendorff requested the German government to sound out the

[33]
United States concerning peace, and followed this seven days later with a statement to the effect that the German

[33]
situ- ation was so desperate that no further delay was possible. The effect of this precipitate action was

[33]
that the government, com- pletely taken by surprise, was half out of its wits; and a new chancellor, Prince Max of Baden,

[30]
was appointed. This change was made in accordance with the belief of the Foreign Office that only a

[33]
'democratic' government could successfully ap- proach President Wilson. Unfortunately the Social Democrats now made

[32]
a serious blunder. They refused to enter a govern- ment in which the Conservative Party was represented

[33]
a stipulation which was later, of course, to give that party a chance to throw all blame on the other groups. While the

[32]
new chancellor was endeavoring to sound out the Allies, Ludendorff again intervened to say that at any moment the

[34]
enemy might break through and that therefore a request for an armistice must be despatched immediately. The chan-

[33]
cellor insisted that time was needed to negotiate acceptable terms, again Ludendorff countered, and thereupon

[32]
the first armistice note was despatched to Wilson on October 3. Hin- denburg's letter describing the military

[29]
situation, dated Sep- tember 29, attributed the crisis to the breakdown of the Mace- donian front and the

[33]
inability to get troop replacements. When Walter Rathenau suggested, in the Vossische Zeitung, a levie en masse

[32]
as the only way out, Ludendorff replied that this would do more harm than good. 272 MEIN KAMPF But after an exchange of notes

[32]
between the State Depart- ment of the United States and the German government had shown that the only terms Wilson was

[33]
willing to grant were harsh, Ludendorff changed his mind and declared that a levie m masse might be resorted to, after all.

[32]
But the government now felt that the German people would not understand such a change of face, that a revolution was

[34]
imminent, and that at- tempted resistance would only make matters worse. Luden- dorff handed in his resignation. He was

[32]
succeeded by General Wilhelm Gr6ner, who saw at once that further resistance was out of the question. On November 8, the

[32]
Kaiser was advised to abdicate. It is, therefore, apparent that Ludendorff was sure the War had been lost

[32]
before any revolutionary movement had broken out in Germany. This view is confirmed by all who, on the

[34]
Allied side, knew the situation that existed between Septem- ber 29 and November 8. As a matter of fact, the American

[32]
commanders were so certain that a triumphal march on to Berlin would cost relatively little that some of them

[32]
accepted the armistice with bad grace. Marshal Foch has often been severely criticized (e.g., by General

[32]
Mordacq) for the 'human- itarianism' which induced him to end the struggle before the German border was reached.

[33]
German deficiencies in supplies, man-power, and armament were so marked that, despite the stubbornness with which picked

[31]
troops defended themselves, any other outcome than the utter rout of the German army was unthinkable. In

[33]
addition the collapse of Austria and the break- down of Bulgaria opened the way for an advance into southern

[33]
Germany. The major reasons why Germany lost the War are seen as inherent in the nature of the political

[33]
action she sponsored. On this virtually all non-German students are agreed. The only real military issues are

[33]
these : whether a different handling of the battle of the Marne might not have led to the speedy defeat of France, and

[32]
whether Ludendorff could have won the Flanders battles of 1918 if he had taken additional troops out of Russia. Neither

[31]
query is answerable. But these facts con- cerning the political situation are established: the march THE

[33]
REVOLUTION 273 through Belgium forced Britain to enter the War; the insistence upon unrestricted U-boat warfare in

[34]
1917 induced the United States to enter the conflict; and the harsh terms of the Treaty of Brest-Litovsk may have dissuaded

[32]
(cf. The Forgotten Peacv, by John W. Wheeler-Bennett) President Wilson from trying to reach a peace with Germany on the basis of the

[32]
'Fourteen Points.' One may add a number of minor political misadven- tures: the fantastically mismanaged

[33]
attempt to obtain Polish support by setting up a vassal kingdom of Poland; the murder of Edith Cavell ; the bombing of

[32]
London ; the contemptuous at- titude adopted towards the Austrians; and the strange maneu- vers of Colonel von

[33]
Papen in Washington. Those who deny the validity of these contentions and they include all Germans who cherish

[33]
some fondness for the Pan-German program maintain that if so magnificent an army failed under such leadership to win

[33]
the War, the reason can only lie within Germany itself. In essence, the credibility of such a view must be sought

[32]
in the realm of idea rather than in that of fact. The Prussian war machine was created to be the ideally perfect

[33]
instrument of national action. If everything that could render it in practice what it was in theory had been done,

[33]
it could not have been defeated. For what is absolutely right in conception must also be absolutely right in

[33]
practice. The realm of the real is only the logical counterpart of the realm of the ideal. This conception of the army

[30]
of 1914 is at the back of many German minds; and a similar attitude of mind is at the bottom of the doubts

[31]
entertained by many about the army of 1938. They would not argue that France has a poorer or better army than

[33]
Germany's, but only that the German army has defects. Now what was wrong with the German instrument during the War? The answer

[33]
is that, as a result of Marxist agitation, germs of sabotage were introduced into the German system which

[33]
developed into veritable cancers; and that, as a conse- quence of the 'pacifism' which formed part of the normal

[33]
bourgeois outlook, large sections of the public were victims of the dishonest alien propaganda dispensed by

[31]
President Wilson ahd others. Evidence to support these contentions was ad- 874 MEIN KAMPF vanced on three important

[32]
occasions during the history of the Weimar Republic; the controversy between Erzberger and Helfferich during 1919; the

[33]
Magdeburg Trial of December, 1924, when President Friederich Ebert defended himself against a reactionary journalist's

[33]
assertions that he had committed high treason by helping to organize the Munitions Strike of 1918; and the Munich 'Stab in

[31]
the Back' Trial, conducted during October and November, 1925, at which leading Social Democrats were the plaintiffs. It is

[34]
impossible to do more here than summarize very briefly the facts and surmisals then advanced. The charge against

[33]
Erzberger was that by sponsoring the Peace Resolution of 1917, which disclaimed any desire by Germany to annex

[34]
territory or to hold other peoples under economic tutelage, he had under- mined the belief of the German

[33]
people in ultimate victory and therewith weakened their morale. President Ebert was ac- cused of having

[33]
sought to end the War by depriving the army of needed munitions; and his enemies insisted that all along he and his

[32]
fellow-Marxists had waited for the chance to spring at the throat of a fatherland left prostrate before the enemy. The

[32]
Munich Trial was far more important because the whole question of Social Democratic attitudes during and

[32]
immediately after the War was threshed out. Sensational testimony was offered by General Gr6ner and

[32]
others. The Erzberger case may be dismissed; for though it was of great importance to the history of the Weimar

[32]
Republic, it offers nothing to substantiate the 'stab in the back' theory. The Reichstag Resolution failed to affect the

[30]
conduct of the War either at home or abroad, and nothing Erzberger did checked in the least either Ludendorff's

[33]
dictatorial policy or the flan of the army. The second and third cases are more perti- nent. As a matter

[33]
of fact, the Minority (Independent) So- cialists did refuse, as the War went on, to vote the necessary credits

[33]
to continue the conflict; a few of them maintained rela- tions with dissatisfied sailors, who then provoked the mutiny

[34]
of 1918 which halted the German navy's projected sensational last-minute attack on the British fleet; and a number were in-

[33]
volved both in the Munitions Strike and in the revolutionary THE REVOLUTION 275 activities which led to open

[30]
revolt in November. Moreover, the extreme Spartacist movement, which during the War pub- lished subversive

[32]
literature and which afterward led to the establishment of the Communist Party, was led by former Socialists

[31]
among whom Karl Liebknecht and Rosa Luxemburg were the most important. It is therefore possible to say that

[32]
opposition to the War did exist inside Germany, and that efforts were made to awaken in the masses

[31]
a spirit of resistance to the Kaiser and the High Command. Liebknecht did obtain world-wide prominence for his

[32]
pacifistic utterances, which no parliamentarian in any Al- lied country duplicated. Yet one notes

[33]
immediately that the anti-war movement was utterly insignificant until late in 1918, when the half -starved

[33]
population lost all hope of victory. The effects of the blockade were horrible and the physical health as well

[32]
as the morale of Germany suffered greatly. When in history has a people been called upon to shoulder a

[32]
heavier bur- den, and when has one responded to the summons with such astounding patience? Yet none of the agents of

[32]
subversive activity helped to form the government of November, 1918. The men who undertook that difficult task knew

[33]
exactly what they were doing. The Social Democrats had debated a long while before assenting to a suggestion

[32]
that came from the High Command and the Foreign Office. Some of the ablest among them were certain that to accept

[33]
responsibility under such circumstances would later on mean being charged with the defeat and its conse- quences. Ebert

[32]
took up the Chancellor's duties on the basis of a secret understanding with the generals, as Groner explained at the

[33]
Munich Trial. Neither he nor his fellows wanted the Revolution. The Republic was proclaimed, a little hastily, by

[32]
Philip Scheidemann in order to forestall Liebknecht's declara- tion to the same effect. The Minority Socialists

[34]
were, of course, far more pacifistic and revolutionary. Yet even the leading members of this group were stunned

[31]
by the sudden collapse of the nation and were not prepared to deal with the situation thus created. The most

[33]
serious blot on the national escutcheon was the 276 MEIN KAMPF mutiny in Wilhelmshaven on October 30. This was preceded by

[34]
scattered instances of insubordination to some of which politi- cal intent was ascribed. Yet the situation

[33]
was peculiar. Peace negotiations were under way; the abdication of the Kai- ser had been demanded ; and still the men

[33]
were ordered to get ready for a sudden sortie which was virtual suicide. Therefore they had a certain right

[33]
to assume that their own commanders were guilty of insubordination, and could justify their conduct accordingly.

[32]
At any rate the navy had done its duty for four years; and to attribute Germany's loss of the War to their

[31]
sabotage of a romantic and desperate maneuver is to strain credulity to the breaking point. CHAPTER

[32]
VIII BEGINNING OF MY POLITICAL ACTIVITY AT THE end of November, 1918, I came back to Munich. I went

[34]
again to join the reserve battalion of my regiment which was now in the hands of 'Soldiers' Councils.' The entire business

[32]
disgusted me to such a degree that I decided at once to go away again if possible. Together with my

[33]
faithful war comrade, Schmiedt Ernst, I now came to Traunstein and remained there till the camp was broken up. In March, 1919, we again

[33]
returned to Munich. Hitler, with no home to which to return he had been out of touch with his family for years walked to

[32]
Munich, and arrived there shortly after the murder of Kurt Eisner, who had headed the revolution that had driven the

[34]
Wittelsbachs from their thrones and had then up to the time of his assassina- tion by Count Arco-Valley been Prime Minister

[33]
of Bavaria. Eisner, a Jew and not a native Bavarian, was an idealist who had been jailed during the War for

[33]
writing pacifist tracts. The account of his reign reads like a fairy tale. Refusing to curb free speech or to put through any

[31]
rash socialization measures, he set about attempting to prove to the Allies that Germany's workers fully

[33]
acknowledged the guilt of the former Imperial government in starting the War and were therefore entitled to

[30]
278 MEIN KAMPF The situation was untenable and urged necessarily towards a further continuation of the

[33]
Revolution. Eisner's death only hastened developments and led finally to the Soviet dictatorship, or, in other

[33]
terms, to a temporary reign of the Jews as it had been originally intended by the originators of the whole

[33]
revolution. In those days endless plans chased each other in my head. For days I pondered what could be done at all, but

[32]
the end of all reflections was always the sober conclusion a just peace. In addition he proved himself a violent

[33]
Bavarian particularist, and gave his government an artistic setting by staging festivals at which orchestral

[33]
overtures preceded his addresses. The Eisner regime was succeeded by a Socialist government which in turn was

[33]
driven out of Munich by a 'Soviet dictator- ship. 9 This did little except watch the various factions which comprised it fight one

[32]
another. Just previously Sovietism had triumphed in Hungary; and not a few intellectuals were now of the

[33]
opinion that the Russian idea was about to conquer the world. Several Moscow agents appeared in Munich, and two

[33]
of them were Jewish. In addition a couple of unworldly Jew- ish poets, Ernst Toller and Gustav Landauer, joined the new

[31]
movement. This extraordinary revolution, which the Munich citizenry welcomed as they would the plague, did

[31]
irreparable damage to the cause of labor by murdering ten hostages, mem- bers of a Rightist secret

[31]
society. In addition Jewish participa- tion in it opened the doors to anti-Semitic agitation.

[33]
Angered and embittered citizens were now willing to ascribe all evils to the Hebrew race. Eisner's example

[33]
had encouraged other dreamers to think that they, too, could renew the face of the earth. Government troops were sent to restore

[34]
order in Munich. They were joined by a number of volunteer military organiza- tions, and on May 2, 1919, took the city

[32]
after a stiff fight. Frightful vengeance was taken. Some estimates place the num- ber of those shot with or without

[32]
court-martial at more than a BEGINNING OF MY POLITICAL ACTIVITY 279 that I, as one without name, did not

[33]
possess even the least presupposition for any useful activity. I will speak latei on of the reasons for which

[30]
even then I could not make up my mind to join one of the existing parties. In the course of the Councils'

[32]
Revolution I acted for the first time in a manner which invoked the displeasure of the Central Council. On

[33]
April 27, 1919, early in the morn- ing, I was supposed to be arrested; but in facing the rifle I presented, the three fellows

[32]
lacked the necessary courage and marched away in the same manner in which they had come. A few days after the

[30]
liberation of Munich, I was sum- moned to join a commission for the examination of the events of the

[33]
Revolution in the Second Infantry Regiment. This was my first more or less purely political activity.

[33]
thousand. Poor Landauer was among those slain. Therewith Bavaria became what it had never previously been the most

[31]
reactionary part of Germany. Inside its borders, Rightist rebels against the Republic, putschists and patriotic

[33]
assassins found refuge. No doubt the major cause of the whole sad affair was the mur- der of Eisner. He was on his way

[33]
to the Bavarian Landtag, and would there have turned over the government to the Majority Socialists, when he was

[32]
felled; and some of his followers, not knowing what forces were responsible, committed other mur- ders that led to

[34]
desperate and fateful strife between the factions which alone could govern. To Count Arco- Valley, whom he imprisoned

[32]
in 1933, Hitler owes a debt he can never repay. The earliest reports concerning Hitler's political activities arc

[32]
interesting. He was housed in barracks with a number of ' Red ' soldiers. When the army took the city, these barracks were

[33]
seized, Hitler was first called aside, and then every tenth man was shot. The inference is that he was already in

[33]
the service of the army. 880 MEIN KAMPF A few weeks later I was given orders to take part in a 'course' which was being held

[32]
for the members of the army. There the soldier was to receive certain foundations of civic education. For me the

[30]
value of the whole performance lay in the fact that now I was given the possibility of be- coming

[32]
acquainted with some comrades who were of the same conviction and with whom I would then be able to discuss

[32]
thoroughly the situation of the moment. All of us were more or less firmly convinced that Germany could no

[32]
longer be saved from the approaching collapse by the parties of the November crime, the Center Party and Social

[32]
Democracy, but that even the so-called 'bourgeois national' formations would never be able to remedy this

[33]
despite their best intentions. Here quite a series of assump- tions were lacking, without which such a task could not succeed.

[31]
The time that followed proved our opinions of those days to be right. Thus in our small circle one discussed the

[32]
formation of a new party. The basic ideas which we had in mind thereby were the same which were realized

[33]
later on by the 'German Workers' Party.' The name of the new move- ment to be founded was to offer, from the beginning,

[32]
the possibility of approaching the great masses; for without these qualities the whole work seemed senseless and

[32]
super- fluous. Therefore we arrived at the name 'Social-Revolu- tionary' Party; this for the reason that the

[33]
social ideas of the new foundation indeed meant a revolution. He became one of the group of soldiers selected

[31]
to receive in- struction in methods of 'political enlightenment.' Such courses were normal in many parts of

[32]
Germany during the period of Reichswehr reorganization. Cf. Gen. L. R. G. Maercker, Vom Kaiserheer zur Reichswehr (From the Imperial

[31]
Army to the Reich Army). Early biographers state that Hitler almost im- mediately attracted attention.

[33]
BEGINNING OF MY POLITICAL ACTIVITY 281 But the deeper cause for this was found in the following: No matter how much

[33]
I had occupied myself even previ- ously with economic problems, this had always remained more or less within

[31]
the limits which resulted from consider- ing social questions in themselves. Only later this frame expanded in

[33]
consequence of my examining the German policy of alliances. The latter was to a great extent the result

[32]
of a wrong estimation of economics, as well as the confusion about the possible bases of a feeding of the

[33]
German people in the future. But all these thoughts were still rooted in the opinion that capital in every case

[33]
was only the result of labor and, therefore, like the latter, was subject to the correction of all those factors

[33]
which are either able to stimulate or to hinder human activity. Therein was supposed to be found also

[34]
the national importance of capital, as capital itself in turn was supposed to depend so entirely upon

[32]
the greatness of the State's, that is, the nation's, liberty and power; that this relation alone was bound to lead to an

[33]
advancement of the State and the nation on the part of capital out of the mere urge for self- preservation or

[33]
increase. This dependency of capital upon the independent and free State forces it also in its turn to stand

[34]
up for this freedom, power, strength, etc., of the nation. Therefore, the State's task towards capital was com- paratively simple

[32]
and clear: it had only to take care that the latter remained the servant of the State and did not pretend to be the

[33]
master of the nation. This attitude, therefore, could confine itself within two borderlines: preser- vation of

[34]
a prosperous national and independent economy on the one hand, securing social rights of workers on the other.

[32]
In previous times I was not yet able to recognize the difference between this capital as purely the

[33]
ultimate result of creative labor as compared with a capital the existence 282 MEIN KAMPF and nature of

[33]
which rests exclusively on speculation. For this I lacked the first stimulation, for it had not come to me. This now

[32]
was carried out thoroughly by one of the various gentlemen, lecturing in the course already men- tioned : Gottfried

[33]
Feder. For the first time in my life I now heard a discussion, in principle, of the international exchange and

[33]
loan capital. Immediately after I had listened to Feder's first lecture, the idea flashed through my mind that

[33]
now at last I had found the way to one of the most essential principles for the foundation of a new party. In my eyes,

[32]
Feder's merit was that he outlined, with ruthless brutality, the character of the stock exchange and Gottfried Feder,

[33]
engineer born in Wtirzburg, was one of many persons moved by the disarray of post- War national economy to

[32]
solve the monetary problem. In the United States he would doubtless have urged the coinage of silver at

[33]
a ratio of 32 to I. 'Breaking the slavery of interest is,' he declared, 'the steel axle round which everything turns.'

[31]
The meaning is: instead of taking up loans when it needs money, the govern- ment should, when undertaking public works, issue

[33]
treasury certificates of the same value as the value of the structures erected. Thus, for example, a gas

[33]
plant would be worth, say, $1,000,000. This value the government could then transmute into certificates. Opponents pointed out that Feder

[31]
erred in assuming that money in circulation was covered by real values inside the country. Feder's most

[31]
elaborate exposition of the point, which he maintained was his most original contribution to Party

[33]
doctrine, is contained in his Brechung der Zinsknecht- schaft. Goebbels' verdict on the book is interesting but un- translatable:

[33]
'Brcchcn muss dabei nur dcr, der diesen Unsinn lesen muss.' Other Nazis also attacked Feder, but the Party never officially

[32]
repudiated him. After 1933, however, he was BEGINNING OF MY POLITICAL ACTIVITY 283 loan capital that was

[32]
harmful to economy, and that he exposed the original and eternal presupposition of interest. His

[33]
arguments were so correct in all fundamental questions that those who criticized them from the beginning denied less

[33]
the theoretical correctness of the idea but rather the practical possibility of its execution. But what in

[33]
the eyes of the others was a weakness of Feder's arguments was in my eyes their strength. fThe task of a program-maker is not to

[33]
state the various degrees of a matter's realizability, but to demonstrate the matter as such ; that means, he has

[33]
to care less for the way but more for the goal. Hereby an idea's correctness in principle is decisive and not

[33]
the difficulty of its execution. relegated to a minor r&le. When Hitler began to make impor- tant friends, his

[33]
adviser in financial matters became Dr. Paul Bang, an intimate friend of Dr. Hugenberg's and one of the directors of

[33]
the Alldcutschcr Verband. After 1933 Dr. Hjalmar Schacht was installed as the official wizard, to be replaced in 1938 by Walther Funk. The best

[33]
brief commentary on the significance of these mat- ters for National Socialist propaganda we have seen was

[33]
writ- ten by Alfred Braunthal for Die Gcsellschaft, Vol. VII, nr. 12. (Decomer 1930). 'The National Socialist movement has had two peaks the first

[33]
half of 1924, and the fall of 1930. At both times there existed a peculiar economic situation. The first half of 1924 was

[33]
the time when the stabilization crisis was at its worst. Interest rates were fantastically high in the money

[34]
market. During January the rate was between 90 and 100 per cent, sinking then in July to "only " 20 per cent. At the same time,

[33]
however, the Reichsbank discount rate was only 10 per cent. Thereupon everything depended upon whether one had good

[34]
banking connections and could, by using these, get to the Reichsbank and its cheap credits. The life and death of an enterprise was

[33]
in the hands of the bank. 284 MEIN KAMPF As soon as the program-maker tries to take into account the 'useful reality' instead

[33]
of absolute truth, his work will cease to be a pole star for inquiring mankind, becomes instead a prescription for

[32]
everyday life. He who draws up the program of a movement has to fix its goal, the politician has to aim

[30]
towards the fulfillment of the goal. Therefore, the one's thinking is governed by eternal truth, the other's

[34]
activity more by practical reality of the moment. The greatness of the one is founded in the absolute and

[31]
abstract correctness of his idea, that of the other in the right attitude towards given facts and their useful

[33]
application, whereby the aim of the program-maker has to serve as his leading star. While a politician's plans

[33]
and acts that means their becoming reality may be looked upon as the touchstone for his importance, the program-maker's

[33]
ultimate intention can never be realized, as the human mind is well able to grasp facts of truth and to establish

[30]
crystal-clear goals, but their complete execution will necessarily fail because of the general human

[33]
incompleteness and inadequacy. The more abstractly right and therefore powerful this idea may be, the more

[32]
impossible remains its complete fulfill- ment as long as it depends on human beings. Therefore the program-maker's

[34]
importance must not be measured by 'In 1930 also the interest rates for long-term credits were, despite the depression,

[32]
almost as high as they had been during the boom period (when the rates were unduly high even for such times). And

[32]
again the Reichsbank discount rates were much lower. Therefore the producers of consumers' goods and the merchants (by

[30]
reason of their inventories) suffered under the heaviest interest burden, in relation to the general

[33]
economic situation, during 1924 and 1930. The middle classes naturally felt it most, since its members could less easily

[32]
find the way to the sources of credit. For this reason the middle classes turned with pleasure in such periods to a

[34]
movement which promised to "break the slavery of interest." ' BEGINNING OF MY POLITICAL ACTIVITY 285 the fulfillment

[33]
of his aims, but rather by their correctness and the influence which they have taken on in the develop- ment of mankind. If

[33]
it were different, one could not count the founders of religions among the greatest men on this earth, since the fulfillment

[33]
of their ethical intentions can never be even a nearly complete one. Even the religion of love, in its

[33]
effects, is only a weak reflection of the volition of its sublime founder; but its importance is to be sought in

[34]
the orientation which it tried to give to a cultural, ethical, and moral development in general. The extremely

[33]
great difference in the tasks of the pro- gram-maker and the politician is also the reason why a combination

[32]
of both in one person is almost never to be found. This may be said especially of the so-called ' success- ful ' small

[31]
politicians whose activity is for the most part only an 'art of the possible 9 as Bismarck described,

[33]
somewhat modestly, politics in general. The freer such a 'politician' keeps himself from great ideas, the easier and

[33]
frequently also the more visible, yet always faster, will his successes be. Of course, they are thereby also

[31]
subject to worldly evanes- cence and sometimes they do not outlive the death of their fathers. The work of such

[33]
politicians is, on the whole, un- important for posterity, since their successes in the present are based

[33]
only on warding off all really great and incisive problems and ideas, which as such would also have been of value for

[33]
coming generations. The execution of such aims as are of value and importance for the distant future brings

[33]
little reward to him who de- fends them and finds little understanding with the great masses who, at the first, understand enactments

[33]
concerning beer and milk better than farseeing plans for the future, the execution of which could arrive only later

[32]
on, but the use- fulness of which would be of value only to posterity. Thus, out of a certain vanity which is

[32]
always a relative of stupidity, the great mass of all politicians will keep away 286 MEIN KAMPF from all really

[31]
difficult plans for the future, in order not to lose the sympathy of the mob of the present. The success and the

[33]
importance of such politicians are to be found, therefore, exclusively in the present and they do not

[31]
exist for posterity. For little minds this is not embarrassing ; they are content with this. With the program-maker the

[30]
situation is different. His importance lies always almost exclusively in the future, as not

[33]
infrequently he is what is described by the words 'se- cluded from the world.' For, if the politician's art may be looked

[34]
upon really as an art of the possible, then the pro- gram-maker may be counted among those of whom it is said that the gods

[30]
like them only if they ask for, and desire, the impossible. Nearly always he will have to renounce the

[30]
recognition of the present, but in turn he will harvest, provided his ideas are immortal, the fame of

[31]
posterity. During long periods of human life it thus may sometime happen that the politician

[32]
unites with the program-maker. But the closer this amalgamation is, the greater are the obstacles which resist the

[33]
politician's work. Then he works no longer for the requirements which are clear to any philis- tine, but for aims which

[33]
are understood only by few. There- fore his life is torn between love and hate. The protest of the present, which

[33]
does not understand this man, wrestles with the acknowledgment of posterity for which, after all, he works. For the greater a man's

[33]
works for the future are, the less is the present able to understand them, and the more diffi- cult also is the fight

[33]
and the more rare the success. But if, nevertheless, in the course of centuries one man succeeds in this, then he may

[32]
perhaps, in his later years, be surrounded by a faint glimmer of the coming glory. But these great ones are only the

[33]
marathon runners of history; the laurel wreath of the present only just touches the temples of the dying hero. BEGINNING

[31]
OF MY POLITICAL ACTIVITY 28? But among them must be counted the great fighters in this world, those who, although not

[33]
understood by their time, are nevertheless ready to fight the battle for their ideas and ideals. They are those who

[33]
once will be nearest to the heart of the people; it almost seems as though everyone would then feel it his duty now to make

[33]
good in the present what the past had once sinned against the great. Their life and work is followed in touchingly grateful

[31]
admiration, and especially in gloomy days, it will be able to uplift broken hearts and despairing souls. These,

[32]
however, are not only the really great statesmen, but also all other great reformers. Side by side with Fred-

[33]
erick the Great stands a Martin Luther as well as a Richard Wagner. < When listening to Gottfried Feder's first lecture about

[33]
the ' Breaking of the Tyranny of Interest,' I knew immediately that the question involved was a theoretical

[31]
truth which would reach enormous importance for the German people's future. The sharp separation of the stock exchange

[33]
capital from the national economy offered the possibility of fighting the internationalization

[33]
of German economic life, without threatening with the fight against capital in general, also the > l>asis of an

[33]
independent folk autonomy. Germany's de- velopment already stood before my eyes too clearly for me not to know

[32]
that the hardest battle had to be fought, not against hostile nations, but rather against international cap- ital. In

[33]
Feder's lecture I sensed a powerful slogan for this coming fight. But here, too, the later development proved how

[30]
correct our feeling of those days was. Today we are no longer laughed at by the sly-boots of our bourgeois

[34]
politicians; today even they, provided they are not conscious liars, see that the international stock exchange capital

[33]
was not only the great instigator of war, but that just now, after the fight has been ended, it does not refrain from turning peace

[33]
into hell. 888 MEIN KAMPF The fight against international finance and loan capital has become the most important point in

[33]
the program of the German nation's fight for its independence and freedom. But as regards the objections of the so-called

[33]
'practi- cians/ one can give the following answer: all your fears about the terrible economic consequences of

[33]
carrying out the 'breaking of the tyranny of interest' are superfluous; because, first of all, the prescriptions you gave

[32]
the German people so far have not done it any good at all; your attitude towards the questions of national

[34]
autonomy remind us very much of the reports of similar experts of times past, for example of the Bavarian

[30]
Medical Board on occasion of the question of introducing the railroads; it is well known that all the fears of this

[33]
venerable corporation of those days were never justified; the passengers in the trains of the new 'steam horse' did

[34]
not become dizzy, the spectators, too, were not taken ill, and one abandoned the wooden fences for making the new

[31]
institution invisible; only the wooden fence in the head of all the so-called 'experts' was preserved for

[33]
posterity. Secondly, however, one should remember the following: every and even the best idea becomes

[33]
a danger as soon as it pretends to be an end in itself, but in reality only represents a means to an end; but for

[33]
myself and all true National Socialists there is only one doctrine: people and country. What we have to fight for

[30]
is the security of the existence and The meaning of 'international capital' at this time was

[33]
'capitalistic England. 1 Party philosophers saw in perfidious Albion a spider in a counting-house. With the help of

[34]
smaller Jewish spiders, it had enmeshed Germany in its net and devoured it. France was looked upon as a mere tool

[31]
in the hands of the London 'City.' Gradually the term took on other mean- ings: the authors of the Dawes and Young Plans,

[32]
investors in German bonds, and great speculators like Ivan Kreuger. BEGINNING OF MY POLITICAL ACTIVITY 289 the

[33]
increase of our race and our people, the nourishment of its children and the preservation of the purity of the blood,

[33]
the free- dom and independence of the fatherland in order to enable our people to mature for the fulfillment

[32]
of the mission which the Creator of the universe has allotted also to them. Every thought and every idea,

[31]
every doctrine and all knowledge, have to serve this purpose. From this point of view everything has to be

[33]
examined and to be employed or to be rejected according to its usefulness. Thus no theory can stiffen into

[33]
a mortal doctrine, since everything serves only for life. Gottfried Feder's conclusions, however, were the cause

[32]
which made me occupy myself thoroughly with this domain which had hitherto been little familiar to me. Now I

[31]
began to learn again, and now for the first time I came to the understanding of the contents and the meaning of the

[32]
life-work of the Jew Karl Marx. Only now his ' Cap- ital f became really comprehensible to me, as well as Social

[33]
Democracy's fight against the national economy, the aim of which is to prepare the ground for its domination of

[31]
the truly international finance and stock exchange capital. But these courses had the greatest effective

[33]
consequence in still another direction. One day I wanted to speak in the discussion. One of the participants

[33]
thought it his duty to enter the lists for the Jews, and he began to defend them in lengthy arguments. This aroused me to

[33]
reply. An overwhelming number of the pupils who were present were of my point of view. The result was that a few days

[31]
later I was ordered to report to one of the erstwhile Munich regiments as a so-called 'in- struction

[32]
officer.' In those days the discipline among the troops was still rather weak. It suffered from the after-effects of the

[32]
period 290 MEIN KAMPF of Soldiers' Councils. Only very slowly and cautiously could one change over to introducing,

[32]
instead of the 'volun- tary' obedience as one so nicely named the pigsty under the rule of Kurt

[33]
Eisner military discipline and subordi- nation. In the same way the unit was now to learn to feel and to think

[32]
in terms of nation and fatherland. In these two directions lay the domains of my new activity. I started full of

[32]
ambition and love. For thus I was at once offered the opportunity to speak before a large audi-

[33]
ence; and what previously I had always presumed, merely out of pure feeling without knowing it, occurred now:

[33]
I could 'speak.' My voice also had already improved so much that I could be heard sufficiently at least in the small squad rooms.

[32]
No other task could make me happier than this one, because now I was able, even before my discharge, to

[33]
render useful services to that institution which had been infinitely near to my heart, the army. Also, I could

[33]
speak of some success. I thus led back many hundreds, probably even thousands, in the course of my lectures to their people

[31]
and fatherland. I 'nationalized' the troops, and in this way I was able also to help to strengthen the general

[33]
discipline. Again I became thereby acquainted with a number of comrades with the same convictions who

[33]
later began to form the basic stock of the new movement. CHAPTER IX THE GERMAN WORKERS 1 PARTY ONE day I received

[33]
orders from my headquarters to find out what was behind an apparently political society which, under the name of

[32]
' German Workers' Party,' intended to hold a meeting on one of the following days, in which also Gottfried Feder was

[32]
supposed to speak; I was to go there and to look at the society and to report upon it. One could easily

[31]
understand the curiosity which in those days the army showed towards political parties. Revolu- tion had

[33]
bestowed the right of political activity on the sol- dier, and now those of them who were least experienced made

[32]
ample use of it. Only in the moment when the Center Party and Social Democracy had to realize, to their

[31]
regret, that the soldiers' sympathy began to turn away from the revolutionary parties towards the national

[32]
movement and resurrection, one saw fit to deprive the soldiers again of the right of franchise and to forbid

[33]
political activity. It was, therefore, clear that the Center Party and Marx- ism took up this measure, for, if one

[32]
had not undertaken this curtailment of 'civil rights' (as one called the political equality of the soldier

[32]
before the Revolution), there would have been no revolution a few years later, and therefore also no

[32]
further national degradation and dishonor. In 292 MEIN KAMPF those days the troops were well on the way towards reliev- ing the

[33]
nation of its bloodsuckers and the Entente's handy- men in the interior. That now also the so-called 'national 9 parties

[33]
voted enthusiastically for the correction of the pre- vious opinions of the November criminals, and thus helped

[33]
to render innocuous the instrument of the national rising, only shows where the purely doctrinary ideas

[33]
of these most harmless of the harmless could lead to. The bourgeoisie, which was really suffering from mental senility, was,

[33]
in all sincerity, of the opinion that now the army would again become what it had been, namely, a stronghold of

[33]
German fighting power, while Center and Marxism thought only to break out its dangerous national poisonous fang, without which,

[32]
however, an army will forever remain only 'police/ but will not be a 'troop' able to fight against the foreign

[32]
enemy; something that later on was amply proved. Or did perhaps our ' national politicians ' believe that the

[34]
army's development could be other than national? That really would be just like them. But this is the consequence of the fact

[32]
that, instead of being a soldier in the War, one is a babbler, that means a parliamentarian, and that one has no

[33]
idea what goes on in the minds of men who are reminded by the most glorious past that they were once the first soldiers

[33]
of the world. Thus I decided to go to the abovementioned meeting of that party which was until then still entirely

[32]
unknown to me. When in the evening I entered the 'Leiber' room which later on was to become of historical

[32]
importance for us, of the former Sterneckerbrau in Munich, I met there about twenty to twenty-five people,

[32]
chiefly from among the lower walks of life. Feder's lecture was already familiar to me from the courses, and

[33]
therefore I could devote myself to looking at the assembly proper. THE GERMAN WORKERS' PARTY 293 Its impression on

[32]
me was neither good nor bad; a new foundation like so many others. It was the time when every- one who was

[33]
dissatisfied with the development things had taken so far, and who no longer had confidence in the existing parties,

[31]
felt called upon to launch a new party. Thus such societies sprang up everywhere, only to disap- pear again

[33]
silently after some time. The founders, in most cases, had no idea what it means to develop a society into

[32]
a party or even into a movement. Thus these foundations nearly always suffocated in their ridiculous

[32]
bourgeois at- mosphere. After listening for about two hours I did not judge the 4 German Workers' Party ' from any

[34]
different point of view. I was glad when Feder finally finished. I had seen enough and was just about to go when the open

[33]
discussion, which In Bavaria after the War strong groups, particularly among the peasants, came to the conclusion that

[31]
Germany was ir- retrievably lost, and that the sole hope was to erect a Bavarian State, larger, if

[33]
possible, than the Bavaria of pre-iSyo days. It was also believed that if such a State were formed, it would

[32]
be granted concessions in the matter of reparations. The chief protagonist of these ideas was Dr. Georg Heim, a Center

[32]
Party politician with a great following among the peasants. He sounded out President Wilson on the probable

[31]
attitude of the Allies towards a separate Bavaria, and made a considerable effort to

[32]
persuade Austria the Tyrol in particular to join the projected State. Nothing came of it, first of all

[31]
because the Crown Prince kept aloof. But the agitation did have one consequence of fateful import the

[33]
separation of the Bavarian People's Party from the Center Party, and therewith the weak- ening of the position

[32]
of Catholics in the Reich as a whole. la the initial appeal issued by the sundered group, it was pro- claimed that

[33]
Germany was only a 'uniting of the German States on a federal basis,' that any Constitution adopted

[33]
by the nation as a whole would need ratification by the separate 294 MEIN KAMPF was announced at that moment, made me

[33]
decide to stay after all. But here also everything seemed to take an unim- portant course, till suddenly

[33]
a 'professor' was given the floor who first expressed doubts of the correctness of Feder's reasons, and then, after the latter had

[34]
replied very ably, planted himself on the ground of ' facts,' not without recom- mending, however, to the young party to take up

[33]
the 'severance' of Bavaria from 'Prussia' as an especially im- portant point of the party program. The man had the cheek

[34]
to pretend that, in that case, German Austria espe- cially would immediately link itself to Bavaria, and that then the peace

[33]
would be a far better one, and other similar nonsense. Thereupon I could not help but announce my intention to

[33]
speak, in order to give this learned man my opinion on this point, with the result that the gentleman who had just spoken left

[30]
the scene like a drenched poodle, even before I had finished.fWhen I spoke they had listened with

[32]
astonished faces, and only when I was about to say good-night to the assembly, a man came running after me,

[32]
introduced himself (I even did not understand his name, correctly), and handed me a small booklet, obviously

[32]
a political pamphlet, with the urgent request that I read this by all means. This was very agreeable to me, for now

[32]
I could hope that States, and that Bavaria would join the Reich only on the con- dition that the especial political,

[31]
cultural, and economic rights to which it was entitled were respected 'in constitutional law.' It was a

[33]
spokesman for this point of view whom Hitler ha- rangues out of the meeting like a 'drenched poodle.' Hitler had now proved that

[30]
he could 'orate' as effectively as Feder and the other instructors appointed by his military

[32]
superiors, one of whom a Captain Mayr later on joined the Social Democratic Party and the military

[31]
organization (the Rcichsbanncr) associated with it. THE GERMAN WORKERS' PARTY 295 perhaps in this way I could become

[32]
acquainted with this boring society in an easier manner, without being forced again to attend such interesting

[33]
meetings. For the rest, this man who was apparently a worker, had made a good impression on me. With this now I went away.

[33]
In those days I still lived in the barracks of the Second Infantry Regiment, in a tiny room which still showed very

[32]
clearly the traces of the Revolution. During the day I was out, mostly with the Rifle Regiment 4, or at meetings or

[32]
lectures with some other army unit, etc. Only at night I slept in my quarters. As I used to wake up in the

[33]
morning before five o'clock, I had gotten into the habit of throwing pieces of bread or hard crusts to the little mice

[33]
which spent their time in the small room, and then to watch these droll little animals romp and scuffle for these few delicacies.

[32]
I had already known so much misery during my lifetime that I was able to imagine only too well the

[33]
hunger, and there- fore also the pleasure, of the little things. On the morning after this meeting, towards five o'clock,

[32]
I was lying awake in my cot and looking at this bustle and activity. Since I could not go to sleep again, I

[33]
suddenly thought of the previous evening, and now I remembered the booklet which the worker had given to me. And so

[31]
I began 3 The author of this pamphlet was Anton Drexler, a simple and sickly man who had been declared unfit for

[34]
military service. A few copies of the brochure have been preserved. Its principal argument was that the German

[33]
worker must turn, if he hoped for a decent livelihood, from internationalism to nationalism. If he remained

[33]
addicted to the first, he would forever be gouged by a hostile international finance. During the War Drexler

[33]
had joined the Vaterlandspartei and so expressed his disapproval of the Reichstag Peace Resolution of 1917. He called

[33]
his first unit ' Freier Arbeiterauschuss fuer einen guten Frieden' (Com- mittee of Free Workers for a Good Peace) ; and after

[32]
the War he 296 MEIN KAMPF to read. It was a little pamphlet in which the author, this particular worker, described how, out of the

[33]
medley of Marxist and unionist phrases, he again arrived at thinking in national terms; this explained the title, 'My

[33]
Political Awakening/ Once I had started, I read the entire little document with interest; for in it an

[33]
event was reflected which I had gone through personally in a similar way twelve years ago. Involuntarily

[33]
I saw thus my own devel- opment come to life again before my eyes.-^ In the course of the day I thought about it

[32]
several times and was finally just about to put it away when, less than a week later, to my astonishment, I

[33]
received a postcard with the news that I had been accepted as a member of the ' German Workers' Party'; I was requested

[32]
to express my opinion about this, and for that purpose I was expected to come to a committee meeting of the

[33]
party on the following Wednesday. I was actually more than astonished at this manner of 'winning' members, and

[32]
I did not know whether to be an- noyed or to laugh at it. I had no intention of joining a changed the name to 'Deutsche

[32]
Arbeiterpartei' (German Work- ers' Party). A few similar groups sprang up here and there in Germany, advocating

[34]
a Socialistic program to be realized out- side the Marxist sphere because internationalism had failed. The most

[33]
famous exponent of this point of view in North Ger- many was to be August Winnig. The chairman of the German Workers' Party

[33]
was Karl Harrer, a journalist who almost from the beginning took a dis- like to Hitler. He was opposed to violent

[32]
anti-Semitism (as were the majority of Germans in that time), and he was not a man to wield the bayonet too

[30]
ferociously. A year went by be- fore the recalcitrant Harrer could be ousted from his position. In retrospect the

[32]
historian must conclude: at that time the question was not merely whether Hitler would join the Party but whether the

[32]
Party would have Hitler. THE GERMAN WORKERS' PARTY 291 ready-made party, but wished to found a party of my own. This

[33]
unreasonable demand was really out of the question for me. I was just about to send the gentlemen my written reply,

[33]
when curiosity gained the upper hand and I decided to appear on the day fixed in order to define my

[34]
reasons orally. Wednesday arrived. The restaurant in which the said meeting was to take place was the Alte Rosenbad

[33]
in the Herrenstrasse; a very poor restaurant, to which only once in a blue moon somebody seemed to find his way

[33]
by mis- take. This was not surprising in the year 1919, when the menus of even the larger restaurants were able to attract

[33]
customers but very modestly and poorly. But until then I had not known this inn at all. I passed through the sparsely lit

[34]
guestroom where not a soul was present, looked for the door to the adjoining room, and then I was face to face with the ‘meeting.

[33]
9 In the twilight of a half-demolished gas lamp four young people were sitting at a table, among them also the author

[33]
of the little booklet, who immediately greeted me in the most friendly terms and welcomed me as a new member of

[31]
the ‘German Workers’ Party.’ Now I was somewhat taken aback. As I was informed that the actual ‘ Chairman for the

[31]
organization in the Reich ‘ was still to come, I intended holding back my explanation. The latter finally

[33]
appeared. He was the chairman of the meeting in the SterneckerbrSu on the occasion of Feder’s lecture. Meanwhile my

[32]
curiosity was again aroused and I was full of expectation for the things to come. Now I finally learned the

[32]
names of the various gentlemen. The chairman of the ‘organization in the Reich’ was a Herr Harrer, that of the Munich

[31]
district, Anton Drexler. Now the minutes of the last session were read, and the confidence of the assembly was

[33]
expressed to the secretary t 298 MEIN KAMPF Next followed the treasury report (there were all in all 7 Marks and 50 Pfennings in

[33]
the possession of the party), for which the assurance of the general confidence was ex- pressed to the treasurer.

[33]
Now this again was put down in the minutes. Then followed the First Chairman's reading of the answers to a letter from Kiel to

[34]
one from Diisseldorf and to one from Berlin; everybody agreed to them. Now the documents received were read

[33]
: a letter from Berlin, one from Diisseldorf, and one from Kiel, the arrival of which seemed to be accepted with great

[31]
satisfaction. One ex- plained this growing correspondence as the best and most visible symptom of the spreading

[31]
importance of the 'Ger- man Workers ' Party.' Then a lengthy discussion about the answers to be made took place.

[33]
Terrible, terrible; this was club-making of the worst kind and manner. And this club I now was to join? Then the new memberships were

[32]
discussed, that means, my being caught. Now I began to ask questions. Apart from a few leading principles, nothing existed; no

[31]
party program, no leaflets, nothing in print at all, no membership cards, not even a miserable rubber stamp; only

[33]
visibly good faith and good will. My smile had disappeared again, for what was all this but the typical symptom of utter

[34]
helplessness and complete despair covering all previous parties, their programs, their intentions and their activities? What made these

[34]
four young people come together to an outwardly so ridiculous activity was actually only the expression

[33]
of their inner voice which, emotionally rather than consciously, made all the previous doings of parties appear as no longer

[33]
suitable for a rise of the German nation as well as for the healing of its internal damages. I quickly read through

[33]
the leading principles which were available in a typed copy, and in them I saw a seeking rather than knowledge.

[33]
Many tilings THE GERMAN WORKERS' PARTY 299 'rere dim or uncertain, many things were missing, but nothing was there which in

[33]
its turn could not be looked upon as a symptom of struggling toward realization. I, too, knew what these people felt; it was

[33]
the longing for a new movement which was to be more than a party in the previous sense of the word. When I went home

[33]
to the barracks on that evening, I had already formed my opinion of this society. Now I was faced by perhaps

[32]
the most serious question of my life: was I to join or was I to refuse? My reason could only advise me to

[33]
refuse, but my feeling would not let me find peace, and the more often I tried to keep the absurdity of this entire

[32]
club before my eyes, the more often did feeling speak in favor of it. In the days that followed I was restless. I

[33]
began to ponder about the pros and cons. I had long since made up my mind to take up political activity;

[32]
that this could be only in a new movement was also clear to me, so far only the instigation for action had not

[32]
come. I do not belong to those who start something one day in order to end it again the next day or to change

[32]
over, if possible, to another affair. But this very conviction was the chief rea- son, among others, why it was so

[33]
difficult for me to make up my mind to found such a movement. I knew that for me this would mean a decision forever,

[33]
where there would never be a 'turn back.' For me it was not a temporary game, but dead earnest. Even in those days

[32]
I had always had an instinctive aversion to people who start something without, however, also carrying it out; 1

[31]
loathed these jacks-of-all-trades. I considered the activity of these people worse than doing nothing. This

[34]
opinion, however, was one of the chief reasons why I was not able, like perhaps so many others, to decide to

[33]
found something which either was to become everything or which else, more suitably, should not be carried out atalL

[33]
300 MEIN KAMPF Now Fate itself seemed to give me a hint. I should never have joined one of the existing parties, and

[33]
later on I will state the reasons for this; for this reason, however, this ridiculously small foundation with its handful

[32]
of members seemed to me to have the advantage that it had not yet hardened into an 'organization/ but

[33]
seemed to offer to the individual the chance for real personal activity. For this was the advantage which

[33]
was bound to result: here one would still be able to work, and the smaller the movement was, the easier it would be to bring

[32]
it into the right shape. Here the contents, the goal, and the way could still be fixed, something that with the existing great

[33]
parties was impossible from the beginning. The longer I tried to think about it, the more the con- viction grew in my mind

[31]
that just here, out of such a small movement, some day the rise of the nation could be pre- pared, but never from the

[33]
political parliamentarian parties which clung much too much to the old ideas or even shared the advantages of

[33]
the new regime. For what was to be announced now was a new view of life and not a new elec- tion slogan. t However,

[33]
it was an infinitely hard decision to wish to transform this intention into reality. What prerequisites did

[32]
I myself bring to this task? That I had no means and was poor seemed to me the most easily endurable, but it was more

[32]
difficult that I sim- ply belonged to the great crowd of nameless people, that I was one among the millions who are

[31]
allowed to continue to live by sheer accident, or who are called from life again without even their

[33]
surroundings condescending to take notice of it. To this came the difficulty which was bound to result from my lack

[31]
of schools. The so-called 'intelligentsia 9 at any rate looks down with really infinite condescension on

[32]
everyone who has not been pulled through the obligatory schools in order to have the THE GERMAN WORKERS' PARTY 301

[34]
necessary knowledge pumped into his brains. Actually, the question is never, What can this man do, but what has he learned?

[32]
To these 'educated' ones the greatest empty- head, provided he is only wrapped in a sufficient number of

[32]
certificates, is worth more than even the most clever boy who does not possess these priceless paper bags. I was

[33]
able to imagine in what way this 'educated' world would con- front me, and in that I was wrong only in so far as in

[32]
those days I still believed people to be better than they unfor- tunately are, for the greater part, in sober

[31]
reality. This, of course, as everywhere else, lights up the exceptions much more brightly. Thus I learned to

[31]
distinguish all the more between the eternal ' pupils ' and the really competent. < After two days of agonized

[31]
pondering and reflection I finally arrived at the decision to take the step. It was the most decisive

[32]
decision of my life. There could not, and must not, be a retreat. Thus I registered as a member of the German

[33]
Workers' Party and received a provisional membership ticket with the number seven. CHAPTER X THE CAUSES OF THE COLLAPSE

[34]
E depth of the fall of a body is always the measure for the distance of its momentary situation from the one

[33]
it had originally. The same may also be said of the fall of nations and States. With this, however, a deci- sive

[32]
significance must be attributed to the previous situation or rather height. Only that which usually rises

[31]
above the general level can also fall or tumble visibly deep. This makes the collapse of the Reich so

[33]
serious and terrible for every thinking and feeling man, that it brought the fall from a height hardly still imaginable

[34]
in the face of the mis- ery of the present degradation. Even the very foundation of the Reich seemed to be gilded

[31]
by the charm of an event that elated the entire na- tion. After an incomparably victorious course there

[33]
arises finally, as the reward for immortal heroism, a Reich for the sons and the grandsons. Whether consciously or uncon-

[32]
sciously, it makes no difference, all the Germans had the feeling that this Reich, which did not owe its existence to the

[34]
cheating of parliamentary factions, stood out over the measure of other States solely by the sublime manner

[32]
of its foundation; for, not in the cackling of parliamentary word battles, but under the thundering and roaring of the

[33]
Parisian blockade front took place the solemn act of the THE CAUSES OF THE COLLAPSE 303 manifestation of the will,

[32]
that the Germans, lords and people, were determined to form one realm in the future and again to elevate the

[33]
imperial crown as a symbol; not with assassination had this been carried out, not deserters and duty-shirkers were the

[32]
founders of the State of Bis- marck, but the regiments of the front. This unique birth and baptism of fire alone wove

[34]
around the Reich a glimmer of historic fame, such as was but rarely the lot of the oldest States. And what a rise now

[33]
set in! The freedom towards the exterior gave the daily bread to the interior. The nation became rich in numbers and

[33]
worldly goods. The honor of the State, however, and with it that of the entire people, was guarded and protected by an

[33]
army which most visibly showed the difference from the one-time German Union. So deep is the fall which hits the Reich

[33]
and the German people that at first everybody, as if seized with dizziness, seems to have lost feeling and consciousness;

[34]
one can hardly remember the previous height, so dreamlike and unreal appears, measured by the misery of the present,

[33]
the greatness and splendor of that time. Thus it may also be explained that one is only too blinded by the sublime,

[32]
and thereby forgets to look for the omens of the enormous collapse which certainly must have somewhere been

[33]
present. This may be said, of course, only of those for whom Germany was more than a mere dwelling-place for making

[34]
and spending money, as only they are able to experience the present condition as a breakdown, while to the others

[33]
it is the fulfillment of their hitherto unsatisfied wishes, long desired. ^4- These omens, however, were visibly

[34]
present at that time, though only very few tried to draw a certain lesson from them. 304 MEIN KAMPF Today this is more necessary

[34]
than ever. Just as one is only able to arrive at the cure of an illness if the cause of it is known, the same

[34]
may be said also as regards curing political evils. Of course, one usually sees and recognizes the outward

[32]
form of an illness, the symp- toms that catch the eye, more easily than its inner cause. This is also the reason why so

[32]
many people never go beyond the discovery of outward symptoms and therefore even confuse the symptoms with the

[33]
cause, nay, even preferably try to deny the presence of such a cause altogether. There- fore also, most

[32]
of us primarily see the German collapse only as a result of the general economic distress and its

[33]
conse- quences. Almost everyone, however, has to share in carry- ing the burden of this distress, so that here is

[33]
found a cogent reason for every single individual to understand the catas- trophe. But the great masses see far

[33]
less the collapse in the political, cultural, and ethical-moral direction, etc. Here, feeling and also reason

[33]
fail completely with many people. That this is so with the great masses may be allowable, but that also in the circles

[33]
of the intelligentsia the German collapse is looked upon primarily as an 'economic catas- trophe,'

[31]
and that therefore the cure is expected to come from economy, is one of the reasons why so far

[32]
recovery has been impossible. Only if one realizes that here, too, econ- Criticism of the so-called

[32]
'business enterprise State' i.e., the State which looks upon economic enterprise as the chief source of

[33]
riches and therefore of well-being was a favorite topic of post-War Rightist literature. Oswald Spengler held

[32]
that the basis structure of modern society is national and politi- cal, so that industry depends upon its

[33]
fundament, the State. On the other hand, it is independent in the sense that leader- ship must be developed inside

[33]
the industry itself. Hence the necessity for personal leadership and initiative. (Cf . Neubau dtische THE CAUSES

[33]
OF THE COLLAPSE 305 erniy is only of second or even third importance, but that political, ethical-moral, as

[34]
well as factors of blood and race, are of the first importance, then one will strive at an under- standing of the causes

[33]
of the present misfortune, and with it, one will be able to find means and ways to recovery. The quest for the causes

[33]
of the German collapse is there- fore of decisive importance, above all for a political move-

[33]
ment, the very goal of which is to be the conquest of the defeat. But also with such research into the past one has to guard

[32]
very much against confusing the effects, which more surely catch the eye, with the less visible causes. The easiest and

[33]
therefore also the most widespread ex- planation of today's misfortune is that the consequences involved are

[33]
those of the lost war, and that therefore the latter is the cause of the present evil. Now there may be many who

[32]
will seriously believe this nonsense, but there are many more out of whose mouths such an explanation can

[33]
only be a lie and conscious un- truth. This may be said of all those who today have their place at the government's mangers.

[33]
For, did not once the very announcers of the Revolution most urgently point out, again and again to the people, that

[32]
for the great masses it would make no difference whatsoever how this war Oddly enough this is virtually the same

[33]
reasoning to which the Majority Socialists resorted during the War in order to at- tack Minority Socialists

[32]
who maintained that the worker had no interest in the struggle, and that therefore his party was not justified in

[32]
supporting the government either by voting credits or by rendering patriotic service. Scheidemann, David, and

[33]
Ebert maintained that if Germany did not defend herself to the utmost of her ability, German industry would lose

[33]
its markets and therewith its ability to pay wages. But they all repudiated ware of conquest. 106 MEIN KAMPF would end?

[32]
Have they not, on the contrary, asserted most seriously that at the utmost only the ' great capitalist 9 could have

[32]
any interest in the victorious end of this colossal wrestling of nations, but never the German people itself, or

[31]
even the German worker? Indeed, on the contrary, did not these apostles of world reconciliation assert

[33]
'militarism' could only be destroyed by the German defeat, but that the German people would celebrate its most glorious

[32]
resur- rection? Did one not praise in these circles the benevo- lence of the Entente, and did one not charge

[33]
Germany with the entire guilt of bloody struggle? But would one have been able to do so without the explanation

[34]
that even defeat would have no special consequences for the nation? Was not the entire Revolution trimmed with the phrase

[33]
that through it the victory of the German flag would be pre- vented, and that thereby the German people would face all the more

[33]
its inner and outer freedom? Was this perhaps not so, you miserable and lying fel- lows? It really takes a truly Jewish

[33]
impudence to attribute the cause of the collapse to the military defeat, while the cen- tral organ of

[33]
all traitors of nations, the Vorwaerts of Berlin, wrote nevertheless that this time the German people would not be allowed

[33]
to bring its flags home with victory! And this is now supposed to be the cause of our collapse? It would naturally

[33]
be quite useless to quarrel with such forgetful liars, and therefore I would also not waste one word about

[32]
it, if unfortunately this nonsense were not repeated parrot-like by so many entirely thoughtless

[31]
people, without that maliciousness or conscious untruth- fulness that would give the cause for this. But, further- more, these

[33]
explanations are intended to be helpful to our fighters for enlightenment, which is very necessary anyhow

[32]
in a time when the spoken word is usually twisted in one's very mouth. THE CAUSES OF THE COLLAPSE 307 Thus in

[34]
reply to the statement that the lost war is guilty of the German collapse, the following is to be said : The loss of the War

[33]
was certainly of terrible importance to the future of our fatherland, but this loss is not a cause, but, in turn,

[33]
again only a consequence of other causes. That an unfortunate end of this fight for life and death was bound to

[32]
lead to very disastrous consequences was cer- tainly entirely clear to every sensible and not malicious

[33]
person, but unfortunately there were also those whose intelligence seemed to be lacking at the right

[32]
time, or who, contrary to their better knowledge, nevertheless first disputed and denied this truth; these were for the

[33]
greater part those who, after the realization of their secret wish, now suddenly receive the belated realization

[33]
of the catastrophe which they helped to bring about. They, therefore, are the culprits of the collapse, and not the lost

[30]
war, as it now This passage is first of all a defense of General Ludendorfl and of the dictatorship he

[33]
exercised during the War. The argument is characteristic. Unfortunately the Pan-German element had to

[33]
concede that the sacrifices of four years had been in vain ; and it determined now to fight down the popular feeling that

[34]
war itself, as an instrument of national policy, had been repudiated. Therefore the argument that peace is

[32]
the most effective solvent of national greatness re-appears in a thousand forms. Nevertheless relatively few

[32]
Nazis have ven- tured to assert that war itself is good. Normally they shrink a little from drawing all the conclusions

[33]
latent in Spengler's phrase, ' Man is a beast of prey.' What they generally advo- cate is an army ideally perfect, so

[32]
that Germany may impose its peace upon the world without the shedding of blood. For as Houston Stewart Chamberlain said

[33]
during the War, only the German word for peace Friede expresses what the world needs, a Masting realm of love and tenderness'

[32]
(a kind of ex- tension of the last act of Tristan und Isolde). The French word Paix stands for nothing except a pact, a treaty.

[30]
Hitler 308 MEIN KAMPF pleases them to say and to believe. For the loss of the Wai was only the consequence of their

[33]
activity, and not, as they now assert, the result of 'bad' leadership. The enemy, too, did not consist of cowards; he, too,

[34]
knew how to die; his number was, for the first day, greater than that of the Ger- man army, his technical armament had the arsenals

[34]
of the whole world at his disposal; thus the fact that the German victories which were gained by fighting against a whole world

[32]
during four years were due, with all heroic courage and all 'organization/ only to superior leadership, cannot be

[31]
denied in the face of reality. The organization and the leadership of the German army were the most

[31]
colossal affair which the earth has ever seen so far. Its deficiencies were within the bounds of general human

[31]
imperfection as a whole. That this army broke down was not the cause of our pre- sent misfortune, but only the

[33]
consequence of other crimes, a consequence which in its turn, however, introduced the beginning of a further

[32]
and this time more conspicuous col- lapse. That this is the case may be derived from the following: When, then, is

[34]
a military defeat bound to lead to such a complete breakdown of a nation and a State? Since when is this the result

[33]
of an unlucky war? Do nations perish at all by a lost war as such? in office is fond of demanding that every

[34]
German must be- come, physically and mentally, an instrument of the High Command, and of the turning the next minute to

[33]
a proclama- tion of his ardent desire for peace. One may, perhaps, put the matter in a nutshell by saying: for Mr. Neville

[33]
Chamberlain 1 peace' is something that will permit the British investor to keep on excelling at the hunt; for Mr. Hitler it is

[33]
something that results from the scare that follows a mobilization of the German army. THE CAUSES OF THE COLLAPSE 309

[33]
The answer to this can be very short: Whenever nations receive in their military defeat the return for their inner

[34]
corruption, cowardice, and lack of character, in short, for their unworthiness. If this is not the case, then the military

[33]
defeat will become the impulse for a coming greater rise rather than the tombstone of a nation's existence.

[32]
History offers no end of examples for the correctness of this assertion. Unfortunately, the military

[33]
defeat of the German people is not an undeserved catastrophe, but rather a deserved punishment by eternal

[33]
retribution. We more than de- served this defeat. It is only the greatest outward symp- tom of decay among quite a

[33]
series of internal ones which perhaps would have remained hidden to the eye of most people, or which perhaps one, in

[31]
ostrich-like manner, did not want to see. One should only look at the accompanying symptoms with which the German people

[34]
accepted this defeat. Had one not in many circles actually expressed joy at the mis- fortune of the fatherland

[33]
in the most shameless way? But who does this if he does not really deserve such punish- ment? Indeed, did one not even go

[32]
farther and boast of finally having caused the front to retreat? And it was not the enemy who did this, no, no, it was

[33]
Germans who piled such disgrace upon their heads! Did misfortune perhaps hit them unjustly? Since when, however, does one

[32]
step forward in order to attribute the war guilt to oneself? And this, despite realization and knowledge to the

[32]
contrary! No, and again no: in the way and in the manner in which the German people accepted its defeat one is

[33]
able to recog- nize most clearly that the true cause of our collapse is to be found in a place quite apart from

[33]
the purely military loss of some positions or in the failure of an offensive; for if the front as such

[33]
had really failed and if, by its misfortune, the doom of the fatherland had been caused, the German 310 MEIN KAMPF people would have

[33]
accepted defeat in quite a different way. Then, with clenched teeth, one would have endured the misfortune that now

[32]
followed, or one would have lamented it, overcome by pain; then wrath and fury against the en- emy who had

[33]
become victorious by the cunning of chance or by the will of Destiny would have filled the hearts; then, like to

[30]
the Roman Senate, the nation would have stepped up to the defeated divisions with the fatherland's thanks for the

[32]
sacrifices made so far, and with the request not to despair of the Reich. Even the capitulation would have been

[33]
signed only by force of reason, while the heart would have already beaten in expectation of the coming rise.

[33]
After the War a strange frenzy of jubilation was indulged in by various groups of Germans. There was dancing all night

[32]
in the streets of villages and towns; delirious welcomes to homecoming sweethearts shocked the sedate. The German

[32]
government sent emissaries to welcome troops returning to Berlin and to invite their support in putting the new

[33]
govern- ment on a firm basis; but few consented to stay, and those who did were normally soon out of control. Soldiers who

[33]
took up quarters in the Berlin Schloss at Liebknecht's behest re-emerged decked in the ex-Kaiser's uniforms, their pockets stuffed

[33]
with silver from the Imperial cupboards. Most striking detail of all, Berlin was on Christmas Eve, 1918, perilously close to

[31]
the brink of revolution. The government had no armed forces on which it could rely; the revolutionaries had

[32]
amassed considerable strength. But as if at a prearranged signal, everybody went off to celebrate and the

[33]
crisis was over. One of the most serious charges brought against Erzberger was that he had written an old Suabian

[33]
toast in a tavern book at Weimar. All this was, of course, the result of the attack of giddiness which followed a sudden

[33]
release from four years of pressure such as no other people had ever been called upon to bear. For years nationalists

[33]
referred to these things as indi- cations of the base Qualities that were hidden in the German peyche THE CAUSES

[33]
OF THE COLLAPSE 311 In such a manner one would have accepted a defeat which would have been due to Fate alone.

[33]
Then one would not have laughed and danced, then one would not have boasted of one's cowardice, and one would not

[32]
have glori- fied the defeat; one would not have jeered at the fighting troops and one would not have torn its flag and

[33]
cockade down into the dirt, but above all : then it would never have come to that terrible condition which caused

[33]
an English officer, Colonel Repington, to utter the contemptuous re- mark: 'Among the Germans every third man is

[34]
a traitor.' No, this pestilence would never have been able to swell up to such a suffocating flood which now for five years

[33]
has drowned even the last remainder of respect on the part of the rest of the world. From this can best be seen the lie contained

[32]
in the asser- The spectacle of Germany in defeat was in some respects undignified. Neither, for that matter, was the

[32]
spectacle of Allied countries reveling in victory a highly edifying one. On both sides orgies of lust and

[33]
madness, for which Europe could hardly parallel in history, marked the end of the conflict. In Germany, American

[33]
and British observers saw passers-by young loafers and deserters for the most part beset officers, tear the insignia from

[34]
their shoulders, and bash their sabres against the pavement. One such observer wrote in his diary at the time: 'There will

[33]
be a reaction against these things^and it will not be pleasant to contemplate.' Yet such phenomena did not illustrate the

[33]
sentiment of either the people or the army as a whole. In November, 1918, a battalion of veterans, covered with

[33]
gray mud, starved to the bone, marched home- ward through the streets of Mtinster. On they came with firm tread, rifles slung on their shoulders,

[32]
looking for all the world like a procession of wraiths arisen from the battlefields of the Marne. The thousands gathered

[33]
along the streets stood in awe-struck silence, until finally a universal sob that shook the crowd seemed to come from

[33]
every throat. In a small Moselle 312 MEIN KAMPF tkm that the lost war was the cause of the German col' lapse. No, the military

[33]
collapse was in its turn only the consequence of quite a series of the symptoms of an illness and their causes, which

[33]
had visited the German nation even in time of peace. It was this the first catastrophic conse- quence of moral

[34]
poisoning, visible to all, the consequence of a decrease in the instinct of self-preservation and of the conditions

[33]
for it, which had already begun to undermine the foundations of the people and the Reich many years ago. But it took

[34]
the entire bottomless lying of Jewry and its Marxist fighting organization to burden with the guilt of the collapse just

[31]
that man, the only one who tried, with superhuman will power and energy, to prevent the catas- trophe he saw

[31]
approaching and to spare the nation the time of the deepest degradation and dishonor. By stamping village,

[33]
officers of the Fourth Army Corps, A.E.F., attended a Christmas midnight Mass, in 1918. Widows in black ushered their little children,

[33]
dressed in white, into the church from out of the snow-filled night; and not one of them stood dry-eyed as the music of ancient

[33]
carols eddied round the tombs of village warriors dead a thousand years ago. No, it is historically un- just to cast

[31]
aspersions on the German people. They were utterly stunned by the suddenness of their defeat, for which nothing had

[33]
prepared them. And they were left to carve out their own destiny by officers who, after years of dictatorship, wished

[33]
now to get the ruins off their hands. The most effective critics of Ludendorff were not 'Jewish writers' or 'Marxist journals, 9 but

[33]
gentlemen of the Right Virtually no one in the Foreign Office at the end of the con- flict entertained any

[32]
doubt that the General had ruined Ger- many, and the memoirs of Bernstorff, Solf, Ktthlmann, and others bear witness to this fact Nor has

[33]
military criticism been less outspoken. THE CAUSES OF THE COLLAPSE 313 Ludendorff aa the culprit of the loss of the World

[32]
War, one took away from the hand of the only dangerous accuser, who was able to stand up against the traitors to the

[33]
father- land, the weapon of moral right. Therewith one started out with the very correct assumption that in the size of

[34]
the lie there is always contained a certain factor of credibility, since the great masses of a people may be more

[31]
corrupt in the bottom of their hearts than they will be consciously and intentionally bad, therefore with the primitive

[33]
simplicity of their minds they will more easily fall victims to a great lie than to a small one, since they themselves

[32]
perhaps also lie sometimes in little things, but would certainly still be too much ashamed of too great lies. Thus such an

[33]
untruth will not at all enter their heads, and therefore they will be unable to believe in the possibility of

[33]
the enormous impu- dence of the most infamous distortion in others; indeed, they may doubt and hesitate even when

[34]
being enlightened, and they accept any cause at least as nevertheless being true; therefore, just for this reason some part

[33]
of the most impudent lie will remain and stick; a fact which all great lying artists and societies of this world know only too well and

[33]
therefore also villainously employ. Those who know best this truth about the possibilities of the application

[34]
of untruth and defamation, however, were at all times the Jews; for their entire existence is built on one single

[32]
great lie, namely, that here one had to deal with a religious brotherhood, while in fact one has to do with

[33]
a race what a race! As such they have been nailed down forever, in an eternally correct sentence of funda-

[33]
mental truth, by one of the greatest minds of mankind; he called them 'the great masters of lying.' He who does not realize this or

[34]
does not want to believe this will never be able to help truth to victory in this world. 314 MEIN KAMPF For the sake of the German

[32]
people one has to consider it almost a piece of good fortune that the time of its latent illness was not

[34]
suddenly cut short by such a terrible catas- trophe, because otherwise the nation would probably have perished

[32]
more slowly, but nevertheless all the more cer- tainly. The illness would then have become a chronic dis- ease,

[33]
whereas now in the acute form of the collapse it be- came clearly and distinctly visible at least in the eyes of

[29]
a larger crowd. It was not by accident that man became master of the plague more easily than of

[33]
tuberculosis. The one comes in terrible death waves, scourging mankind, the other sneaks in slowly; the one leads to

[34]
terrible fear, the other to gradual indifference. But the consequence was that man opposed the one with the whole

[33]
ruthlessness of his energy, while he tries to check consumption with weak means. Thus he mastered the plague, while he in turn

[33]
is mastered by tuberculosis. Exactly the same is also the case with diseases of national bodies. If

[33]
they do not appear in the form of a catastrophe, man begins gradually to get used to them and finally he will

[34]
perish by them, though only after a long time, but never- theless more certainly. Then it is a good fortune (however

[32]
bitter) if Destiny decides to intervene in this slow process of putrid corruption and, at one blow, to put

[34]
before the eyes of him who is stricken the end of the disease. For this is what such a catastrophe amounts to more than

[32]
once. Then it may easily become the cause of a recovery which sets in with utmost determination. But

[33]
also in such a case the prerequisite is again the real- ization of the inner reasons which cause the disease

[33]
in question. What is most important also here is the distinction be- tween the causes and the conditions they bring about. This

[34]
will be the more difficult the longer the contagious matter has been in the nation's body and the more it had THE CAUSES

[33]
OF THE COLLAPSE 315 already become a natural part and parcel of that body. For it may very easily happen

[33]
that after a certain time one no longer considers an absolutely noxious poison as 'alien' as such,

[32]
but that one looks upon it as consistent with one's nationality or tolerates it, at the utmost, as a

[32]
necessary evil, so that one no longer considers imperative the search for the cause of the morbific

[30]
agent. During the long pre-War years of peace certain patho- logic features had certainly appeared and been

[32]
recognized as such, whereas, apart from a few exceptions, one did not at all take the morbific agent into

[33]
account. It might be said that here again it was most of all the symptoms of eco- nomic life which became conscious to

[34]
the individual more than perhaps the injurious consequences in quite a series of other domains. There were

[33]
many signs of decay which ought to have stimulated serious reflection. In this respect, from the purely economic

[33]
point of view, the following may be said : By the rapid increase of the German people's number before the War, the question

[33]
of supplying the daily bread stepped into the foreground of all political and economic thought and activity in

[32]
a more and more acute manner. Unfortunately, one could not make up one's mind to arrive at the

[33]
only correct solution, but believed that one could reach the goal in a cheaper way. As soon as one renounced gaining

[33]
new territory and, instead, entangled oneself in the delusion of a world-wide economic conquest, the end was

[32]
bound to lead to an industrialization that was as limitless as it was detrimental. The first consequence of

[33]
gravest importance was the weakening of the peasant class. In the same measure in which the latter class diminished,

[32]
the mass of the prole-, 316 MEIN KAMPF tariat of the great cities grew more and more, till finally the balance was lost

[33]
entirely. Now the sharp contrast between poor and rich became really apparent. Superabundance and misery now

[33]
lived so dose together that the consequences of this could be and were bound to be necessarily very dreary.

[31]
Distress and frequent unemployment began to play their game with people and left discontent and embitterment as a

[31]
memory behind them. The consequence of this seemed to be the political class split. Thus, with all economic

[33]
prosperity, discontent nevertheless became greater and deeper, and it even went so far that the conviction, 'it can

[33]
no longer go on like this,' became a general one, without people forming or being able to form a definite

[32]
idea of what should perhaps have come. These were the typical symptoms of a deep discontent which tried to express

[34]
itself in such a manner. But worse than this were other consequential symptoms Which the economization of the nation

[32]
brought with it. In the measure in which business rose to become the de' termining master of the State, money

[33]
became the god whom now everybody had to serve and to worship. Now the celestial gods were put more and more

[32]
into a corner as outmoded and old-fashioned, and instead of to them, in- cense was offered to the idol of

[33]
mammon. A truly evil degeneration thus set in, especially evil for the reason that this took place at a time

[31]
when the nation, more than ever, would probably need the highest heroic conviction at a threatening critical hour;

[33]
Germany had to be prepared with the help of the sword to stand up some day for her attempt to secure her daily bread

[33]
by way of a 'peaceful economic work.' Unfortunately, the domination of money was sanctioned also by

[34]
that authority which should have resisted it most of all: His Majesty the Kaiser acted unluckily when he THE CAUSES

[33]
OF THE COLLAPSE 317 drew the aristocracy particularly into the orbit of the new fiscal capital. Here, of

[33]
course, one has to admit to his credit that in this respect unfortunately even Bismarck did not recognize the

[33]
impending danger. With this, however, the ideal virtues had practically stepped back behind the value of money, for it

[33]
was obvious that once one had started out on such a way, the nobility of the sword would very shortly have to

[33]
take its place behind the aristocracy Attacks on the German nobility were to remain character- istic

[33]
of National Socialism. Among nationalists, the princes were reproached for their poor war record. More generally,

[33]
feeling waxed strong against the caste on social and economic grounds. Even the Center Party struck noblemen off its list

[30]
of candidates a revolutionary action of which it was to re- pent later. The question concerning what

[29]
disposition was to be made of the fortunes of the princes rocked German politics for years, leading

[33]
eventually to a referendum which cut across all party alignments. Hitler's criticism seems to have been based

[32]
primarily on intermarriages between the scions of noble houses and Jewish maidens. Such alliances were, as

[31]
a matter of fact, common, many dating back to Napoleonic times. Anyone who takes the trouble to study the

[32]
dedications of memoirs that appeared after the middle of the nineteenth century will find that in a great many

[34]
instances this rule ap- plies: the nobler the author, the more certain he is to boast a Jewish grandmother. The late eighteenth

[30]
century period of Lessing's Nathan der Wcisc was characterized by the homage paid to brilliant and

[33]
beautiful Jewish women. Some of the marriages were, of course, based on money, but it must be added that

[33]
the Jews brought from Vienna and Frankfort a culture superior to any that then existed in northeast Germany. The most

[30]
voluminous Nazi critic of the German nobility is, however, R. Walther Darrfe, Hitler's Minister of

[33]
Agriculture. Born in the Argentine and said to have specialized in veterinary science, Darr6 is above

[33]
all the author of Neuadel aus Blut und Boden. He summarizes the faults of the princes as these have 318 MEIN KAMPF of

[34]
finance. Financial operations succeed more easily thtin battles. Also, it was no longer inviting now for the real

[33]
hero or statesman to be brought into contact with the next- best Jew banker, so that the really meritorious man could no

[32]
longer have an interest in the bestowal of such cheap decorations, but refused them with thanks as far as he was

[33]
concerned. This development was profoundly saddening also from the point of view of blood ; the nobility lost more long

[33]
since been chalked up by Lagarde, Langbehn, Treitschke, and others. Then he attributes most of the blame to Charle- magne,

[33]
who because the fact that he favored Roman law and custom proved that he 'no longer possessed a sense of the im-

[33]
portance of the German nobility, by reason of the fact that he was deficient in the heritage of German blood,

[34]
1 The battle of Verden (782) was, he thinks, the deciding point. For there Charlemagne defeated the ' Saxon nobles.' From that time on,

[33]
'a Christian nobility is dominant in Germany, formed for the most part of Prankish noblemen-officials, whose blood was

[33]
of dubious purity in the Germanic sense, though in the course of time . . . this was replaced by or improved by

[29]
better blood. But this history of the development of the German Christian nobility out of the Prankish

[32]
noblemen-official caste is very basically the cause why, in contradistinction to the heathen Germanic

[32]
nobility, it no longer acts as a leadership embedded in the people, but as a caste set apart by itself

[33]
above the German people a caste which was dissolved only after the Crusades.' (Dane's diction and syntax retain

[33]
certain veter- inarian characteristics.) How, then, is the situation to be remedied? In the Vdlkischer Bcobachter

[33]
(1923) Darr proposed the establishment of Zucht- ivarten that is, offices for breeding control whose duty it would be to keep

[33]
records of German breeding. German girls were to be divided into four classes: the ten per cent shown by inspectors to have

[33]
the best German blood were to be set apart as the group from which the 'new German nobility' might freely choose ; the rest of

[33]
those girls against whose blood streams THE CAUSES OF THE COLLAPSE 319 and more the racial presumption for its existence. For

[30]
a greater part the designation 'non-nobility' would have been far more suitable. A symptom of serious

[32]
economic decay was the slow ex- tinction of the personal right of possession and the gradual handing-over of the

[34]
entire economy into the possession of stock- holders' companies. Only with this had labor truly sunk to the level

[34]
of an object of speculation of unscrupulous hagglers; but the nothing important could be said were also to be within

[32]
the 'new nobleman's' purview, provided he could obtain the Zuchtwarfs permission to wed with one of them; the group against which

[33]
pertinent criticism could be advanced were to be free to marry, provided they were sterilized in advance;

[33]
and those unfortunates whose blood proved to be beneath contempt were to be held away from the altar under all

[30]
cir- cumstances. To these ideas Darr6 has often returned, particularly in the famous seventh chapter of

[33]
Neuadel aus Blut und Boden, in which he attempts to apply the laws of breeding to the German people. Here also is

[33]
the often quoted passage in which he maintains that an illegitimate child of 'good blood' is to be ranked higher than

[31]
a legitimate child of 'bad blood.' The distinction is of importance, since girls of 'bad blood' are no longer

[34]
permitted to marry peasants whom the law permits to inherit land. How much of this theory has been put into practice cannot

[34]
be determined. The most important of the published decrees are the sterilization laws. No figures on the total

[33]
number of operations are available, nor is there any certainty that 'feeble-mindedness' has been the major

[33]
argument resorted to. Physicians recently employed in German hospitals estimate that the total number of

[34]
operations since 1933 the law was decreed during July of that year exceed 200,000. migrt authorities whose veracity there is

[33]
no reason to doubt insist that a good portion of these sterilizations were carried out for racial or political

[33]
reasons. Some Catholic physicians have been 320 MEIN KAMPF alienation of property from the employee, however, was

[33]
now increased ad infinitum. The stock exchange began to triumph and proceeded to take slowly but gradually

[33]
the life of the nation in its charge and control. The internationalization of German economic life had

[33]
been introduced even before the War by the roundabout way of the stock issues. Indeed, one part of German indus-

[33]
try still tried to guard itself with determination against this fate; but then, in turn, it fell victim to the combined attack

[33]
removed from their positions for unwillingness to enforce the law. (Cf. also Nazi Germany: Its Women and Family

[34]
Life, by Clifford Kirkpatrick.) In addition the 'new nobility' is in process of formation. The most important caste is

[31]
formed by the S.S. the black- garbed Schutzstaffd (Safety Staff) commanded by Himmler; and this is now governed by a rigid

[32]
marital code. The Nttrn- berg Laws on Race and Citizenship, passed in 1935, provide (Articles I and 2 of Section II):

[33]
'Marriages between Jews and subjects of German or kindred blood are forbidden. Marriages contracted despite this law

[32]
are invalid, even if they be con- cluded abroad in order to circumvent this law. . . . Extra- marital relations

[34]
between Jews and subjects of German or kindred blood are forbidden.' In addition, certain 'experi- ments' in breeding have been

[32]
conducted. Finally it may be added that the most famous recruit to National Socialism from the ranks of the German

[33]
nobility is Prince August Wilhelm, fourth son of the ex-Kaiser. He was a familiar addendum to Nazi rallies

[33]
prior to the Machtcr- greifung (seizure of power). But during the 'blood purge' of 1934 he was suddenly ordered by General

[31]
Goering to take a holiday in Switzerland, with which request he conformed without delay. During the 'crisis' that

[33]
developed in 1938 out of Hitler's relations with the Reichswehr, the ex-Crown Prince was despatched on a similar excursion

[33]
into the Swiss Alps. THE CAUSES OF THE COLLAPSE 321 of greedy capital which fought this battle especially with the aid of its

[31]
faithful comrade, the Marxist movement. The continued war against the German 'heavy industry' was the visible

[31]
beginning of the German economy's inter- nationalization, aimed at by Marxism's victory in the Rev-

[33]
olution. While I am writing this, the general attack against the German State Railways, which is now handed over to

[32]
the international capital, has finally been successful. With this the 'international' Social Democracy has

[33]
again reached one of its high objectives. How far one had succeeded in this 'economization' of the German

[31]
people is probably most visible from the fact that finally after the War one of the leading heads of German

[32]
industry, and above all, German trade, was able to express the opinion that economy as such would be in

[32]
a position to re-erect Germany, nonsense which was dished up in a very moment when France again based

[33]
instruction in her schools primarily on the humanistic principles, in order to prevent the opinion that the nation

[34]
and the State owed their exist- ence to business and not to eternally ideal values. The remark which in those days

[32]
a Stinnes gave the world caused After the platform of the Social Democratic Party had be- come ' reformist ' in

[33]
character, attention was devoted primarily to the question: 'What industries are ripe for socialization?' When

[33]
the War was over, two commissions were appointed by the Reich government to look into the matter. The principal result

[33]
was a theoretical decision that the coal industry ought to be socialized. Nothing else was accomplished, unless

[32]
the law establishing 'industrial workers' councils' be considered an advance. Under the Dawes Plan, the German

[31]
Railroads were organized into a separate 'company' (Reichsbahn-GeseUschaft) in the management of which the

[33]
Reparations Commission had a share. The idea was to collect reparations money from the proceeds of the railroads, which

[33]
remained, however, the property of the Reich. 322 MEIN KAMPF the most unbelievable confusion; because it was taken up

[33]
immediately in order to become, with marvelous speed, the leit-motiv of all quacks and prattlers whom Heaven had let

[33]
loose over Germany in the capacity of 'statesmen' since the Revolution. One of the most evil symptoms

[31]
of decay in pre-War Germany was the constant spreading of half measures in all and every- thing. It is always the

[34]
consequence of one's own uncer- tainty about some affair as well as of a cowardice resulting from these and

[31]
other reasons. This disease is promoted further by education. German education before the War was

[33]
afflicted with an extremely great number of weaknesses. Its intention was cut out, in a very one-sided manner,

[33]
for the purpose of breeding pure 'knowledge'; it was orientated less towards 'abilities,' and far less emphasis was

[33]
put on the cultivation of character in the individual (as far as this is at all pos- sible!), very little on

[33]
the promotion of the joy of accepting Compare Spengler (Zucht oder Bildung?): 'First comes con- duct, and then knowledge. But as

[33]
a nation we are not at all aware of what conduct is, and we have had far too much "education." We have been

[33]
crammed full of knowledge that has no bearing on life, which is purposeless and directionless, by indefatigable

[33]
teachers unable to propose to themselves any other task. But it is one thing to be pedantic, and another

[34]
to possess prudence, knowledge of life, and experience in the ways of the world. ... I would place Latin in the foreground,

[31]
even today. Germany owes to the thorough training in Latin af- forded by its gymnasia during the past

[31]
century more than it realizes. To that training it owes its intellectual discipline, its talent for

[34]
organization, and its progress in technology. 1 Spengler adds, in prophetic words, that teaching history and 'educting the people

[33]
politically' are one and the same thing. THE CAUSES OF THE COLLAPSE 323 responsibility, and none at all

[32]
on the training of will power and determination. Its results were really not the strong man, but rather the pliable

[33]
'know-all/ as which we Ger- mans were generally looked upon before the War and were esteemed accordingly. One

[33]
liked the German, as he was very useful, but one respected him too little, just in conse- quence of his weakness

[32]
of will. Not without reason was it above all he, who of all people most easily lost his nation- ality and his

[34]
fatherland. The nice proverb, ' M it dem Hute in der Hand komnti man durch das ganze Land' [with one's hat in one's hand one can

[32]
go through the whole land], says all there is to say. This pliability became really disastrous, however, when it

[33]
determined the forms with which alone one was per- mitted to approach the monarch ; that means, never to con- tradict him, but

[33]
to agree to all and everything that His Majesty pleases to ordain. The free dignity of man was most needed just in

[33]
this very place, if otherwise the mon- archistic institution was not to perish some day just because of this

[33]
cringing; for it was cringing and nothing else, and only to miserable cringers and sneaks, in short, to the whole decadent

[33]
pack which has always felt at home around the highest thrones more than the honorable, decent, and hon- est souls, this can pass

[30]
for the only given form of contact with the wearers of a crown. These 'most humble 9 crea- tures, however, with all

[32]
humility towards their master and bread-provider, have forever demonstrated their greatest impudence towards the

[34]
other part of mankind, and most of all when it pleased them to have the cheek to present them- selves as solely 'monarchistic'

[33]
to the other sinners; a gen- uine impudence which only such a titled or untitled maw- worm can exhibit. For in

[33]
truth these people have been the gravediggers of the monarchy and especially of the mon- archistic idea. This is

[33]
conceivable in no other way. A man who is ready to stand up for a cause will and can never be a 324 MEIN KAMPF sneak and

[33]
a characterless cringer. He who is really seri- ously concerned about the preservation and the furtherance of

[33]
an institution will cling to it with the last fiber of his heart, and will never be able to get over the fact if evils

[31]
of some kind become apparent in that institution, but such a man indeed will not cry this out publicly, as the

[33]
democratic 'friends' (?) of the monarchy did in exactly the same men- dacious manner, but he will most seriously warn and try

[33]
to influence His Majesty in person, the bearer of the crown. Thereby he will not and must not take the point of view that

[33]
His Majesty will nevertheless be at liberty to act according to his will, even if this may and is bound to lead to

[33]
disaster, but in such a case he will have to protect the monarchy against the monarch, and this at any risk. For, if

[32]
the value of this institution were to be found in the per- son of the monarch who happens to reign at the time in-

[34]
volved, then this would be the worst institution conceiv- able as a whole, for only in the rarest cases are the monarchs

[33]
the 61ite of wisdom and reason, or even of character, as one likes to describe them. Only the professional

[31]
cringers and sneaks believe this, but all straightforward people and these are nevertheless still the most valuable

[31]
individuals of the State will feel repulsed by the representation of such an absurd opinion. For them

[32]
history is only history, and truth is truth, even if the parties involved are monarchs. No, the fortune to

[34]
possess a great monarch in the person of a great man falls only so rarely to the share of the people that they have to

[34]
be content if the malice of Fate at least abstains from making the very worst mistake. Thus the value and the importance

[33]
of the monarchistic idea cannot lie in the person of the monarch himself, except Heaven resolves to place the crown

[32]
on the temples of an heroic genius like Frederick the Great or of a wise character like Wilhelm I. This

[33]
happens once in the course of cen- turies, and hardly more often. For the rest, however, the THE CAUSES OF THE COLLAPSE

[31]
325 idea takes precedence of the person, since the meaning of this arrangement lies exclusively in this

[33]
institution itself. But with this the monarch himself falls into the circle of service. Now he, too, is only a wheel in

[31]
this work, and in this capacity he is obligated to the work. He, too, has now to submit to the higher end, and

[33]
'monarchist' is no longer he who silently lets the bearer of the crown sin against him- self, but he who prevents this. If it were

[32]
different, not even the dethronement of an obviously mentally deranged prince would be permissible, if the

[33]
meaning were not found in the idea, but in the ' sacred ' person at any price, t Today it is really necessary to

[33]
put this down, as recently These remarks are, in view of much that has been entered into the ledger since 1923, a fairly

[33]
beguiling temptation to be retrospective. The relationships between Hitler and Wilhelm II are worth studying for

[33]
the light they throw on German psychology. In both cases oratorical talent was used to flutter the dovecotes

[31]
in the majority of European capitals. Both were disciples of Chamberlain, and both believed firmly in the

[31]
inevitable 'war of races. 1 God was with Wilhelm as he is with Hitler. Under the old regime, there was Prince

[33]
Eulenberg; under the new there is Rudolf Hess. The court pianist tradi- tion survived into the Third Reich. The craving to

[33]
be re- ceived into British society has endured, together with the same inability to 'arrive. 1 Before

[32]
the War, naval officers preparing to receive the Kaiser on a tour of inspection, were surprised to find that

[33]
a lofty pedestal had been erected, to the top of which a staircase led. The riddle was solved when Wilhelm ascended

[33]
to that lofty perch and talked down to his dear navy. In 1 935 1 a similar pedestal was constructed for the Niirnberg Party

[30]
Conference. Hitler mounted, and talked down to his beloved S.A. The Kaiser's picture, in days gone by, was

[31]
ubiquitous; Hitler's is now, if possible, still more universal. But to date the fondness for uniforms has

[32]
apparently been bequeathed to General Goering. 326 MEIN KAMPF more and more of those types begin again to

[33]
emerge from obscurity to whose wretched attitude the collapse of the monarchy must be ascribed not in

[33]
least degree. With a certain naive imperturbability, these people now talk again only of 'their' king (whom, however,

[32]
they had nevertheless left in the lurch in the most wretched manner, in the criti- cal hour only a few years ago), and they

[33]
begin to describe as a bad German every man who is not willing to tune in with their mendacious tirades, while

[33]
in truth these are exactly the same poltroons who in the year 1918 dispersed and rushed away from each and every red

[32]
arm badge, who let their king be king, immediately exchanged halberd for the walking stick, donned neutral neckties, and

[33]
disap- peared, as peaceful 'citizens,' actually without leaving a trace. At that time they had disappeared at

[30]
one blow, these royal champions, and only after the revolutionary hurricane had calmed down, thanks to the

[33]
activity of the others, so that one could again blare out into the air one's ' Hail to the King, Hail,' these 'servants'

[32]
and 'councillors' of the crown began again to emerge cautiously. But now they are all here, and they cast their eyes

[31]
longingly backwards towards the fleshpots of Egypt, they hardly can restrain themselves for loyalty towards the king and for

[32]
eagerness to accomplish great feats, till perhaps the first red arm badge will some day appear again, and the ghostly crowd of the

[33]
parties inter- ested in the monarchy bolts again, like mice before the cat. If the monarchs themselves were not

[32]
guilty of these things, one could only pity them most heartily because of their defenders of today. But they can be

[32]
convinced, at any rate, that with such knights one loses perhaps one's throne, but that one does not fight for crowns. This

[33]
devotion, however, was a fault of our entire educa- tion, a fault which took its revenge now in this place in an

[33]
especially terrible manner. For in consequence of this, these wretched types were THE CAUSES OF THE COLLAPSE 387

[33]
able to hold their ground at all courts and to undermine gradually the foundations of the monarchy. But when the building

[33]
then finally began to shake, they were blown away as it were and disappeared. Naturally: cringers and flunk- ies

[33]
do not let themselves be killed for their master. That the monarchs never know this and on principle fail to learn this has been their

[33]
doom of old. One of the worst symptoms of decay was the increasing cow- ardice towards responsibility as well as

[32]
the half-heartedness in all things resulting from it. t The starting-point of this plague, however, lies with us to a great part in the

[33]
purest cultivation of irresponsibility in our parliamentary institution: unfortunately, this

[32]
plague invaded slowly also the remaining domains of life, most of all that of the State. Everywhere one

[32]
began to evade re- sponsibility and for this reason one preferred to take up half and insufficient

[33]
measures; because by their application the measure of the responsibility to be borne personally seems

[33]
to be screwed down to the smallest size. One need only look at the attitude of the various govern- ments towards

[33]
a series of really detrimental symptoms of our public life, and one will easily recognize the terrible

[31]
meaning of this general half-heartedness and cowardice towards responsibility.-^ Here again Spengler is

[33]
interesting. 'We must set to work here and now,' he declared in Der Sumpf, 'relentlessly finding the sore on the German

[34]
body, if a long-drawn-out, creeping illness is to be cured.' But Spengler detected the evil, not in the parliamentary

[33]
system as such, or even in Marxism, but rather in the mechanics of party life. Parties, he contended, became ends

[32]
in themselves, and lost all relation to the bane central concerns of the nation. 328 MEIN KAMPF I take up only a few

[33]
cases out of the vast number which is at our disposal: Just in journalistic circles one usually prefers to call

[30]
the press a 'great power' of the State. As a matter of fact its importance is truly enormous. It cannot be

[33]
overestimated ; it is indeed actually the continuation of the education of youth in advanced age.

[33]
t Thereby one can divide the readers as a whole into three groups: First, those who believe everything they read;

[33]
Secondly, those who no longer believe anything; Thirdly, those who critically examine what they have read

[34]
and judge accordingly. The first group is numerically by far the greatest. It con- sists of the great masses of the people and

[31]
therefore repre- sents the mentally simplest part of the nation. But it can- not at all be expressed in terms of

[33]
professions, but, at the utmost, in general grades of intelligence. To it belong all those to whom independent

[30]
thinking is neither inborn nor instilled by education, and who, partly through inability and partly through

[32]
incompetence, believe everything that is put before them printed in black on white. Also those lazy-

[33]
bones belong to it who are well able to think for themselves, but who, out of sheer mental inertia, gratefully pick

[34]
up anything that someone else has thought before, with the modest assumption that the latter will probably have exer-

[31]
cised the right kind of effort. Now with all these people, who represent the great masses, the influence of the press will be

[33]
enormous. They are not in a position, or they do not wish personally, to examine what is offered to them

[32]
so that their entire attitude towards all current problems can be led back almost exclusively to the outward

[32]
influence of others. This may be of advantage in case their enlightenment is carried out by a sincere and

[33]
truth-loving party, but it is evil as soon as scoundrels or liars do this. THE CAUSES OF THE COLLAPSE 329 The second group is

[33]
much smaller even in number. It is composed of the greater part of elements which first be- longed to the first group, and who

[33]
after long and bitter dis- appointments changed over to the contrary and believe no longer in anything at all that

[33]
comes in the form of print before their eyes. They hate every newspaper; either they do not read it at all or they are

[33]
annoyed at the contents without exception, since in their opinion it is composed only of lies and untruths. These people

[33]
are very difficult to handle, as they will also always face the truth mistrustingly. Therefore they are lost

[34]
to every positive work. The third group finally is by far the smallest; it consists of the mentally truly fine heads

[32]
whom natural gifts and education have taught to think independently, who try to form a judgment of their own about

[30]
everything, and who submit most thoroughly everything they have read to an examination and further

[31]
development of their own. They will not place a newspaper before their eyes without making their brains co-operate

[33]
continuously, and then Mr. Author will not easily hold his own. The journalists therefore like such a reader only

[32]
with reserve. For this third group, indeed, the nonsense which a newspaper may scribble together is of little danger or

[34]
impor- tance. They have accustomed themselves anyhow in the course of their lifetime to see as a rule in

[33]
every journalist a scoundrel who tells the truth only occasionally. Unfortu- nately, however, the importance

[34]
of these excellent people lies only in their intelligence and not in their number; a mis- fortune in a time in

[34]
which wisdom is nothing and the major- ity everything. Today, where the ballot of the masses de- cides, the decisive

[33]
value lies with the most numerous group and this is the first one: the crowd of the simple ones and the credulous." It is in

[32]
the paramount interest of the State and the na- tion to prevent these people from falling into the hands ot 330 MEIN KAMPF

[33]
evil, ignorant, or even malevolent educators. The State, therefore, has the duty to supervise their

[33]
education and to prevent any nuisance. Therefore, it has to watch especially the press, for its influence is

[33]
by far the strongest and most penetrating on these people, as it is applied not temporarily but permanently. In

[33]
the persistent and eternal repetition of this instruction lies its entire unheard-of importance. Therefore,

[33]
if in any place at all, the State must not forget that just in here all means must serve an end ; it must not let itself

[33]
be misled by the boast of a so-called ' freedom of the press/ and must not be persuaded to fail in its duty and to put

[33]
before the nation the food that it needs and that is good for it; it must assure itself with ruthless determination of

[33]
this means for educating the people and to put into the service of the State and the nation. But what food was it that

[33]
the German press of the pre-War time put before these people? Was it not the worst conceivable poison? Was not the worst

[32]
kind of pacifism inoculated into the heart of our people, at a time when the rest of the world was about to

[34]
throttle Germany slowly but surely? Did not this press, even in times of peace, instill into the brains of the people doubts

[33]
about the rights of their own State, in order to restrict it from the beginning in the choice of the means for its defense?

[33]
Was it not the German press which knew how to make palatable to our people the nonsense of 'Western Democracy/ till

[33]
finally, captured by all these enthusiastic tirades, it thought that it could en- trust its future to a League

[34]
of Nations? Did it not help in educating our people towards a wretched immorality? Did it not ridicule morals

[33]
and customs, interpreting them as being old-fashioned and humdrum, till finally our people actually became 'modern'?

[33]
Did it not, by continued attack, undermine the fundamentals of State authority for so long till a single blow

[32]
was sufficient to cause the collapse of this building? Did it not once fight against every mani- THE CAUSES OF THE

[31]
COLLAPSE 331 festation of the will to give to the State what belongs to it, did it not fight with all means, did it not

[31]
disparage the army by continued criticism, did it not sabotage general conscription, and did it not

[32]
solicit the refusal of military credits, etc., till the results could not fail to arrive? The activity of the

[32]
so-called liberal press was the work of gravediggers for the German people and the German Reich. One can pass by in

[33]
silence the Marxist papers of lies; to them lying is as necessary to their life as catching mice is to the cat; but

[33]
its task is only to break the people's folkish and national spine, in order to make it ripe for the yoke of slav-

[32]
ery of international capital and its masters, the Jews. But what did the State do against this mass poisoning of the

[33]
nation? Nothing, actually nothing. A few ridiculous decrees, a few fines against too great villainies, and that was all.

[33]
But instead, one hoped perhaps to gain the favor of this pest by bringing forth flatteries and acknowledgments of the 'value'

[33]
of the press, its 'importance,' its 'educational mission,' and the other nonsense of that kind, which the Jews, slyly smiling,

[34]
received and accepted with cunning thanks. The cause for this miserable failure, however, was not the non-recognition

[33]
of the danger but rather a cowardice, crying to Heaven, and the half-heartedness of all resolu- tions and measures, born

[33]
out of it. Nobody had the cour- age to take up thoroughgoing radical means, but here, as everywhere else,

[33]
one bungled about with half prescriptions, and, instead of delivering the coup de grdce, one perhaps only irritated

[33]
the viper, with the result that not only every- thing remained as it had been, but that, on the contrary, the power of

[33]
the institution to be fought increased from year to year. The German government's defensive against the press horde, slowly

[31]
corrupting the nation, of chiefly Jewish origin and of Jewish journals, was without a straight line, without 332 MEIN KAMPF

[32]
determination, but above all without any visible goal. Here the brains of the privy councillors gave out

[30]
completely, in the estimation of the importance of this fight as well as in the choice of the means, and the

[32]
establishment of a clear plan. Planlessly one doctored about; at a time when one had been bitten too much one

[33]
locked up such a journalistic viper for a few weeks or months, but one left the snake's nest as such well alone. This was

[32]
partly, of course, also the consequence of the infinitely sly tactics of Jewry on the one hand and of

[33]
a stupidity or harmlessness typical amongst privy councillors on the other. The Jew was much too clever to permit

[34]
his entire press to be attacked uniformly. No, the purpose of a part of it was to cover up. While the Marxist

[33]
papers, in the meanest way, went to battle against everything that The 'Jewish press 1 was a slogan then, as it has since been

[32]
in other lands. As a matter of fact, a few of the ablest 'liberal' journals in Germany were edited by Jews.

[33]
Nevertheless, when one views the press of the country as a whole, the Jewish in- fluence appears to have been limited

[32]
to the 'democratic' news- papers of Berlin and Frankfort. More emotion was aroused by a number of vigorous

[33]
Jewish opposition journalists of an in- dependent stamp Maximilian Harden, Kurt Eisner, L. Schwarzschild, Georg Bernhard. Since 1933

[32]
the German press has been completely 'subordi- nated' (gleichgeschaltet). The first to go were the labor news- papers, not the

[33]
Marxist ones merely, but particularly those of the trade unions. Der Deutsche the paper which Dr. Hein- rich Brflning founded

[34]
and which he once edited had been the organ of the Christian unions; now it was transformed into the daily mouthpiece of

[32]
Dr. Robert Ley, leader of the Arbeitsfront (Labor Front). Oddly enough the Jewish-owned journals were the ones to retain

[30]
longest a measure of inde- pendence, because they had been sold in time to powerful industrial

[33]
organizations. The Frankfurter Zcitung, for ex- THE CAUSES OF THE COLLAPSE 333 may be sacred to man, while they attacked

[33]
State and gov- ernment in the most infamous manner and set great parts of the people by the ears, the bourgeois democratic

[33]
Jewish papers knew how to give themselves the air of the well- known 'objectivity'; they carefully avoided all strong

[33]
language, well knowing that all empty-heads are able to judge all things only according to their appearance and that

[34]
they never have the ability to penetrate into the interior, so that for them the value of a cause is

[32]
judged by the ex- terior instead of by the contents ; a human weakness to which they fortunately owe also the

[31]
attention they receive. For these people the Frankfurter Zeitung was and is in- deed the incorporation of all

[33]
decency; for it never employs ample, had a fairy godmother in I. G. Farben, the chemical trust. Religious dailies,

[32]
many of which had been strong and influential concerns, were thoroughly curbed. The editors were fired in lots of a

[33]
dozen. What remained were journalistic torsos, which should have been permitted to die a respectable death. For a while

[34]
Colonel Franz von Papen held a jittery protecting hand over the Catholic Germania of Berlin, once the organ

[33]
to which all had turned for information concerning the views of the powerful Center Party. Then at last the miserable

[34]
remnant of former glories was snuffed out in 1938. The Vienna Reichspost, organ of Dollfuss and Schuschnigg, collapsed far more rapidly.

[32]
The provincial newspapers became mere reprints of hand-outs from the Propaganda Office. The press is the Nazi

[31]
Party's greatest source of income, being a monopoly of tremendous dimensions. The Volkische Beobachter is the

[32]
official paper, but almost every Nazi chieftain has a journal peculiarly his own. Particular value is

[33]
attached to the illustrated weeklies, many of which are highly effective propaganda media. Every

[33]
Nazi event is a photographers' holiday. During a single Rosenberg speech in 1933, official cameramen took 456 flashlight

[34]
pictures. The Party also main- tains a considerable number of newspapers in foreign countries. 334 MEIN KAMPF crude expressions,

[33]
it rejects all physical brutality, and always appeals to fight with 'spiritual' means which, strangely enough, is nearest

[33]
to the heart of just the most unintelligent people. This is a result of our semi-education which detaches the people

[31]
from the instinct of nature, pumps a certain knowledge into them without being able to lead them to the ultimate

[33]
realization, as for this purpose industry and good will alone are not useful, but the neces- sary reason

[33]
has to be present, and not only that, it has to be inborn. The ultimate realization, however, is always only

[34]
the understanding of the causes of the instinct; that means, man will then never fall into the lunacy of believing that he has

[33]
now really advanced to the position of master and lord of Nature, which the conceit of a semi-education brings

[31]
about so easily, but he will then understand all the more the fundamental necessity of the working of

[33]
Nature, and he will realize how far also his existence is subjected to these laws of the eternal battle

[33]
and struggle in an up- ward direction. We will then feel that, in a world in which the planets circle around the sun, where moons ride

[34]
around planets, where power alone is always the master of weakness and forces it into obedient service or

[32]
else breaks it, there can be no special laws valid for man. For him also the eternal principles of this ultimate

[32]
wisdom apply. He can try to comprehend them, but he will never be able to free himself from them. But it is just for our

[33]
intellectual demi-monde that the Jew writes his so-called intellectual press. For them the The Berliner Tageblatt,

[33]
edited by Theodor Wolff, was the paper the Nazis most hated, excepting the much less influential Gerade Weg, of Munich.

[32]
On the day the Party came to power, offices of the second journal were smashed to bits and the editor Dr. Fritz

[34]
Gerlich was jailed. He was eventually executed. Theodor Wolff escaped from Germany in 1933. THE CAUSES OF THE COLLAPSE

[32]
335 Frankfurter Zeitung and the Berliner TageblaU are made, for them their tone is tuned, and on them finally they

[32]
exer- cise their influence. By avoiding most carefully all forms seeming outwardly rude, they nevertheless pour the

[32]
poison from other vessels into the hearts of their readers. Under a geseires [Yiddish; from the Hebrew gezera, meaning

[31]
unnec- essary talk] of nice sounds and phrases they lull them into the faith as though really pure science or even

[33]
morality were the driving forces behind their activity, while in reality it is only the ingenious

[32]
and cunning art of stealing in this man- ner from the hand of the enemy the weapon against the press. For while some are

[32]
dripping with decency, all weak heads are the more inclined to believe that with the others it is a case of

[34]
only minor excrescences, which, however, should never be allowed to lead to an infringement of the freedom of the press

[32]
(as one calls this nuisance of unpunish- able lying to, and poisoning of, the people). Thus one shies from proceeding

[33]
against this banditry, as one fears that in such a case one will immediately have the 'decent' press against

[34]
oneself; a fear that is only too justified. For, as soon as one tries to proceed against one of these disgraceful

[33]
papers, immediately all the others will take its side, but by no means perhaps in order to endorse its kind

[32]
of fight, Heaven forbid ; only the principle of the freedom of the press and of public opinion are involved ; this

[33]
alone has to be defended. But the strongest man weakens in the face of this clamor, since it comes from the mouth of

[33]
only ' decent ' papers. . . . Thus the poison could penetrate into and work in the system of our people without hindrance and

[32]
without the State having the power to master the disease. In the ridicu- lous and half-hearted means which it applied

[32]
against it is shown the threatening decay of the Reich. For an institu- tion which is no longer determined to defend

[31]
itself with all weapons practically gives itself up. Every half measure is then the visible symptom of

[32]
internal decay which will 336 MEIN KAMPF and must be followed, sooner or later, by external col- lapse. I believe that the

[33]
present generation, rightly guided, will more easily overcome this danger. It has experienced several things

[34]
which were able to strengthen the nerves of those who did not lose them altogether. Surely in the future, the Jew

[33]
will certainly raise an enormous clamor in his newspapers, once the hand is put on his favorite nest and an end

[34]
is made of the misuse of the press, and once also this instrument of education is put into the service of

[33]
the State and is no longer left in the hand of strangers and enemies of the people. But I also believe that this will

[31]
annoy us younger ones less than it once did our fathers. A 30 cm. shell has always hissed more than a thousand Jewish

[32]
newspaper vipers; therefore let them hiss. t A further example for the half-heartedness and the weak- ness of the leading

[33]
authority in pre-War Germany in the most important vital questions of the nation can be the following: Parallel

[34]
with the political and moral infection of the people went a no less terrible poisoning of the health of the national

[31]
body. Syphilis began to spread more and more, especially in the great cities, while tuberculosis was

[32]
steadily reaping its harvest of death almost throughout the entire country. Although in both cases the consequences for the

[31]
nation This extensive philippic against syphilis is among the most interesting passages in Mein Kampf. Much

[34]
medical or pseudo- medical speculation has been built up round about it, with which we do not associate ourselves.

[32]
The essential point is that syphilis and Rassenschande (i.e., cohabitation between a German and a person of

[32]
impure blood) are placed on the same level. The first can be cured, however. The second i irre- parable. THE

[32]
CAUSES OF THE COLLAPSE 337 were terrible, one could no longer bring oneself to take decisive measures.

[32]
Towards syphilis especially one can describe the attitude of the national and State authority

[31]
only with the words, complete capitulation. If one wanted to fight it seriously, one had to take quite

[33]
different steps than was actually the case. The invention of a remedy of a questionable character as well

[34]
as the commercial exploitation of the latter are able to help but little with this plague. Also here only the fight

[33]
against the causes should be considered and not the aboli- tion of the symptoms. The cause, however, lies primarily

[33]
in our prostitution of love. Even if the result of this were not this terrible disease, yet it would still be of

[33]
deepest danger for the people, for the moral devastation which this depravity brings with it are sufficient to destroy

[32]
a people slowly but surely. The Judaization of our spiritual life and the mammonization [sic] of our

[31]
mating impulse sooner or later befouls our entire new generation, for instead of vig- orous children of

[33]
natural feeling, only the miserable speci- mens of financial expedience come forth. For this becomes more

[33]
and more the basis and the only prerequisite for our marriages. Love, however, finds an outlet somewhere

[32]
else. Naturally, one can also here mock Nature for a certain time, but the revenge will not fail to

[32]
appear, it only will appear later, or rather, it is often recognized too late by the people. However, how

[33]
devastating are the consequences of a continued disregard of the natural presuppositions for mar- riage

[33]
can be demonstrated by our aristocracy. Here one is presented with the results of a propagation which has

[31]
been based for one part on purely social compulsion, for the other on financial reasons. The one leads to

[32]
weakening altogether, the other to blood poisoning, as now every department-store Jewess is considered

[29]
suitable to augment the offspring of 'His Highness. 9 The latter then looks like 131 MEIN KAMPF it. In both cases complete

[33]
degeneration is the consequence. Our 'middle class 9 takes pains today to walk the same way and it will end at the same

[33]
goal. With indifferent haste one tries to pass by disagreeable truths, as though by such an attitude one could make

[33]
these things undone. No, the fact that the population of our big cities is prostituted more and more in its love

[32]
life, and that just through this it falls victim to syphilis in more and wider circles, cannot just be abolished by

[32]
denying it; it is there. The most obvious results of this mass contagion can be found on the one hand in the lunatic

[33]
asylums, and on the other, unfortunately, in our children. These es- pecially are the sad certificates

[32]
of misery of the irresistibly advancing tainting of our sexual life; in the diseases of the children the

[30]
vices of the parents are revealed. Now there are different ways to reconcile oneself with this

[33]
disagreeable, even terrible fact: some do not see any- thing at all, or rather they do not want to see anything:

[33]
this is of course by far the most simple and cheapest 'atti- tude'; others wrap themselves in a saintly cloak of prudish- ness

[33]
that is as ridiculous as it is also mendacious; they only talk of this entire domain as if it were a great

[30]
sin, and, above all, in the presence of every sinner caught in the act, they express their deeply felt inner

[32]
indignation in order then to close their eyes in pious disgust towards this vicious disease and to ask God (if possible

[33]
after their own death) to rain fire and brimstone upon this Sodom and Gomorrah in order once again to make an

[32]
elevating example of this disgraceful mankind ; a third group see very well the terrible consequences which this

[32]
disease is bound to, and will, bring with it, but nevertheless they only shrug their shoulders, convinced that they can do nothing

[33]
against this danger, anyhow, so that one has to let things go as they are going. All this is of course comfortable and

[34]
simple, only one must not forget that a nation will fall victim to such inertia' THE CAUSES OF THE COLLAPSE 339 The excuse

[32]
that the other nations are no better off of course can hardly change anything In respect to the fact of their own

[33]
decline, except perhaps that the feeling that others also meet with misfortune would bring for many a mitigation of

[33]
their own pains. However, the question is then all the more which nation first and by itself is able to master this plague, and

[33]
which nations cannot help per- ishing. But that is what matters in the end. This also is only a touchstone for the value of

[33]
a race, and that race which does not pass the test will die and make room for races healthier or at least tougher and of greater

[33]
resistance. For, since this question primarily concerns the coming generation, it belongs to those of whom it is

[33]
said, with terrible correctness, that the sins of the fathers are visited upon the tenth generation. But this is valid

[29]
only for the sins against blood and race. The sin against the blood and the degradation of the race are the

[31]
hereditary sin of this world and the end of a mankind surrendering to them. But how truly miserably did the

[31]
Germany of pre-War times face just this one question. What was done in order to check the tainting of our young

[33]
generation in the big cities? What was done to attack the infecting and mam- monization [sic] of our love life?

[33]
What, in order to fight the resulting syphilization of our national body? The answer is most easily given by

[33]
stating what should have been done. First, one should not be allowed to take this question too easily, but to understand

[33]
that upon its solution will depend the happiness or the unhappiness of generations, nay, that it may be or even

[32]
must be decisive for the entire future of our people. Such a realization, however, required ruthless

[34]
measures and interventions. At the top of all re- flections the conviction should have been placed that first of all the attention

[32]
of the entire nation has to be concen- 340 MEIN KAMPF trated on this terrible danger, so that every single indi-

[33]
vidual becomes conscious in his mind of the significance of this fight. One can bring obligations and burdens which are

[33]
incisive, and sometimes hard to bear, to a general effec- tiveness only when, apart from compulsion, also

[32]
the real- ization of the necessity of this activity is given to the individual. But this demands an

[33]
enormous enlightenment to the exclusion of all current questions which have an otherwise deviating effect. In

[32]
all cases which involve the fulfillment of apparently impossible demands or tasks, the entire attention of

[34]
a people has to be united uniformly on this one question in such a manner as though indeed its existence or

[31]
non-existence de- pended upon its solution. Only thus will one make a people willing and able to

[33]
undertake truly great achievements and efforts. This principle is valid also for the individual, as far as

[34]
he wishes to attain great goals. He, too, will be able to do this only in step-like sections. He, too, will then always have to

[34]
unite his entire efforts on the reaching of a certain limited task, until this seems to be fulfilled and the marking

[33]
of a new section can be undertaken. He who does not carry out the partition of the way to be conquered into single

[34]
sections, and then tries to conquer them plan- fully with sharpest concentration of all forces, one by one, will never be able

[31]
to arrive at the goal, but he will remain lying somewhere on the way, perhaps even by the side of it. This

[32]
gradual approach to a goal by work is an art and it requires at a time the staking of actually the utmost

[33]
energy in order to conquer the way, step by step. This is, therefore, the very first preliminary condition which

[33]
is necessary for the attack on so difficult a part of the human way, the condition that the leadership succeeds in

[33]
presenting to the masses of the people just that part of the goal which has to be reached, or, rather, which has to THE CAUSES OF

[32]
THE COLLAPSE 341 be fought for, as the one that is now solely and alone worthy of human attention, and upon the

[33]
conquest of which everything depends. The great masses of the people, anyhow, can never see the whole way before them

[33]
with- out getting tired and without despairing of the task. They will keep the goal before their eyes only to a certain extent,

[33]
but they will be able to visualize the way only in small sections, similar to the wanderer who also knows and

[33]
is aware of the end of his journey, but who overcomes the endless road better if he cuts it up into sections and

[31]
now marches ahead towards each single one, as though this were the desired goal. Only thus he advances without

[33]
despairing. Thus, by employing all propagandistic auxiliary means, one should have made the fight against syphilis

[33]
appear as the task of the nation, not as one task among others. For this purpose one should have hammered into

[30]
the people its evils as the most terrible misfortune in its full extent, and under application of all

[33]
auxiliary measures, till the whole nation should have come to the conviction that upon the solution of this

[33]
question really everything depends, future or doom. Only after such a preparation, carried out for years ifTo date

[33]
the 'extensive propaganda' anent syphilis has not been one of the principal achievements of the Third Reich. In

[33]
1933 strong measures were taken to curb prostitution. Under the Republic, the Berlin Department of Health had taken the view

[32]
that all the State could intelligently do was to control the health of the street- walker. The changes in the law resulted,

[33]
however, in 40,000 new cases of syphilis within a few months (according to an official report). Recently there has been

[33]
a tendency to control the effects of social disease by examining persons who wish to marry, especially if

[33]
they seek a loan from the government in accordance with the laws provid- ing grants of aid to prospective bridegrooms. 342 MEIN KAMPF

[33]
necessary, will the attention, and with it also the determina- tion, of a whole people be awakened to such

[33]
an extent that now one will be able to take very difficult and sacrificial measures without running the risk

[33]
that one will not be understood or that one will suddenly be left in the lurch by the willingness of the masses. For, in

[32]
order to attack this plague seriously, enormous sacrifices and works just as great are necessary. The fight

[31]
against syphilis requires a fight against prosti- tution, against prejudices, old habits, against previous ideas,

[33]
general opinions, amongst them last but not least, against the mendacious prudishness in certain circles, etc. The first condition for

[30]
only the moral right to fight against these things is to make early marriage possible for the coming

[33]
generation. In late marriages alone lies the compulsion for keeping an institution which, no matter how much

[33]
one may turn and twist oneself, is and remains a disgrace to mankind, an institution which damned badly suits a being

[33]
who otherwise in modesty likes to consider itself the 'image' of God. Prostitution is a disgrace to

[32]
mankind, but one cannot abolish it by moral lectures, pious intentions, etc., but its limitation and its final

[32]
elimination warrant the abolition of quite a number of preliminary conditions. But the first is and

[33]
remains the creation of the possibility of early marriage, according to human nature, above all for

[30]
the man; because the woman is here only the passive part, anyhow. However, how erring, even how

[33]
incomprehensible the people have partly become today may be derived from the fact that one not seldom hears

[33]
mothers of the so-called 'better' society say that they are grateful to find a husband for their child who has 'already

[33]
sown his wild oats/ etc. As in this direction there is in most cases less shortage than would be the case the other way round,

[33]
the poor girl THE CAUSES OF THE COLLAPSE 343 therefore will fortunately find such a de-horned Siegfried, and the children

[33]
will be the visible result of such a 'sen- sible 1 marriage. If one considers that, apart from this, a restriction

[31]
of propagation itself, as far as possible, takes place, so that Nature is barred from all choice, as now

[34]
naturally every human being, no matter how miserable, has to be kept alive, there remains only the question

[33]
why then such an institution still exists at all and what purpose it is supposed to have? Is this then not exactly

[33]
the same as prostitution itself? Does then the duty towards poster- ity no longer play any r&le at all? Or does one

[31]
not realize with what curse one burdens oneself, towards children and children's children, by such a criminally

[33]
careless manner in the guarding of the ultimate right of Nature and even of the ultimate obligation

[34]
towards Nature? Thus the cultured people degenerate and perish gradually. Marriage also cannot be an

[33]
end in itself, but has to serve the one greater aim, the propagation and preserva- tion of the species and the race.

[33]
Only this is its meaning and its task. But if this is true, then its soundness can be measured only by the manner in which it

[33]
fulfills this purpose. Evea for this reason, an early marriage is right, as it gives the young marriage still that force

[33]
from which alone a healthy generation, capable of resisting, can ensue. Of course, to make this possible, quite

[30]
a series of social conditions are necessary without which one cannot think of an early marriage.

[32]
Therefore, the solution of this question, which is so small, cannot take place without incisive measures in

[33]
Prior to 1925, the Republic had, it is true, been able to do very little towards solving the problem of housing. The end of

[33]
the War not only brought the army back home, but also forced into the larger cities a constant stream of refugees from

[34]
territories sundered from Germany by the peace treaties. 344 MEIN KAMPF social regard. What importance must be attributed

[33]
to these should be understood most of all in a time when the so-called 'social' republic, by its inability in

[32]
the solution of the housing question alone, simply prevents numerous marriages and thus favors prostitution. The

[32]
absurdity of our way of arranging salaries, which considers the question of the family and its support far too

[32]
little, is also a reason which makes so many an early marriage impossible. Therefore, one can

[34]
approach a real fight against prosti- tution only if, by a fundamental change of social condi- tions, earlier marriage than

[32]
can take place now is made It is sometimes estimated that 1,000,000 persons migrated from the regions ceded to

[33]
Poland. In addition the country was overrun with fugitives from Russia and the Baltic States. The government had

[33]
no money; and during the period of in- flation the very sources from which revenue might have been obtained dried up. But

[33]
as soon as the Dawes Plan went into effect, housing plans of vast dimensions got under way. During the four years beginning with

[32]
1925, Germany erected more homes than did any other European country in the same period. There was much

[31]
argument concerning the character of the work done. Socialist municipal governments, often committed to

[33]
family limitation, favored apartment houses; Catholic and Protestant agencies, which sought to promote 'normal'

[31]
family life, tried whenever possible to erect one- family houses. Sometimes, as in Cologne, the

[33]
expenditures drew from critics the complaint that bankruptcy was inevitable. Under National Socialism, the trend has

[32]
predominatingly been towards one-family housing. This has been aided by a marked tendency on the part of

[33]
middle-class families to place their savings in real property. Yet there is no essential differ- ence between 1928 and 1935 in

[33]
this regard, though such a build ing as the huge apartment-house erected in Neu-K6lln. Berlin, under the Republic would hardly

[33]
be erected today. THE CAUSES OF THE COLLAPSE 345 generally possible. This is the very first preliminary con-

[30]
dition for a solution of this question. In the second place, however, education and training have to

[32]
eliminate quite a series of evils about which one hardly cares at all today. Above all, in our

[33]
present-day education a balance between intellectual instruction and physical training has to take place.

[33]
What today calls itself a gymnasium is an insult to the Greek example. With our education one has entirely

[33]
forgotten that in the long run a healthy mind is able to dwell only in a healthy body. Especially when, with a few

[33]
exceptions, one looks at the great masses of the people, this principle receives absolute validity. In pre-War

[33]
Germany there was a time when one no longer cared for this truth. One simply went on sinning against the body,

[32]
and one thought that in the one-sided training of the 'mind' one possessed a safe guaranty for the greatness of the

[34]
nation. A mistake which began to avenge itself much sooner than one thought. It is no acci- dent that the bolshevistic

[32]
wave found nowhere a better ground than in those places where a population, degener- ated by hunger and

[32]
constant undernourishment, lives: in Central Germany, Saxony, and the Ruhr district. In all these districts, however,

[33]
a serious resistance on the part of the so-called ' intelligentsia ' to this Jewish disease hardly takes

[30]
place any longer for the simple reason that the in- telligentsia itself is physically completely

[33]
degenerated, though less by reasons of distress than by reasons of education. The exclusively intellectual

[34]
attitude of our edu- cation of the higher classes makes them unable in a time where not the mind but the fist

[32]
decides even to preserve themselves, let alone to hold their ground. In physical deficiencies there lies not

[33]
infrequently the first cause of personal cowardice. The exceeding stress on a purely intellectual training

[33]
346 MEIN KAMPF and the neglect of physical training favor also in much too early youth the formation of sexual conceptions.

[33]
The boy who, by sports and gymnastics, is brought to an iron- like inurement succumbs less to the need of sensual grati-

[33]
fication than the stay-at-home who is fed exclusively on intellectual food. A reasonable education,

[31]
however, must take this into consideration. Further, it must not forget that on the part of the healthy young man the

[33]
expectations of the woman will be different than on the part of a prematurely corrupted weakling.^ Thus the entire

[34]
education has to be directed towards employing the free time of the boy for the useful training of his body. He has

[34]
no right to loaf about idly in these years, to make streets and movie theaters insecure, but after his daily work he has

[32]
to steel and harden his young body so that life will not find him too soft some day. To get this under way and also to

[33]
carry it out, to guide and to lead is the task of the education of youth, and not the exclusive infiltration of

[33]
so-called wisdom. It has also to do away with the conception that the treatment of the body were the concern of each

[31]
individual. There is no liberty to sin at the expense of posterity and, with it, of the race.

[33]
Parallel with the training of the body, the fight against the poisoning of the soul has to set in. Our entire public life

[33]
today resembles a hothouse of sexual conceptions and stimulants. One has only to look at the menus of our

[33]
movie houses, vaudevilles, and theaters; and one can hardly deny that this is not the right kind of food, above all for

[33]
youth. In shop windows and on billboards one works with the basest means in order to attract the atten- tion of the masses. That this

[33]
is bound to lead to serious damage to youth is probably clear to everyone who has not lost the ability to

[33]
imagine himself in the place of a youth's soul. This sensual sultry atmosphere leads to THE CAUSES OF THE COLLAPSE

[33]
347 ideas and stimulations at a time when the boy ought not yet to have an understanding for such things. The result of this

[33]
education can be studied in a not very enjoyable way with the youth of today. From the courtrooms events sometimes

[33]
penetrate to the public which permit a horrible insight into the inner life of our fourteen- and fifteen-year- old

[33]
youths. Who will wonder, therefore, that even in the circles of this age syphilis begins to seek its victims? And is it

[30]
not a misery to see how so many physically weak, and also mentally corrupt, young men receive their

[30]
initiation into marriage by a whore of the big cities? No, he who wants to attack prostitution must

[31]
primarily help to abolish the mental presupposition for it. He has to clear away the filth of the moral

[32]
contamination of the ' culture' of our big cities, and this ruthlessly and without There is no doubt that one of the

[33]
sources of Nazi strength lies in the sanity of its attitude towards youth as compared with the view taken on the whole

[32]
by German Communism. This last had a baneful hedonistic core : the result of the fact that it stressed the rights of the

[33]
masses far more effectively than it did their duties. A good many sound people turned to Hitlerism because they

[32]
could not stomach such Communist demands as these : free contraceptives, family aid to unmarried lovers, and 'week-ends.'

[30]
However arguable it may be that young people without money will not abstain from love rela- tionships, it is

[33]
nevertheless a prevalent belief that society ia something more than just an institute for having a 'good

[33]
time.' However sinister the ultimate objectives of the Nazis may be, there is no doubt that Hitler's soldier

[30]
helpers have often in- culcated a healthier attitude towards life. Unfortunately, the good thus

[29]
accomplished has in part been destroyed again by forces inherent in the Nazi dynamic. The Nazi youth

[31]
organizations take up ao much of the boy or girl'i leisure time that little is left for the hearth-side.

[33]
Moreover, the 'anti-bourgeois' doctrine inculcated tends to make th 348 MEIN KAMPF hesitating despite all clamor and

[33]
lamentations which then, of course, will be let loose. If we do not lift our youth out of the morass of its present surroundings,

[34]
it will be sub- merged in it. He who does not want to see these things supports them and becomes thus a fellow culprit in the slow

[32]
prostitution of our future, for the latter lies in the coming generation. This cleaning-up of our culture must

[33]
extend to nearly all domains. Theater, art, literature, movies, the press, billposters and window displays must be cleaned of

[34]
the symptoms of a rotting world and put into the service of a moral idea of State and culture. Public life has

[33]
to be freed from the suffocating perfume of our modern eroticism, exactly as also of all unmanly prudish

[33]
insincerity. In all these things the goal and the way have to be determined by the care for the preservation

[33]
of our people's health in body and soul. The right of personal freedom steps back in the face of the duty of the preserva-

[34]
tion of the race. f Only after the execution of these measures can the medical fight against this disease itself

[33]
be carried on with some prospects of success. However, here, too, the ques- tion involved cannot be that of half measures,

[33]
but also here one will have to come to the most serious and most incisive decisions. It is a half measure

[32]
to allow incurably ill people the permanent possibility of contaminating the domestic virtues seem

[31]
tame. Henri Lichtenberger concludes (The Third Reich) that 'the gulf between generations, far from being bridged, is only

[33]
becoming greater under the Spartan regime installed by Hitlerism.' Moral conditions are often deplorable,

[33]
judged by standards of Christian or bourgeois morality. The fact that an illegitimate child, if born of 'good stock/ is

[33]
considered an asset to the Reich seems to have made many young girls lose their heads; and an increase in the practice

[32]
of homosexual vice is conceded on all sides. THE CAUSES OF THE COLLAPSE 349 other healthy ones. But this

[33]
corresponds entirely to a humaneness which, in order not to hurt one individual, lets hundreds of others

[31]
perish. The demand that for de- fective people the propagation of an equally defective off- spring be made

[33]
impossible is a demand of clearest reason and in its planful execution it means the most humane act of mankind.

[33]
It will spare undeserved suffering to millions of unfortunates, but in the future it will lead to an increas-

[32]
ing improvement of health on the whole. The determina- tion to proceed in this direction will also put up a dam

[31]
against the further spreading of venereal diseases. For here, if necessary, one will have to proceed to the

[33]
pitiless isolation of incurably diseased people; a barbaric measure for one who was unfortunate

[32]
enough to be stricken with it, but a blessing for the contemporaries and for posterity. The temporary pain of

[33]
a century may and will redeem millenniums from suffering. The fight against syphilis and its pacemaker, prostitu-

[33]
tion, is one of the most colossal tasks of mankind, colossal for the reason that it does not involve the solution of

[32]
a single question in itself, but rather the abolition of quite a series of evils which, as their consecutive

[33]
symptoms, give the cause for this disease. For the illness of the body is here only the result of an illness of

[33]
moral, social, and racial instincts. If this fight, by reason of inertia or also cowardice, is not fought out, then one should

[33]
look upon the nations five hundred years from now. Then one would be able to find only a few images of God, without

[33]
deliberately insulting the All Highest. But how, in the old Germany, had one tried to deal with this plague? Upon

[31]
quiet examination there results a really distressing answer to this. In the circles of the government one

[30]
certainly knew the terrible ravages of this illness very well, though one was perhaps not quite able to

[31]
visualize 350 MEIN KAMPF the consequences; but in the fight against it one failed completely, and instead of

[34]
thoroughgoing reforms one preferred to take miserable means. One doctored about with the disease and one let

[31]
the causes be causes. One subjected the individual prostitute to a medical examina- tion,

[34]
supervised her as well as might be possible, and in case of an ascertained illness put her into some hospital,

[33]
from which, after being outwardly cured, she was let loose again on the rest of mankind. Of course, one had introduced

[33]
a 'protective paragraph, 9 according to which a person who was not quite healthy or cured had under penalty to

[33]
avoid sexual intercourse. This measure is certainly right in itself, but in its practical execution it fails

[33]
almost completely. First, the woman, in case she is met by misfortune in this way, solely in conse- quence of

[32]
our, or rather of her, education, will in most cases refuse to let herself be dragged into the courtroom (under

[33]
accompanying circumstances which are certainly often embarrassing) as a witness against the wretched thief of her health.

[33]
Just to her this is of little use; anyhow, in most cases, she will be the one who has to suffer most from this; because

[33]
she is hit much harder by the contempt of her heartless surroundings than would be the case with the man. But finally, imagine

[33]
her situation if the conveyer of the disease is her own husband. Is she to put him on trial? Or what else, then, is

[34]
she to do? But in the case of the man the fact is added that he unfortunately runs only too often into the way

[34]
of this plague after ample consumption of liquor, as in this state he is least in a position to judge the qualities

[32]
of his 4 beauty ' ; a fact that is only too well known to the prostitute who is sick, anyhow, and that, for this reason,

[33]
causes her always to fish for men in this ideal condition. But the end is that he, disagreeably surprised later on,

[34]
is not able to remember his one-time compassionate benefactress, despite frantic THE CAUSES OF THE COLLAPSE

[33]
351 reflections, something that must not be surprising in a city like Berlin or even Munich. To this is added further

[33]
that the persons involved are frequently visitors from the pro- vinces who in any case face the whole humbug

[33]
of the big cities with complete perplexity. Finally, however, who is able to know whether he is sick or healthy?

[31]
Do not numerous cases occur where an apparently cured person suffers relapses and now causes the most

[34]
terrible evil, without himself being aware of it in the end? Thus the practical effect of this protection by the legal

[33]
penalty of a guilty infection is in reality equal to naught. Exactly the same can be said of the control of

[33]
the prosti- tutes, and finally also the cure itself is still uncertain and doubtful even today. Only one thing

[31]
is certain : the disease spreads more and more despite all the preventive measures of that time. By this,

[33]
however, the ineffectiveness of these measures is proved in the most striking way. For everything that was done

[33]
besides this was as ridicu- lous as it was insufficient. The fight against the prostitu- tion of the people's soul failed

[32]
on the entire line; that means more rightly that here one did nothing at all. But he who wants to understand this

[34]
easily need only study the statistical basic facts about the spreading of this plague, compare its growth during the last

[33]
hundred years, and try to imagine this further development and he really would have the simple-mindedness of an ass

[31]
if then an uncomfortable chill did not run down his spine. The weakness and the half-heartedness with which even then one

[32]
defined one's attitude towards such a terrible symptom can be evaluated as a visible sign of the

[33]
decay of a people. When the energy for the fight for one's own health is no longer present, the right of living in this world

[33]
of strength begins gradually to withdraw. It belongs really only to the powerful 'whole' and not to the weak 'half/ 352 MEIN KAMPF

[33]
One of the most visible symptoms of the old Reich's decay was the slow sinking of the general level of culture; by

[32]
culture I do not mean what is called today by the word 'civilization.' The latter seems to be, on the contrary,

[32]
rather an enemy of true spiritual and living levels. As early as before the turn of the century an

[33]
element began to push its way into our att which up to that time could be looked upon as entirely alien

[31]
and unknown. Per- haps in previous times errors of taste happened some- times, but the cases involved were

[32]
artistic derailments to which posterity at least gave a certain historical value, rather than products of a

[32]
degeneration which was no longer artistic at all but rather senseless. Through them the political collapse, which

[30]
later on, of course, became better visible, began to announce its arrival in the cultural field. The

[29]
bolshevism of art is the only cultural form of life, Here Hitler states, without philosophical

[34]
elaboration, the doctrine which some groups of German intellectuals accepted as a bridge across which the German

[33]
mind could pass to Na- tional Socialism. Civilization means the application of reason to life, a process which scored

[33]
its greatest triumphs while Germany was struggling to emerge from the debris of the Thirty Years' War Goethe, Schiller, Kant, not

[32]
to mention Lessing and Wieland, are reflections of the Western mind rather than original creations of the German soul.

[33]
Even the great medieval Empire was based upon the triumph of Chris- tianity. Therefore the patriot prefers

[33]
to seek out the 'life forces,' the irrational impulses, which seem to him more chat- acteristic of the German mind. This

[33]
decision is sometimes couched in desperate phraseology: 'When I hear the word culture,' wrote Hans Johst (the first

[31]
official Nazi playwright), 1 release the safety catch on my revolver.' And F. G. Jtinger that half-mad but gifted poet who

[32]
eventually found Hitlerism tale and unprofitable, and went to prison for having indited, THE CAUSES OF THE

[33]
COLLAPSE 353 and the only intellectual manifestation possible to bolshc- vism on the whole. He to whom this may seem

[32]
strange should only subject to an examination the art of those States which have had the good fortune of being

[33]
bolshevized, and to his horror he will observe the sickly excrescences of lunatics or of degenerate people

[31]
which since the turn of the century we have learned to know under the collective conception of cubism or

[33]
dadaism as the official art of those States. This phenomenon had become apparent even in the short dura- tion

[33]
of the Bavarian Soviet Republic. Even here one could see how all the official billposters, propaganda draw- ings

[33]
in the newspapers, etc., showed the stamp of not only political, but also that of cultural, decay. As little as one

[33]
could imagine about sixty years ago a political collapse of the greatness now arrived at, just as little

[33]
was a cultural breakdown thinkable as it began to show itself in futuristic and cubistic representations since

[33]
1900. Sixty years ago an exhibition of so-called dadaistic the most violent attack on the Party ever penned inside

[33]
Germany asks, 'Why do we need four walls? One wall is enough!' The wall is that against which the enemy is stood and shot. But one

[32]
is not quite sure that J linger isn't being ironical. In so far as the philosophers (Klages, Heidegger, Baumler) are

[32]
concerned, this development means a revival of certain aspects of early nineteenth-century idealism, with a

[33]
militaristic emphasis. (Cf. Mensch und Erdc, by Dietrich Klages.) Hitler's views, re-emphasized in his Munich art lecture of

[31]
1937, crystallize in the teaching that there is only one art German-Nordic art. All attempts to sunder painting, for

[33]
example, into various schools are mistaken. The most impor- tant exponent of these views is Professor Paul Schultze-

[30]
Naumburg, who achieved fame when he was appointed director 354 MEIN KAMPF 'experiences' would have seemed simply

[33]
impossible, and the sponsors would have been sent to the madhouse, while today they even preside in 'artists' unions.'

[33]
This plague could not have appeared at that time, because neither would public opinion have suffered it nor would

[33]
the State have looked on quietly. For it is an affair of the State that means of the government to prevent a people

[33]
from being driven into the arms of spiritual lunacy. For in lunacy such a development would end one day. For

[33]
on the day that this kind of art were actually to correspond to the general conception, one of the most severe

[33]
changes of mankind would have begun ; the backward development of the human brain would have begun with this, but one would

[32]
hardly be able to conceive the end. As soon, however, as from this point of view one lets pass before one's eyes the

[34]
development of our cultural life of the Weimar Art School after the Nazi triumph of 1930. He immediately caused

[33]
to be removed from the Weimar Museum all examples of expressionistic art, on the ground that this was an expression of

[33]
a mankind subnormal from the racial point of view. Later on he delivered what was then considered a startling address,

[31]
claiming that race dictated one's response to art, and that anyone who found esthetic pleasure in expres-

[30]
sionism was not a German. Schultze-Naumburg contends that an artist cannot help reproducing 'the most signal racial

[33]
characteristics of his own figure.' Therefore distortions, as practiced by the modernists, imply that the painter

[31]
or sculptor is himself deformed in a racial sense. Many Nazis have accepted these teachings with a wry

[30]
grimace, pointing out that on such a basis the museums ought also to be cleansed of primitive, Egyptian,

[32]
Byzantine, and even Italian art. On the subject of music, Hitler has been equally categorical: To me

[33]
a single German military march is worth more than all the junk of these new musicians these people belong in

[33]
a sanatorium.' THE CAUSES OF THE COLLAPSE 355 in the past twenty-five years, one will be shocked at seeing how far

[33]
we already are on the way to this backward devel- opment. Everywhere we meet germs that represent the beginning

[34]
of excrescences by which our culture is bound to perish sooner or later. Also, we are able to recognize in

[33]
them the symptoms of decay of a slowly rotting world. Woe to the nations which are no longer able to master this disease

[31]
! One was able to find such diseases in almost all domains of art and general culture in Germany. Here

[33]
everything seemed to have already passed the climax and to hurry towards the abyss. The theater sank visibly

[33]
deeper and it would probably have retired completely as a cultural factor even then, had not at least the Court

[32]
Theaters turned against this prostitution of art. If one leaves these and a few praiseworthy exceptions out of

[33]
account, the perform- ances of the stage were such that for the sake of the nation it would have been more useful

[33]
to avoid visiting them en- tirely.^- It was a sorrowful sign of inner decay that one no longer might send the young

[33]
people to most of these so- called 'abodes of art,' which was openly and shamelessly admitted with the general

[33]
warning of the penny arcades 1 Children are not admitted ! ' One should consider that one had to take such precau-

[33]
tions in those places which primarily should exist for the education of youth and not for the amusement of old blast

[33]
generations. What would the great dramatists of all times have said to such a rule and what, above all, about the cir-

[33]
cumstances which gave the causes for them? How would perhaps a Schiller have flared up and a Goethe have turned away

[33]
in indignation! However, what are Schiller, Goethe, or Shakespeare as compared with the 'heroes' of the new German

[33]
dramatic art? Old, worn-out, and outlived, nay, 'conquered' types. For this was the characteristic of this time: not that it

[31]
356 MEIN KAMPF itself produced only dirt; what is more, it sullied everything that was really great in the past. This is,

[32]
however, a symptom which one can see always at such times. The more villainous and wretched are the products of

[33]
a time and its people, the more one hates the witnesses of a former greater time and dignity. But most of

[33]
all in such times one would like to eliminate altogether the memory of the past of mankind, in order

[32]
to disguise thus, by the exclusion of every possibility of comparison, one's own trash as 'art.' For this

[32]
reason, the more wretched and miserable any new institution is, the more will it endeavor to extin- guish

[33]
even the last traces of past times, whereas any really valuable renovation of mankind can also continue,

[33]
with an easy mind, the good achievements of past generations, even often now tries to make them stand out. Then it has no

[32]
fear to fade perhaps as compared with the past, but for its own part it makes such a valuable contribution to the

[33]
general treasure of human culture that often, for the very evaluation of the latter, it wishes to keep

[33]
awake the memory of the former achievements in order to secure thus all the more the full understanding

[33]
of the present for the new donation. Only he who is not able to give anything valuable out of himself to

[34]
the world, but tries to act as though he wants to give it God knows what, will hate Yet oddly enough it is precisely Goethe who,

[33]
by reason of his bourgeois background, is today characteristic of the 'civi- lization' which the Nazi Revolution

[32]
discountenances. Some- times he has been hated because foreigners relish his poetry; sometimes he has been

[32]
tossed aside scornfully as the 'man without a musket.' The first generation of Nazi philosophers Rosenberg,

[33]
Klages still numbered him among the nation's great. The second generation no longer reads him. Hauer's attempt to make him

[32]
the 'prophet of the new German religion" has failed. THE CAUSES OF THE COLLAPSE 357 everything that has already been

[32]
given and would most of all like to deny it or even to destroy it. t This may be said not only for 'novelties' in the

[31]
domain of general culture, but also for those of politics. Revolutionary new movements, the more

[33]
inferior they themselves are, the more will they hate the old form. Also here one can see how the striving to

[32]
make one's own trash appear as something leads to blind hatred towards the superior good of the past. As long as, for

[33]
example, the historical memory of a Frederick the Great has not died, a Friedrich Ebert is only able to create

[33]
moderate astonishment. The hero of Sans Souci is to the former barkeeper of Bremen approximately like

[33]
the sun is to the moon. Only when the rays of the sun are gone is the moon able to shine. There- fore, the hatred

[33]
of all new moons of humanity towards their fixed stars is only too understandable. In political life such naughts

[33]
usually, if Fate throws the reign tempo- rarily into their laps, not only soil and stain the past with untiring zeal, but

[33]
they also withdraw themselves, by ex- treme measures, from general criticism. As an example for this the protective

[33]
legislation of the Republic may be considered. If, therefore, any new idea, a new doctrine, a view of

[33]
life or also a political as well as an economic movement tries to deny the entire past, or wants to

[32]
deride it and to make it valueless, for this reason alone one has to be extremely cautious and

[32]
mistrusting. In most cases the reason for This attack on Ebert, first President of the Republic, is entirely in the

[34]
spirit of the conservative opposition, which forgot that Ludendorff had said hopefully, 'Ebert will manage.' The laws

[31]
referred to were passed after the murder of Rathenau to protect the government and its officials against

[33]
arbitrary attacks from Rightist organizations. Spengler inveighs against them in much the same way. 358 MEIN KAMPF such hatred is

[33]
either one's own inferiority or even an evil intention in itself. A genuinely blissful renovation

[33]
of man- kind would always and forever have to continue to build in that place where the last foundation ends. It will not

[32]
have to be ashamed of using existing truths. The entire human culture, as well as man himself, is only the

[33]
result of one long single development, during which every genera- tion added to, and built in, its building stones.

[33]
The mean- ing and the aim of revolutions is not to wreck the entire building, but rather to take away unsuitable

[33]
stuff which has been badly fitted in and to continue to build on and add to the healthy spot that has been made free. Thus alone

[33]
will one be able and allowed to speak of a progress of mankind. In the other case the world is never redeemed

[33]
from chaos, as the right of rejection of the past would fall to every generation, and with this every genera- tion would

[29]
be allowed, as the presupposition for its own work, to destroy the works of the past. The saddening fact of the

[33]
deterioration of our culture of the pre-War time lay, however, not only in the complete impotency of

[34]
the artistic and generally cultural creative force, but rather in the hatred with which the memory of the greater

[33]
past was soiled and extinguished. In nearly all domains of art, and especially of the theater and of literature,

[32]
one began to produce less important novelties at the turn of the century, in order, however, to deride

[31]
instead the best old creations and to present them as inferior and conquered, as though this period of the most shameful

[33]
inferiority would be at all able to 'conquer' anything. Out of this striving to remove the past out of the sight

[33]
of the present, the evil intention of these 'apostles' of the future could clearly and distinctly be seen. From this one

[32]
should have recognized that one had to deal, not with certain cultural intentions, even though they were wrong, but with

[30]
a process of destruction of the basis of culture as a whole, THE CAUSES OF THE COLLAPSE 359 and with a

[32]
ridiculing of sound art appreciation, made possible by this and with the intellectual preparation for

[30]
political bolshevism. For if the time of Pericles appears incorporated in the Parthenon, so does the

[33]
bolshevistic present in a cubistic grimace. In this connection one has also to point to the cowardice which

[33]
again becomes visible through this of part of our people which by virtue of its education and its position should have

[33]
been obliged to make front against this cul- tural disgrace. Out of pure fear of the clamor of these bolshevistic

[33]
art apostles who most violently attacked and nailed down as an old-fashioned philistine everyone who did not

[32]
want to recognize in them the crown of creation, one renounced any serious resistance and gave in to what

[33]
seemed inevitable after all. One was seized with genuine fear of being denounced for lack of understanding by

[30]
these half-wits or scoundrels; as though it were a^disgrace not to understand the products of intellectual

[33]
degenerates or cunning deceivers. These disciples of culture, however, The hatred of expressionism which had

[33]
its roots in Nietzsche is bound up in Hitler's mind with admiration foi Wagner's writings on art. The composer of Gotierddmmerung

[31]
was a great musician, but he was in some ways a philistine; and it was against that philistinism that Nietzsche

[30]
protested bitterly. Speaking in Dresden in 1848, Wagner said: 'What is the German thing? It is, it must be, the right thing!' In the

[32]
apotheosis of Germanism which Wagner represents, Chamber- lain found a living justification of his theories. And through

[33]
Chamberlain (whom he once met in Bayreuth, and from whom he received an emphatic endorsement) Hitler has learned how to

[32]
expound Wagner. In a Wagnerian universe, there is room for expressionism (which the war experience greatly

[31]
furthered) because there is no nakedness of soul in Wagnerianism. There is only soulfulness a great

[33]
quality, but one tinged constantly in the damp that rises from the waters of banality. 360 MEIN KAMPF had a very simple

[33]
means to stamp their nonsense into God knows how enormous an affair by presenting to the astonished world as so-called

[33]
'inner experience' any unin- telligible and visibly crazy stuff, taking in this cheap man- ner the word of reply

[33]
from the mouths of most people at the start. For there was no reason to doubt that this also could be an inner experience, but

[34]
one could doubt whether it was permissible to put before the same world the hal- lucinations of insane people or

[32]
criminals. The works of a Moritz von Schwind or of a Boecklin were also an 'inner experience' at that, of artists

[33]
endowed with the grace of God, and not of fools. But here one could so well study the miserable cowardice of

[33]
our so-called ' intelligentsia ' which shuns every serious resistance against this poisoning of the sound instinct

[30]
of our people and left it to the people itself to be content with this impudent nonsense. In order not to be

[33]
considered lacking in art understanding, one took then every derision of art into the bargain in order to

[32]
become finally actually uncertain in the judgment of good or bad. Taken all in all, these were signs of

[33]
a world getting worse and worse. As a doubtful symptom the following has to be stated : During the nineteenth century

[33]
our cities began to lose more and more the character of 'culture places' in order to sink to mere 'human

[32]
settlements.' The weak connection which our present-day proletariat of our big cities has with its dwelling-place is just the

[29]
consequence of the fact that here really only the accidental local place of residence of the

[32]
individual is involved and nothing else. This is partly connected with the frequent change of residence,

[33]
caused by the social conditions, which does not grant sufficient time to man for closer connection with his city, THE CAUSES

[32]
OF THE COLLAPSE 361 and partly the cause of this must be sought also in the general cultural unimportance and

[33]
poverty of our present cities themselves. Still at the time of the Wars of Liberation, the German cities were not

[33]
only few in number but also modest in size. The few really big cities were for the greatest part Court cities, and as

[33]
such they possessed nearly always a certain cultural value and mostly also a certain artistic picture. The few

[33]
places of more than fifty thousand inhabitants were, as compared with cities of the same population today,

[34]
rich in scientific and artistic treasures. When Munich counted sixty thousand souls, it began to become one of the first

[32]
German art centers ; today nearly every manufac- turing place has reached, if not even exceeded, this figure

[33]
many times, without, however, sometimes being able to call its own even the most humble of genuine values. Pure

[34]
collections of flats and dwelling-houses, nothing more. How, with such lack of importance, a special attachment to these places

[33]
can originate must be a riddle. Nobody will be specially attached to a city which has nothing else to

[31]
offer than what any other city has; one which lacks any individual touch and where everything is

[34]
carefully avoided that could even look like art or something similar. But, as if this were not enough, the really

[33]
big cities also become poorer and poorer in works of art, in proportion with the rising increase in the number of

[32]
population. They appear more and more polished off and they present ex- actly the same picture, though on a

[33]
larger scale, as the small and miserable factory towns. What modern times added to the cultural contents of our big

[32]
cities was com- pletely insufficient. All our cities feast on the glory and the treasures of the past. It takes from the

[32]
Munich of today everything that was created under the reign of Ludwig I ; one will be shocked at seeing how poor the

[32]
addi- tion of important artistic creations since that time is. The 368 MEIN KAMPF same applies to Berlin and to most of the

[31]
other big cities. The essential thing, however, is nevertheless the follow- ing: our present big cities have no

[33]
monuments, dominating the entire picture of the city, which could somehow be called the symbol of the time.

[30]
But this was the case in the cities of old, since nearly all of them had a special monument of its pride. The

[34]
characteristic of the antique city was not found in the private buildings, but in the monuments of the community

[32]
which seemed destined not for the moment but for eternity, for they were supposed to reflect not the riches of the

[29]
individual owner but rather the greatness and the importance of the community. Thus monuments

[32]
originated which were suited to attach the individual in- habitant to his city in a manner which

[34]
today seems to us sometimes almost incomprehensible. For what he had before his eyes were not the miserable

[33]
houses of private owners but the magnificent buildings of the whole commun- ity. Compared with them the living house

[33]
was actually reduced to an insignificant object of secondary importance. For, only when comparing

[31]
the dimensions of the antique State buildings with the contemporary private houses will one understand the

[34]
overpowering sweep and force of this stress on the viewpoint to allot the first place to the public works. What today we admire

[33]
in the wreckage and fields of ruins of the old world as the few still outstanding colos- Buses are not business palaces

[34]
of the time but temples and State buildings; that means works the owner of which was the public. Even in the splendor of the later

[33]
Rome, first place was not taken by the villas and the palaces of individual citizens, but by the temples and

[33]
the thermae, the All this has now been changed. Munich has its Kunsthalle, Berlin its new Chancellery and Olympic Village.

[32]
Millions have been spent on such buildings, and unlimited millions mav still be poured out. i THE CAUSES OF THE COLLAPSE 363

[33]
staia, circuses, aqueducts, basilicas, etc., of the State; that means of the entire people/' Even the Germanic

[33]
Middle Ages maintained this point of view, though also under quite different conceptions of art as the leading principle.

[34]
That which in antiquity found its expression in the Acropolis or in the Pantheon, now clad itself in the forms of the Gothic

[33]
cathedrals. Like giants they stood out over the swarm of small frameworks, wooden or brick buildings of the medieval town, and thus

[33]
they became symbols which today still define the character and the picture of these places, while at their sides

[34]
the tene- ment-house blocks climb higher and higher. Cathedrals, town halls, and grain markets, as well as watch-towers, are the visible

[31]
sign of a conception which ultimately cor- responded to that of antiquity. But how truly miserable the

[33]
relation between State and private buildings has become today. If Berlin were to meet the fate of Rome, then

[30]
the coming generations could one day admire the department stores of some Jews, and the hotels of some

[32]
corporations the most imposing works of our time, as the characteristic expression of the culture of our days.

[34]
Compare, therefore, the unfavorable disparity that prevails, even in a city like Berlin, between the build-

[33]
ings of the Reich and those of finance and commerce. Even the amount of money allotted to the State buildings is

[33]
in most cases truly ridiculous and insufficient. No works are created for eternity, but at the most those for

[33]
the momentary need. No higher idea is at all predominant in this. The Schloss of Berlin was at the time it was built

[32]
quite a different work from perhaps the new Library in the frame of the present. While one single battleship

[33]
repre- sented a value of around sixty millions, hardly half of this amount was granted for the first magnificent building

[33]
of the Reich, which was intended for eternity, the Reichstag Building. Indeed, when the question of the interior deco- 364 MEIN KAMPF

[33]
ration was decided upon, the 'high' House voted against the use of stone, it ordered the walls trimmed with plaster;

[33]
and this time the 'parliamentarians' had acted correctly for once: plaster heads do not belong between walls of stone.

[32]
Thus our cities of the present lack the outstanding symbol of national community, and hence it is no wonder that the

[33]
community does not see any symbol of itself in its cities. This must lead to a spiritual dullness which mani- fests

[32]
itself in practice in a wholesale indifference of the present-day city dweller towards the lot of his

[33]
city. This also is a sign of our declining culture and of our general collapse. The time is suffocated

[33]
in petty expedi- ency, in other words, in the service of money. Thus one must not be surprised if under such

[33]
a deity little under- standing for heroism remains. The present only harvests that which the immediate past has sown. All

[30]
these symptoms of decay are ultimately only conse- quences of the lack of a certain, commonly

[33]
acknowledged view of life and of the general uncertainty in the judgment, and the definition of an attitude

[33]
towards the various great questions of the time, resulting from it. Therefore, everything, beginning with education,

[33]
is half-hearted and wavering, shuns responsibility and ends thus in cowardly tolerance of even recognized

[31]
evils. Dreamy humaneness becomes the fashion, and by a weak surrender to the ex- crescences and in sparing the

[33]
individuals, one sacrifices in turn the future of millions.-' How much the general destruction spread is also

[33]
appar- ent when looking at the religious conditions before the War. Here too, uniform and effective convictions,

[33]
through a view of life, had long been lost in great parts of the nation. In this the adherents, freeing themselves officially from

[34]
the Church, play a less important r61e than those who are THE CAUSES OF THE COLLAPSE 365 indifferent as a whole. While both

[32]
denominations keep up missions in Asia and Africa, in order to lead new followers to the doctrine (an

[32]
activity, which, compared with the advance of the Mohammedan faith, can show only very modest successes), in

[31]
Europe proper they lose millions and again millions of adherents of inner homogeneousness, who now face

[31]
religious life either as strangers or at least walk ways of their own. The consequences, especially as regards

[32]
morality, are unfavorable ones. Remarkable is also the more and more violent fight begun

[32]
against the dogmatic fundamentals of the various churches, without which, however, the practical existence of

[33]
a religious faith is unthinkable in this world of man. The great masses of a people do not consist of philosophers,

[33]
and it is just for them that faith is frequently the sole basis of a moral view of life. The various substitutes

[32]
have not proved so useful in their success that one would be able to see in them a useful exchange for the

[34]
former religious creeds. But if religious doctrine and faith are really meant to seize the great masses, then the absolute

[32]
authority of the contents of this faith is the basis of all effectiveness. What, then, the customary style of

[33]
living is for general This is the reverse of 'religion is the opium of the people. 1 Rauschning (cf . his Revolution

[32]
des Nihilismus) has pointed out Hitler's deep respect for the Catholic Church and in particular for the Society of

[33]
Jesus. In this he resembles Auguste Comte, who once proposed a liaison between Positivism and Rome.

[33]
Both sundered their admiration from any kind of belief. Hitler praises the ability (as he sees it) of the Church to

[33]
keep on resolutely proclaiming an article of faith, however powerful the arguments arrayed against it may be.

[34]
If the nation can build dogmas about its new 'myth' and propagate them aa stubbornly, it may (so it is thought) give Germany

[33]
a new faith, which the masses will cherish as tenaciously as they have until latterly cherished Christianity. 366 MEIN KAMPF

[32]
life, without which certainly hundreds of thousands ol well-bred people would live sensibly and wisely, but mil- lions of

[31]
others certainly would not, the organic laws are for the State and dogma is for religion. Only by this is the

[33]
wavering and infinitely interpretable, purely spiritual idea definitely limited and brought

[31]
into a shape, without which it could never become faith. In the other case, the idea would never grow beyond a

[31]
metaphysical conception, in short, beyond a philosophical opinion. The attack upon the dogma in itself

[33]
resembles, therefore, very strongly also the fight against the general legal fundamentals of the State, and, just

[32]
as the latter would find its end in a com- plete anarchy of the State, thus the other in a worthless religious

[32]
nihilism. But for the politician the estimation of the value of a religion must be decided less by the

[33]
deficiencies which it perhaps shows than by the presence of a visibly better substitute. As long as there is no

[34]
apparent substitute, that which is present can be demolished only by fools or by criminals. Of course, not the smallest

[33]
share of the guilt of the unenjoyable religious conditions lies with those who burden the religious conception too much

[33]
with worldly things, An attack on the Center Party, the official spokesmen for which were often priests and prelates. The fact

[33]
that a Catholic Party entered into a coalition with Social Democracy in the Reich and in several States

[32]
was described as a 'betrayal' of Christian principles not only by Right radicals with axes to grind, but also by a

[33]
number of wealthy and conservative Catholics. As a matter of fact, that collaboration not only had the sanction

[29]
of the highest ecclesiastical authorities in the land but was unimpeachable on any basis. The

[34]
'liberalism' of the 'political Catholics' was a favorite shibboleth among Jew baiters. THE CAUSES OF THE COLLAPSE

[33]
367 thus bringing it frequently into a quite unnecessary con- flict with so-called exact science. Here the victory

[33]
will, though after a serious struggle, nearly always fall to the latter, but religion will suffer serious damage in the eyes

[33]
of all those who are not able to raise themselves above purely outward knowledge. But worse than all are

[34]
the devastations which are brought about by the abuse of religious convictions for political purposes. One can

[32]
really not proceed too sharply against those wretched profiteers who like to see in religion an instrument which may

[33]
render them political, or rather com- mercial, services. These impudent liars, however, shout their creed into the world with

[30]
a stentorian voice so that the other sinners can surely hear it, but not in order to die for it, if

[33]
necessary, but in order to live better. For one single political job they offer the meaning of an entire

[32]
faith for sale; for ten parliamentary mandates they ally themselves with the Marxist mortal enemies of all

[32]
reli- gion and for one minister's seat they would certainly also marry the Devil, in so far as the latter would not be

[30]
deterred by a remnant of decency. If in pre-War Germany the religious life had for many an

[31]
after-taste, this was attributable to the misuse which was inflicted on Christianity on the part of a

[32]
so-called 1 Christian ' party, as well as to the impudence with which one tried to identify the Catholic faith with

[33]
a political party. This substitution was a fatality which perhaps brought parliamentary seats to a number

[30]
of good-for-nothings, but injury to the Church. The result, however, had to be borne by the whole nation, as the

[33]
consequences of the loosening of religious life caused by this occurred just in a time when everything

[33]
began to give way and to change, anyhow, and when the traditional fundamentals of behavior and moralitv threat-

[33]
ened to collapse. 368 MEIN KAMPF This, too, represented cracks and rifts in our national body which might well be harmless as long as

[33]
no special strain occurred, but which were bound to cause disaster whenever, by the impetus of great events, the question

[31]
of the inner solidarity of the nation became of decisive importance. ' Also in the field of

[33]
politics, when looked at with observant eyes, there were evils which might and must appear as symptoms of a coming decay

[33]
of the Reich, provided no improvement or change were soon brought about. The aimlessness of German domestic and foreign

[32]
politics was visible to anyone who did not deliberately wish to be blind. The business of compromise

[33]
seemed to agree most of all with Bismarck's opinion that ' politics is the art of the pos- sible.' Now, however, there was

[32]
just a slight difference between Bismarck and German chancellors who followed, which permitted the former to drop such a

[32]
remark about the nature of politics, while the same opinion out of the mouths of his successors was bound to

[33]
assume quite a different significance. For Bismarck only wished to express with this sentence that, in order

[31]
to reach a certain political goal, all possibilities may be applied, or, one can proceed according to all

[32]
possibilities; but his successors saw in this utterance only the solemn exemption from the necessity of

[33]
having political thoughts or even aims at all. But political aims were really no longer present at that time for

[30]
the leading authorities of the Reich; because for this the neces- sary foundation of a view of life and the

[33]
necessary clarity on the laws of inner development of political life as a whole were missing. There

[33]
were not a few to whom the prospects in this direction appeared dim and who castigated the planless- ness and thoughtlessness

[33]
of the policy of the Reich, and THE CAUSES OF THE COLLAPSE 369 were, accordingly, very well aware of its inner

[32]
weakness and hollowness, but they were only the outsiders of political life; the official authorities of the

[33]
government passed by the observations of a Houston Stewart Chamberlain just as indifferently as this is still the case

[33]
with us today. These people are too stupid to think for themselves, and too vain to learn which is necessary from others.

[33]
Thus one sees incorporated in almost every councillor of the ministry an atom of that eternal truth which

[32]
caused Oxenstierna to exclaim: 'The world is ruled only by a fraction of wisdom.' (This is no longer the case since

[32]
Germany has become a republic. Therefore, it has also been forbidden by the law for the Protection of the

[33]
Republic to believe, or even to discuss, anything like that. But Oxenstierna was lucky that he lived at that

[33]
time and not in this wise republic of today.) As early as in pre-War times, that institution was recog- nized

[31]
in which the strength of the Reich was to incorporate itself as the greatest weakness: the parliament, the Reich- stag. Here

[33]
cowardice and irresponsibility presented them- selves in a rarely finished type. It is one of

[32]
the greatest thoughtless observations which one may hear not infrequently, especially in these days, that in Germany

[33]
parliamentarism 'has failed since the Revolution.' By this the appearance is only too easily given as

[32]
though this had perhaps not been the case before the Revolution. But this institution can in reality have no

[33]
other effect than a devastating one and this at a time when most people, still clad with blinders, did not or did not want

[31]
to see anything. For, that Germany actually was crushed was not a little due to this institution, but that the

[29]
catastrophe had not occurred before cannot be con- sidered as the merit of the Reichstag, but was

[33]
attributable to the resistance which, still in the years of peace, con- fronted the activity of this gravedigger

[33]
of the German nation and the German Reich. 370 MEIN KAMPF Out of the vast number of devastating evils which came forth from, or were

[33]
caused by, this institution, 1 will point only to a single one which, however, exhibits most of all Ac inner nature

[33]
of this most irresponsible institution of all times. The terrible half measures and weakness of the political

[34]
guidance of the Reich in domestic and foreign affairs was due primarily to the working of the Reichstag; it became one

[32]
of the chief causes of the political collapse. Half measure was everything that in any way was sub- ject to the

[31]
influence of this parliament, no matter how one looks at it. Half measure and weak was the Reich's policy of

[29]
alliances in foreign politics. While thus one wanted to preserve peace, one was bound to drive

[34]
unresistingly towards war. Half measure was furthermore the policy towards Poland. The restraint of this passage is

[32]
noteworthy. Prior to the War, the energetic Germanizing of Poland Was fostered by such men as Dr. Hugenberg,

[34]
afterward leader of the Nationalist Party and pivot man in the deal which put Hitler in power. Disgusted with the failure

[32]
of the pre-War Prussian government to stamp out all Polish opposition, Hugenberg resigned as an official, became

[33]
a director of Krupp, and there made himself the systematic mole who ate away the financial underpinning

[32]
of large portions of the German press and then boasted that he could make Germany read whatever he wanted it to read.

[31]
After the War he took up the same work anew. Sums gathered from Chambers of Commerce, etc., to 'fight Bolshevism' were

[31]
diverted into the purchases of daily and weekly papers until Hugenberg, as the controlling influence in the

[33]
Scherl-Verlag, had under his thumb a multitude of German metropolitan and provincial dailies. He also acquired

[33]
UFA, largest German film concern, which has more recently become the property of the German government. After 1922 when

[33]
the Polish uprisings, intended to wrest from Germany more territory than the peace treaties had taken THE CAUSES

[32]
OF THE COLLAPSE 971 One irritated without, however, ever proceeding seriously. The result was neither a

[31]
reconciliation with the Poles nor a German victory, but instead enmity with Russia. Half measure was the

[31]
solution of the question of Alsace- from her were in full swing Germany was again characterized by a

[31]
resentment of Polish activities which often contrasted strangely with efforts to regulate the trade and

[33]
minority problems. The Corridor, a strip of territory separating East Prussia from the main portion of the Reich

[33]
and leading to the new harbor city of Gdynia, was considered a major political problem, and the fate of

[33]
Danzig was kept dangling before the consciousness of the League of Nations. But when Hitler came to power, an attempt was made

[33]
to counter Polish opposition by establishing friendly relations with that country. It was pointed out that after all both

[34]
countries enjoyed the blessings of dictatorship. Many predicted that the Poles and the Germans would march arm in arm to the conquest

[32]
of Russia. The Poles, however, were playing a difficult and crafty game. For a time they appeared to have

[34]
rather the better of it. They kept a protecting hand over the Polish minority in Danzig, and at the same time did

[31]
not relax the pressure that was brought to bear on German minority groups in Poland. It was the annexation of

[33]
Austria that first tipped the scales in Hitler's favor. Almost immediately there appeared in various parts of

[33]
the diplomatic world a ' memorandum ' purporting to be a plan for a 'Catholic group' of States in Central Europe,

[33]
running from Italy through Croatia and Hungary to Slovakia and Poland. When the Czechoslovakian crisis was settled by

[32]
giving Hitler what he wanted, the Poles acted quickly, but were unable to secure what, perhaps, they most needed

[34]
a clear route tc the South. They did acquire the Teschen region, which is doubtless the richest morsel taken from the State once so

[32]
hope- fully created by Masaryk and Wilson. But the inability of Slovakia and Hungary to reach a

[33]
modus vivendi blocked any further progress. Most of the inhabitants ceded to Hungary changed their allegiance

[33]
most unwillingly; and on both sides 372 MEIN KAMPF Lorraine. Instead of smashing with brutal fists once and for all times the head

[32]
of the French hydra, or granting equal rights to the Alsatian, one did neither. (One was not even able to do so,

[32]
because in the ranks of the greatest of the new boundaries the strange phenomenon of a National Socialism

[33]
making great headway among the peasants though they were Slavs or Maygars completely changed the situa- tion. The swastika

[32]
became a popular symbol. To some extent this was due to propaganda, but a more important factor was the

[32]
feeling that under Hitler agriculture would be more prosper- ous, Jewry at a disadvantage, and all Leftist

[32]
theories of social improvement for the masses abrogated. Poland tried very hard to effect the separation of

[33]
Ruthenia from Czechoslovakia. So far it has failed. Far more significant, however, is the fact that the collapse

[31]
of Prague as a center of military strength has radically altered the position of Poland. Its major

[30]
natural resources and its armament manufactories are in the West, within range of German heavy

[33]
artillery. Therefore its very good army (many rank its infantry with the best in Europe) was left dangling by

[32]
a thread, and it had perforce to seek safety by trying to improve relations with Russia. The implications of the

[30]
Ukrainian question have already been discussed, but one may add in addition that German control of

[32]
Czechoslovakia can make this a haven for Ukrainian separatist agitators. Therefore Poland is

[31]
imperiled. It is difficult to see why Warsaw could desire the dismemberment of the State on its southern

[33]
boundaries, even if Teschen was a rich and long- coveted prize. Yet it could hardly be to Germany's advantage to

[34]
threaten Poland with war. The cost of such a struggle, in treasure and possibly also in prestige, would not compensate for

[32]
the possible gains, among which reacquisition of the Silesian coal and ore fields may be listed. After the War of 1870,

[30]
Alsace-Lorraine was incorporated in the new German Empire; it eventually became an

[32]
Imperial domain. The Alsatians did not conceal their desire for au- THE CAUSES OF THE COLLAPSE 373 parties there sat

[32]
also the greatest traitors to the country. In the Center Party, for instance, Herr Wetterl6.) But all this would still have been

[34]
bearable if that power had not also fallen victim to the general half measures, that power on the existence of

[33]
which finally the existence of the Reich depended : the army. The way in which the so-called 'German Reichstag' had sinned

[31]
here is enough alone to burden it for all times with the curse of the German nation. For the most wretched

[33]
tonomy, which in many cases was more strictly a wish to return to France. Bismarck wisely refused to exert

[33]
untoward pressure, believing that after a few generations the feeling would die out of its own accord. Nevertheless,

[30]
he permitted himself to be involved in the Kulturkampf, and therewith also in ambitious programs for

[33]
Protestantizing Catholic Alsace. The University of Strassburg was the symbol of the 'cultural reconstruction'

[32]
sponsored by Prussia. Naturally the clergy now led the opposition, having in Abb6 Haegy a highly gifted

[33]
leader. When the Kulturkampf was over, the Center Party took up the task of cementing relationships between Alsace and

[31]
the Reich. It was sometimes sabotaged by the Prussian bu- reaucracy and the army (witness theZabern

[33]
incident of 1913), but was none the less so effective on the whole that the vast majority of Alsatians fought loyally

[30]
for Germany during the War and afterward became autonomists as a result of their opposi- tion to the

[33]
annexation by France decreed by the Treaty of Versailles. Hitlerism abruptly broke off this development, although

[33]
as a result of the Blum policies a new wave of opposi- tion arose during 1936. The Abb6 Wetterl6 was the leader of

[32]
those who after the War welcomed enthusiastically the coming of the French. Very considerable Nazi

[33]
propaganda efforts were uncovered in Alsace, especially in Strassburg, during 1938. The appeal seems to have been

[32]
made on the basis of relative economic prosperity. Peasants in particular were induced to

[33]
believe that a millennium had dawned across the Rhine. 374 MEIN KAMPF reasons, these parliamentary party rascals

[33]
have stolen and struck from the hands of the nation the weapon of self- preservation, the only protection of the freedom and

[33]
inde- pendence of our people. If today the graves of Flanders Field were to open, out of them would rise the bloody

[33]
accusers, hundreds of thousands of the best young Germans, who were driven into the arms of death, badly and half-trained, due to

[33]
the unscrupulousness of these parliamentary criminals; the fatherland has lost them and millions of cripples and dead,

[30]
simply and solely in order to make possible for a few hundred traitors to the people, political

[30]
wirepulling, extor- tion, or even the rattling forth of doctrinary theories. While Jewry, through its Marxist and

[31]
democratic press, proclaimed to the whole world the lie of German 'mili- tarism' and thus strove to incriminate

[32]
Germany with all possible means, the same parties refused any large-scale training of the strength of the German

[33]
people. Thus the enormous crime which was brought about by this must at once become clear to everyone who even stops

[31]
to think that in case of a coming war the entire nation would have to take up arms, that therefore by the

[33]
rascality of these nice representatives of their own so-called 'representation of the people ' millions of

[33]
Germans would be driven towards the enemy with bad, insufficient, or half-finished training. But even if one does not

[29]
take into consideration at all the consequences of the brutal and rude unscrupulousness of the

[33]
parliamentary panders, brought about in this manner, one must nevertheless not forget that the shortage of trained

[30]
soldiers could easily lead, at the beginning of a war, The pre-War Reichstag had the power to veto budget ap-

[33]
propriations. It is not correct to say that it hampered the development of the army of the ill-starred navy, though

[32]
certain extreme demands put foward by Pan-Germanists were not found acceptable. THE CAUSES OF THE COLLAPSE 375 to

[33]
losing that war, something that happened in the great World War in such a terrible manner. The loss of the fight for the freedom

[33]
and independence of the German nation is the result of the half measures and the weakness carried out even in peace

[33]
in drafting the entire force of the people for the defense of the fatherland. t If too few recruits were trained on

[34]
land, the same half measures were at work at sea, so that the weapon of na- tional self-preservation was made more or

[32]
less worthless. Unfortunately, however, here the heads of the navy them- selves were infected by this poison. The

[33]
tendency to build all ships, on the stocks, always a little smaller than the English ships launched from the stocks at the same time,

[33]
waa little farseeing and still less ingenious. A navy which from the beginning cannot be brought to the same level with its

[32]
prospective enemy, purely in terms of numbers, must try to replace the lack in numbers by the superior

[30]
fighting power of the single ships. It is the superior fighting power that matters and not a legendary

[31]
superior 'quality/ which is nonsense as long as it does not express itself in fighting power. In fact, modern

[32]
technique has now ad- vanced to such an extent and has arrived at so great a uniformity in the various

[30]
civilized States that it must be considered impossible to give to the ships of one power a

[33]
considerably greater fighting value than to the ships of the same tonnage of another State. But it is far less

[32]
con- ceivable to attain superiority with smaller displacement as compared with a greater. Indeed, the small

[34]
tonnage of the German ships could be brought about only at the expense of speed and armament. The phrase with which one now

[32]
tries to justify this fact shows, however, a very serious lack of logic on the part of the authority which was

[32]
responsible for this in peace 376 MEIN KAMPF times. For one explained that the material of the German guns was so

[33]
visibly superior to that of the British that the German 28 cm. gun barrel did not fall behind the British 30.5 cm. barrel in firing

[33]
efficiency!! But just for this reason it would have been the duty now also to change over to the 30.5 cm. cannon, as the goal

[33]
should not have been to reach the same, but a superior, fighting power. Otherwise the ordering of the 42 cm. mortar would

[33]
have been superfluous as the German 21 cm. mortar was in itself superior to any French high-angled cannon, present at

[33]
that time, but the forts would have fallen also before the 30.5 cm. cannon. The leaders of the land army thought correctly, but those

[33]
of the navy unfortunately did not. The abandonment of a superior effect of the artillery as well

[33]
as of a superior speed was founded entirely in the so-called 'idea of risk,' which was basically wrong. The heads

[31]
of the navy, by the very form of its construction, re- nounced the offensive and thus necessarily stressed the

[31]
defensive. But with this one also renounced ultimate suc- cess, which lies, and can lie forever, only in the

[33]
offensive. A ship with less speed and weaker armature will in most It would be difficult to buttress these assertions

[31]
with facts. It is surely not the fault of the Reichstag that the Admiralty adopted a type of gun later found

[33]
inadequate. As a matter of fact, not a few Reichstag delegates notably Matthias Erzberger were almost

[31]
pathetic in their efforts to induce Admiral von Tirpitz to speed up armament. The development of naval

[32]
aviation was urged in particular. But Tirpitz, who did not wish to commit himself to any instrument of war

[32]
until its efficiency had been established, was slow to act. In the end he was, of course, found to have guessed wrong.

[34]
Believing that the War would necessarily be of brief duration, he had supposed that the British fleet would attack in the North

[33]
Sea. and had not reckoned with the blockade. THE CAUSES OF THE COLLAPSE 377 cases be sent to the bottom by the speedier and

[32]
more heavily armed enemy with the firing distance which is more favorable to the latter. Quite a

[34]
number of our cruisers had to experience this in the bitterest manner. However, the War showed how absolutely wrong

[34]
was this opinion of the heads of the navy in peace time which, wherever possible, forced us to change the armature

[32]
of the old, or to improve that of the new, ships. But if in the battle of the Skagerrak the German ships had had the same

[33]
tonnage, the same armament, and the same speed as the British ships, then, under the hurricane of the better-hitting

[31]
German 38 cm, shells, the British fleet would have sunk into a watery grave. Japan at one time had carried out a

[32]
different policy for her navy. There one principally stressed the point of having in each single new ship a

[31]
superior fighting power against the prospective enemy. This corresponded to the possi- bility of

[31]
utilizing the navy in the offensive. While the leaders of the land] [army still kept themselves free from such

[32]
fundamentally wrong trains of thought, the navy, which unfortunately was represented ' parliamenta- rily ' in

[33]
a better way, succumbed also to the mentality of this institution. It was organized by halfway viewpoints and

[32]
was later on also used according to similar ones. What nevertheless appeared in the form of immortal

[29]
glory was attributable only to the solid German craftsmanship as well as to the ability and the

[33]
incomparable heroism of the various officers and crews. But if the former headquarters of the navy had also been

[31]
up to this in ingenuity, the sacri- fices would not have been in vain. Thus perhaps it was just the superior

[31]
parliamentary ability of the leading head of the navy in peace time that turned out to be its

[31]
misfortune, since, unfortunately also in its structure, instead of purely military viewpoints,

[33]
parliamentary viewpoints began to play the decisive r61e. The half measures and the weakness, as well as the scanty

[31]
378 MEIN KAMPF logic which is the parliamentary institutions 9 own, began to tint also the heads of the navy. As

[31]
already pointed out, the land army still refrained from such trains of thought, which were basically wrong. Especially the

[31]
colonel in the Great General Staff of that time, Ludendorff , led a desperate fight against the criminal half

[33]
measures and weakness with which the Reichstag faced the vital questions of the nation, and mostly denied them. If the battle which

[33]
this officer fought at that time was nevertheless futile, the fault rested half upon parlia- ment, but half upon the,

[33]
if possible, still more wretched attitude and weakness of the Reichs-Chancellor Bethmann- Hollweg. But this does not in the least

[34]
hinder the culprits of the German collapse from trying to attribute today the guilt to the very man who alone turned

[34]
against this negli- gent treatment of national interests. (One betrayal more or less never makes any difference to

[31]
these born wire- pullers.) He who thinks over all these sacrifices which were bur- dened upon the nation by the

[31]
criminal carelessness of these most unscrupulous men, he who leads before his eyes all the dead and the cripples,

[33]
sacrificed in vain, as well as the boundless disgrace and dishonor, the unspeakable misery which now has met us, and

[29]
he who knows that all this came only in order to open the way towards the minister's seat for a crowd of

[33]
unscrupulously pushing persons and job- hunters, will also understand that one can call these crea- tures really only

[34]
by words like scoundrel, villain, rascal, and criminal, because otherwise the meaning and the pur- pose of the existence

[32]
of these expressions in the usage of the language would be incomprehensible. For, in compari- son with these

[33]
traitors to the nation, every pimp is a gentle- man. . THE CAUSES OF THE COLLAPSE 379 But it is strange that all real shadow

[32]
sides of the old Germany caught the eye only whenever by this the inner solidarity of the nation had to

[31]
suffer injury. Indeed, in such cases, the disagreeable truths were simply shouted out to the great masses, while

[33]
otherwise one preferred shame- fully to pass by in silence many things, even partly to deny them. This was

[33]
the case whenever an improvement could perhaps have been carried out by public treatment of a question. In addition,

[31]
the authoritative parties of the government understood next to nothing of the value and the nature of

[33]
propaganda. That by propaganda, with permanent and clever application, even heaven can be palmed off on a people

[33]
as hell, and, the other way round, the most wretched life as paradise, this only the Jew knew, who then acted accordingly;

[34]
the German, or rather his government, had not the faintest idea of this. This was to take its most serious revenge during

[33]
the War. All the numerous evils of the German life before the War, as pointed out here, and others, were set off

[32]
also by many advantages. With a just examination one must even acknowledge that, to a great extent, the

[33]
other countries and peoples also called most of our ills their own, and that Before the War, Germany had relied in the main

[33]
on industrial rather than investment expansion. Branch plants were es- tablished in well-nigh all foreign countries; centers of

[33]
trade influence were built up, often at great cost. When the War was lost, it was argued that the friendship which had bound the Allied

[33]
countries together was a consequence of the financial ties which existed between them. A favorite thesis has been,

[34]
for example, that Germany's freedom from indebtedness to the 'bankers 9 had been a great disadvantage, since no one had

[33]
interests at stake inside her boundaries. German Jewish news- 380 MEIN KAMPF in many things they overshadowed us by far,

[32]
while they did not possess many of our actual advantages. The loremost of these advantages may be said,

[33]
among other things, to be the fact that the German people among nearly all European nations still tried most of all to pre- serve

[33]
the national character of its economy, and that, despite many evil premonitions, it was least of all subject

[32]
to the international finance control. A dangerous ad- vantage, however, which later on also became the

[32]
greatest instigator of the World War. If one sets aside this and many other facts, then three institutions stand out

[33]
among the vast number of the healthy sources of the nation's power which in their kind presented themselves as exemplary

[32]
as well as partly unexcelled. There was first the State form in itself and the dis- tinct stamp which it had received in the

[32]
Germany of modern times. Here one may set aside the various monarchs, who, as human beings, could not help being

[33]
subject to all weak- nesses which are usually visited upon this world and its children, for otherwise one would

[32]
really have to despair al- together of the present; for the representatives of the pres- ent regime, looked

[31]
upon just as personalities, are perhaps mentally and morally the most modest that one is able to

[34]
Imagine, even after prolonged reflection. He who measures the ' value' of the German Revolution with the value

[32]
and the greatness of the personalities which it has given to the German people since November, 1918, will cover his face

[30]
papermen and pacifists were (so ran the tale) employed to weaken the army of the fatherland. While they

[32]
undermined German resistance, their brethren outside stirred up the rest of the world against Germany. Doubtless no

[31]
astute Nazi leader has ever credited these hypotheses, which were designed for the consumption of the

[34]
infantile. THE CAUSES OF THE COLLAPSE 381 in shame before the judgment of posterity which one will not be able

[34]
to stop from talking by protective laws, etc., and which therefore will say what all of us nevertheless recognize today,

[32]
that is, that the brains and the virtues of our neo-German leaders are in the inverse proportion to the snouts and vices. The

[34]
monarchy was certainly estranged from many, es- pecially from the great masses of the people. This was the consequence of

[33]
the fact that the monarchs were not always surrounded let us say by the most brilliant, and particu- larly not by the most

[33]
honest, heads. Unfortunately, they partly preferred the flatterers rather than the straightfor- ward natures, and therefore

[33]
they were also ' instructed ' by flatterers. A very grave evil in a time when the world had undergone a great

[30]
change in many old opinions, a change which now naturally did not stop before the judgment of many

[33]
old-established traditions of the Courts. At the turn of the century, therefore, the common man and human being was no

[33]
longer able to show special ad- miration for a princess clad in a uniform, riding along a front. It is obvious that

[33]
one was not able to imagine the effect of such a parade in the eyes of the people, because otherwise

[33]
such unfortunate incidents would probably never have taken place. Also, the humane dreams of these cir- cles,

[33]
which were not always quite genuine, had a repelling rather than an attractive effect. If, for example, the Prin-

[33]
cess X 'deigned' to taste a sample of the food in a people's kitchen with the wiell-known result, it might perhaps have looked well

[33]
enough in former times, but the success at that time was to the contrary. In this case one may well assume that

[33]
Her Highness had really no idea that on the day of her inspection the food was a little different from that of the other

[33]
days ; but it was quite sufficient that the people knew this. Thus the best possible intention became ridiculous, if not

[32]
actually irritating. 382 MEIN KAMPF Descriptions of the always proverbial frugality of the monarch, his much too

[32]
early rising as well as his veritable drudgery till late at night, besides, with the continued danger of his

[33]
threatening undernourishment, nevertheless caused very doubtful comments. One certainly did not want to know what and how

[33]
much the monarch had the grace to take in; one did not begrudge him a 'sufficient 1 meal; also, one did not set out

[33]
perhaps to deny him the necessary sleep; one was content if as a man and as a char- acter he only honored

[32]
the name of his house and the nation and fulfilled his duty as a ruler. The telling of fairy tales was of

[31]
little use, and it was all the more harmful." However, this and many similar things were only trifles. But,

[33]
unfortunately, the conviction that one was ruled any- how from above, and that the individual need not

[33]
care for anything further, had a worse effect on very great parts of the nation. As long as the government was really

[33]
good or at least had the best intentions, things might be all right. But alas! if in the place of the old government, which in it- self

[33]
had good intentions, a new, less decent one, were to step in, then the irresolute obedience and the childlike

[32]
faith were the most serious misfortune conceivable. But all these and many other weaknesses were set off

[32]
also by undeniable values. There was the stability of the entire State authority, caused by the

[33]
monarchistic State form, as well as the immunizing of the highest State posts from the turmoil of the speculations of

[34]
ambitious politicians. Further, the respectability of the institution in itself, as well as the authority

[33]
caused even by this; finally, the uplifting of the body of officials and especially of the army above the

[30]
level of the obligations of political parties. To this was added the advantage of the personal

[33]
representation of the head of the State by the monarch as a person, and the example of a responsibility

[33]
which the monarch has to shoulder more THE CAUSES OF THE COLLAPSE 313 than the accidental crowd of a parliamentary

[33]
majority. (The proverbial incorruptibility of the German administration was primarily due to this.)

[33]
But finally the cultural value of the monarchy was a high one for the German peo- ple and it was well able to

[33]
balance other disadvantages. The German monarchs 1 residential towns were still the abodes of an artistic sense

[33]
which nevertheless threatens to die out more and more in our materialistic time. What the German princes did for

[32]
art and science even during the nineteenth century was exemplary. In any case, the present time must not be

[29]
compared with this. t But as the greatest factor of value, in this time of the beginning and slowly spreading

[32]
decomposition of our na- Perhaps the German army is rivaled only by the French army as an historical

[31]
institution. Both were developed during that heyday of European nationalism which coincided with the French

[33]
Revolution. Both taught discipline, health, con- duct. But whereas the French look back upon a national history more or less

[32]
continuous since the days of ancient Rome, the Germany of 1913 was still a country of peoples, almost of tribes, held

[32]
together by military leaders. The heroes were Frederick the Great, Bismarck, Moltke; and however deeply any

[30]
citizen might resent drill and warfare, he could not escape the fact that Germany was the army. That is why the

[32]
abdication of the army in 1918 the trans- fer of authority and responsibility to a government without a

[33]
military foundation was so appalling even to the men who took up the burden of government. They had suddenly, in

[33]
an hour of demoralizing defeat, to find some principle of unity which was not military in character. To

[31]
have succeeded would have meant, not merely the creation of a new Germany, but also the creation of a new

[32]
ideology. And unfortunately most of the leaders had to face the fact that the majority of their 384 MEIN KAMPF

[32]
tional body, we have to list the army. It was the mightiest school of the German nation, and for no other reason did the

[33]
hatred of all enemies direct itself precisely against this protection of national self-preservation and freedom.

[33]
One cannot present a more glorious monument to this unique institution than the establishment of the truth that

[31]
it was calumniated, hated, fought, but also feared, by all inferior people. That at Versailles the wrath of the

[33]
international exploiters of the nation directed itself primarily against the old German army makes it all

[32]
the more recognizable as the protection of the freedom of our people against the power of the stock exchange.

[33]
Without this warning power, the meaning of Versailles would long have been executed upon our people. What the German people

[32]
owes to the army may be simply summed up in one single word, namely: every- thing. The army trained for

[32]
absolute responsibility at a time when this quality had become very rare and the shunning of

[32]
responsibility had more and more become the order of the day, starting from the model example of all

[34]
unscrupu- lousness, the parliament; the army further taught personal courage in a time when cowardice threatened

[33]
to become a spreading disease, and when the willingness to sacrifice, to stand up for the general welfare, was

[33]
almost looked upon as stupidity, and when only he seemed to be clever who un- derstood best how to spare himself

[33]
and to advance his own 'ego'; it was the school which still taught the individual supporters wanted, not something new, but

[32]
the restoration of the old. Not to have foreseen these things was the tragic psychological blunder of Woodrow

[33]
Wilson a blunder which was really worse than a crime. Wilson came from a people unified, as probably no other

[31]
people has ever been, by an ac- cepted tradition of constitutional law; and he imagined that this happy

[33]
situation could be exported to other lands. THE CAUSES OF THE COLLAPSE 385 German to seek the salvation of the nation,

[33]
not in the men- dacious phrases of international fraternity between negroes, Germans, Chinese, French, British, etc., but rather

[32]
in the strength and the unity of his own nationality. The army taught determination, while otherwise in

[33]
daily life lack of determination and doubt began to govern the actions of people. It actually meant something,

[33]
at a time when the super-wise people set the fashion everywhere, of keeping up the principle that a command

[33]
is still better than no command. In this sole principle was contained a still unspoiled, robust health which would long since have

[32]
dis- appeared from the remainder of our life if the army and the education it gave had not provided for the

[33]
continued re- newal of this primordial strength. One only has to see the terrible lack of determination of our

[33]
present Reichs leaders who are not able to pull themselves together, unless they have to deal with the forced signing of

[33]
a new dictate of ex- ploitation; in this case, of course, they decline all responsi- bility and with the speed of

[33]
a court stenographer they sign everything that one may deem fit to put before them, for in this case the decision

[33]
is easily taken: it is 'dictated' to them.-' The army further taught idealism and devotion to the fatherland and its

[32]
greatness, while life had otherwise become the sole domain of greed and materialism. It educated

[32]
a uniform people as compared with the separation into classes, and here it perhaps showed its only fault, the

[32]
institution of the voluntary enlistment for one year. A fault for the reason that the principle of absolute

[31]
equality was broken and the man with a higher education was lifted out of the frame of the general

[33]
surroundings, while just the contrary would have been of advantage. With the seclusion from the world of our upper classes

[32]
which was so great even then, as well as the always increasing estrangement from their own people, the army would have been

[31]
able to have an especially 386 MEIN KAMPF beneficial effect if in its ranks at least it avoided every

[33]
separation of the so-called 'intelligentsia. 9 That this was not done was a mistake; but what institution in

[33]
this world is without mistakes? With this institution the good sides were predominant to such an extent that the few ills

[33]
were far below the average of human imperfection. But the greatest service of the army of the old Reich was

[33]
that, in a time of the general 'counting by majority' of the heads, it put the heads above the majority. In

[29]
the face of the Jewish democratic idea of a blind worship of numbers, the army upheld the faith in

[33]
personality. Thus it also bred what the newer times need most of all: men. Yes, indeed, in the swamp of a generally

[33]
spreading softening and ef- feminacy, out of the ranks of the army there shot up every year 350,000 vigorous young men who

[32]
in two years' train- ing had lost the softness of youth and had gained bodies hard as steel. The young man, however, who during this time

[33]
practiced obedience, also learned to give commands. Even by his step, one recognized the trained soldier.

[33]
This was the high school of the German nation, and it was not for nothing that the grim hatred of those who, out of envy and greed,

[33]
needed and desired the weakness of the Reich and the defenselessness of its citizens, was concen- trated on the army.

[34]
What many Germans in blindness or malicious will did not wish to see, the foreign world recog- nized in the German army; the most

[34]
powerful weapon in the service of the freedom of the German nation and the nourishment of her children. Added to the State

[33]
form as well as to the army came, as the third in the alliance, the incomparable body of officials of the old

[33]
Reich. Germany was the best organized and the best adminis- tered country in the world. One could well accuse it of

[32]
THE CAUSES OF THE COLLAPSE 387 bureaucratic red-tape, but this was no different in all the other States, even

[33]
rather worse. But what the other States did not possess was the wonderful solidarity of this appara- tus as well

[33]
as the incorruptible, honest loyalty of its repre- sentatives. Better to be a little pedantic, but honest and

[33]
loyal, rather than enlightened and modern, but inferior of character, and, as is frequently shown today, ignorant and

[33]
incompetent. For, if one likes to pretend that the German administration of the pre-War time was thought bureau-

[33]
cratically genuine, but bad from the business point of view, to this one can answer only the following: Which land of

[33]
the world had a better managed and commercially better or- ganized administration in her State railways than Ger-

[33]
many? It was reserved only for the Revolution to destroy this model apparatus till finally it appeared

[33]
ripe to be taken out of the hands of the nation and to become 'socialized' in the sense of the founders of this

[33]
republic; that means, to serve the international stock exchange capital, the prin- cipal instigator of the German

[32]
Revolution. What thereby distinguished especially the body of Ger- man officials and the apparatus of

[33]
administration was its independence of the various governments whose political convictions were not able

[33]
to exercise any influence on the position of German State officials. Since the Revolution, however,

[31]
this has changed thoroughly. The place of com- petence and ability was taken by party conviction and a

[32]
self-reliant and independent character was now an impedi- ment rather than an advantage. On the State form, the

[32]
army and the body of officials rested the wonderful power and strength of the old Reich. These were primarily the

[32]
causes of a quality which the pre- sent-day State lacks completely: the State authority! For this does not rest on

[33]
drivel in the parliaments or diets, and also not on the laws for their protection, or on court sen- tences for the frightening

[31]
of impudent deniers of this au- 388 MEIN KAMPF thority, but on the general confidence which may and can be shown in the

[33]
management and the administration of a community. But this confidence is in turn only the result of an

[33]
unshakable inner conviction of the unselfishness and the honesty of the government and the administration of

[31]
a country as well as of a harmony between the meaning of the law and general moral views. For, in the long run,

[33]
government systems are not held together by the pressure of force, but rather by the belief in the quality and

[30]
the truthfulness with which they represent and promote the interests of a people. Therefore, no matter how

[33]
seriously certain evils of the pre-War time ate into the inner strength of the nation and threatened to hollow it

[30]
out, one must not forget that other States suffered from these diseases still more than Ger- many, and that

[33]
nevertheless in the critical hour of danger they did not fail and did not perish. But if one considers that the German

[32]
weaknesses before the War were balanced by strong sides which were just as great, then the ultimate cause for the

[34]
collapse can and must be found in still an- other field; and this was also the case. The deepest and the ultimate cause for

[33]
the ruin of the old Reich was found in the non-recognition of the race problem and its importance for the historical

[33]
development of the people. For events in the lives of the nations are not expressions of chance, but, by the laws of

[34]
nature, happen- ings of the urge of self-preservation and propagation of species and race, even if the people are

[32]
not conscious of the inner reasons for their activitv. CHAPTER XI NATION AND RACE are statements of truth which are so

[33]
obvious that just for this reason the common world does not see, or at least does not recognize, them. At times the world passes

[33]
these well-known truisms blindly and it is most astonished if now suddenly somebody discovers what everybody

[33]
ought to know. The ' Columbus eggs ' are lying about by the hundreds of thousands, only the Columbuses are rarely seen.

[32]
Thus, without exception, people wander about in Na- ture's garden; they think they know almost everything, and yet, with few

[32]
exceptions, they walk blindly by one of the most outstanding principles of Nature's working: the inner seclusion of the

[34]
species of all living beings on earth. Even the most superficial observation shows, as an almost brazen basic principle of

[31]
all the countless forms of expression of Nature's will to live, her limited form of propagation and increase,

[33]
limited in itself. Every animal mates only with a representative of the same species. The titmouse

[33]
seeks the titmouse, the finch the finch, the stork the stork, the field mouse the field mouse, the common mouse the common mouse, the wolf

[32]
the wolf, etc. Only exceptional circumstances can change this; first of all the compulsion of captivity, as well as

[33]
any other impos- 390 MEIN KAMPF sibility of mating within the same species. But then Nature begins to resist this

[32]
with the help of all visible means, and her most visible protest consists either of denying the bas- tards further procreative

[33]
faculty, or she limits the fertility of the coming offspring; but in most cases she takes away the capacity

[33]
of resistance against disease or inimical at- tacks. This is then only too natural. Any crossing between two

[34]
beings of not quite the same high standard produces a medium between the standards of the parents. That means: the young one will

[33]
probably be on a higher level than the racially lower parent, but not as high as the higher one. Consequently,

[34]
it will succumb later on in the fight against the higher level. But such a mating contradicts Nature's will to breed life as

[32]
a whole towards a higher level. The presumption for this does not lie in blend- ing the superior with the inferior, but

[32]
rather in a complete victory of the former. The stronger has to rule and he is not to amalgamate with the

[34]
weaker one, that he may not sacrifice his own greatness. Only the born weakling can consider this as cruel, but at that he is

[33]
only a weak and limited human being; for, if this law were not dominating, all conceivable development towards

[33]
a higher level, on the part of all organically living beings, would be unthinkable for man. The consequence of this

[31]
purity of the race, generally valid in Nature, is not only the sharp limitation of the races

[33]
outwardly, but also their uniform character in themselves. The fox is always a fox, the goose a goose, the tiger

[31]
a tiger, etc., and the difference can lie, at the most, in the different measure of strength, force, cleverness, skill,

[32]
perseverance, etc., of the various specimens. But there will never be found a fox which, according to its inner

[31]
nature, would per- haps have humane tendencies as regards the geese, nor will there be a cat with a friendly

[30]
disposition towards mice. NATION AND RACE 391 Therefore also, here the fight amongst one another

[32]
originates less from reasons of inner aversion than from hunger and love. In both cases, Nature looks calm and

[32]
even satisfied. The fight for daily bread makes all those suc- cumb who are weak, sickly, and less determined, while the

[33]
males' fight for the female gives the right of propagation, or the possibility of it, only to the most healthy.

[33]
But the fight is always a means for the promotion of the species' health and force of resistance, and thus a cause for its

[33]
de- velopment towards a higher level. If it were different, every further development towards higher levels

[33]
would stop, and rather the contrary would happen. For, since according to numbers, the inferior ele- ment always outweighs

[29]
the superior element, under the same preservation of life and under the same propagating

[33]
possibilities, the inferior element would increase so much more rapidly that finally the best element

[33]
would be forced to step into the background, if no correction of this condi- tion were carried out. But just this is done by

[34]
Nature, by subjecting the weaker part to such difficult living conditions This appeal to the sacred norm of the 'survival

[32]
of the fittest' customary in Pan-German literature had been resorted to as well by critics of Socialism. The

[33]
'tearful sentimentality' of the humanitarians, forever attempting to salvage what had better be left to

[30]
die, is denounced by Spengler and many others. But the application of 'fitness' to mating is something else

[32]
entirely, deriving from Plato through a number of intermedi- aries some of whom can be sought out in modern

[34]
anti-Semitic literature. There are considerable differences. Thus, Ludwig Schemann thinks that Nature does

[33]
not mean the same thing by 'fitness' that man does, and that therefore any vigorous re- course to eugenics except in

[33]
so far as purely negative matters (health, etc.) are concerned would prove impossible and impractical. Others

[32]
have gone the whole way and advocated rigid public regulation of procreation. 392 MEIN KAMPF that even by this the

[33]
number is restricted, and finally by preventing the remainder, without choice, from increasing, but by making here a

[31]
new and ruthless choice, according to strength and health. Just as little as Nature desires a mating between weaker

[33]
individuals and stronger ones, far less she desires the mix- ing of a higher race with a lower one, as in

[33]
this case her en- tire work of higher breeding, which has perhaps taken hun- dreds of thousands of years, would tumble at one blow.

[33]
-4- Historical experience offers countless proofs of this. It shows with terrible clarity that with any mixing of the blood

[33]
of the Aryan with lower races the result was the end of the culture-bearer. North America, the population of

[32]
which consists for the greatest part of Germanic elements which mix only very little with the lower, colored races

[31]
displays a humanity and a culture different from those of Central and South America, where chiefly the

[34]
Romanic immigrants have sometimes mixed with the aborigines on a large scale. By this example alone

[31]
one may clearly and dis- tinctly recognize the influence of the race mixture. The Germanic of the North

[34]
American continent, who has re- mained pure and less intermixed, has become the master of that continent, he will

[34]
remain so until he, too, falls victim to the shame of blood-mixing. f The result of any crossing, in brief, is always the follow-

[32]
ing: (a) Lowering of the standard of the higher race, (&) Physical and mental regression, and, with it, the be- ginning of

[33]
a slowly but steadily progressive lingering ill- ness. To bring about such a development means nothing less than sinning

[33]
against the will of the Eternal Creator. This action, then, is also rewarded as a sin. Man, by trying to resist this iron

[33]
logic of Nature, be- comes entangled in a fight against the principles to which NATION AND RACE 393 alone he, too,

[30]
owes his existence as a human being. Thus his attack is bound to lead to his own doom. Of course, now comes the

[32]
typically Jewish, impudent, but just as stupid, objection by the modern pacifist: 'Man conquers Nature!' Millions

[31]
mechanically and thoughtlessly repeat this Jewish nonsense, and in the end they imagine that they themselves

[33]
represent a kind of conqueror of Nature; whereas they have no other weapon at their disposal but an 'idea,' and

[33]
such a wretched one at that, so that accord- ing to it no world would be conceivable. But quite apart from the fact that so

[33]
far man has never conquered Nature in any affair, but that at the most he gets hold of and tries to lift a flap of her

[32]
enormous, gigantic veil of eternal riddles and secrets, that in reality he does not 'invent' anything but only

[32]
discovers everything, that he does not dominate Nature, but that, based on the know- ledge of a few laws and

[33]
secrets of Nature, he has risen to the position of master of those other living beings lacking The argument has

[33]
been put another way by Professor Carl Schmitt (cited by Kolnai) : 'A universal organization in which there is no

[33]
place for warlike preservation and destruction of human life would be neither a State nor an Empire : it would

[31]
lose all political character/ Yet this is not Jewish but Christian teaching that is under criticism. Cardinal

[32]
Faulhaber, meeting the objection that the Old Testament is filled with 'hymns of hate/ responded that Christianity had

[31]
indeed changed those hymns into canticles of love, and added: 'There is no alterna- tive: either we are

[29]
disciples of Christ, or we lapse into the Judaism of antiquity with its hymns of hate/ The letter which the

[33]
evangelical churches addressed to Hitler in June, 1936, contained these words: 'When blood, race, creed, nationality and

[33]
honor are thus raised to the rank of qualities that guarantee eternity, the Evangelical Christian is bound, by

[32]
the first commandment, to reject the assumption/ 394 MEIN KAMPF this knowledge; but quite apart from this, an idea cannot conquer the

[33]
presumptions for the origin and the existence of mankind, as the idea itself depends only on man. With- out men there

[33]
is no human 'idea' in this world; thus the idea is always caused by the presence of men, and, with it, of all those laws

[33]
which created the presumptions for this existence. And not only that! Certain ideas are even tied to cer- tain men. This can

[34]
be said most of all of just such thoughts the content of which has its origin, not in an exact scientific truth, but rather in the world

[32]
of feeling, or, as one usually expresses oneself so nicely and 'clearly' today, which re- flects an 'inner

[33]
experience.' All these ideas, which have nothing to do with clear logic in itself, but which represent mere expressions

[33]
of feelings, ethical conceptions, etc., are tied to the existence of those men to whose spiritual force of

[33]
imagination and creation they owe their own existence. But precisely in this case the preservation of these

[32]
certain races and men is the presumption for the existence of these 'ideas/ For example, he who actually

[30]
desires, with all his heart, the victory of the pacifistic idea in this world would have to stand up, with all

[33]
available means, for the conquest of the world by the Germans; for if it should come about the other way round, then, with the last

[32]
German, the last pacifist would die off, as the other part of the world has hardly ever been taken in so deeply by this

[32]
nonsense, ad- verse to nature and to reason, as unfortunately our own people. Therefore, whether one

[33]
wanted to or not, if one had the serious will, one would have to decide to wage war in order to arrive

[33]
at pacifism. This and nothing else was what the American world-redeemer Wilson wanted to have done, at least our

[33]
German visionaries believed in this. With this, then, the purpose was fulfilled.-' Indeed, the pacifist-humane idea

[33]
is perhaps quite good whenever the man of the highest standard has previously NATION AND RACE 395 conquered and subjected

[33]
the world to a degree that makes him the only master of this globe. Thus the idea is more and more deprived of

[33]
the possibility of a harmful effect in the measure in which its practical application becomes rare and

[33]
finally impossible. Therefore, first fight, and then one may see what can be done. In the other case, mankind has

[33]
passed the climax of its development, and the end is not the rule of some ethical 'idea/ but barbarism, and, in

[32]
consequence, chaos. Naturally, here the one or the other may laugh, but this planet has driven on its course through the

[33]
ether for millions of years without men, and the day may come when it will do so again, if people forget that they owe their

[34]
higher existence, not to the ideas of some crazy ideologists, but to The foregoing passages are derived

[33]
in the main from Houston Stewart Chamberlain, but with nuances that suggest the influence of Rosenberg, or at least of the Free

[33]
Corps which imported so much militaristic anti-Semitism into Germany after the War. For Chamberlain the moral

[31]
superiority of the 'Aryan' is undeniable; and therefore, if humanity is not to decline

[33]
morally, it must hope for the victory of the 'Aryan' over lesser peoples. But Chamberlain is quite honest: for him

[33]
a ' German ' and an ' Aryan ' are the same thing. He was bitterly disappointed when 1918 seemed to mean perpetual moral

[33]
de- gradation for the human race. In his famous letter to Hitler, following their meeting in 1923, he wrote, therefore:

[33]
4 At one blow you have transformed the state my soul was in. Germany's vitality is proved if in this hour of its

[33]
deepest need it can produce a Hitler/ Perhaps the basis of this attitude as a whole must be sought in those fears

[32]
of an eventual 'war be- tween races' which were aired as early as the eighteenth cen- tury, but reached a kind of

[31]
apogee during the nineteenth. Then the inferiority of the 'colored races ' was taken for granted, though the

[29]
interest taken in a newly discovered Indian litera- ture, ascribed in theory to an '

[34]
Indo-Germanic invasion 9 of Asia, tended to make many place the Brahmins on a somewhat 396 MEIN KAMPF the knowledge

[33]
and the ruthless application of Nature's brazen laws. Everything that today we admire on this earth science and art,

[34]
technique and inventions is only the creative product of a few peoples and perhaps originally of one race.

[33]
On them now depends also the existence of this entire cul- ture. If they perish, then the beauty of this earth sinks

[32]
into the grave with them. t No matter how much the soil, for instance, is able to in- fluence the people, the result will

[32]
always be a different one, according to the races under consideration. The scanty fertility of a

[32]
living space may instigate one race towards the highest achievements, while with another race this may

[32]
only become the cause for the most dire poverty and ulti- mate malnutrition with all its consequences. The

[33]
inner dis- position of the peoples is always decisive for the way in which outward influences work themselves out. What

[32]
leads one people to starvation, trains the other for hard work. All great cultures of the past perished only because the

[33]
originally creative race died off through blood-poisoning. The ultimate cause of such a decline was always

[33]
the for- getting that all culture depends on men and not the re- verse; that means, that in order to save a certain culture

[33]
the man who created it has to be saved. But the preservation is bound to the brazen law of necessity and of the right

[31]
of the victory of the best and the strongest in this world. higher level. Later on the 'negroid characteristics' of the

[32]
Mediterranean races were stressed by Pan-German writers. The Latin, the Catholic, was of highly questionable

[33]
value. The Germanic Aryan had a right to dominate, and eventually he surely would. After the War the stress

[33]
was shifted to the Jew, partly because French 'inferiority' had not been satis- factorily demonstrated, after

[34]
all, and partly because the Free Corps encouraged the view that Jewry was responsible for Germany's acquiescence in

[33]
Allied demands. NATION AND RACE 397 He who wants to live should fight, therefore, and he who does not want to battle in this world

[33]
of eternal struggle does not deserve to be alive. Even if this were hard, this is the way things are. But it is

[33]
certain that by far the hardest fate is the fate which meets that man who believes he can 'conquer' Nature, and yet, in truth,

[33]
only seems to mock her. Misery, distress, and diseases are then her answer! The man who misjudges and disdains the laws of

[33]
race actually forfeits the happiness that seems destined to be his. He prevents the victorious march of the best race

[34]
and with it also the presumption for all human progress, and in con- sequence he will remain in the domain of the animal's

[34]
help- less misery, burdened with the sensibility of man. It is a futile enterprise to argue which race or

[34]
races were the original bearers of human culture and, with it, the actual founders of what we sum up with the word

[33]
'mankind.' It is simpler to put this question to oneself with regard to the present, and here the answer follows easily

[33]
and dis- tinctly. What we see before us of human culture today, the results of art, science, and techniques, is almost

[34]
exclusively the creative product of the Aryan. But just this fact admits of the not unfounded conclusion that he alone

[32]
was the founder of higher humanity as a whole, thus the prototype This idyl of 'Aryan ' pre-history is

[32]
interesting because of the definition of 'culture' that is involved. For 'culture' in this sense is once

[31]
again become the principal concern of Europe. The 'Aryan' succeeds in pushing his way onward and upward by

[33]
conquering lesser peoples and using them as 'helping forces' (slaves). Then, however, master and slave intermarry, and tho

[33]
' culture ' decays. Perhaps this is only an analogy borrowed from some pictorial history of European

[33]
colonizing effort: perhaps it is more philosophical. Spengler had taught in 398 MEIN KAMPF of what we understand by the word

[32]
'man.' He is the Prometheus of mankind, out of whose bright forehead springs the divine spark of genius at all times,

[33]
forever re- kindling that fire which in the form of knowledge lightened up the night of silent secrets and thus made man

[32]
climb the path towards the position of master of the other beings on this earth. Exclude him and deep darkness will again fall

[33]
upon the earth, perhaps even, after a few thousand years, human culture would perish and the world would turn into a desert.

[33]
-4- If one were to divide mankind into three groups: culture- founders, culture-bearers, and culture-destroyers, then, as

[33]
representative of the first kind, only the Aryan would come in question. It is from him that the foundation and the walls

[32]
of all human creations originate, and only the external form and color depend on the characteristics of the

[32]
various peoples involved. He furnishes the gigantic building-stones and also the plans for all human progress, and

[32]
only the exe- cution corresponds to the character of the people and races in the various instances. In a few

[33]
decades, for instance, the entire east of Asia will call a culture its own, the ultimate bases of which

[32]
will be Hellenic spirit and Germanic tech- nique, just as is the case with us. Only the external form will (at least

[31]
partly) bear the features of Asiatic character. It is not the case, as some people claim, that Japan adds

[29]
European techniques to her culture, but European science and techniques are trimmed with Japanese

[33]
characteristics. the Decline of the West that cultures arise and fall cyclically; and Hitler here provides

[33]
a convenient illustration of why they fall. Therewith the riddle proposed by Spengler is solved; the 'culture-making'

[34]
folk is that which, obeying the law that only the fittest survive, embarks on conquest and exploitation; and the 'culture-destroying

[32]
folk 9 is the slave breed which tempts the aristocratic group into intermarriage. This i Nietzsche materialized.

[32]
NATION AND RACE 399 But the basis of actual life is no longer the special Japanese culture, although it

[32]
determines the color of life (because out- wardly, in consequence of its inner difference, it is more

[33]
visible to European eyes), but it is the enormous scientific and technical work of Europe and America, that

[33]
is, of Aryan peoples. Based on these achievements alone the East is also able to follow general human

[32]
progress. This creates the basis for the fight for daily bread, it furnishes weapons and tools for it, and only the external

[33]
makeup is gradually adapted to Japanese life. But if, starting today, all further Aryan influence upon

[33]
Japan should stop, and supposing that Europe and America were to perish, then a further development of Japan's

[33]
present rise in science and technology could take place for a little while longer; but in the time of a few

[33]
years the source would dry out, Japanese life would gain, but its culture would stiffen and fall back into the sleep out of which

[32]
it was startled seven decades ago by the Aryan wave of culture. Therefore, exactly as the present

[32]
Japanese development owes its life to Aryan origin, thus also in the dim past foreign influence and

[32]
foreign spirit were the awakener of the Japanese culture. The best proof of this is the fact that the latter

[29]
stiffened and became completely paralyzed later on. This can only happen to a people when the

[31]
originally crea- tive race nucleus was lost, or when the external influence, which gave the impetus and the

[32]
material for the first de- velopment in the cultural field, was lacking later on. But if it is ascertained that

[33]
a people receives, takes in, and works over the essential basic elements of its culture from other races, and

[33]
if then, when a further external influence is lack- ing, it stiffens again and again, then one can perhaps call such a race

[33]
a 'culture-bearing' one but never a 'culture-cre- ating' one. An examination of the various peoples from

[30]
this view- point evidences the fact that in nearly all cases one has to 400 MEIN KAMPF deal, not with originally

[33]
culture-creating, but rather always with culture-supporting peoples. It is always about the following picture of

[33]
their develop- ment that presents itself: Aryan tribes (often in a really ridiculously small number of their own people)

[30]
subjugate foreign peoples, and now, stimulated by the special living conditions of the new terri- tory

[30]
(fertility, climatic conditions, etc.) and favored by the mass of the helping means in the form of people of

[33]
inferior kind now at their disposal, they develop the mental and organizatory abilities, slumbering in

[32]
them. Often, in the course of a few millenniums or even centuries, they create cultures which originally

[33]
completely bear the inner features of their character, adapted to the already mentioned special qualities of

[33]
the soil as well as of the subjected people. Finally, however, the conquerors deviate from the purity of their

[31]
blood which they maintained originally, they begin to mix with the subjected inhabitants and thus they end their own

[32]
existence; for the fall of man in Paradise has always been followed by expulsion from it. f Often, after a

[33]
thousand and more years, the last visible trace of the one-time overlords is shown in the fairer com- plexion which their

[32]
blood has left, in the form of the color, to the subjected race, and in a petrified culture which they had founded as the

[32]
original creators. For, just as the actual and spiritual conqueror lost himself in the blood of the sub- jected, thus

[33]
also the fuel for the torch of human culture progress was lost! As through the blood the color of the former masters keeps a faint

[32]
glimmer as a memory of them, thus also the night of the cultural life is faintly brightened by the creations that

[33]
remained of the erstwhile bearers of light. These now shone through all the barbarism that has returned, and in the thoughtless

[32]
observer of the moment they awaken only too frequently the opinion that he sees the picture of the present

[32]
people, whereas it is only the mir- ror of the past at which he is looking. NATION AND RACE 401 Then it may happen that such

[33]
a people for a second time, nay, even more often in the life of its history, comes into touch with the race

[31]
of its one-time suppliers of culture, without a memory of former meetings necessarily being present. The

[32]
remainder of the blood of the one-time mas- ters will unconsciously turn to the new apparition, and what first was only

[33]
possible by compulsion will now succeed with the help of their own will. Then a new culture wave makes its entrance and

[33]
lasts until its bearers have once more been submerged in the blood of foreign peoples. It will be the task of a future

[33]
culture and world history to make researches in this sense and not to suffocate by re- flecting external facts,

[33]
as this is unfortunately only too often the case with our present science of history. Merely from this sketch

[33]
of the development of ' culture- bearing' nations results also the picture of the origin, the work, and the decline

[32]
of the true culture-creators of this globe, the Aryans themselves. Just as in daily life the so-called genius

[33]
requires a special No definition of the word 'Aryan' is acceptable. German lexicographers were hard pressed

[33]
to hit upon an accurate description. The term itself is probably of Sanskrit origin, and seems to have meant 'friends/

[32]
It was next assumed that these 'friends' were Indo-Germans, who (it was further as- sumed) had invaded India and

[31]
subjugated the 'lesser breeds/ Finally 'Aryan' became just a synonym for 'Indo-German.' The 1931 edition of the

[33]
encyclopedia Der grosse Herder said: 'Recently some have used (ethnologically, in an incorrect way)

[32]
'Aryan' to indicate Indo-Germans in general. In this case, the term is used as in the nature of a

[32]
slogan in the struggle over the self-determination and preservation of our race against Jewry, which is of a

[30]
different order.' For this and similar definitions (surely discreet enough), the earlier volumes of this

[33]
encyclopedia were ordered withdrawn from circulation. In practice the word is officially used today as

[32]
a racial term 402 MEIN KAMPF cause, often even a real impetus in order to be made con- spicuous, the same is

[33]
also the case with the ingenious race in the life of the peoples. In the monotony of everyday life

[33]
even important people often seem unimportant and they hardly stand out over the average of their surroundings; but

[33]
as soon as they are faced by a situation in which others would despair or go wrong, out of the plain average child

[33]
the ingenious nature grows visibly, not infrequently to the astonishment of all those who hitherto had an

[33]
opportunity to observe him, who had meanwhile grown up in the small- ness of bourgeois life, and therefore, in

[32]
consequence of this process, the prophet has rarely any honor in his own coun- try. Never is there a better

[33]
opportunity to observe this than during war. In the hours of distress, when others de- spair, out of apparently harmless

[32]
children, there shoot sud- denly heroes of death-defying determination and icy cool- ness of reflection. If this hour of

[32]
trial had never come, then hardly anyone would ever have been able to guess that a young hero is hidden in the

[32]
beardless boy. Nearly always such an impetus is needed in order to call genius into action. excluding Jews and

[33]
negroes. The second are frowned upon because (i.a.) they are admitted into the French army; and because, it

[31]
is hoped, sympathy for the Nazi cause may be thus awakened among Southerners in the United States.

[34]
Delegations of 'Brahmins 1 have, however, been cordially welcomed to the New Germany. Parallels to this can be found

[33]
in the writings of Pan-Germans like Heinrich Class and Count Reventlow. In an address delivered during 1932, Hitler declared;

[33]
'Let them call us in- human! If we save Germany, we shall have done the greatest deed in the world. Let them call us unjust!

[33]
If we save Ger- many, we shall have repaired the greatest injustice in the world. Let them say that we are without

[33]
morality! If our people is saved, we shall have paved the way for morality!' NATION AND RACE 403 Fate's hammer

[33]
stroke, which then throws the one to the ground, suddenly strikes steel in another, and while now the shell of everyday life

[33]
is broken, the erstwhile nucleus lies open to the eyes of the astonished world. The latter now re- sists and does not want to

[33]
believe that the apparently 'identical' kind is now suddenly supposed to be a 'differ- ent' being; a process which

[33]
repeats itself with every eminent human being. Although an inventor, for instance, establishes his fame only

[33]
on the day of his invention, one must not think that perhaps his genius in itself had entered the man only just at

[33]
this hour, but the spark of genius will be present in the forehead of the truly creatively gifted man from the hour of

[33]
his birth, although for many years in a slumbering condi- tion and therefore invisible to the rest of the world. But some

[33]
day, through an external cause or impetus of some kind, the spark becomes fire, something that only then be- gins to

[33]
stir the attention of other people. The most stupid of them believe now in all sincerity that the person in ques- tion

[32]
has just become 'clever,' whereas in reality they them- selves now begin at last to recognize his greatness; for true

[33]
genius is always inborn and never acquired by education or, still less, by learning. This, however, may be said, as

[33]
already stressed, not only for the individual man, but also for the race.-'- Creatively active peoples are

[31]
creatively gifted from the very bottom and forever, although this may not be recognizable to the eyes of the

[32]
superficial observer. Here, too, external recogni- tion is always only possible as a consequence of

[31]
accom- plished facts, as the rest of the world is not able to recognize genius in itself, but sees only its

[33]
visible expressions in the form of inventions, discoveries, buildings, pictures, etc. ; but even here it often takes

[33]
a long time till it is able to struggle through to this knowledge. Exactly as in the life of the in- dividual

[32]
important man his genius or extraordinary ability 404 MEIN KAMPF strives towards its practical realization

[33]
only when urged on by special occasions, thus also in the life of the peoples the real use of creative forces

[32]
and abilities that are present can take place only when certain presumptions invite to this. We see this most

[34]
clearly in that race that cannot help having been, and being, the supporter of the development of human culture the Aryans.

[33]
As soon as Fate leads them towards special conditions, their latent abilities begin to develop in a more and more

[33]
rapid course and to mold them- selves into tangible forms. The cultures which they found in such cases are nearly always

[31]
decisively determined by the available soil, the climate, and by the subjected people. The latter,

[33]
however, is the most decisive of all factors. The more primitive the technical presumptions for a cultural

[33]
activity are, the more necessary is the presence of human auxiliary forces which then, collected

[30]
and applied with the object of organization, have to replace the force of the ma- chine. Without this

[32]
possibility of utilizing inferior men, the Aryan would never have been able to take the first steps

[33]
towards his later culture; exactly as, without the help of various suitable animals which he knew how to tame,

[33]
he would never have arrived at a technology which now allows him to do without these very animals. The words

[33]
'Der Mohr hoi seine Schuldigkeit getan, er kann gehen' [The Moor has done his duty, he may go] has unfortunately too

[33]
deep a meaning. For thousands of years the horse had to serve man and to help in laying the foundations of a development which

[33]
now, through the motor-car, makes the horse itself superfluous. In a few years it will have ceased its activity, but

[31]
without its former co-operation man would hardly have arrived at where he stands today. Therefore, for the

[33]
formation of higher cultures, the exist- ence of inferior men was one of the most essential presump- tions, because

[30]
they alone were able to replace the lack of NATION AND RACE 405 technical means without which a higher

[32]
development is un- thinkable. The first culture of mankind certainly depended less on the tamed animal, but

[32]
rather on the use of inferior people. Only after the enslavement of subjected races, the same fate

[33]
began to meet the animals, and not vice versa, as many would like to believe. For first the conquered walked be-

[33]
hind [in later editions read : before] the plow and after him, the horse. Only pacifist fools can again look upon this

[33]
as a sign of human baseness, without making clear to themselves that this development had to take place in order

[32]
to arrive finally at that place from where today these apostles are able to sputter forth their drivel

[32]
into the world. The progress of mankind resembles the ascent on an end- less ladder; one cannot arrive at the top

[32]
without first hav- ing taken the lower steps. Thus the Aryan had to go the way which reality showed him and not that of which the

[33]
imagination of a modern pacifist dreams. The way of real- ity, however, is hard and difficult, but it finally

[32]
ends where the other wishes to bring mankind by dreaming, but un- fortunately removes it from, rather than brings it

[32]
nearer to, it. Therefore, it is no accident that the first cultures origi- nated in those places where the

[33]
Aryan, by meeting lower peoples, subdued them and made them subject to his will. They, then, were the first technical instrument

[31]
in the serv- ice of a growing culture. With this the way that the Aryan had to go was clearly lined out. As a

[32]
conqueror he .subjected the lower peoples and then he regulated their practical ability according to his

[32]
command and his will and for his aims. But while he thus led them towards a useful, though hard activity, he not only

[32]
spared the lives of the subjected, but perhaps he even gave them a fate which was better than that of their former

[33]
so-called ' freedom/ As long as he kept up ruthlessly 406 MEIN KAMPF the master's standpoint, he not only really remained 'mas- ter' but

[30]
also the preserver and propagator of the culture. For the latter was based exclusively on his

[33]
abilities, and, with it, on his preservation in purity. But as soon as the subjected peoples themselves began to

[33]
rise (probably) and approached the conqueror linguistically, the sharp separat- ing wall between master and slave fell.

[34]
The Aryan gave up the purity of his blood and therefore he also lost his place in the Paradise which he had

[33]
created for himself. He be- came submerged in the race-mixture, he gradually lost his cultural ability

[32]
more and more, till at last not only mentally but also physically he began to resemble more the sub-

[33]
jected and aborigines than his ancestors. For some time he may still live on the existing cultural goods, but

[33]
then petri- faction sets in, and finally oblivion. In this way cultures and realms collapse in order to make room for

[33]
new formations. The blood-mixing, however, with the lowering of the racial level caused by it, is the sole cause of

[33]
the dying-off of old cultures; for the people do not perish by lost wars, but by the loss of that force of resistance which

[33]
is contained only in the pure blood. All that is not race in this world is trash. All world historical events, however,

[32]
are only the expres- sion of the races' instinct of self-preservation in its good or in its evil meaning. That is,

[33]
security is better than freedom. And security, carried to its ultimate in the 'total mobilization 9 of

[32]
the nation, is very well analyzed by Rauschning. The masses still cling to the residue of personal liberty, of

[31]
self-determination, which has been left to them. Yet all such things must disappear com- pletely before the absolute

[33]
'security' which is the inherent ob- jective of the Hitlerite revolution has been reached. NATION AND RACE 407

[33]
t The question about the inner causes of the overwhelming importance of Aryanism can be answered to the effect

[32]
that they are to be sought less in a greater potentiality of the instinct of self-preservation in itself, than in the

[34]
special way in which the latter expresses itself. The will to live, looked at subjectively, is the same everywhere

[32]
and it is dif- ferent only in the form of its actual effect. With the most original living beings the instinct of

[33]
self-preservation does not go beyond the care for their own 'ego.' Here the i ego- ism,' as we call this urge, goes so far

[33]
that it even comprises time, so that the moment itself claims everything and be- grudges everything to the coming

[33]
hours. The animal lives in this state only for itself, seeks food only whenever it feels hungry, and fights only for its

[34]
own life. But as long as the instinct of self-preservation expresses itself in this way, every basis for the formation

[32]
of a community, be it even the most primitive form of the family, is lacking. Even the community

[33]
between male and female, beyond the mere mating, requires a broadening of the instinct of self-preser- vation, as now

[33]
the care for their own 'ego' extends also to the other part; sometimes the male seeks food for the female, but not

[33]
infrequently both of them for the young ones. Nearly always the one steps in for the protection of the other, so that here

[32]
the first though infinitely simple forms of a readiness to sacrifice present themselves. As soon as this instinct

[33]
extends beyond the limits of the narrow frame of the family, the prerequisite for the formation of greater unions

[33]
and finally formal States is given. With the lowest people of the earth we find this quality only to a very small

[33]
extent, so that often nothing but a family is formed. The greater the individual's readiness to subordinate

[32]
his own purely personal interests is, the more increases also the ability for the establishment of

[33]
extensive communities. This will to sacrifice in staking his personal labor and, if 408 MEIN KAMPF necessary, his

[33]
own life for others, is most powerfully de- veloped in the Aryan. He is greatest, not in his mental capacities

[33]
per se, but in the extent to which he is ready to put all his abilities at the service of the community. With

[34]
him the instinct of self-preservation has reached the most noble form, because he willingly subjects his own ego to the life

[31]
of the community and, if the hour should require it, he also sacrifices it. Not in the intellectual

[34]
abilities lies the Aryan's culture- creating and building ability. If he had only these, he would always be able

[31]
to work only destructively, but in no case 'organizingly'; for the innermost nature of all organ-

[33]
ization is based on just the fact that the individual re- nounces representing his personal opinion and his

[33]
interests and sacrifices both in favor of a majority of people. Only The Aryan is therefore the best

[33]
soldier. But he will also be the best 'worker,' in the sense adopted by Prussian Socialism, which is in theory a system

[32]
rewarding men on the basis of the service they render the State, the community, as a whole. Today the world

[34]
confronts the fact that German labor has, by and large, acquiesced in this theory. Its former Marxism has to a large extent

[33]
been shuffled off; and perhaps it was the most fundamental characteristic of that Marxism that it based a conception of

[33]
class warfare on an assumption of uni- versally valid human rights. The individual worker was held entitled

[31]
to certain inalienable privileges, and for the sake of these the struggle against a society that

[33]
refused to grant them was imperative. But just because Marxism respected human rights however secularistic

[33]
its understanding of them may have been its revolutionary initiative was necessarily lamed. The shock

[33]
which the best German Socialists felt when they confronted the Bolshevist regime was the result of their feeling that Lenin had

[33]
betrayed the fundamental creed of Marxism. He had sold the faith in order to dominate. The Third Reich began by depriving

[33]
the German worker of NATION AND RACE 409 by way of the general community is his share returned to him. Now, for

[33]
instance, he no longer works directly for himself, but with his activity he joins in the frame of the community,

[31]
not only for his own advantage, but for that of all. The most wonderful explanation of this disposition is

[33]
offered by his word 'work/ by which he does not mean an activity for gaining his living, but only a creative toil that

[33]
does not contradict the interests of the community. In the other case he calls the human activity, in so far

[34]
as it does not serve the instinct of self-preservation without consideration for the welfare of the contemporary

[33]
world, by the words theft, usury, robbery, burglary, etc. This disposition now, which causes the individual's ego to

[33]
step back in the face of the preservation of the commun- ity, is really the first prerequisite for any truly

[32]
human cul- ture. Only out of this all the great works of mankind are able to originate, works which bring little

[31]
reward to the exactly what the Third Internationale had taken from him freedom of assembly, traditional

[33]
organizations, the right to designate his leaders. But it manifested, in a manner in which the Republic could not

[33]
manifest, its need for workers. And therewith (despite all material privations, such as bad bread, lack of fats, lower pay,

[32]
harder work) the way was prepared for a revolution of the working class a revolution the dim outlines of which

[30]
undoubtedly fascinate the German toiler today. For by abolishing the individual, the Third Reich

[30]
automatically created the mass. And by establishing dominion, power, as the sole ethical norm, it

[32]
automatically created a longing for power on a scale hitherto unknown. Sooner or later the two the new

[33]
masses, and the new ethical absolute must coincide. Marxism is out of date in Germany, there- fore, simply

[32]
because the theory of human rights is out of date. With that those who have destroyed Marxism will have to reckon. (Cf. Dcr

[34]
Arbcitcr: Herrschaft und Gestalt, by Rrn$t Jtinger.) 410 MEIN KAMPF founder but the richest blessing to posterity. Out of this alone one can

[33]
understand how so many are able to sustain a poor life in honesty, which imposes only poverty and mod-

[32]
esty on themselves, but which guarantees the fundamen- tals of the community's existence. Every laborer,

[33]
every peasant, every inventor, official, etc., who works without ever being able to attain happiness and well-being,

[33]
is a carrier of this high idea, even if the deeper meaning of his actions remained hidden to himself forever. But

[31]
what applies to work as the basis of human nutrition and all human progress applies to a far greater extent to the

[32]
protection of man and his culture. In giving up one's own life for the existence of the community lies the

[33]
crowning of all will to sacrifice. Only this prevents everything that human hands have built from being overthrown again

[33]
by human hands, or destroyed by Nature for herself. < But just our German language has a word which in a glorious manner

[33]
describes acting in this sense: fulfillment of duty (Pflichterfiillung) ; that means, not to suffice for one- self, but to

[31]
serve the community; this is duty. Now the basic disposition out of which such an activity grows we call

[33]
idealism, to distinguish it from egoism. By this we understand only the individual's ability to sacrifice

[33]
himself for the community, for his fellow citizens, t But how necessary is it to recognize again and again

[33]
that idealism is not perhaps superfluous or even dispensable expression of feeling, but that in truth it was, is, and

[33]
will be the prerequisite for what we call human culture; indeed, that idealism alone has created the notion 'man.'

[33]
To this inner attitude the Aryan owes his position in the world, and to it the world owes man; for this attitude

[34]
alone has shaped the mere intellect into the creative force which now, in its unique blending of the crude fist

[33]
with ingenious intellect, has created the monuments of human culture. Without its ideal attitude all, even

[32]
the most brilliant, abil- NATION AND RACE 411 ities of the intellect would only be intellect in itself, but never

[33]
creative force, outward appearance without inner value. But as true idealism is nothing but subjecting the indi-

[32]
vidual's interest and life to the community, and as this again represents the presumptions for any kind of

[32]
creative organizing forms, therefore in its very heart it corresponds to the ultimate will of Nature.

[33]
Idealism alone leads men to voluntary acknowledgment of the privilege of force and strength and thus makes them

[31]
become a dust particle of that order which forms and shapes the entire universe. Purest idealism is

[30]
unconsciously deepest knowledge. How much this applies and how little genuine idealism has to do with playful

[32]
imagination one can recognize imme- diately if the unspoilt child, the healthy boy, is permitted to

[34]
judge. The same boy who is nauseated by the drivel of an ' ideal ' pacifist is ready to throw away his young life for

[33]
the ideal of his nationality. Here the instinct of realization unconsciously obeys the deeper necessity of

[32]
the preservation of the species, if neces- sary at the expense of the individual, and it protests against the

[33]
visions of the pacifist babbler who in reality as a crudely made-up yet cowardly egoist trespasses against

[33]
the laws of development; for the latter is conditioned by the individual's willingness to sacrifice himself

[33]
in favor of the Someone has written: 'Suffer the little children to come unto me; for theirs is the kingdom of death. 1 Three

[33]
months after Hitler's rise to power, the traveler through Germany could see in school play-yards tots of four and five with sticks on

[34]
their shoulders, going through military evolutions at the command of a drill-master. Austria, in the days following the Anschluss,

[31]
was patrolled by boys of upper grammar school and high school age. They were armed with rifles and drawn bayonets. 412 MEIN KAMPF

[33]
community and not by sickly imagination on the part of cowardly know-alls and critics of Nature, Just in such

[34]
times, when the ideal attitude threatens to disappear, we can at once recognize a reduction of that force which

[34]
forms the community and thus gives culture its presumption. As soon as egoism becomes the ruler of a na- tion, the ties

[31]
of order loosen, and in the hunt for their own happiness people fall all the more out of heaven into hell. Even

[34]
posterity forgets those men who only serve their own advantage, and it praises as heroes those who renounce their

[32]
own happiness. <The Jew forms the strongest contrast to the Aryan. Hardly in any people of the world is the instinct of self-

[33]
preservation more strongly developed than in the so-called 'chosen people/ The fact of the existence of this race

[32]
alone may be looked upon as the best proof of this. Where is the people that in the past two thousand years has been ex-

[33]
posed to so small changes of the inner disposition, of char- acter, etc., as the Jewish people? Which people finally has

[33]
experienced greater changes than this one and yet has always come forth the same from the most colossal catas trophes

[33]
of mankind? What an infinitely persistent will for life, for preserving the race do these facts disclose! Also

[32]
the intellectual abilities were schooled in the course of centuries. Today the Jew is looked upon as

[33]
'clever,' and in a certain sense he has been so at all times. But his reason is not the result of his own development,

[33]
but that of object lessons from without. For also the human mind is not able to climb the heights without steps; for every step

[33]
forward he needs the foundation of the past, and, moreover, in that comprehensive meaning which can be revealed only through

[33]
general culture. All thinking will rest only to a very small extent on one's own realization, but to the greater

[30]
extent NATION AND RACE 413 on the experiences of the time past. The general level of culture supplies the

[33]
individual, mostly without his noticing this, with such a profusion of preliminary knowledge that now, armed

[33]
in this manner, he can set out towards further steps of his own. The young boy of today, for instance, grows up among a truly

[32]
vast number of technical achieve- ments of the past few centuries that now, as being matters of course, he no longer pays

[30]
attention to many things which were still a riddle to great minds a hundred years ago, though for the follow-up and the

[33]
understanding of our progress in this field it is of decisive importance for him. If today even a genius

[33]
of the twenties of the past century were suddenly to leave his grave, he would find it much harder to make his way

[32]
about in the present time than this is the case of an average boy of fifteen of today. For he would lack all the

[33]
infinite prerequisites which the individual takes in, so to speak, unconsciously, during his adolescence

[33]
in the midst of the general culture of the corresponding time. As now the Jew (for reasons which will immediately

[32]
be- come evident from the following) was never in the pos- session of a culture of his own, the bases for his

[32]
spiritual 'The Jews, 1 said Chamberlain, 'are neither a race nor a people They are the unique example of

[33]
a purely parasitic product of decay.' This point of view is based to a certain ex- tent on a corrupt reading of

[29]
a sentence in Mommsen's Roman History, which reads: 'In the Old World, too, Jewry was an active ferment of

[31]
cosmopolitanism and national decomposition, and was for that reason a preferred full-fledged member in the

[32]
Caesarian States, the politics of which were in truth nothing but cosmopolitanism, and the folkdom of which was

[33]
essentially nothing else than humanity/ Mommsen meant that the Jews, uprooted from their Fatherland, lived everywhere

[32]
and served as links to tie Rome to the provinces. Chamberlain built up an elaborate theory to account for this

[33]
'parasitic product.' The 414 MEIN KAMPF activity have always been furnished by others. At all times his intellect has

[33]
developed through the culture that sur- rounds him' Never did the reverse process take place, t For, even if the Jewish

[31]
people's instinct of self-preserva- tion is not smaller, but rather greater, than that of other nations, and even if his

[32]
spiritual abilities very easily create the impression as though they were equal to the intel- lectual

[33]
disposition of the other races, yet the most essential presumption for a cultured people is completely lacking,

[34]
the idealistic disposition. In the Jewish people, the will to sacrifice oneself does not go beyond the bare instinct

[32]
of self-preservation of the indi- vidual. The seemingly great feeling of belonging together is rooted in a

[34]
very primitive herd instinct, as it shows itself Jews were, he thought, a race mixed with other races too diverse in

[29]
character to permit assimilation. They had married with Arabs and Syrians, and were as a result

[33]
degenerate. Original sin as described in the Old Testament was, he held, only the 'sin of blood' i.e., the sin

[33]
of intermarriage with inferior breeds. Few Nazis prior to 1933 put much faith in these teachings, at which Ernst Roehm is known to

[34]
have laughed. To them Jew baiting was merely a highly effective form of drumming up prejudice against the hated

[33]
Republic, which had given jobs to Rathenau, Eisner, Hilferding, and others. Even today one hears honest Nazi dissent

[33]
from the official anti-Semitism, but this is probably more or less in- grained in youth. There was abundant protest

[33]
against the November pogroms, but little of it was publicly manifested. The popular readiness to be stirred to

[33]
a passion over the Jews witness the 'Juda vcrrecke' (May the Jews die) out- cry which the youth organizations in particular

[32]
have taken up seems based partly on willingness to detest all things not strictly German (a consequence, no doubt, of the

[33]
disap- pointments and privations that followed the War) and partly NATION AND RACE 415 in a similar way in many other

[31]
living beings in this world. Thereby the fact is remarkable that in all these cases a common herd instinct leads to

[33]
mutual support only as long as a common danger makes this seem useful or unavoidable. The same pack of

[33]
wolves that jointly falls upon its booty dissolves when its hunger abates. The same is true of horses, which try to ward

[32]
off the attacker in common, and which fly in different directions when the danger is gone. With the Jew the case is

[32]
similar. His will to sacrifice is only ostensible. It endures only as long as the existence of the

[33]
individual absolutely requires this. However, as soon as the common enemy is beaten and the danger

[33]
threatening all is averted, the booty recovered, the apparent harmony among the Jews themselves ceases to make

[32]
way again for on economic unrest. The Jew was represented as one who pro- fited by the inflation, or as the

[33]
major cause of business and professional competition. But it is difficult to make a good argument to show

[33]
Jewish economic dominance in pre-Hitler Germany, nor as Jewish cultural influence noteworthy outside

[32]
Berlin. What can be said is that an unwise cult of publicity sometimes overstressed the importance of

[33]
individual Jews. Many believed that anti-Semitic propaganda could be stopped if it were shown that Jews had

[33]
contributed a great deal to the reputation of Germany abroad. Almost precisely the opposite effect was

[33]
achieved. For a digest of statistics concerning the Jew in business, cultural and professional life, cf. The Jews in

[32]
Nazi Germany, edited by the American Jewish Committee. A somewhat better case could be made out

[29]
against the Jewish proletariat, since it was largely recruited from eastern Europe and was not

[33]
immediately able to throw off the manners of the ghetto. But it was far too small and too isolated to be a

[31]
factor of importance in German life, excepting as a source whence certain types of photography might be

[29]
derived. The labor groups, both Marxist and Christian, frowned upon anti-Semi- tism. 416 MEIN KAMPF the inclinations

[33]
originally present. The Jew remains united only if forced by a common danger or is attracted by a com-

[33]
mon booty; if both reasons are no longer evident, then the qualities of the crassest egoism come into their own, and,

[32]
in a moment, the united people becomes a horde of rats, fight- ing bloodily among themselves. If the Jews were

[33]
alone in this world, they would suffocate as much in dirt and filth, as they would carry on a detest- able struggle to cheat

[33]
and to ruin each other, although the complete lack of the will to sacrifice, expressed in their cowardice, would also

[33]
in this instance make the fight a comedy. <Thus it is fundamentally wrong to conclude, merely from the fact of

[32]
their standing together in a fight, or, more rightly expressed, in their exploiting their fellow human beings, that the Jews have

[34]
a certain idealistic will to sacrifice them- selves. Here, too, the Jew is led by nothing but pure egoism on the part

[32]
of the individual. Therefore also the Jewish 'State' (which is supposed to be the living organism for the

[33]
preservation and the propa- gation of the race) is territorially completely unlimited. For a certain

[32]
limitation of a State formation by space always presupposes an idealistic attitude by the State

[31]
race, espe- cially above all a correct conception of the notion 'work/ In the same measure in which this

[31]
attitude is lacking or absent, every attempt at a formation or even at the preser- vation of a

[30]
territorially limited State fails. But with this also the basis on which a culture alone can

[29]
originate is eliminated. For this reason, however, the Jewish people, with all its apparent

[33]
intellectual qualities, is nevertheless without any true culture, especially without a culture of its

[33]
own. For the sham culture which the Jew possesses today is the property of other peoples, and is mostly spoiled in his

[33]
hands. NATION AND RACE 417 tWhen judging Jewry in its attitude towards the question of human culture, one has to keep

[33]
before one's eye as an essential characteristic that there never has been and con- sequently that today also

[31]
there is no Jewish art; that above all the two queens of all arts, architecture and music, owe nothing

[33]
original to Jewry. What he achieves in the field of art is either bowdlerization or intellectual theft. With

[33]
this, the Jew lacks those qualities which distinguish creatively and, with it, culturally blessed races. But how far the Jew

[32]
takes over foreign culture, only imi- tating, or rather destroying, it, may be seen from the fact that he is found most

[33]
frequently in that art which also appears directed least of all towards invention of its own, the art of acting. But here,

[32]
too, he is really only the 'jug- gler/ or rather the ape; for here, too, he lacks the ultimate touch of real greatness;

[32]
here, too, he is not the ingenious creator, but the outward imitator, whereby all the turns and tricks he applies

[33]
cannot deceive us concerning the inner lack of life of his creative ability. Here the Jewish press alone

[32]
comes lovingly to his aid, because about every, even the most mediocre, bungler, ^provided that he is

[32]
a Jew, it raises such a clamor of hosannas that the rest of the world finally actually believes that it sees

[33]
a real artist before its The statement that there had been no Jewish art in olden times is highly questionable.

[34]
Historians of liturgical art now believe that the decorative schemes of early Christain churches may have been

[32]
derived in part from the Synagogue. At all events, the Gregorian Chant certainly owes much to ancient Jewish

[33]
music. To term all modern Jewish art 'derivative' is injudicious, particularly in Germany, as witness Max

[34]
Lieber- mann in painting and Erich Mendelsohn in architecture. Modern Jewish stars of the stage include Elisabeth

[32]
Bergner, Max Pallenberg, and Fritz Kortner. The most famous Jewish theatrical director was Max Reinhardt. 418 MEIN KAMPF eyes, whereas in

[33]
reality it has only to deal with a wretched comedian. No, the Jew possesses no culture-creating energy what-

[32]
soever, as the idealism, without which there can never exist a genuine development of man towards a higher

[33]
level, does not and never did exist in him. His intellect, there- fore, will never have a constructive effect, but

[34]
only a de- structive one, and in very rare cases it is perhaps stimulat- ing, at the utmost, but then in the form

[32]
of the original pro- totype of that 'Kraft, die stets das Bose will und dock das Gute schafft ' [that force which always wants

[33]
evil and never- theless creates good]. Any progress of mankind takes place not through him but in spite of him. As the Jew

[32]
never possessed a State with definite terri- torial boundary, and as therefore he never called

[33]
a culture his own, the conception arose that one had to deal with a people that had to be counted among the ranks

[33]
of the nomads. This is an error that is as great as it is dangerous. The nomad certainly possesses a definitely

[33]
limited living space, only he does not cultivate it like a sedentary peasant, but he lives on the yield

[30]
of his herds with which he wanders about in his territory. The simplest reason for this is to be seen in the poor

[33]
fertility of a soil which therefore does not permit of settlement. But the deepest cause lies in the dis- parity

[34]
between the technical culture of a time or a people and the natural poverty of a living space. There are

[33]
do- mains in which even the Aryan is unable to become master of the soil in closed settlements and to make a

[33]
living from it, except by the technology he developed in the course of more than a thousand years. If he did not

[33]
have this tech- nology, then he would either have to avoid these territories or he would also have to struggle

[31]
along as a nomad in per- petual wandering (provided that his thousand-year-old education and custom of

[33]
settlement did not make this ap- pear simply impossible to him). One has to consider, how- NATION AND RACE 419 ever,

[33]
that at the time the American continent was opened, numerous Aryans fought for their living as trappers, hunt- ers, etc.,

[32]
and this frequently in large groups with women and children, always wandering about, so that their exist- ence resembled

[33]
completely that of the nomads. Only when their increasing number and better instruments permitted them to clear the wild soil

[32]
for tillage and to resist the abor- igines, more and more settlements sprang up over the country.^The Aryan

[33]
also was probably first a nomad, and in the course of time he settled down, but he never was, for this reason, a Jew!

[33]
No, the Jew, is not a nomad; for the latter already has a definite attitude towards the conception 'work' which

[32]
served as the basis for his later development, inasmuch as the necessary spiritual presumptions for that

[32]
purpose are present. With him also the basically idealistic attitude exists, though in an infinite

[31]
dilution, and therefore through his entire character he appears perhaps alien to Aryan peoples, but not

[33]
uncongenial. With the Jew, how- ever, this attitude is non-existent; therefore he never was a nomad, but

[33]
always only a parasite in the body of other peoples. That thereby he sometimes leaves his previous

[34]
liv- This comment on American history is based upon the writ- ings of Karl May, a famous German 'thriller/ whose stories

[30]
of Indians and pioneers Hitler has deeply relished. An interest- ing related passage on nomads in

[33]
America may be found in Das Schwein als Kritcriuvn fucr nordische Vodker und Semitcn (The Hog as a Criterion for Nordic

[30]
Peoples and Semites) by R. Walther Darr6. There an attempt is made to show that the Jewish prohibition of pork

[32]
indicates that they were a nomadic desert people, while the Nordic addiction to that animal reveals an

[32]
innate tendency to settle down. Hans Guenther also attributes Bodenstdndigktil (settling down instinct) to the Germans. Cf .

[33]
Rasscnkunde des deutschen Volkes. 420 MEIN KAMPF ing quarters is not connected with his intention, but is the simple logic of his being

[30]
thrown out from time to time by the host nation he abuses. But his spreading is the typical symptom of all

[33]
parasites; he always looks for a new feeding soil for his race. t But this has nothing to do with nomadism for the reason

[32]
that the Jew does not think of leaving a territory he occu- pies, but he remains where he is sitting, and that means so

[32]
'sedentary' that he may be expelled only with force and with great difficulty. His spreading to ever new countries

[34]
takes place only in the moment when certain conditions for his existence are apparent there; without that he would

[33]
(like the nomad) change his previous residence. He is and remains the typical parasite, a sponger who, like

[32]
a harmful bacillus, spreads out more and more if only a favorable medium invites 'him to do so. But the

[33]
effect of his existence resembles also that of parasites; where he appears the host people die out sooner or

[32]
later. Thus the Jew lived at all times in the States of other peoples and there he formed his own State, which, though

[33]
disguised by the name of 'religious community/ generally sailed as long as external circumstances did

[32]
not see fit to make a complete revelation of its nature. But once he believed himself strong enough to be

[33]
able to dispense with the protecting cover, then he always dropped the veil and sud- denly he was what so many others

[33]
were unwilling to see and to believe in before : the Jew. In the Jew's life as a parasite in the body

[32]
of other nations and States, his characteristic is established which once caused Schopenhauer to pronounce the

[32]
sentence, already mentioned, that the Jew is the 'great master of lying. 9 Life urges the Jew towards the lie, that is, to

[33]
a perpetual lie, just as it forces the inhabitants of northern countries to wear warm clothes.-' His life within other

[33]
peoples can only exist in the long NATION AND RACE 421 run if he succeeds in creating the impression as though he were not

[33]
a people but only a 'religious community,' though a special one. But with this the first great lie starts. In order to

[30]
lead his existence as a peoples 9 parasite he is forced to deny his inner nature. Now the more

[33]
intelligent the individual Jew is, the more will he succeed in this delusion. It can even go so far that great

[32]
parts of the host nation finally believe in all sincerity that the Jew is really a French- man or an Englishman,

[31]
a German or an Italian, though also of a special 'denomination.' f State authorities, which always seem to be

[33]
animated only by the historical 'frac- tion' of wisdom, fall most easily victim of this infamous deception. In

[33]
these circles independent thinking is looked upon as a genuine sin against the holy advancement, so that one

[33]
must not be surprised that for example even today a Bavarian State minister has not the faintest idea that

[33]
the Jew is a people and not a 'denomination' though only one look into the Jew's own newspaper world ought immedi-

[32]
ately to demonstrate this to even the most modest mind. Of course, the Jewish Echo is not yet an official

[32]
organ and therefore it is 'unauthoritative' for the brains of such a government potentate. The Jews were

[33]
always a people with definite racial qual- ities and never a religion, only their progress made them probably

[31]
look very early for a means which could divert disagreeable attention from their person. But what would have been more

[32]
useful and at the same time more harmless than the 'purloining' of the appearance of being a religious

[32]
community? For here, too, everything is purloined, or rather, stolen. But resulting from his own original

[33]
nature the Jew cannot possess a religious institution for the very reason that he lacks all idealism in any

[33]
form and that he also does not recognize any belief in the hereafter. But in the Aryan conception one cannot

[34]
conceive of a religioo 422 MEIN KAMPF which lacks the conviction of the continuation of life after death in some form.

[32]
Indeed, the Talmud is then not a book for the preparation for the life to come, but rather for a practical and

[34]
bearable life in this world. The Jewish religious doctrine is primarily a direction for preserving the purity

[34]
of the blood of Judaism as well as for the regulation of the Jews' intercourse with one an- other, but even more in

[33]
connection with the rest of the world, that means, with non-Jews. But here, too, the prob- lems involved are not at all ethical, but

[32]
rather extremely modest economic ones. About the moral value of the Jew- ish religious instructions there

[34]
exist today and there have existed at all times rather exhaustive studies (on the non- Jewish side; the drivel

[32]
of the Jews themselves about this is, of course, cut to the purpose) which make this kind of 'religion' appear even

[33]
odious from Aryan viewpoints. But the best stamp is given by the product of this 'religious' education, the Jew himself. His life

[32]
is really only of this world, and his spirit is as alien to true Christianity, for in- Jewish religion does stress

[33]
belief in the immortality of the soul. The earlier portions of the Old Testament do not, it is true, explicitly go

[33]
beyond affirmations concerning the im- mortality of the Jewish people as a whole. Later on, in the Book of Daniel

[33]
and in Maccbabees, the ideas of the survival of the soul and of bodily resurrection are emphasized. Medie-

[33]
val Jewry clung to the belief, and the records of 'saints' who died during persecutions breathe a firm hope of survival in

[33]
God. For a liberal Jewish commentary, cf. A Social and Religious History of the Jews, by Salo Wittmayer Baron.

[33]
The reasoning here is more explicitly formulated in Rosen- berg. Cf. also, St. Paul's Epistle to the Romans, Chapter

[32]
1 1 : 'As concerning the Gospel, they are enemies for your sake; but as touching the election, they are beloved for the

[33]
fathers 9 sake'/ NATION AND RACE 423 seance, as his nature was two thousand years ago to the Sublime Founder of the new

[33]
doctrine. Of course, the latter made no secret of His disposition towards the Jewish people, and when necessary

[33]
He even took to the whip in order to drive out of the Lord's temple this adversary of all humanity, who even

[33]
then as always saw in religion only a means for his business existence. But for this, of course, Christ was crucified,

[33]
while our present party Christianity disgraces itself by begging for Jewish votes in the elections and later tries

[32]
to conduct political wirepulling with atheis- tic Jewish parties, and this against their own nation. Upon this first and

[31]
greatest lie, that the Jew is not a race but simply a religion, further lies are then built up in neces- sary

[32]
consequence. To them also belongs the language spoken at the time by the Jew. For him it is never a means of

[33]
expressing his thoughts, but for hiding them. When he speaks French, he thinks Jewish, and when he turns out German poetry, he only gives an

[32]
outlet to the nature of his people. As long as the Jew has not become the master of the other peoples, he must,

[33]
whether he likes it or not, speak their lan- guages, and only if they would be his slaves then they might all speak a universal

[33]
language so that their domination will be made easier (Esperanto!). How far the entire existence of this people

[33]
is based on a continuous lie is shown in an incomparable manner and certainty in the 'Protocols of the Wise

[33]
Men of Zion/ so The 'Protocols of the Wise Men of Zion' were first circu- lated in Russia during the early years of

[29]
the twentieth century. Apparently they formed part of the literary stock-in-trade of certain secret

[34]
organizations. The tract purports to be an account of a meeting between Jewish leaders in the fall of 1897, which year marked the first

[31]
convention of the Zionist Congress. Since pilgrimages to the Holy Land were popular in Russia, tht 424 MEIN KAMPF

[33]
infinitely hated by the Jews. They are supposed to be a 'forgery' the Frankfurter Zeitung moans and cries out to

[31]
the world once a week; the best proof that they are genuine after all. What many Jews may do unconsciously is here

[32]
exposed consciously. But this is what matters. It makes no difference from the head of which Jew these disclosures

[30]
come, but decisive it is that they demonstrate, with a truly horrifying certainty, the nature and the

[33]
activity of the Jew- ish people and expose them in their inner connection as well as in their ultimate final

[33]
aims. But the best criticism ap- plied to them is reality. He who examines the historical development of the past

[33]
hundred years, from the points of view of this book, will also immediately understand the clamor of the Jewish press. For once

[32]
this book has become the common property of a people, the Jewish danger is bound to be considered as broken.

[33]
combination of Zionism and terrorism was effective propa- ganda. A horrible plot to undermine society,

[30]
overthrow governments, and destroy Christianity is revealed. The 'minutes' are copied verbatim from 'A

[33]
Dialogue in Hades Between Machiavelli and Montesquieu, ' an attack on the Masons and the Bonapartists written

[32]
in French by Maurice Joly in 1868. The 'Protocols' merely substituted the word 'Jew' for Joly's own devils. Another

[30]
probable source is Biarritz, a novel published by John Retcliff in 1868, one scene in which described an

[32]
imaginary annual meeting of 'the prince of the twelve Tribes of Israel' in the Jewish ceme- tery of

[33]
Prague. They discuss measures calculated to destroy all Christians. Editions of the 'Protocols' edited by Rosen- berg

[32]
and others are now widely circulated in Germany and other countries. Noteworthy is the fact that Hitler's

[31]
justifi- cation of them (Count Reventlow had admitted their spuriousness during a sensational trial in 1923) almost

[31]
parallels the explanation given by the Reverend Charles Coughlin at the time they were reprinted in his

[32]
periodical, Social Justice. NATION AND RACE 425 In order to become acquainted with the Jew, it is best to

[32]
study the way he took inside the body of the other peoples in the course of the centuries. It suffices to

[33]
follow this up on the basis of only one example in order to arrive at the necessary conclusions. As

[33]
his development was always and at all times the same, as also the peoples he eats into are always the same,

[31]
it is recommended for such a study to break his development up into certain sections which in this case, to

[33]
simplify matters, I denote with letters. The first Jews came to ancient Germany in the course of the advance of

[33]
the Romans, that is, as tradesmen as usual In the storms of the peoples' migration, however, an end seems to have been

[34]
put also to this, and therefore the time of the first Germanic State formation may be considered the beginning

[34]
of a new and now permanent Judaization of Cen- tral and North Europe. Now a development sets in which was always the same

[33]
or a similar one, wherever Jews met Aryan peoples. (a) With the appearance of the first fixed settlements the Jew

[33]
is suddenly 'there/ He comes as a tradesman, and at the beginning he puts little stress on the disguise of hia

[33]
nationality. He is still a Jew, partly perhaps also for the reason that the external racial difference between

[33]
him and the host nation is too great and his linguistic knowledge too small, and that the seclusion of the host nation is too strong

[33]
for him to venture to appear as something different from a 'foreign tradesman.' With his versatility and the host

[33]
nation's inexperience it is no disadvantage, but rather an advantage, for him to keep up his character as

[33]
'Jew'; one meets the stranger courteously. (ft) Now he gradually begins to become 'active' in eco- nomic life,

[33]
not as a producer, but exclusively as an inter- mediary link. In his versatility of a thousand years'

[33]
trading 426 MEIN KAMPF he is infinitely superior to the clumsy and boundlessly hon- est Aryans, so that after a short

[33]
time trade threatens to become his monopoly. Further, he begins money-lending and that always at usurious

[33]
interest. He actually intro- duces interest by this. The danger of this new institution is not recognized

[30]
at first, but for the sake of the momen- tary advantages it is even welcomed. (c) The Jew has settled down

[33]
completely; that means, he occupies special quarters in the towns and villages and more and more he forms a special State

[33]
within the State. He considers trade as well as all money transactions as his very own privilege, which he exploits

[33]
ruthlessly. (d) Money transactions and trade have now completely become his monopoly. His usurious rates of

[32]
interest finally stir up resistance, his otherwise increasing impertinence causes indignation, his

[31]
riches envy. The cup is filled to overflowing when he draws also the land and the soil into the circle of his

[33]
mercenary objects and degrades it to the level of goods to be sold or rather to be traded. As he him- self never

[32]
tills the soil, but only looks upon it as a property to be exploited, on which the peasant may well remain but only

[33]
under the most wretched extortions on the part of his present master, the aversion against him finally grows into open

[33]
hatred. His blood-sucking tyranny becomes so great that riots against him occur. Now one begins to look more and more

[33]
closely at the stranger and one discovers more and more new repellent features and characteristics in him,

[33]
till the chasm becomes an unsurmountable one. In times of most bitter distress the wrath against him finally breaks out,

[33]
and the exploited and ruined masses take up self-defense in order to ward off the scourge of God. They have got to

[33]
know him in the course of several cen- turies and they experience his mere existence as the same distress as

[32]
the plague. (e) Now, however, the Jew begins to unveil his true qual- NATION AND RACE 427 ities. With disgusting flattery he

[34]
approaches the govern- ments, he puts his money to work, and in this manner he secures again and again the privilege of

[32]
a renewed exploi- tation of his victims. Although sometimes the people's fury against the eternal blood-sucker

[33]
flares up like fire, this does not prevent him in the least from appearing again, after a few years, at the place he had

[32]
barely left and to begin his former life all over. No persecution can deter him from ex- ploiting mankind, can

[32]
expel him; after each one he is here again after a short time, and just the same as he was before. In

[33]
order at least to prevent the worst, one begins to take the soil out of his usurious hands by making the acquisition

[33]
of soil legally impossible for him. [j (/) In the measure in which the power of the monarchs begins to rise, he pushes

[33]
nearer and nearer to them. He begs for 'privileges' and 'charters/ which he willingly re- ceives, against corresponding payment,

[33]
from these gentle- men who are always in need of money. No matter what this costs him, he gets back with interest and compound

[33]
in- terest in the course of a few years the money he has spent. A real blood-sucker which attaches itself to the body of

[33]
the unfortunate people and which cannot be removed until the monarchs themselves again need money and in person

[32]
tap the blood that he has sucked in. This game is repeated again, whereby the r61e of the For a history of these

[33]
pogroms which were caused in the main by the enthusiasm incident to the Crusades cf. 'Die Judcnbck&mpfung im Mittdaltcr,' by Peter

[33]
Browe, S.J., m Zcitschrift jtir katholische Theologie (Vol. LXII, nrs. 2 and 3). Saint Bernard preached against these disorders, and the Papal Bull

[32]
Licet perfidia iudaeorum was published to stop them. Browe's conclusion is that charges of usury, etc.,

[31]
emerge rela- tively late, indicating possibly that the Jews resorted to such measures as means of

[31]
defense. 418 MEIN KAMPF so-called 'German monarchs 9 is just as wretched as that of the Jews themselves. They were really God's

[32]
chastisement for their 'dear' people, these gentlemen, and they find their parallel only in the various ministers of the

[33]
present time. It was thanks to the German monarchs that the German nation was unable to free itself for good from the Jewish

[34]
danger. Unfortunately, this fact did not change later on, so that by the Jew they were only allotted the thousandfold

[32]
reward they deserved for the sins they once committed against their peoples. They had sold themselves to the Devil and had

[33]
landed in his domain. (g) Thus his ensnaring the monarchs led to their ruin. Their attitude towards the peoples loosens slowly but

[30]
surely in the measure in which they cease to serve the interests of the latter and, instead, become the

[34]
usufructuaries of their 'subjects.' The Jew knows their end accurately, and he tries to speed it up if possible. He himself

[34]
advances their eternal financial troubles by diverting them more and more from their true tasks; by toadying to them with the worst

[33]
flattery, he induces them to vice and thus makes himself more and more indispensable. His versatility,

[34]
rather his anscrupulousness, in all money matters knows how to extract, even to extort, more and more money from the ex-

[33]
ploited subjects who tread the path to nothing in shortei and shorter periods of time. Every Court thus has its 4 Court Jew.' (This

[33]
is the name of the monsters who tor- ture the beloved people to the point of despair and who pre- pare the eternal

[31]
pleasure of the monarchs.) Who will won- der, then, that these 'ornaments' of the human race are finally also

[33]
outwardly decorated and rise to the ranks of the hereditary 'nobility/ and thus help not only in making

[33]
this institution ridiculous, but even in poisoning it. Another allusion to the Habsburgs, accused of having

[33]
pro- tected the Jews and of having assured their rise in the world. NATION AND RACE 429 Now he is all the more able to

[32]
use his position for the sake of his advancement. Finally, he only needs to submit himself to baptism in

[33]
order to come into the possession of all possibilities and rights of the natives of the country. He puts through this

[33]
'business' not infrequently to the joy of the churches over the 'son' they have won and to Israel's joy at the successful

[33]
swindle. (fi) Now a change begins to take place within Jewry. So far they were Jews; that means they did not want to appear

[32]
as something else, and also they could not do so with such extremely pronounced race characteristics on both

[33]
sides. Still at the time of Frederick the Great nobody would think of seeing in the Jew something other than a ' foreign

[33]
1 people, and Goethe is still horrified at the idea that in future matri- mony between Christians and Jews would no longer

[32]
be for- bidden by law. Now Goethe was, God knows, certainly no reactionary, far less a helot; what spoke out of him was

[33]
nothing but the voice of blood and of reason. Thus, despite all disgraceful actions of the Courts, the people instinctively

[33]
sees in the Jew the alien element in its own body and it takes a corresponding attitude towards him. This

[33]
was to become different now. In the course of a thousand years he has learned to master the language of his host people

[33]
to such an extent as to believe that he can in the future risk to accent his Judaism a little less and to put his

[33]
' Germanity ' more into the foreground ; for no matter how ridiculous, nay, absurd, it may seem at first, yet he permits

[32]
himself the impudence of changing himself into a 'Ger- manic'; in this case therefore a 'German.' Thereby

[31]
begins one of the most infamous lies conceivable. Since of Ger- manity he possesses really nothing but the

[33]
ability to speak its language badly in the most terrible manner, since for the rest, however, he never blended

[33]
with it, therefore his whole Germanitv rests only on the language. The race, however, 430 MEIN KAMPF ia not based

[33]
upon the language, but upon the blood exclu- sively, something that nobody knows better than the Jew, who puts only

[34]
very little value upon the preservation of his language, but everything on the preservation of the purity

[33]
of his blood. One can change the language of a man with- out ado, that means he can use another language; but then

[33]
he will express his old thoughts in his new language, his inner nature will not be changed. This is shown best of all by the Jew

[31]
who is able to speak in a thousand languages and yet remains always the one Jew. His character qualities have

[33]
remained the same, whether two thousand years ago he spoke Roman as a grain merchant in Ostia or whether as a flour

[31]
profiteer of today he haggles German like a Jew. He is always the same Jew. That this matter of course is

[33]
naturally not understood by a normal councillor of the min- istry or a higher police official of today

[32]
is also a matter of course, as hardly any person endowed with less instinct or intellect walks about than these

[33]
'servants' of our exem- plary 'State authority 1 of the 'present time/ The reason why the Jew decides now suddenly

[33]
to become a ' German ' is obvious. He feels that the power of the mon- archfe begins slowly to tumble, and therefore

[33]
he seeks to get a platform under his feet in time. Further, his financial rule of the entire business life has

[33]
already progressed so far that, without the possession of all the 'civil' rights, he is no longer able to support the whole

[32]
enormous building, in any case no further increase of his influence can take place. But he wishes both; for the

[32]
higher he climbs, the more allur- ingly rises out of the veil of the past his old goal, once pro- mised to him, and with

[30]
feverish greed he watches in his brightest heads the dream of world domination step into tangible proximity.

[33]
Therefore, his sole endeavor is aimed at putting himself into complete possession of the ' civil f rights. This is

[33]
the reason for the emancipation from the ghetto NATION AND RACE 431 Thus the Court Jew develops slowly into the folk Jew;

[33]
that means, of course, the Jew remains now as before in the surroundings of the high gentlemen, he even tries to push still more

[33]
into this circle ; but at the same time another part of his race chums up to the 'dear people.' If one considers

[32]
how much he has sinned against the masses in the course of the centuries, how again and again he squeezed and ex-

[31]
torted without mercy, if one considers further how the people gradually learned to hate him for this and

[33]
finally saw in his existence really nothing but a punishment of Heaven, then one can understand how hard this change

[33]
must be for the Jew. Yes, it is tiresome work to present oneself suddenly again as ' friend of mankind ' to the skinned

[32]
victims. At first, therefore, he begins to make good, in the eyes of the people, what so far he had sinned against it. He

[32]
begins his change as 'benefactor' of mankind. As his new benevolence has a genuine foundation, he cannot

[33]
very well keep to the old words of the Bible that the left hand must not know what the right hand gives, but whether he wants it or not,

[33]
he has to be content with letting as many people as possible know how much he feels the sufferings of the masses and what

[32]
sacrifices he offers personally for this. In the form of this inborn ' modesty ' he calls out his merits to the rest

[32]
Goethe, born in Frankfort, describes the ghetto as he had known it during his boyhood. In Berlin there was already a

[32]
somewhat different situation, although Jews coming there to engage in business were obliged to pay

[34]
tribute. Thus Moses Mendelssohn, founder of the famous banker family, was obliged to put down the purchase price for

[32]
twelve porcelain monkeys of a kind then being produced at the Royal Factory. Emancipation of the Jew was not in

[33]
effect everywhere in Ger- many until 1869. As a boy, Heinrich Heine knew no German. How many Jews had been converted

[34]
previously the ghetto was a religious dividing line we have no means of telling. 432 MEIN KAMPF of the world until the world

[33]
begins really to believe in them. Those who do not believe this do him a great injustice. After a short time he

[33]
begins even to twist these things in such a way as to make it appear as though so far one had only wronged him, and

[33]
not vice versa. Those who are especially stupid believe this and they cannot but have sympathy with the poor

[33]
'unfortunate' one. For the rest one ought to remark here that the Jew, despite all willingness to sacrifice,

[31]
naturally never becomes poor. He knows very well how to manage; indeed, his char- ity is sometimes

[31]
actually comparable to the manure which is spread on the field, not out of love for the latter, but out of

[33]
precaution for one's own benefit later on. But in any case, everybody knows after a comparatively

[32]
short time that the Jew has now become a ' Benefactor and friend of mankind.' What a strange change ! But for this reason

[32]
alone, what to others is more or less natural now creates astonishment, and among many even visible

[33]
admiration. Thus it happens that for this reason one gives him much more credit than to the rest of man- kind, for in their

[33]
case it is considered a matter of course. But even more: the Jew becomes suddenly also 'liberal' and

[32]
he begins to rave of the necessary 'progress' of man- kind. Thus he gradually makes himself the spokesman of

[32]
a new time. Of course, he destroys then also more and more thoroughly the foundations of a truly useful

[33]
national economy. By the roundabout way of the 'share' capital he pushes his way into the circulation of

[33]
national production, he makes the latter an object of usury by way of buying or rather of trading, and thus he robs

[33]
the organizations of the basis of a personal ownership. Only thus there arises that inner estrangement

[32]
between employer and employee which leads to the following political class cleavage. NATION AND RACE 433 But finally, where

[34]
economic interests are concerned, the Jewish influence through the stock exchange grows with ter- rifying speed. He becomes

[33]
the owner, or at least the con- troller, of the national labor force. For the strengthening of his political position

[33]
he tries to pull down the racial and civil barriers which at first still restrain him at every step. For this purpose he fights with

[33]
all his innate thoroughness for religious tolerance and in the completely deteriorated Freemasonry

[34]
he has an excel- lent instrument for fighting out and also for 'putting over' his aims. By the strings of Freemasonry the circles

[33]
of the government and the higher layers of the political and economic bourgeoisie fall into his nets without their

[33]
even guessing this. Only the people as such, or rather that class which is now about to wake up, which fights for its own rights and

[33]
its freedom, cannot yet be sufficiently seized by this in its deeper and broader layers. But this is more necessary than

[33]
everything else; for the Jew actually feels that the possi- bility for his rising to a dominating r61e is

[32]
only given if there is a 'pacemaker' before him; but the latter he believes he can recognize in the

[33]
bourgeoisie, and this in its broadest lay- ers. But one cannot catch glovemakers and linen weavers in the fine net of

[33]
Freemasonry; for this one has to apply more coarse but not less thorough means. Thus to Free- masonry the second weapon

[31]
in the service of Jewry is Hence Rosenberg's crusade against Freemasonry. After 1933, powerful business

[32]
influences were able to halt for a time the dissolution of the lodges. Masonry was inconsequential in

[33]
Germany, the total number of initiates being 76,360 in 1931. They divided into two groups, one of which was 'Christian- national'

[31]
(i.e., conservative), while the other was 'liberal. 9 The first group comprised more than two-thirds of the total

[31]
membership. 434 MEIN KAMPF added ; the press. He puts himself into possession of it with all toughness, but also with infinite

[32]
versatility. With it he begins slowly to grasp and to ensnare, to lead and to push the entire public life,

[31]
because now he is in a position to pro- duce and to conduct that power which under the name of 'public

[31]
opinion' is better known today than it was a few decades ago. But thereby he always presents himself as

[32]
infinitely thirsty for knowledge, he praises all progress, but most of all, of course, that progress which leads others to

[31]
destruc- tion; for in all knowledge and every development he sees forever only the possibility of the

[33]
advancement of his own nationality, and, where this possibility does not exist, he is the inexorable

[33]
and mortal enemy of all light, the despiser of all true culture. Thus he applies all knowledge which he takes in in

[31]
the schools of the others, only to the service of his race. This nationality, however, he guards as never

[33]
before. While he seems to overflow with 'enlightenment,' 'pro- gress/ 'freedom/ 'humanity,' etc., he exercises the strictest

[33]
seclusion of his race. Although he sometimes hangs his women onto the coattails of influential Christians, yet he always

[32]
keeps his male line pure in principle. He poisons the blood of the others, but he guards his own. The Jew does not marry

[32]
a Christian woman, but always the Chris- tian a Jewess. Yet the bastards take to the Jewish side. Especially a part of the

[34]
higher nobility degrades itself com- pletely. He knows this only too well, and for this reason he systematically

[32]
carries out this kind of 'disarmament' of the A very curious generalization. Researches in several German

[31]
Jewish family trees reveal the fact that since the emancipation, the majority of extra-confessional

[33]
marriages were those of Jewish men marrying Christian girls. In the United States, Abie's Irish Rose emphasizes

[34]
the same trend. NATION AND RACE 435 spiritually leading class of his racial adversaries. Yet, in order to disguise his

[31]
activity and to put his victims to sleep, he speaks now more and more of the equality of all men, without

[34]
consideration of race and of color. And those who are stupid begin to believe him. But as his entire being

[34]
still smells too strongly of the stranger for the great mass of the people especially to fall without ado into his nets, he makes

[33]
his press give a picture of himself which corresponds to reality as little as it serves, nevertheless, the purpose

[32]
he intended. Especially in car- toons one endeavors to present the Jew as a harmless little folk which cannot help

[33]
having its characteristics (as others also), but which even by its manners, appearing perhaps a little strange, gives

[34]
forth symptoms of his possibly comic, yet always fundamentally honest and benevolent soul. On the whole one strives

[34]
at making him always appear more 4 unimportant ‘ than dangerous. His final goal in this State, however, is the victory

[33]
of ‘democracy/ or as he understands it: because it eliminates Certainly no orthodox Jews on record have

[32]
subscribed even to the Christian version of the doctrine that all men are equal. This teaching has, indeed, no meaning

[33]
unless it signifies the equality of persons before the law, whether Divine (i.e., religious) or human.

[34]
One of the most remarkable anti-Semitic addresses delivered by Hitler is dated from April, 1922. The following

[32]
passage may be cited: ‘Jewry has tried a ruse which, from the political point of view, is really very clever. This

[33]
capitalistic people, which was the first on this earth to introduce the enslavement of men, has managed to take the

[33]
leadership of the Fourth Estate into its hands. In so doing it had adopted two lands of tactic, one of the Right and one

[33]
of the Left, since it has apostles in both camps. The Jew on the Right tries to make all faults that exist stand out so clearly that

[31]
the man on the street, poor 436 MEIN KAMPF the personality and in its place it puts the majority of stupidity,

[32]
incapacity, and last, but not least, cowardice. The final result of this development will be the overthrow of the

[32]
monarch which is bound to arrive sooner or later. -4- The enormous economic development leads to a change in the

[33]
social classification of the people. While the small craftsmen die out gradually and thus the worker's possi- bility

[33]
of winning an independent existence becomes more and more rare, the worker becomes more visibly

[33]
prole- tarian. The industrial 'factory worker 1 comes into being whose essential characteristic is to be seen in

[33]
the fact that he hardly ever reaches the position of founding an existence of his own in his later life. He is

[31]
' without property' in the truest meaning of the word, so that his old age means a tor- ture rather than life. Even

[30]
previously a similar position had been created devil, will be irritated to the nth degree greed for money,

[33]
unscrupulousness, hardness of heart, disgusting displays of wealth. More and more Jews had slid into the better families, you

[33]
see, and therefore the ruling class has become estranged from its people. 'This was the premise on which work on the Left

[33]
was under- taken. For he was there, to the Left the cheap little dema-gogue. He made it impossible for patriots

[31]
of intelligence to accept positions of leadership in the workers' organizations, first by adopting an

[33]
internationalist point of view, and then by sponsoring a Marxist theory which proclaimed that property as such is theft. Now

[32]
the leadership of industry, in so far as it was patriotic-minded, also could not put up with what was happening.

[33]
Therewith the Jew succeeded in bringing about the isolation of this movement from all nationalist elements. Next,

[33]
through clever management of the press, he so influenced the masses that the Right looked upon the mistakes of the Left as

[33]
mistakes of the German worker, while the mistakes made on the Right in their turn seemed to the German worker NATION

[32]
AND RACE 437 which also categorically urged towards a solution which then also took place. To the peasant and

[32]
draftsman, the official and employee, especially of the State, were slowly added as an additional class. They were

[33]
'without pro- perty' in the truest meaning of the word. The State at last helped itself out of this unsound state in a way by

[32]
taking into its hands the provision for the State employees who could not provide for themselves in their old age and

[32]
intro- duced the pension. Slowly more and more private enter- prises followed this example, so that today

[31]
almost every intellectual, permanently employed, draws a pension later, provided the corporation has

[34]
already reached or surpassed a certain size. Only the security of the State official in his old age was

[33]
able to educate him to that unselfish loyalty to duty which in pre-War times was the most noble quality of

[32]
German officialdom. Thus an entire class, which remained without property, was in a clever manner pulled out of

[31]
social misery and thus joined in the entity of the people. Now this question again approached the State and the

[31]
mistakes of the so-called bourgeois. And neither of the two noticed that the mistakes on both sides were the

[34]
objectives sought by these devilish alien agitators. Thus did there come to pass the ghastliest joke in the world

[32]
history Jewish specu- lators became Jewish labor leaders. While Moses Cohn, stock- holder, stiffens the backs of his

[33]
company until it becomes as stern and uncompromising as possible towards the demands of its workers, Isaac Cohn,

[33]
labor-leader, is in the courtyard of the factory rousing the workers. "Look at them," he cries, "they seek only to crush you. Throw your

[32]
chains away." And up above his brother helps make it possible that the chains are forged at all. The people is to

[33]
destroy the backbone of its independence its own industry in order that it may sink the more surely into

[33]
the golden chains of the slavery of interest imposed by this race.' 438 MEIN KAMPF nation, and this time in a much greater

[32]
extent. More ana more millions of people moved from peasant villages to the big cities in order to earn their

[33]
daily bread as ' factory work- ers ' in the newly founded industries. Working and living conditions of the new class were more

[33]
than pitiful. Even the former working methods of the one-time craftsmen 01 peasants, carried over mechanically to

[32]
the new forms, were unsuitable in every respect. The activity of the one and the other was no longer

[32]
comparable with the efforts which the industrial factory worker has to afford. With the old crafts- manship, time might

[33]
perhaps play far less a r61e than was all the more the case with the new working methods. The formal taking-over of the old

[33]
working hours to the great industrial enterprises had indeed a disastrous effect; for the actual work done before

[33]
was only very little, in conse- quence of the absence of our present intensive working methods. Therefore,

[33]
if at that time one was still able to bear a working day of fourteen or fifteen hours, one could no longer do so at

[33]
a time when every minute is used and applied to the fullest extent. The result of this senseless transfer of

[33]
old working hours to the new industrial activity was really an unfortunate one in two respects: it ruined

[32]
health and destroyed confidence in a higher law. To this was added, finally, the miserable wages as well as, on the

[34]
other hand, the visibly so much better position of the employer. In the country there was no social question, as the master

[34]
and the servant did the same work, and, above all, they ate out of the same dish. But all this had now become different

[33]
at one blow. The separation of the employee from the employer now seems to be carried out in all domains of life. How far

[32]
in this the inner Judaization of our people has progressed can be seen from the low respect, not to say disdain, which is

[33]
awarded the craftsman's work in itself. For this is not Ger- NATION AND RACE 439 man. Only the tainting of our life with foreign

[33]
elements, which was in truth a 'Judaization,' turned the one-time respect for craftsmanship into a certain disdain of

[33]
all physi- cal work as a whole. Thus a new class, which was very little respected, was actually created, and some day

[32]
the question was bound to arise whether the nation would by itself have the energy to make this new class again

[33]
a member of general society, or whether the social difference would widen into a class-like cleavage. But

[32]
one thing was certain: the new class contained not the worst elements in its ranks, but the most energetic ones. Here the

[32]
over-refinements of the so-called i culture ' had not yet exercised their deteriorating and destroying

[33]
influences. In its broad masses, the new class was not yet infected by the poison of pacifist weakness; it was robust, and, if

[33]
necessary, even brutal. While the bourgeoisie does not care at all about this enor- mously important question,

[33]
but indifferently lets things take their course, the Jew seizes the unlimited opportunity for the future which

[33]
is offered here, and while on the one side he organizes the capitalist methods of exploiting human

[33]
beings to the ultimate consequence, he approaches the very victims of his spirit and his activity, and after

[30]
a short time he becomes even the leader of their fight against himself. 'Against himself is, of course, only

[34]
metaphorically ex- pressed, for the great master of lies knows how to make himself appear always as the 'pure 1 one and

[32]
to charge the guilt to the others. As he has the impudence to lead the masses in such a manner, the latter does not

[34]
even think at all that this could mean the most villainous betrayal of all times. And yet it was so. As soon as, out of the general

[33]
economic transformation, the new class develops, the Jew sees also before him, dearly 440 MEIN KAMPF and distinctly, the new

[33]
pacemaker of his own further ad- vancement. First he uses the bourgeoisie as the battle ram against the feudal world,

[33]
then the worker against the bour- geois world. Just as at one time he knew how to gain by sneaking the civil rights for himself

[32]
in the shadow of the bourgeoisie, thus he hopes now that in the worker's fight for his existence, he will find the way

[32]
towards a leadership of his own. From now on the worker only has the task of working for the future of the Jewish

[32]
people. He is unconsciously put into the service of that power which he believes he is fight- ing. By making him

[33]
apparently storm against capital, one can most easily make him fight just for the latter. Thus one always cries out

[32]
against international capital, whereas in reality one means the national economy. The latter is to be

[33]
demolished so that on its field of carnage the triumph of the international stock exchange may be celebrated.

[32]
The Jew's procedure in this is, in short, the following : He approaches the worker, pretends to have pity on him, or

[33]
even to feel indignation at his lot of misery and poverty, in order more easily to gain his confidence

[32]
in this way. He takes pains to study all the actual (or imagined) hardships of his life and to awaken a

[31]
longing for changing such an existence. In an infinitely sly manner, he stimulates the need for social

[32]
justice, dormant in every Aryan, to the point of hatred against those who have been better favored by for-

[34]
tune, and thus he gives the fight for the abolition of social evils a definite stamp of a view of life. He founds

[32]
the Marxist theory. By presenting it as inseparably connected with quite a number of socially justified

[33]
demands, he promotes its spread, and, on the other hand, the decent people's aversion to fulfilling demands which, presented in

[33]
such a form and accompaniment, appear unjust, nay, impossible from the beginning. For under this cloak of social thought, there

[31]
are NATION AND RACE 441 hidden some more truly diabolic intentions, or they are reported in all

[33]
publicity with the most impudent clarity. This doctrine is an inseparable mixture of reason and human

[31]
frenzy, but always so that only lunacy can become reality, and never reason. By the categorical

[31]
rejection of personal- ity and, with it, of the nation and its racial contents, it destroys the elementary

[34]
foundations of the entire human culture which depends on just these factors. This is the true inner nucleus of the Marxist

[33]
' view of life,' as far as one may call this monstrous product of a criminal mind a 'view of life.' With the destruction of

[32]
the personality and the race in this world, there vanishes the essential obstacle for the domination of the

[33]
inferior: this, however, is the Jew. fThe meaning of this doctrine lies just in the economic and the political

[33]
frenzy. For by this all truly intelligent Karl Marx, author of Das Kapital, was the son of Protestant parents, converts from

[30]
Judaism. Like many others who later on identified themselves with Socialism, known previously in its

[32]
Utopian forms in France, he was educated in the neo- Hegelian philosophy. At the time this markedly

[33]
evolutionistic doctrine ran foul of Lutheran Christianity in a conventional and fundamentalistic form.

[33]
There appeared to be no chance for reconciliation between philosophy and religion. The phrase, 4 Religion

[32]
is the opium of the people,' comes, however, not from Marx but from Bruno Bauer. Marx definitely turned to

[29]
Social- ism during his exile, which followed the Revolution of 1848. His strength lies in his sharp insight into

[29]
capitalistic procedure, not in his materialistic dialectic. This last, the especial theme of the

[33]
neo-Hegolians, is much better exemplified in Ludwig Feuerbach and Arnold Rugo. It is difficult, therefore,

[33]
to see how Marx's teaching can be linked up with Judaism in particular. The popular statement of his theory is the work

[33]
of Friedrich Engels, an Aryan; and his philosophy is derivative from Hegel, another Aryan. More- over, Marx

[33]
was a bitter critic of orthodox Judaism. A much 442 MEIN KAMPF members of the nation are kept from putting themselves into

[33]
its service, while those who are mentally less active and economically badly trained, join its ranks with

[31]
flying colors. The intelligentsia, however, which of course also needs this movement for its existence, is

[31]
'sacrificed' by the Jew from his own ranks. Thus there arises a movement of mere handicraft workers under

[32]
exclusively Jewish leadership, apparently aiming at improving the situation of the worker, but in truth

[30]
intend- ing the enslavement, and with it the destruction, of all non-Jewish peoples. The general pacifistic

[30]
paralyzation of the national in- stinct of self-preservation, introduced into the circles of the more

[34]
typically Jewish labor leader was Ferdinand Lassalle, whom the Nazis almost never attack because he affirmed

[32]
the nationalist State and influenced Bismarck. Lassalle's influence also survived in the Christian Labor Union

[33]
movement. How eager the early capitalistic entrepreneurs of Germany were to fulfill 'just' social demands may

[31]
be seen from the history of the miners ' unions, where there was for a long time no question of 'Marxism. 1 But though the

[33]
underfed and ex- ploited workers were led by their clergy, and though they 4 reverenced ' the ' human personality,' their fight

[32]
for recognition met with a rebuff from Emperor and industry alike. Jewish intellectuals, rebuffed by the

[32]
Stoecker movement which during the iSSos blended anti-Semitism with social reform on a conservative basis,

[32]
turned quite generally to democratic ideas. In addition the Social Democratic Party, seldom getting

[31]
recruits from 'Aryan 1 academic life, offered some opportunity to Jews. Their influence was, however,

[30]
limited. In 1914 the Executive Committee of the Party had one Jewish member. In the trade unions

[34]
organized under the Marxist banner, Jewish influence was virtually non-existent. But several Jews were Reichstag

[33]
deputies, or were employed on Party journals. NATION AND RACE 443 so-called 'intelligentsia' by Freemasonry, is

[33]
transmitted to the great masses, but above all to the bourgeoisie, by the activity of the great press, which today is

[32]
always Jewish. To these two weapons of deterioration now comes as the third, and by far the most terrible, the or

[31]
brutal force. Marxism, as the column of at should finish what the work of attrition of ripe in preparation of the

[32]
collapse. Therewith a truly masterful that one really must not be surprised if just those institutions fail

[32]
completely rrl much to present themselves as the bearers legendary State authority. At all times the a few

[33]
exceptions) has found the most his work of destruction in our high and highest or of the State. Cringing submissiveness towards

[33]
‘ above ‘ and arrogant superciliousness towards ‘below’ mark this class as much as a narrow-mindedness that often cries

[33]
to Heaven, which in turn is surpassed only by a sometimes truly aston- ishing presumption. These, however, are

[33]
the qualities which the Jew wants of our authorities and which he correspondingly loves. The practical fight, sketched in broad

[32]
outlines, which now sets in takes the following course : -4- Corresponding to the final aims of the Jewish fight which limit

[32]
themselves not only to the economic conquest of the world, but which also demand the political subjection of the

[32]
latter, the Jew also divides the organization of his Marxist world doctrine into two parts, which, apparently

[30]
separated from each other, nevertheless in truth form one inseparable whole, the political and the

[33]
trade-union move- ment. The union movement is that which is solicitous. To the worker in his difficult struggle for

[31]
existence which he has to fight thanks to the greed or the short-sightedness of many 444 MEIN KAMPF employers, it offers help and

[34]
protection, and with it the possibility of fighting for better living conditions. If the worker does not want to give up

[33]
the representation of his human living rights to the mercy of people who are little conscious of responsibility

[33]
and who are often also heartless, in times when the organized national community, that is, the State, cares

[34]
next to nothing about him, then he has to take the defense of these rights into his own hands. In the same measure in

[33]
which the so-called national bourgeoisie, blinded by financial interests, puts the severest obstacles into the way

[30]
of this struggle for life, and not only resists all attempts at shortening the inhumanly long working hours, at

[33]
abolishing child labor, safeguarding and protecting the woman, raising of the sanitary conditions in workshops and

[32]
homes, but frequently actually sabotages them, the cleverer Jew takes charge of the thus oppressed people. He

[33]
gradu- ally becomes the leader of the unionist movement and this the more easily as he is not concerned,

[32]
in honest conviction, about an actual abolition of social evils, but rather about the formation of an

[33]
economic fighting troop, blindly de- voted to him, for the destruction of the national economic independence.

[33]
For, while the leaders of a sound social pol- icy will permanently movte between the directions of the preservation

[33]
of national health on the one hand and the safeguarding of an independent national economy on the other,

[33]
for the Jew these two viewpoints are not only dis- missed from his fight, but their abolition is, among others, the goal of

[32]
his life. He does not wish the preservation of an independent national economy, but its destruction. Conse-

[32]
quently, no pangs of conscience can prevent him, the leader of the unionist movement, from making demands which not only

[31]
exceed the goal, but the fulfillment of which is either practically impossible or means the ruin of a national

[33]
economy. But, further, he does not want to see before him a healthy, sturdy generation, but a decayed herd, able

[33]
to NATION AND RACE 445 be subjected. This wish, however, again permits him to make demands of the most senseless kind, though

[34]
to his own knowledge their practical fulfillment is impossible, and which therefore could not at all lead to a change of

[34]
condi- tions, but at the utmost to a devastating stirring-up of the masses. This, then, is his concern, and not the genuine and

[32]
honest improvement of its social condition. For this reason, however, Jewry's leadership of unionist affairs is

[33]
uncontested until an enormous work of enlighten- ment supports the great masses and sets them right about their never ending

[33]
misery, or until the State deals with the Jew and his work. For so long as the insight of the masses remains as limited

[32]
as it is now, and the State remains as indifferent as it is now, the masses will always follow mostly him who first

[32]
offers the most impudent promises in regard to economic affairs. But in this the Jew is master. For his entire

[31]
activity is unrestricted by moral objections ! After a short time he thus necessarily expels all

[33]
competi- tors from this field. According to his entire inner rapacious brutality, he first of all adapts the unionist

[32]
movement to the most brutal application of force. The resistance and realiza- tion of those whose insight

[33]
resists the Jewish allure is broken by terror. The successes of such activity are enormous. With the help of

[33]
the union, which could be a blessing to the nation, the Jew actually wrecks the foundations of the national economy.

[33]
Parallel with this the political organization advances. It plays hand in glove with the unionist movement in

[33]
so far as the latter prepares the masses for the political organ- ization, and even drives them into it by

[29]
the whip of force and compulsion. It is further the permanent financial source from which the political

[33]
organization feeds its enor- mous apparatus. It is the controlling organ for the political activity of

[33]
the individual, and in all great demonstrations 446 MEIN KAMPF of a political nature, it does the touting service.

[33]
At last, however, it no longer represents economic concerns at all, but, in the form of the mass and general strike,

[32]
it puts its main fighting means, the laying-down of work, at the disposal of the political idea. By the creation of a press, the

[32]
contents of which is adapted to the mental horizon of people with the lowest education, the political and

[32]
unionist movement finally is given an institution which, by its stirring effects, makes the lowest classes of the

[33]
nation ripe for the most reckless acts. Its task is not to lead the people from the swamp of base mentality to a higher

[34]
level, but rather to meet their lowest instincts. A business that is as speculative as it is remuner- ative with

[33]
the masses, which are as inert as they are some- times also presumptuous. But it is the press above all which

[32]
now, in a truly fanatic fight of calumny, derides everything which could be looked upon as the support of

[33]
national independence, cultural height, and economic self-dependence of the nation. It continuously drums

[30]
upon all those characters which do not want to bow to the Jewish assumption of rule, or whose ingenious

[33]
ability in itself appears a danger to the Jew. For in order to be hated by the Jew, it is not necessary

[33]
to fight him, but it is enough that he suspects the other may either be able to arrive some time at such thoughts or,

[33]
based on his superior genius, to strengthen the force and the height of a nationality, hostile to the Jew. His

[33]
unfailing instinct for such things senses in each indi- vidual the original soul, and his hostility is assured

[30]
to him who is not the spirit of his spirit. As the Jew is not the one who is attacked, but the attacker,

[33]
consequently his enemy is not only he who attacks, but also he who resists him. The means, however, by which he tries

[31]
to break such daring but upright souls is not called honest fight, but lie and calumny. Here he is not frightened by

[33]
anything at all, and his base- NATION AND RACE 447 ness becomes so gigantic that nobody need wonder that in our people

[32]
the personification of the Devil, as the symbol of all evil, assumes the living appearance of the Jew. The

[33]
ignorance of the great masses about the inner nature of the Jew, the lack of instinct and narrow-mindedness of our

[33]
upper classes, make the people easily fall victim to this Jewish campaign of lies. While the upper classes, out of their

[33]
inborn cowardice, turn from a man who is attacked by the Jew in such manner with lie and calumny, the great masses, out

[32]
of stupidity or simplicity, usually believe everything. But the State authorities either wrap

[33]
themselves in silence, or, as is mostly the case, they persecute him who is unjustly at- tacked, in order to

[33]
make an end to the nuisance of the Jewish press, something which then, in the eyes of such an official idiot, appears

[32]
as the preservation of State authority and as safeguarding peace and order, t Slowly the fear of the Marxist

[33]
weapon of Jewry sinks into the brains and souls of decent people like a nightmare. One begins to tremble before the

[33]
terrible enemy, and thus one has become his final victim. The Jew's rule in the State now appears secured

[30]
to such an extent that he may not only again call himself Jew, but ruthlessly admits his final thoughts as regards

[32]
nationality and politics. A part of his race even admits quite openly that it is a foreign people,

[33]
however, not without again lying in this respect. For while Zionism tries to make the other part of the world believe that

[33]
the national self- consciousness of the Jew finds satisfaction in the creation of a Palestinian State, the Jews again most

[32]
slyly dupe the stupid goiim. [Jewish colloquial expression : Gentile men or women.] They have no thought of

[31]
building up a Jewish State in Palestine, so that they might perhaps inhabit it, but they only want a central

[34]
organization of their inter- national world cheating, endowed with prerogatives, with' 448 MEIN KAMPF drawn from the seizure of

[32]
others: a refuge for convicted rascals and a high school for future rogues. But it is the sign, not only of their

[33]
rising confidence, but also their feeling of safety, that now, at a time when one part of them still mendaciously

[33]
plays the German, the French- man, or the Englishman, the other part impudently and openly documents itself as the Jewish

[34]
race. How far they keep the approaching victory before their eyes is seen from the terrible manner which their inter- course with

[33]
the members of other peoples assumes. For hours the black-haired Jew boy, diabolic joy in his face, waits in ambush for

[32]
the unsuspecting girl whom he defiles with his blood and thus robs her from her people. With the aid of all means he tries to ruin the

[32]
racial founda- tions of the people to be enslaved. Exactly as he himself systematically demoralizes

[33]
women and girls, he is not scared from pulling down the barriers of blood and race for others on a large scale. It was and

[32]
is the Jews who bring the negro to the Rhine, always with the same concealed During the War, French colonial troops were

[30]
engaged at the front. Afterward some contingents of these formed part of the French Army of Occupation.

[33]
Estimates of the 'morality' of this procedure naturally vary. The Germans, especially those who had

[33]
been brought up on the 'war of races' doctrine, looked upon Senegambians encamped along the Rhine as the worst of

[34]
all possible profanations. The normal French attitude was that if these troops were good enough to live under the French

[33]
flag, they were also good enough to live in Germany. Yet there is no doubt that the use of colored troops caused

[33]
the French considerable unnecessary loss of good will. The Jews, argues Hitler, were responsible, because the French

[32]
nation (a satrap of England) is the tool of international Jewish bankers. In the background are exaggerated

[32]
conceptions of the influence of the Grand Orient. No protest came from Germany over the use of Moorish troops by

[33]
Insurgent Spain. NATION AND RACE 449 thought and the clear goal of destroying, by the bastardiza- tion which would necessarily set in,

[34]
the white race which they hate, to throw it down from its cultural and political height and in turn to rise personally

[33]
to the position of master. For a racially pure people, conscious of its blood, can never be enslaved by the Jew. It will

[33]
forever only be the master of bastards in this world. Thus he systematically tries to lower the racial level by

[32]
a permanent poisoning of the individual. In the political sphere, however, he begins to replace the

[33]
idea of democracy by that of the dictatorship of the proletariat. In the organized mass of Marxism

[33]
he has found the weapon which makes him now dispense with democracy and which allows him, instead, to enslave and to 'rule'

[33]
the people dictatorially with the brutal fist. He now works methodically towards the revolution in a twofold

[33]
direction: economically and politically. Thanks to his international influence, he ensnares with a net

[33]
of enemies those peoples which put up a too violent resistance against the enemy from within, he drives them

[30]
into war, and finally, if necessary, he plants the flag of revolution on the battlefield. In the field of

[33]
economics he undermines the States until the social organizations which have become unprofitable

[33]
are taken from the State and submitted to his financial control. Politically he denies to the State all means

[34]
of self- preservation, he destroys the bases of any national self-dependence and defense, he destroys the confidence

[33]
in the leaders, he derides history and the past, and he pulls down into the gutter everything which is truly great. In

[33]
the domain of culture he infects art, literature, the- ater, smites natural feeling, overthrows all conceptions

[31]
of 450 MEIN KAMPF beauty and sublimity, of nobility and quality, and in turn he pulls the people down into the

[32]
confines of his own swinish nature. Religion is ridiculed, customs and morality are presented as

[33]
outlived, until the last supports of a nationality in the fight for human existence in this world have fallen.

[33]
(e) [sic] Now begins the great, final revolution. The Jew, by gaining the political power, casts off the few cloaks which he still

[33]
wears. The democratic national Jew becomes the blood Jew and the people's tyrant. In the course of a few years he tries to

[31]
eradicate the national supporters of intelligence, and, while he thus deprives the people of their

[32]
natural spiritual leaders, he makes them ripe for the slave's destiny of permanent subjugation. The most

[34]
terrible example of this kind is offered by Rus- sia where he killed or starved about thirty million people That

[32]
Bolshevism was a creation of Jewry has long been a favorite anti-Semitic assertion. In 1920 Hitler met Dietrich

[33]
Eckart, a journalist of ability who for some years edited the Vdlkischer Bcobachtcr. Mein Kampf closes with his name, and

[33]
some of it reflects his style. It may be that Eckart suggested writing the book. His statue, festooned with wreaths, is the ptice

[33]
de resistance of the Brown House, Munich. Eckart was the author of a pamphlet, Der Bolschewismus von Moses bis Lenin

[33]
(Bolshevism from Moses to Lenin). It was believed at the time that Lenin was a Jew. The Russian Revolution had

[33]
its roots in bad government. Jews suffered from this at least as much as did other groups, but in addition they had to contend with

[33]
fanatical anti-Semitic organizations for which the Czar was not radical enough. That does not explain, however,

[33]
why the Kerensky Revolution was undermined by Bolshevists, and the door is left open to specula- tion. Lenin was

[33]
transported from Switzerland to Russia in 1917 in a sealed railway coach by order of General Ludendorff. The hope was

[32]
that he would be able to wean the Russian army NATION AND RACE 451 with a truly diabolic ferocity, under

[32]
inhuman tortures, in order to secure to a crowd of Jewish scribblers and stock exchange robbers the rulership

[34]
over a great people. But the end is not only the end of the freedom of the peoples oppressed by the Jew, but also the end

[32]
of these peoples' parasites themselves. With the death of the victim this peoples' vampire will also die sooner or

[33]
later. < If we let all the causes of the German collapse pass before our eyes, there remains as the ultimate and

[33]
decisive cause the non-recognition of the race problem and especially of the Jewish danger. The defeats in

[32]
the battlefield of August, 1918, would have been easily bearable. They were out of proportion to the victories of our

[32]
people. Not the defeats have over- thrown us, but we were overthrown by that power which prepared these defeats by

[31]
robbing our people systemati- cally, for many decades, of its political and moral instincts from thoughts of

[31]
continuing the War, and thus make possible a separate peace with Germany. It is usually held that the

[32]
original idea came from Dr. Helphand, an adventurer with a flair of genius and a gift for intrigue. Lenin,

[32]
aided by Trotski, gained control of Russia, and the separate peace which al- most cost Lenin his prestige was

[33]
negotiated at Brest- Litovsk. That (if one excepts Trotski) Jews had an unduly important part in these developments

[33]
is disproved by two facts: that only a small percentage of either the Communist Party leadership or its following

[33]
was Jewish ; and by the reac- tion of leading Jewish Socialists not favorable to the Bolshevist minority. There is

[32]
little evidence to support any current as- sumptions that international Jewish aid was given to Lenin. In

[34]
America, England, and France, Jewish groups naturally favored Kerensky. 452 MEIN KAMPF and forces which alone enable

[34]
and entitle peoples to exist in this world. The old Reich, by inattentively passing by the question of the preservation

[33]
of the racial foundations of our nation- ality, disregarded also the sole right which alone gives life in

[33]
this world. Peoples which bastardize themselves, or permit themselves to be bastardized, sin against the will of eternal

[33]
Providence, and their ruin by the hand of a stronger nation is consequently not an injustice that is done to them,

[33]
but only the restoration of right. If a people no longer wants to respect the qualities which Nature has given it

[33]
and which root in its blood, then it has no longer the right to complain about the loss of its worldly existence. Everything

[33]
in this world can be improved. Any defeat can become the father of a later victory. Any lost war can become

[31]
the cause of a later rise, every distress the fertiliza- tion of human energy, and from every

[32]
suppression can come the forces of a new spiritual rebirth, as long as the blood remains preserved in purity.

[33]
Alone the loss of the purity of the blood destroys the inner happiness forever; it eternally lowers man, and

[34]
never again can its consequences be removed from body and mind. Only upon examining and comparing, in the face

[34]
of this sole question, all the other problems of life, one will be able to judge how ridiculously small the latter

[33]
are as compared with the former. How all of them are only temporal, while the question of the preservation of

[33]
the blood is one of human eternity. All really important symptoms of decay of the pre-War time ultimately

[33]
go back to racial causes. No matter whether questions of general law or excres- cences of economic life, whether

[30]
cultural symptoms of de- cline or political processes of degeneration, whether ques- tions of faulty

[33]
education at school or evil influence on the grown-ups by the press, etc., are involved, always and NATION AND RACE 459

[33]
everywhere it is fundamentally the non-recognition of racial considerations of one's own people or

[32]
the non-recog- nition of a foreign, a racial, danger. Therefore, all attempts at reforms, all works of social aid and

[32]
political efforts, all economic rise, and every apparent increase of spiritual knowledge were

[33]
nevertheless unimpor- tant in their consecutive symptoms. The nation and that organism which enables and preserves

[33]
its life on this earth, that is, the State, did not become internally healthier, but they visibly languished more and

[32]
more. All the sham pro- sperity of the old Reich could not conceal the inner weak- ness, and any attempt at an actual

[32]
strengthening of the Reich failed again and again on account of passing by the most important question. It would be wrong to

[33]
believe that the adherents of the various political doctrines which doctored about the Ger- man national body,

[32]
nay, that even the leaders, to a certain extent, were bad or malevolent men. Their activity was condemned to

[30]
unproductiveness for the sole reason that, in the most favorable case at best, they saw and tried to fight the

[30]
symptomatic forms of our general sickness, but passed blindly by the germ. He who systematically follows the

[33]
political development of the old Reich is bound to arrive, upon quiet examination, at the realization

[33]
that even at the time of unity, and thus of rise of the German nation, the inner decay was already on its

[33]
way, and that, despite all apparent political successes and rising economic wealth, the general situation

[31]
became worse from year to year. Even the elections for the Reichstag, with their outward swelling of the Marxist votes,

[33]
announced the more and more rapidly approaching internal, and, with it, external, collapse. All the successes of

[33]
the so-called bourgeois parties were of no value, not only because they were unable to check the increasing

[33]
numbers of the Marxist flood even with so-called bourgeois electoral victories, but because above all even

[32]
454 MEIN KAMPF they themselves harbored the ferment of deterioration. The bourgeois world itself, without its knowing it, was

[33]
infected with the cadaveric poison of Marxist ideas, and its resistance originated frequently rather from

[30]
the competi- tive envy of ambitious leaders than from a rejection in prin- ciple of the adversaries,

[32]
determined to fight to the extreme' There was only one who, during these long years, fought with imperturbable

[33]
regularity, and this was the Jew. His star of David then rose higher and higher in the same measure in which our

[33]
people's will for self-preservation vanished. Therefore, in August, 1914, it was not a people, deter- mined to attack, which

[33]
rushed to the battlefield, but what took place was only the last flaring-up of the national instinct of self-preservation

[34]
in face of the progressing paci- fist Marxist paralyzation of our national body. As even in those fateful

[33]
days one did not recognize the internal enemy, all outward resistance was in vain, and Providence gave the

[33]
reward, not to the victorious sword, but it followed the law of eternal revenge. Out of this inner realization there

[33]
were to be formed lor us the leading principles, as well as the tendency of the new movement which alone, in our

[31]
conviction, was enabled to For assertions like these, General Ludendorff is primarily responsible.

[32]
Irritated by failure and by some rather tactless attempts to taunt him for that failure, he took refuge in

[30]
anti- Semitic utterances, and lent his great name to reckless calumnies. Had either he or von Hindenburg

[31]
remembeied the Jewish dead of their armies and stopped the tirades with one dear word of disapproval, the whole

[30]
anti-Semitic campaign would have collapsed. It may be that this was too much to expect of men smarting under

[33]
humiliation and defeat. In addition Ludendorff retreated into the shadows of a mystical German faith that lent

[32]
fervor and significance to his attacks. NATION AND RACE 455 bring the decline of the German people not only to

[31]
a stand- still, but also to create the granite foundation upon which one day there can exist a State which

[33]
represents not a mech- anism of economic considerations and interests, alien to the people, but a f olkish

[34]
organism : A Germanic State of the German Nation CHAPTER XII THE FIRST PERIOD IN THE DEVELOPMENT OF THE NATIONAL

[33]
SOCIALIST GERMAN WORKERS 1 PARTY IF NOW at the end of this book I describe the first period of development of our

[34]
movement and deal briefly with a series of questions caused by it, it is not done in order to give a treatise on

[33]
the spiritual aims of the move- ment. The goal and the task of the new movement are so enormous that one can deal

[34]
with them only in a volume of their own. Therefore, in a second volume I will deal in de- tail with the foundations

[33]
(and their programs) of the move- ment and will try to draw a picture of what we conceive by the word 'State. 1 With 'we' I mean

[33]
all those hundreds of thousands who fundamentally long for the same thing with- out their finding the words in detail to describe

[33]
the outward appearance of what is before their inner eye. For with all great reforms the remarkable thing is that at first

[33]
they have as their champion perhaps only a single individual, but as their supporters many millions. For centuries

[31]
their goal is often the inner ardent wish of hundreds of thousands, till one man stands up as the proclaimer of such a

[32]
general will DEVELOPMENT OF THE N.S.G.W.P. 457 and as the flag-bearer of an old longing he helps it to victory in the form of

[33]
a new idea. That millions harbor in their hearts the longing for a fundamental change in the existing circumstances is

[33]
proved by the deep discontent from which they suffer. It is ex- pressed in thousandfold forms of symptoms, with some in despair and

[33]
hopelessness, with others in aversion, in wrath and indignation, with the one in indifference and with the other

[33]
in furious exuberance. Also those who are sick and tired of elections, as well as the many who tend towards

[33]
the most fanatical extreme of the left, may be looked upon as witnesses to this inner discontent. It was the aim

[33]
of the young movement to appeal first of all to these elements. It ought not to form an organization of those who

[33]
are content and satisfied, but to bring together those who are tortured by suffering, those who are without

[33]
peace and unhappy and discontented, and above all it must not swim on the surface of the national body, but

[32]
has to root in its foundations. fTaken from the purely political point of view, the fol- lowing picture presented

[32]
itself in 1918: a people is torn into two parts. The one, by far the smaller, comprises the layers The elections of May, 1924, which

[33]
followed the most hectic period in the history of the short-lived Republic the Ruhr invasion, inflation, the Hitler

[33]
putsch, revaluations of the cur- rency, and the parleys that led to the signing of the Dawes Plan was marked by a trend to

[33]
the Left and Right extremes. The conservative German National Party became the second strongest group in the Reichstag,

[33]
the number of Communist deputies rose to 62 (there had been only 2 in 1920), and the DciUsch-voelkischc Frcihcitspartei (German Folkish

[33]
Freedom Party), founded by Right radical dissidents from the conservm- 458 MEIN KAMPF of national intelligence with exclusion

[32]
of all those who are physically active. It is outwardly national, but by this word it is unable to

[33]
imagine something different from a very lukewarm and weak representation of so-called State in- terests

[33]
which in turn seem identical with dynastic interests. It tries to fight for its ideas and aims with spiritual weapons which

[31]
are as fragmentary as they are superficial, but which in themselves fail completely in the face of the

[33]
enemy's brutality. With one single terrible stroke this class, which just previously was still the ruling one, is

[33]
thrown over, and now, in trembling cowardice, it bears every humiliation on the part of the ruthless victor. It is

[33]
faced, in the form of the second class, by the great mass of the working population. This class is integrated in more or

[33]
less radical Marxist movements, determined to break any spiritual resistance by the power of force. It

[33]
does not want to be national, but it consciously rejects any promotion of national interests as, in turn, it promotes

[33]
all suppression on the part of foreign powers. Measured by figures it is the stronger party, but it comprises above

[33]
all those elements of the nation without which a national re- surrection is unthinkable and impossible. For as

[32]
early as 1918 one had to see clearly about this. tive group, elected 32 men. Under the circumstances, it looked as if

[32]
dissatisfaction with the policies sponsored by the Re- publican governments was growing rapidly, and that the ‘ Re-

[32]
volution ‘ was in danger. In many respects this election resem- bles that of 1930. Yet six months later December, 1924 another

[32]
Reichstag election completely changed the picture. The Communists elected only 32 deputies, and the National

[33]
Socialists 14. The number and percentage of citizens voting increased. Doubtless the principal causes of this reversal

[33]
were two the manifest inability of the extremists to accomplish anything, and the beneficent effect to

[34]
the capital that flowed into Germany under the Dawes Plan. DEVELOPMENT OF THE N.S.G.W.P. 459 Any resurrection of the German

[33]
people can take place only by way of regaining external power. But the prerequisites for this are not arms

[34]
as our bourgeois 'statesmen' always babble, but the forces of will power. At one time the Ger- man people had more than

[31]
enough arms. They were not able to secure its freedom, because the energies of the na- tional instinct of

[33]
self-preservation, the will for self-preserva- tion, was lacking. The best arms are dead and useless ma- terial as long as

[32]
the spirit is missing which is ready, willing, and determined to use them. Germany became defenseless, not

[32]
because there was a shortage of arms, but because the will was missing to guard the arms for the preservation of the

[34]
nation. If today especially our politicians of the left try to point to the lack of arms as the necessary cause of

[34]
their irresolute and yielding policy, which in reality is a policy of betrayal to foreign powers, then one must

[32]
answer them only one thing: No, the contrary is right. You have surrendered the arms by your anti-national and

[33]
criminal policy of giving Bitterness was so great that moderate defenders of the poli- cies adopted since 1918

[33]
resorted to the defense that an unarmed Germany had no choice save acquiescence in Allied decrees. Hence

[32]
Hitler's rejoinder. An attack on the German National Party, which had gained so dominant a position in 1924. If this

[33]
party really succeeded in retaining large groups of Nationalist voters, Hitler's move- ment was doomed to failure.

[33]
Therefore he taunted the con- servatives with their 'cowardice' in 1918 an epithet invented by Philipp Scheidemann,

[32]
Socialist leader, after the War. The attack was politically shrewd. In this and subsequent passages, the especial

[33]
situation of 1924-25 is hinted at. The German National leader up until October, 1924, was Oskar Hergt, an honest veteran

[33]
civil servant, without the skill or callousnrsi needed to guide a party through such difficult times. 460 MEIN KAMPF up national

[34]
interests. Now you are trying to present the shortage of arms as the fundamental cause of your misera- ble wretchedness.

[33]
This is, as everything in your activity, lie and fraud. But this reproach applies just as much to the politicians of

[33]
the right. For thanks to their miserable cowardice, the Jewish rabble who had come into power in 1918 was able to steal

[30]
the arms from the nation. They, too, have there- fore no reason and no right to palm off the present lack of arms as the

[31]
necessity for their clever caution (say 4 coward- ice'), but the defenselessness is just the consequence of their

[33]
cowardice. -< Therefore, the question of regaining Germany's power is not, perhaps, How can we manufacture arms?

[34]
but, How can we produce that spirit which enables a people to bear arms? Once this spirit dominates a people, the will

[34]
finds a thousand ways, each of which ends with arms! But even if you put ten guns into the hands of a coward, yet he will be unable

[33]
to fire one single shot in the event of an attack. They are therefore of less value to him than a knotty

[33]
stick to a courageous man. Even for this reason the question of regaining the politi- cal power of our people is

[30]
primarily a question of the recovery of our national instinct of self-preservation, since any

[33]
preparatory foreign policy as well as every evaluation of a State in itself is directed, as

[32]
experience shows, less Conservatives had inaugurated during this period a cam- paign for equality of

[33]
armament. The argument which would become very familiar later on was that either the Al- lies must carry out their

[30]
promise to disarm, or that Germany must be permitted to rearm. As such the plea was popular enough, at least

[33]
potentially. Hitler and the Nazis generally retorted that arms would be worthless until the people had been inflamed

[33]
with a desire to use them. DEVELOPMENT OF THE N.S.G.W.P. 461 at existing arms than at the deliberate and acknow- ledged,

[31]
or at least the presumed, moral capacity of re- sistance of a nation. A people's ability to form

[33]
alliances is far less determined by a dead lot of existing arms than by the visible presence of a flaming

[33]
will of self-preservation and heroic death-defying courage. For an alliance is not concluded with arms, but with human

[32]
beings. Therefore, the English people must be looked upon as the most valu- able ally in the world as long as its

[33]
leaders and the spirit of its great masses permit us to expect that brutality and toughness which is determined to fight

[33]
out, by all means, to the victorious end a struggle once started, without con- sidering time and sacrifices, in which

[32]
case the actual mili- tary armament need not be in any proportion to that of other States. But if one

[30]
understands that the resurrection of the Ger- man nation is a question of regaining our political will of

[31]
self-preservation, it is also clear that this is not fulfilled by winning elements which are national at least

[32]
according to their will, but only by the nationalization of the deliberately anti-national masses.

[30]
A young movement that sets before itself the goal of the re-establishment of a German State with its own

[33]
sovereignty will have to direct its fight completely at winning the broad masses. No matter how wretched in general

[33]
our so-called 'national bourgeoisie 9 is, how insufficient its national loyalty appears, it is just as certain that from

[31]
this side a serious resistance to a powerful national internal and external policy is not to be

[33]
expected. Even if, for notoriously nar- row-minded and short-sighted reasons, the German bour- geoisie were to remain

[33]
in passive resistance, as once it faced Bismarck in the hour of a coming liberation, nevertheless, with its

[33]
acknowledged and proverbial cowardice, an active resistance need never be feared. The situation is

[32]
different with the masses of our fellow 462 MEIN KAMPF citizens who are internationally minded. In their primitive

[34]
originality they are not only directed more towards the idea of force, but their Jewish leaders are more

[32]
brutal and more ruthless. They will beat down any German rise just as once before they broke the German army's

[33]
backbone. But above all, in this parliamentarily ruled State, by force of the superiority of

[32]
their number, they will not only prevent any national foreign policy, but they will further exclude any higher

[33]
evaluation of the German strength and with it any chance of potential alliances. For the weak momentum which lies in

[33]
our fifteen million Marxists, Democrats, Paci- fists, and representatives of the Center is not only known to us, but is

[32]
recognized even more by the foreign powers which measure the value of a possible alliance with us

[32]
according to the weight of this burden. One does not form an alliance with a State in which the active part of the

[33]
population has at least a passive attitude towards any resolute foreign policy. To this is added

[33]
the fact that the leaders of these parties of national betrayal, merely out of their instinct of self- preservation, must and

[33]
will be hostile to any rise. From the historical point of view it is simply inconceivable that the German people

[33]
could once more take its former position without settling accounts with those who were the cause and the occasion

[33]
of the unheard-of collapse which afflicted our State. For before the tribunal of posterity November, 1918, will not

[33]
be evaluated as high treason, but as treason against the country. Thus the regaining of German independence in

[32]
foreign affairs is primarily connected with the regaining of the domestic willful unity of our people. f But

[33]
looked at from the purely technical point of view the thought of a German rise as regards foreign politics seems absurd

[31]
as long as the great masses are not ready to enter into the service of this idea of freedom. Taken from

[33]
DEVELOPMENT OF THE N.S.G.W.P. 463 the purely military viewpoint, with a little reflection it will become clear, above all

[32]
to every officer, that one cannot war against foreign powers with the help of students' battalions, but that for this

[31]
purpose one needs, apart from the brains of a people, also its fists. Thereby one has to keep in mind that a

[32]
national defense, which is based only upon the circles of the so-called 'intelligentsia/ would only spoil the

[34]
price- less goods of the nation. The young German intelligentsia, which found its death with the voluntary regiments in the fields

[33]
of Flanders in the fall of 1914, was sorely missing later on. They were the best property the nation possessed, and this loss

[33]
could never be replaced in the course of the War. But it is not only impossible to carry through the fight it- self if

[33]
the charging battalions do not have the masses of the workers among their ranks, but it is also impossible to carry

[33]
out the technical preparation where the unifying will of the national body is missing. Just our people, which, under

[33]
the thousand eyes of the Treaty of Versailles, has to live dis- armed, will be able to make technical arrangements

[33]
for On November n, 1914, German regiments comprised of student volunteers stormed the French positions at Langhe- marcq (near Ypres)

[33]
in Belgium, singing the DeutscUand song. The losses were fearful. This deed is looked upon as the most heroic in the German

[32]
war record. The theory that the November Revolution was an act of high treason often led to highly emotional

[33]
outbursts. Thus Dr. Wilhelm Frick declared in January, 1928: 'To the gallows with the criminals who have misgoverned us during

[32]
the past ten years!' But oddly enough the Nazis also attacked the November Revolution on the ground that it was no

[33]
genuine revolution. Speaking in Munich during 1929, Goering said: 'Our misfortune was that this "revolution" was no German

[31]
revolution. Therefore we know the revolution is still coming, and that it must, bring the release of German

[33]
energies.' 464 MEIN KAMPF regaining its freedom and human independence only if the host of professional informers is

[33]
decimated to those whose inborn lack of character permits them to betray everything to everybody in

[32]
return for the well-known thirty pieces of silver. One can manage these people. Unmanageable, how- ever, seem the

[33]
millions of those who oppose the national rise out of political resistance, unless the cause of their ac-

[33]
tivity, their international Marxist view of life, is fought and torn out of their hearts and brains. No matter, therefore, from

[33]
which point of view one ex- amines the possibility of regaining the independence of our State and nation,

[33]
whether from that of the preparation of foreign politics, that of technical armament, or from that of the struggle itself,

[32]
there remains the preliminary winning over of the great masses of our people for the idea of our national

[32]
independence as the presupposition for everything. But without regaining our external freedom, every

[29]
idea of an inner reform itself remains, in the most favorable case, only the increase of our

[34]
productivity as a colony. Every so-called economic uplift renders its surplus only to the commissions

[32]
of international control, and every social improvement increases, in the most favorable case, only the

[33]
capacity of working for them. Cultural achievements will no longer fall to the share of the German nation at all,

[33]
they are too closely connected with the political independ- ence and dignity of a nationality. If,

[33]
therefore, the German future's favorable solution is connected with the national winning of the great masses

[33]
of our people, then this must also be the highest and the greatest task of a movement the activity of which is not to

[30]
be exhausted in the satisfaction of the moment, but which has to examine every hour and every

[33]
activity only as to their consequences for the future."
DEVELOPMENT OF THE N.S.G.W.P. 465 Thus we realized as early as

[33]
1919 that the new movement has to carry out, first, as its highest aim, the nationaliza- tion of the masses. As regards tactics,

[34]
a series of demands resulted from this. (1) In order to win the masses for the national rise, no social sacrifice is

[33]
too great. No matter how many economic concessions are offered to the classes of our workers and employees today,

[33]
they are not in proportion to the gain for the entire nation whenever this helps to give back their nationality

[32]
to the broad masses. Only short-sighted narrow-mindedness, as unfortunately is often found in the circles of our

[33]
business men, can fail to acknowledge that in the long run there can be no economic rise for them also, and with

[33]
this no economic profit, as long as the inner national solidarity of the nation is not restored. Hitler

[33]
never went farther than this in criticizing the capital- ist system after his release from prison. Other members of

[33]
the Party objected, and Otto Strasser openly charged him with having sabotaged the 'revolution. 1 (Adolph Hitler:

[33]
Wilhelm III, by Weigand von Miltenberg.) During September, 1930, this difference between Hitler and the Strasser group was brought

[33]
out into the open when three army officers were tried in Ulm for high treason, on the ground that they had attempted to build

[32]
Nazi 'cells' within the Reichswehr. Hitler repudiated the revolutionary ideas of Strasser, but added that if the

[34]
Nazis came to power they would court-martial the 'Novem- ber criminals.' The result was that Lieutenant Scheringer, one of

[33]
the officers tried, switched to the Communist Party. The incident throws much light upon the strength of anti-capitalis- tic

[34]
sentiment in Germany at the time. Scheringer and Strasser charged that Hitler had sold out for money. Therewith the question

[33]
as to how the Nazi Party was financed had been raised, but no satisfactory answer nas ever been given. During

[33]
its early years, funds were obtained from Munich friends, from the Reichswehr, and probably from White 466 MEIN KAMPF If the German unions

[33]
had ruthlessly guarded the interest of the workers during the War, they would have extorted a thousand times, by strike,

[34]
the demands of the workers from the then dividend-hungry employers, even during the War, but if, as regards the considerations

[33]
of the national defense, they had acknowledged their German nationality just as fanatically, and with the same

[32]
ruthlessness, they would have given to the fatherland what is due the fatherland, then the War would not have been lost. But how

[31]
ridiculous all and even the greatest economic concessions would have been as compared with the enormous

[34]
importance of the War one would have won. Thus a movement which intends to give the German worker back to the German

[31]
people has to be clear about the fact that economic sacrifices play no r61e whatsoever in this question, unless the

[31]
preservation and the independence of the national economy are threatened by this. (2) The national

[33]
education of the great masses can only take place through the d6tour of a social uplift, since ex- clusively by

[33]
this all those general economic presuppositions are created which permit the individual to take part

[33]
in the cultural goods of the nation. Russians who had access to foreign money. Whence came the stream of gold that poured

[33]
through White Russian fingers is, indeed, one of the unsolved mysteries of post-War history. Certain organizers,

[31]
e.g. Kurt Luedecke (cf. I Knew Hitler), have supplied further hints as to the sources whence support came. In later years

[32]
abundant aid came from German industry and landed interests. Then the approved formula for contributions was

[33]
a so-called 'loan' for which a 'receipt' was issued. The actual Mender' remained unknown, the money passing through the hands of

[32]
some real or imaginary 'association.' How much Italian cash was furnished is not known. Evidence was

[33]
intro- duced by the district attorney's office in Munich to show that Mussolini had helped to finance the putsch

[33]
of 1923. DEVELOPMENT OF THE N.S.G.W.P. 467 (3) The nationalization of the great masses can never take place by way of half measures,

[33]
by a weak emphasis upon a so-called objective viewpoint, but by a ruthless and fanatically one-sided

[32]
orientation as to the goal to be aimed at. That means, therefore, one cannot make a people 'na- tional' in the

[33]
meaning of our present 'bourgeoisie,' that is, with so and so many restrictions, but only nationalistic with the entire

[29]
vehemence which is harbored in the extreme. Poison is only checked by antidote, and only the

[32]
insipidity of a bourgeois mind can conceive the middle line as the way to heaven. The great mass of a people

[33]
consists neither of professors nor of diplomats. The small abstract knowledge it possesses directs its sentiments rather to

[33]
the world of feeling. In this is rooted either its negative or positive attitude. It is open only to

[30]
the expression of force in one of these direc- tions, and never to a half measure swaying between them. This

[33]
hysteria was an important discovery. It was created by a kind of hypnotic influence seemingly exerted

[32]
by the Party assemblies on people undoubtedly not wholly normal as a re- sult of the privations through which they had

[33]
passed. Extraor- dinary phenomena of a similar kind were numerous during the post- War years e.g., the curious

[32]
'healer' of Hamburg, Hauser, who was followed by immense crowds; the Bibelfor- scher (Bible Students), who raised tides of

[31]
adventistic emotion in Silesia and elsewhere; Rudolph Steiner, the anthropologist, who built houses

[33]
resembling trees; etc. Those who heard Hitler during those years are unanimous in saying that he en- gendered a kind of

[32]
emotional trance with methods quite his own. Party guards moved continuously round the place of as- sembly, and

[33]
usually some interloper was found who could be dramatically shaken and bounced. Then there was a pause. Had

[32]
anything gone wrong? Then Hitler appeared, looking as if he had run the final two hundred yards in record time, to

[32]
unleash a torrent of words, working himself into a frenzy of 468 MEIN KAMPF Their sentimental attitude, however, is

[33]
caused by their ex- ceeding stability. It is more difficult to undermine faith than knowledge, love succumbs to

[32]
change less than to re- spect, hatred is more durable than aversion, and at all times the driving force of the most

[32]
important changes in this world has been found less in a scientific knowledge animating the masses, but rather in a

[34]
fanaticism dominating them and in a hysteria which drove them forward. He who would win the great masses must know the key

[33]
which opens the door to their hearts. Its name is not ob- jectivity, that is, weakness, but will power and strength. (4) One can only

[32]
succeed in winning the soul of a people if, apart from a positive fighting of one's own for one's own aims, one

[34]
also destroys at the same time the supporter of the contrary. In the ruthless attack upon an adversary the people

[33]
sees half-somnambulistic energy that lasted for hours, and reveling in climaxes that were more like motifs in

[33]
Wagnerian drama than like any kind of discourse. Perhaps he would suddenly break into a sort of weeping, pause,

[33]
and shout ' Dcutschland, Dcutschland, Dcutschlandl' However the foreigner might react, even quite normal Germans were swept off their feet. Hitler's

[31]
very entrance had effected an emotional release. Then his oratory wrung every listener dry

[32]
provided that is, that he could bring himself to be en rapport with what was being said. In short, the psychology of the crowd that

[33]
comes to see a prize-fight. The modern masses are not impressed with argu- ments directed against an opponent. They

[34]
must see him actu- ally downed. And if they could then be cajoled further with bloodcurdling promises, all was well. The following

[33]
quotation from the National- Sozialistischc Blatter was not intended to be meticulous prophecy, but its effect

[33]
was calculated: 'During this fight, heads will roll in the sand, and they will be either ours or the others. Let us see to it, then, that

[32]
those heads belong to the others! 9 DEVELOPMENT OF THE N.S.G.W.P. 469 at all times a proof of its own right, and it perceives the re'

[32]
nunciation of his destruction as an uncertainty as regards its own right, if not as a sign of its own wrong. The great

[32]
masses are only a part of nature, and this feeling does not understand the mutual handshake of peo- ple who

[34]
assert that they want various things. What they want is the victory of the stronger and the annihilation or the unconditional

[33]
surrender of the weaker, t The nationalization of our masses will only be successful if, along with all positive

[33]
fighting for the soul of our people, its international poisoners are extirpated. (5) All great questions of the times are

[32]
questions of the moment, and they represent only consequences of certain causes. Only one of them is of causal

[33]
importance, that is, the question of the racial preservation of the nationality. In the blood alone there rests

[34]
the strength as well as the weakness of man. As long as the people do not recognize and pay attention to the importance of

[33]
their racial founda- tion, they resemble people who would like to teach the grey- hound's qualities to poodles, without realizing that

[33]
the greyhound's speed and the poodle's docility are qualities which are not taught, but are peculiar to the race.

[33]
Peoples who renounce the preservation of their racial purity re- nounce also the unity of their soul in all its

[33]
expressions. The torn condition of their nature is the natural, necessary consequence of the torn condition of

[32]
their blood, and the change in their spiritual and creative force is only the effect of the change in their racial

[31]
foundations. He who wants to redeem the German people from the qualities and the vices which are alien to its

[33]
original nature will have to redeem it first from the alien originators of these expressions. Without

[33]
the clearest recognition of the race problem and, with it, of the Jewish question, there will be no rise of the German

[32]
nation. 470 MEIN KAMPF The race question not only furnishes the key to world history, but also to human culture as

[32]
a whole. (6) Making the great mass of our people, which today stand in the international camp, a member of a national

[33]
people's community does not mean to renounce the repre- sentation of justified class interests. Class and professional

[30]
interests are not identical with class dissension, but they represent a natural consequence of our

[31]
economic life. The division into professional groups is in no way opposed to a genuine people's

[33]
community, as the latter expresses itself just in the nationality's unity in all those questions which concern

[30]
this very nationality. Making a professional group which has become a class a member of the people's

[34]
community, or even of the State, is not carried out by the descending of the higher classes, Cf. Rosenberg, Westn Ziele und

[33]
Grundsdtze der N.S.D.A.P. (The Nature, Objectives, and Principles of the N.S.G.W.P.): 'The idea of the genuine folk-State was born out of

[30]
the concept of race. This idea is today the final criterion of our judgment of all we do on earth.' It is

[33]
sometimes thought that after 1933 the Nazis had been willing to mitigate their attack upon the Jews, and that agitation

[33]
by Jews outside Germany e.g., the boycott was responsible for resumption of the attack. Un- doubtedly the Party was

[34]
impressed, especially by the Foreign Office, with the need for care in handling the Jewish problem because relations

[34]
with other States might be impaired. Rosen- berg, for example, then director of the Foreign Affairs Division of the Party,

[32]
declared at the Niirnberg Party Congress of September, 1933, that the Party did not preach, had not preached, race hatred. But

[33]
distinguished German- Americans who visited Hitler during 1933 with a view to counseling moderation were bluntly

[33]
told that they did not understand history or the necessary steps to be taken in regenerating the German people.

[30]
He himself spoke on the subject at the same Niirnberg Congress, and declared: 'National Socialism is a

[34]
DEVELOPMENT OF THE N.S.G.W.P. 471 but by the uplifting of the lower classes. Again, the bearer of this process can never be the higher

[33]
class, but the lower one which is fighting for its equal right. The bourgeoisie of today did not become a member of

[33]
the State by measures of the aristocracy, but by its own energy under its own leader- ship. The German worker

[33]
is not lifted into the frame of the German people's community by the roundabout way of weak fraternizing scenes,

[33]
but by the deliberate uplifting of his social and cultural position, until the most serious dif- ferences may

[33]
be looked upon as overcome. A movement which establishes this development for its goal will have to draw its

[32]
followers primarily from this camp. It is allowed to fall back on the intelligentsia only in so far as the

[33]
latter has understood and realized completely the goal to be view of life. By absorbing the human being who belongs

[33]
to the disciples of this view of life by reason of what is deepest in it, it becomes the Party of those who are

[33]
really, according to their natures, attributable to a certain race. In doing so it recognized the fact that there

[32]
are varying racial substances in our people. It is far removed from repudiating in itself this mixture, which

[34]
constitutes the total picture of the expression given by our people to life. But it wishes that the political

[32]
and cultural leadership of our people should become the function, the expression of that race which, through heroism, and thanks

[33]
solely to its innate virtue, has created what would otherwise not be the German race. National-Socialism

[32]
therewith pro- fesses an heroic teaching of the value of blood, or race and of the personality, as well as of the

[33]
eternal principles on which selection is based, and therewith consciously enters into un- bridgable antitheses to

[32]
the view of life which informs pacifistic- international democracy and its consequences.' That was, at least in

[33]
intention, a philosophical speech; but it ought to have been warning enough that what has happened since was fated to

[33]
happen even then. 472 MEIN KAMPF aimed at. This process of transformation and approach will not be finished in ten or twenty years,

[33]
but experience shows that it will take many generations. -< The most serious reason against the present-day worker's approach

[32]
towards a national people's community does not rest upon the representation of his class interests, but in his

[33]
international leadership and attitude, hostile to people and fatherland. The same unions, led by national

[32]
fanatics where political and folkish considerations are concerned, would make millions of workers the most

[32]
valuable members of their nationality without considering the fights taking place in various instances where

[32]
purely economic considera- tions are involved. A movement which honestly wants to give the German

[32]
worker back to his people and to tear him away from the delusion of internationalism has to attack most sharply

[32]
a conception which is predominate above all in the circles of employers, which, by a national community,

[33]
understands the helpless economic surrender of the employees to the em- ployers, and which chooses to see, in every attempt

[32]
at guarding even the most justified interests of the economic existence of the employee, an attack upon the

[33]
people's com- munity. Such an assertion, then, is not only untrue, but deliberately mendacious, because the people's

[33]
community imposes the same obligations not only on the one side but also on the other. Exactly

[32]
as a worker sins against the spirit of a genuine people's community if, based on his power, he makes ex-

[31]
tortionate demands without consideration for the common welfare and the existence of a national

[33]
economy, an em- ployer breaks this community just as much if he abuses the national working strength by exploitation

[33]
and an inhuman business management, and makes millions out of its sweat. Then he has no right to call himself national,

[33]
he has no right to moan about a people's community, but he is an DEVELOPMENT OF THE N.S.G.W.P. 473 egotistical rascal, who,

[33]
by introducing social discontent, provokes future fights which are bound to injure the nation in one way or

[33]
another. Thus the reservoir from which the young movement is to draw its adherents will primarily be the masses of our

[33]
employees. The task involved is to tear them from the grip of the delusion of internationalism, to free them from their social

[33]
distress, to take them out of their cultural mis- ery, and to lead them into the circle of the people's com- munity as

[34]
a uniform and valuable factor which feels and wants to be national. Now in so far as in the circles of the national

[32]
intelligent- sia there are human beings with very warm hearts for their people and its future, filled with deepest

[33]
knowledge of the importance of the fight for the soul of these masses, they Assertions were many that the suppression

[33]
of Marxist or Christian labor organizations would not mean a disadvantage to labor, since they could be replaced

[33]
with adequate corpora- tive organizations. The question as to what a workers' party ought to be had disturbed

[33]
the German National Socialist Party of Austria, whose ablest leader was Rudolph Jung. The organization dates from

[33]
1904, but the name as stated was adopted at the Vienna convention of 1918. It was Pan- German in outlook, adopted a program

[33]
having much in com- mon with the ideas later formulated by Feder, and was con- cerned primarily with the question as

[33]
to whether a workers' party had necessarily to favor the class struggle. During August, 1920, the party delegates met

[32]
in Salzburg, and Nazi delegates from Munich also attended. The resolutions adopted stressed above all the

[34]
necessity for an ultra-nationalistic point of view. It did not oppose the socialization of some of the means

[33]
of production, but emphasized the inviolability of pri- vate property. Hitler spoke against the class struggle

[33]
at this convention, averring that there was as little room on the N.S.G.W.P: ‘for a class-conscious worker as for a grouo- 474 MEIN KAMPF are most

[32]
welcome in the ranks of this movement as a valuable spiritual backbone. But the winning of the bourgeois

[33]
ballot cattle must never be the aim or even the intention of this movement. In that case it would burden itself with

[33]
a mass which, in its entire nature, would paralyze the force di- rected towards winning the broad layers of the people.

[33]
For notwithstanding the theoretical beauty of the idea of leading together the great masses from above and from

[32]
be- low, inside the frame of the movement and at this moment, yet this is opposed by the fact that by general

[33]
proclama- tions one is perhaps able to create moods or even to render insight, but not qualities of character, or

[33]
rather, that one does not wipe out bad habits the origin and growth of which have embraced centuries. The difference

[33]
as regards the mutual cultural level and the mutual attitude towards the questions of economic concerns is

[29]
still so great at this time that it would immediately manifest itself as an impediment, once the

[33]
intoxication of various demonstrations has passed. But finally the goal is not to rearrange the layers of the camp that

[34]
is national in itself, but to gain the anti-national camp. And this viewpoint is also exclusively decisive for

[32]
the tactical attitude of the whole movement. (7) This attitude, one-sided though clear, has also to express

[31]
itself in the propaganda of the movement, and on the other hand, it is in its turn required by reasons of

[32]
propaganda. conscious bourgeois. 9 A year later, Jung had maneuvered his Aufltrians into accepting a class-conscious but

[33]
anti-Marxist point of view. This action sundered Hitler from the Austrian National Socialists of the period, just as the same

[33]
standpoint would later on sunder him from class-conscious followers in Germany. It is probably for this reason that he nowhere

[33]
mentions Jung and his group. DEVELOPMENT OF THE N.S.G.W.P. 419 If the propaganda IB to be effective for the movement, it has to

[33]
be directed at one side, as in the other case, with the variance of the spiritual training of the two

[33]
camps con- cerned, it would either not be understood by the one or the other would reject it as a matter of course and

[33]
therefore as uninteresting. t Even the manner of expression and the language cannot be equally suitable

[32]
in their effect upon two so extremely dif- ferent layers. If propaganda renounces the originality of

[33]
expression, it will not find its way to the feeling of the great masses. But if in word and gesture it applies the coarseness

[33]
of the masses' feelings and expressions, it will be rejected as rude and vulgar by the so-called intelligentsia.

[32]
Among a hundred so-called speakers there are hardly ten who would be in a position to speak today with the same

[33]
effect to an auditorium composed of street sweepers, locksmiths, sewer cleaners, etc., and to give on the following day

[33]
a lec- ture of necessarily the same intellectual contents to univers- ity professors and students. But

[31]
among a thousand speakers there is perhaps only a single one who is able to speak before locksmiths and

[32]
university professors alike in a form which is equally satisfactory to both sides or even im-

[34]
passions them towards a sweeping storm of applause. But one must keep before one's eyes that if it is to spread even the most

[32]
beautiful thought of a sublime idea, it has to make use of small and smallest minds. It does not matter what These

[33]
assertions may be correct. On the other hand, it is also possible to assume as many do that Hitler's triumph was

[33]
not due to the 'stupid masses 9 which come to hear him peak, but to the intellectual reconstruction which the na- tionalist

[33]
intelligentsia placed on Pan-German Socialism. For an analysis of these intellectuals, cf . Heiden and Kolnai.

[33]
Heiden (who is critical) says they were discalced bourgeois who needed a new basis on which to attain to power and

[33]
station. 476 MEIN KAMPF the ingenious inventor of an opinion has before his eye, but what its announcers transmit to the great

[32]
masses, and in what form and with what success they do so. The strength of Social Democracy, even of the entire Marxist

[33]
movement as a whole, in its capacity of an attract- ing force, rested for the greater part upon the unity

[31]
and thus on the one-sidedness of the public to which they appealed. The more apparently limited, even

[34]
narrow-minded, their trends of thinking were in this, the more easily were they accepted and worked over by the masses,

[33]
the mental level of which corresponded to the food they were offered. But from this resulted also a simple and clear

[31]
line for the new movement:^ Propaganda, in its contents and form, has to be directed at the great masses and its

[32]
efficiency has to be measured exclusively by its effective success. At a meeting of the broad layers of

[33]
a people not that speaker speaks best whose mentality is nearest to the in- telligentsia present, but he who conquers

[32]
the heart of the masses. A member of the intelligentsia who is present at such a meeting and who criticizes the

[30]
speaker, despite his obvious success in respect to the lower classes to be conquered, proves the complete

[33]
inability of his thinking and the use- lessness of his person for the young movement. For this These requirements

[32]
were met perfectly by Dr. Paul Joseph Goebbels. Born in the Rhineland, for a time recipient of a scholarship in a

[31]
Catholic educational institution, later a favorite pupil of Friedrich Gundolf and therewith an

[32]
initiate into the mysteries of the Stefan George school, he was at first doubtless filled with honest resentment of

[32]
social conditions in Germany. He once offered his services to the Social Demo- crats. AM a Nazi he first

[33]
served as an assistant to Gregor Strasaer in Berlin, and then in a moment of crisis abandoned DEVELOPMENT OF

[33]
THE N.S.G.W.P. 477 movement only that intellectual comes into question who has understood the task and the goal of the movement

[33]
to such an extent that he has also learned to judge the activity of propaganda according to its success and

[34]
not according to the impressions which it makes upon himself. For the pur- pose of propaganda is not the amusement

[29]
of people who al- ready are disposed towards nationalism, but the winning of the enemies of our

[31]
nationality, in so far as they are of the same blood. But, generally speaking, those ideas which I have

[31]
already summed up briefly under the heading of war propaganda should become decisive for the kind and the

[30]
execution of the young movement's own work of enlightenment. Its success proved that it was right. (8) The goal of a

[33]
political reform movement will never be reached by a work of enlightenment or by influencing the ruling powers,

[33]
but only by the gaining of the political power. Every idea aimed at changing the world has not only the right

[33]
but also the duty to assure itself of those means which make possible the carrying-out of its ideas. Its success

[32]
is the only wordly judge of the right or the wrong of such an enterprise, whereby the word success one must not

[32]
understand, as in the year 1918, the seizure of power in itself, but its effective consequences beneficial to the

[33]
nationality. Thus a coup d'ttat must not be looked upon as successful, as thoughtless State attorneys of Germany mean

[31]
today, if the revolutionaries succeeded in seizing con- Strasaer and went over to Hitler. Admittedly an

[33]
unprincipled opportunist, he has been termed the 'Nazi Radek' and the 1 Nazi Mephisto.' But behind the exterior

[34]
of club foot, big nose, receding chin, and nervous movements, there is an extraordi- narily mobile intelligence.

[33]
Ae a speaker he still captivates younger German intellectuals as no other man in the Party does. 478 MEIN KAMPF trol of

[31]
the State, but only if from the intentions and aims upon which such a revolutionary action is based there

[32]
arises a higher welfare for the nation than that which existed under the previous r6gime. Something which cannot

[31]
very well be said of the German Revolution as the gangster raid of the fall of 1918 is called. But if the gaining of the

[32]
political power forms the pre- supposition for the practical execution of reformatory in- tentions, then

[32]
a movement with such an intention must consider itself from the first day of its existence as a move- ment of the

[33]
masses and not as a literary tea club or a philis- tine bowling club. (9) The young movement, according to its structure

[33]
and its inner organization, is anti-parliamentarian; that means in general, and in its inner construction, it

[32]
rejects a princi- ple of a decision by the majority, by which the leader is degraded' to the position of the

[32]
executive of the will and the opinion of the others. The movement, in small things as well as big things, represents the

[31]
principle of a Germanic democracy : choice of the leader, but absolute authority of the latter. The

[33]
practical consequences of this principle in the move- ment are the following : The first chairman of a local group is

[33]
elected, but he alone is then also its responsible director. All committees are under his jurisdiction

[33]
and not inversely, he under that of a committee. There are no committees by election, but only committees

[33]
for work. The work is divided up by the re- sponsible director, the first chairman. The same principle applies also to

[33]
the next higher organization, the precinct, the district, or county. The first chairman is always elected, but with this he is

[31]
the exclusive leader of the movement. All committees are subjected to him and not he to the com- mittees. He

[30]
decides, and with this he also takes the re- sponsibility on his shoulders. The followers of the move-

[32]
DEVELOPMENT OF THE N.S.G.W.P. 479 ment are at liberty to call him to account before the forum of a new election, to

[32]
divest him of his office, in so far as he has violated the principles of the movement or has served its

[32]
interests badly. But in his place there then steps the more efficient, the new man, with the same authority, but

[31]
also with the same responsibility. It is one of the primary tasks of the movement to make this the

[33]
determining principle, not only within its own ranks, but also for the entire State. He who wants to be the leader

[34]
bears, with the highest, unrestricted authority, also the ultimate and the most serious responsibility. He who

[33]
is not able to do this or who is too great a coward to bear the consequences of his activity is unsuitable

[33]
to be the leader. Only the hero is chosen for this. Progress and the culture of mankind, however, are not products

[33]
of the majority, but they rest exclusively upon the genius and the energy of the personality. To

[33]
breed and to establish it in its rights is one of the preliminary conditions of regaining our nationality's

[32]
great- ness and power. With this, however, the movement is anti-parliamenta- rian, and even its share in such an

[33]
institution can only have the meaning of an activity for the smashing of the latter, for the abolition of

[31]
an institution in which we see one of the most serious symptoms of mankind's decay. (10) The movement decidedly

[33]
refuses to define its atti- tude towards questions which either lie outside the frame of its political work,

[33]
or which are unimportant for it because they are not of fundamental significance. Its task is not that of

[32]
a religious reformation, but that of a political re- organization of our people. In the two religious

[33]
denomina- tions it sees two equally valuable pillars for the existence of our people, and for this reason it

[31]
fights those parties which wish to degrade this foundation of an ethical, religious, and 480 MEIN KAMPF moral prop of our

[31]
national body to the instrument of their party interests. Finally, the movement sees its task, not in the re-

[32]
establishment of a certain State form or in the struggle against another, but in the creation of those principle-

[32]
foundations without which neither republic nor monarchy can exist in the long run. Its mission is not the foundation of

[31]
a monarchy or the strengthening of a republic, but rather the creation of a Germanic State. The question of the

[30]
external formation of this State, that means, its coronation, is not of fundamental impor- tance, but is

[33]
conditioned only by questions of practical ex- pediency. Once a people has understood the great problems and tasks

[31]
of its existence, the question of external formalities will no longer lead to inner struggles. (n) The question of the

[33]
movement's inner organization is one of expediency and not of principle. The best organization is

[30]
not that which puts the greatest, but that which puts the smallest, apparatus of mediation between the leaders of an

[32]
organization and the individual followers. For the task of the organization is only to trans- mit a

[33]
certain spiritual idea, which first springs from the head At the time this was written, the Party had not yet pledged itself to

[33]
a Fascist ideology. Its organization was modeled after the pattern of the Free Corps, or 'private' soldier groups.

[33]
Some important personalities, notably General von Epp, were still loyal to the monarchical idea. Others felt

[33]
that a republic was the desirable form, provided the right people were running it. In addition the laws forbidding

[33]
agitation against the Republic exacted caution. The precept enjoining restraint in the discussion of religion was

[33]
dictated by similar considera- tions. Openly professed anti-clericalism would have brought down on Hitler's head

[33]
the wrath of the Bavarian government. DEVELOPMENT OF THE N.S.G.W.P. 4S1 of an individual, to a multitude of people,

[32]
as well as the supervision of its execution. With this the organization is in all and everything only

[33]
a necessary evil. In the best case it is a means to an end, in the worst case an end in itself. As the world is

[32]
able to produce more mechanical beings than spiritual and ideal ones, the forms of the organization

[32]
usually form themselves more easily than ideas in them- selves. The practical development of every

[32]
idea that strives for realization in this world, especially that which has a re- formatory character, is, in broad

[32]
outlines, the following: An ingenious idea originates in the brains of a man who now feels himself called

[34]
upon to transmit his knowledge to the rest of mankind : he now preaches his views and gradu- ally he gains a certain circle of

[33]
followers. This state of the direct and personal transmittal of the ideas of a man to the rest of the world is the most

[32]
ideal and the most natural one. With the increase of the followers of the new doctrine, there gradually

[33]
results the impossibility of the bearers of the idea to continue personally to influence and to lead and

[31]
to guide the countless adherents. In the same measure now in which the direct and the shortest intercourse is

[33]
excluded, in con- sequence of the growth of the community, there appears the necessity of connecting members: with

[32]
this the ideal condi- tion is ended, and it is replaced by the necessary evil of an organization. Small

[33]
sub-groups are formed, which in the political movement, for instance in the form of a local group, represent the germ

[32]
cells for the future organization, f If one does not want to lose the uniformity of the doc- trine, this

[33]
subdivision must take place only after the authority of the spiritual founder and the school he has called

[32]
into life may be looked upon as recognized. In con- nection with this, the geo-political importance of

[33]
a center of a movement cannot be overrated. Only the presence of 482 MEIN KAMPF such a center and of a place,

[34]
bathed in the magic of a Mecca or a Rome, can at length give a movement that force which is rooted in the inner

[33]
unity and in the recognition of a head that represents this unity. Thus, when forming the first organizing germ cells,

[32]
one must never forget the need of not only preserving the im- portance of the original starting place of the

[32]
idea, but also to increase it to a superior one. This increasing of the ideal, moral and actual

[34]
transcendent importance of the starting and leading point of the movement, has to be carried out in the same measure in

[33]
which now the lowest germ cells of the movement, the number of which has become countless, demand new alliances in the form

[32]
of organizations. For as soon as the increasing number of single adherents and the impossibility of a

[33]
further direct contact with them leads to the formation of lowest groups, the final countless increase of these lowest forms of

[33]
organization commands the formation of higher groups which, politically speaking, one can then call perhaps county or

[33]
district groups. For no matter how easy it may be to maintain the authority of the original center as compared

[33]
with the lowest local groups, it will be just as difficult to preserve this posi- tion in the face of the higher forms of

[33]
organization now de- veloping. But this is the presumption for the uniform existence of a movement and with

[32]
it for the carrying-out of an idea. Finally, if also the greater middle divisions begin to shape themselves

[32]
into uniform structures, then, even in the This extraordinary code, by which the dynamism of the Party was

[33]
placed on a secure foundation, was pushed through by Hitler at a Party meeting on July 26 and 27, 1921. At the time serious

[33]
divisions among the members threatened to undermine the stability of the whole enterprise. Drexler and most

[33]
of his group resented the influence of Rosenberg, Feder, DEVELOPMENT OF THE N.S.G.W.P. 483 face of these, the difficulty of

[33]
safeguarding the absolutely leading character of the original place of foundation, its school, etc., is also

[33]
increased. Therefore, the mechanical forms of an organization may only be worked out in the same measure

[32]
in which the spirit- ual and ideal authority of a center seems to be uncondi- tionally safeguarded. For

[32]
political formations this guar- anty can often appear to be given only by the practical power. ^ From this short

[33]
description the following lines of direction for the inner structure of the movement result: (a) Concentration of

[33]
the entire work first in a single place, Munich. Formation of a community of absolutely reliable

[32]
adherents and establishment of a school for the future spreading of the idea. The gaining of the future Hess, and

[33]
others. These they considered ‘too intellectual/ Julius Streicher was also not ready to bow to the yoke of

[33]
dictatorship. Hitler had gone to Berlin ostensibly to take lessons in public speaking, and had there discussed

[34]
with several Junkers the feasibility of transferring Party headquarters to Berlin. The meeting led to nothing. The Junkers

[33]
had ex- pected to do all the talking, and instead found themselves listening. Meanwhile Drexler and his friends were also de-

[31]
bating a trek to Berlin, presumably in the hope of thus getting rid of Hitler. The Party meeting, suddenly

[33]
decided upon, was therefore of crucial importance; and the whip was cracked over Drexler's head. Hitler threatened

[29]
to quit, pointed out that the Party's influential friends were his friends, and left the assembly with nothing to do but

[31]
capitulate. Thereupon Max Amann, later on official chief of the Nazi press, was in- stalled as business

[30]
manager of the Party, and Hitler laid down the rules here enumerated. Most interesting doubtless was the

[33]
declaration that no groups outside Munich were to be recognized until they had accepted Munich's leadership. This

[33]
left Streicher feeling the edge of the axe. In 1922 he capitu- lated. 484 MEIN KAMPF necessary authority by successes,

[33]
visible and as great aa possible, in this place only. In order to advertise the movement and its leaders, it

[33]
was necessary not only to shake the confidence in the in- vincibility of the Marxist doctrine in one

[32]
place, visible to all, but also to prove, if possible, the contrary. (b) Formation of local groups only after the

[31]
authority of the central leading group in Munich may be looked upon as unconditionally recognized. f (c) The

[32]
formation of district, county, or country groups also takes place, not only according to the demand in itself, but

[32]
only after the security of an unconditional recognition of the central office has been achieved.

[31]
Further, the formation of organizing structures depends on the heads which are present and which can come under

[32]
consideration as leaders. For this there are two ways: (a) The movement has at its disposal the necessary

[32]
financial means for the training and schooling of able heads for the future leadership. The material it thus has won is

[33]
methodically employed according to the points of view of tactical and other expediency. This is the easier and

[33]
the quicker way; but it requires great financial means, as this leader material is able to work for the movement only

[33]
if it is paid. (&) The movement, in consequence of the lack of funds, is not in a position to install appointed leaders,

[33]
but has to depend on honorary offices at first. This is the slower and the more difficult way. The leadership of

[33]
the movement must leave large fields uncultivated, provided there does not emerge from the followers a head who

[33]
is able and willing to put himself at the disposal of the leaders, and to organize and to lead the movement in

[33]
the particular field. It may happen that in great districts nobody is found, DEVELOPMENT OF THE N.S.G.W.P. 495 but that in other places

[31]
two or even three approximately equally able people come forth. The difficulty which lies in such a

[30]
development is great and can only be overcome after many years. The presumption for the creation of an

[33]
organizing form is, and always remains, a head that is able to take over the leadership. Just as an army has no

[32]
value in its organizing forms without its officers, thus a political movement is just as useless without the

[33]
appropriate leader. When an appropriate leading personality is lacking, the omission of the formation of

[33]
a local group is of greater use to the movement than its organization which failed in consequence of the lack

[31]
of a leading and progressive head.-'- The leadership proper not only demands will power, but also ability,

[33]
whereby one has to ascribe a greater importance to will power and energy than to genius itself, and

[32]
most valuable is a combination of ability, determination, and perseverance. (12) The future of

[33]
a movement is conditioned by the fanaticism, even more the intolerance, with which its ad- herents present

[34]
it as the only right one and enforce it in the face of other formations of a similar kind. It is the greatest

[31]
mistake to believe that the strength of a movement is increased by uniting it with another one of

[33]
similar character. Each enlargement brought about in this way means, first, of course, an apparent increase in its outward

[33]
size and with it also an increase of power in the eyes of superficial observers, but in reality it only

[33]
takes over the germs for an inner weakening that will become effective later. t For no matter what one may say

[33]
of the equality ot two movements, in reality it never exists. For if it did it would practically be, not two,

[32]
but only one, movement. No matter where the differences lie and if they root only in 486 MEIN KAMPF the different

[34]
abilities of the leaders they exist. The coupling of two not quite equal formations does not cor- respond to the natural

[33]
law of evolution, but the victory of the stronger in the tense struggle, and the breeding of the strength and the force of

[33]
the victor made possible by this. By uniting two approximately equal political formations there may

[32]
arise momentary advantages, but every success gained in this way is the cause of inner weaknesses

[33]
appearing later. The greatness of a movement is exclusively guaranteed by the unrestricted development of

[34]
its inner strength and by the latter's permanent increase up to its final victory over all competitors. Yes, one can

[33]
even say that its strength and with it its justification of existence increases only as long as it acknow- ledges

[33]
the principle of fight as the presumption of its devel- opment, and that it has passed the climax of its strength in the moment

[32]
when the complete victory is on its side. Thus it is only useful for a movement to aspire to this

[33]
victory in a form which does not lead to a momentary victory, but which gives it a long period of growth due to

[32]
the long duration of the struggle caused by absolute intol- erance. Movements, which owe their growth only to the

[34]
so-called fusion of similar formations that means compromises are like hothouse plants. They shoot up, but they lack the strength

[31]
to defy centuries and to resist heavy storms. -4- The greatness of every powerful organization as the in-

[33]
corporation of an idea in this world is rooted in the religious This reproduces in part the reasoning of Sorel.

[34]
It is worthy of note that the same idea, which probably originated with the French pholosopher, Auguste Comte,

[34]
now reappears in the ideology of almost every revolutionary movement bent on doing exactly the opposite

[33]
of what Christianity set out to do. DEVELOPMENT OF THE N.S.G.W.P. 487 fanaticism with which it intolerably enforces itself

[32]
against everything else, fanatically convinced of its own right. If an idea is right in itself, and if thus

[32]
armed it embarks on the struggle in this world, it is invincible and every perse- cution will lead to its inner

[32]
strengthening. The greatness of Christianity was not rooted in its attempted negotiations of compromise with perhaps

[33]
simi- larly constructed philosophical opinions of the old world, but in the inexorably fanatical preaching

[31]
and representa- tion of its own doctrine. The apparent advance which movements obtain by fusions is simply

[31]
overtaken by the permanent growth of the strength of a doctrine that remains independent and that defends itself. (13) The

[33]
movement has to educate its members in prin- ciple in a way that in the fight they do not see something that has been

[31]
negligently put together, but something that is aimed at. Therefore, they must not fear the hostility of the

[33]
adversaries, but they should perceive it as the presump- tion for the justification of their own existence. They must not

[33]
shun the hatred of the enemies of our nationality and our view of life and its expressions, but they should long for it.

[33]
But to the expressions of this hatred lie and calumny also belong. He who is not fought that means slandered and abused

[32]
by the Jewish papers is not a decent German and no true National Socialist. The best standard for the value of his

[33]
loyalty, the honesty of his conviction, and the force of his will is the hostility which he encounters on the part of

[33]
the mortal enemy of our people. It must be pointed out again and again to the adherents of the movement, and in

[33]
a wider sense to the entire people, that the Jew always lies in his papers, and that even a once asserted truth

[33]
serves only to cover a greater fraud, and thus in turn it is again deliberate untruth. The Jew 488 MEIN KAMPF is the great

[33]
master of lying, and lie and deception are his weapons in the fight. Every Jewish defamation and every Jewish

[33]
lie is an honorary scar on the body of our fighters. He is nearest to us whom they abuse most, and he is our best

[33]
friend whom they hate most mortally. He who picks up a Jewish newspaper in the morning without finding himself abused in

[33]
it has not usefully applied the previous day; for if it were so, he would be persecuted, slandered, abused,

[29]
cursed, and sullied by the Jew. And only he who most successfully opposes this mortal enemy of our

[34]
nationality and of every Aryan people and culture has the right also to hope for himself for the calumnies

[32]
of this race and thus for the attack of his people. If these principles enter the flesh and the blood of our adherents, the

[29]
movement will become unshakable and invincible. (14) The movement has to promote the respect for the

[32]
personality by all means; it must never forget that the value of all that is human is rooted in the personal

[33]
value, and that every idea and every achievement are the results of the creative force of a man, and

[31]
that the admiration for the greatness is not only a tribute of thanks to the latter, but that it also winds a

[33]
unifying band around the grateful. fThe person cannot be replaced ; especially in cases when it does not represent

[32]
the mechanical, but the cultural and creative, element. As little as a famous master can be replaced and

[33]
another able to complete the painting which he left behind half finished, just as little can one replace the great

[33]
poet and thinker, the great statesman and the great general. For their activity lies always in the field of art; it has not been

[33]
bestowed on them by mechanical education, but is born in them by divine grace. The greatest transformations and

[30]
achievements in this world, their greatest cultural results, the immortal deeds DEVELOPMENT OF THE N.S.G.W.P. 489 in the field of

[31]
statesmanship, etc., are inseparably con- nected forever with a name and are represented by it, The

[33]
renunciation of the homage to a great mind meant the loss of an immense energy which streams forth from the names of

[34]
all great men and also women of this earth. The Jew knows this best of all. Just he, whose great men are only great in the destruction

[33]
of mankind and its culture, sees to their idolatrous admiration. He attempts to pic- ture the people's admiration

[33]
for their own geniuses as unworthy and stamps it with the word 'worship of the person/ As soon as a people becomes so

[32]
cowardly that it succumbs to this Jewish arrogance and impudence, it renounces the powerful energy it

[31]
possesses; for the latter is not based upon the admiration for the masses, but upon the venera- tion of the

[32]
genius and the elation and the devotion brought about by him. If human hearts break and human souls despair, then the great

[32]
conquerors of distress and worry, of shame and misery, of spiritual bondage and physical coercion, look down

[33]
upon them, out of the twilight of the past, and offer their eternal hands to the despairing mortals! Woe to the people that is

[31]
shamed of seizing them! ^ In the first period of the growth of our movement, nothing made us suffer more than our

[33]
insignificance, the very fact that our names were not known made our success doubtful. But the most difficult thing at

[33]
that time, during This has since been done efficiently enough. Hitler is the Messiah, whose faith is that which alone

[31]
can save the world, in to far as the German people are concerned. Wilhelm Kube and Robert Ley, both prominent

[33]
officials, have likened him to Christ. For many for himself, too he is the mouth- 490 MEIN KAMPF which often only six, seven, or

[32]
eight heads came together in order to listen to the words of a speaker, was to awaken the faith in the powerful

[32]
future of the movement and to preserve it in this small circle. fThink of six or seven men, all poor devils without

[33]
names, joining together with the intention of forming a movement which is supposed to succeed some day in doing what

[33]
the powerful great parties of the masses failed to do, the re-erection of a German Reich with greater power and glory!

[33]
If we had been attacked at that time, nay, if one had only laughed at us, we would have been happy in both events.

[30]
For the depressing thing was neither the one nor the other, but it was only the complete lack of attention we

[33]
encountered at that time. This was true most of all for my person. When I entered the circle of the few men, there could

[34]
be the question neither of a party nor of a movement. I have already described my impressions on the occasion

[34]
of my first meeting with this small formation. In the weeks that followed thereafter, I had time and occasion to study the then

[31]
impossible appearance of this so-called party. The picture was, God knows, really a depressing one. There

[32]
existed nothing, really nothing at all. The name of a party, the committee of which represented practically the

[33]
entire body of members, which in one way or another was just that which they tried to fight, a parliament on a small

[33]
scale. Here also voting ruled, and if the great parliaments at least shouted their throats hoarse for months about great problems,

[32]
here in this small circle endless discussions set in piece of German Providence. By others he is surrounded with the

[33]
adjectives once applied to Stefan George by his 'circle.' Still more effective is the slogan, 'Ein Reich, ein Yolk, rin

[33]
Ftihrcr,' which the Nazis chant at every demonstration. The meaning is, 4 One Reich, one folk, one leader/ DEVELOPMENT OF

[33]
THE N.S.G.W.P. 491 about the answer to a letter that had fortunately arrived! The public, of course, knew nothing at all about

[33]
all this. No person in Munich knew the party even by name, except for its few adherents and their few friends. Each Wednesday

[31]
there took place a so-called committee meeting in one of the Munich cafes, once a week a discus' sion

[30]
evening. As all the members of the 'movement' were at first represented in the committee, the persons were

[32]
naturally always the same. The question involved was now to break the small circle at last, to win new followers, but

[32]
above all to make the name of the movement known at any price. The technique of this procedure was the

[33]
following :-4 We tried every month, later on every fortnight, to hold a 'meeting.' The invitations for this were written

[32]
on a typewriter and partly by hand on pieces of paper, and the first few times they were distributed that is,

[33]
carried out by us personally. Each of us turned to his circle of friends in order to move the one or the other

[33]
to visit one of these meetings. The success was a miserable one. I still remember how in this first period

[34]
I myself once carried out about eighty of these bills, and how in the evening we waited for the masses of people that

[34]
were to come. With one hour's delay the chairman had finally to open the meeting. We were again seven men, the old

[33]
seven. We proceeded to have the invitation bills written and multiplied by machine by a Munich stationery

[32]
shop. The result was a few spectators more at the next meeting' Thus the number rose gradually from eleven to

[33]
thirteen, finally to seventeen, to twenty- three, and to thirty-four listeners. The funds were brought together by very small

[32]
collec tions in the circle of us poor devils, so that at last we were 492 MEIN KAMPF able to announce a meeting by an

[33]
advertisement in the then independent Munchner Beobachter in Munich. This time the success was indeed astonishing.

[32]
We had arranged a meeting at the Munich Hofbrauhaus Keller (not to be confused with the Munich Hofbrauhaus Festsaal),

[32]
a small hall which could hardly accommodate one hundred and thirty persons. To me personally the room seemed like

[33]
a great hall, and each of us was afraid whether we would succeed in filling this 'mighty' building with people on the particular

[33]
evening. At seven o'clock one hundred and eleven persons were present, and the meeting was opened. A Munich

[32]
professor made the principal speech, and I for the first time in public was to speak second. In the eyes of the then first

[33]
chairman of the party, Herr Harrer, the affair seemed a great venture. The other- wise certainly decent gentleman could

[33]
not help being con- vinced that I could do everything but speak. Even in the future one could not alter his opinion.

[33]
Events took a different course. I had been granted twenty minutes' speaking time in the first meeting to be addressed

[33]
to the public. I spoke for thirty minutes, and what formerly I had felt in my mind, without knowing it somehow, was

[33]
now proved by reality. I could speak. After thirty minutes the small room filled with people was electrified, and the en-

[33]
thusiasm found its expression first in the fact that my appeal to the willingness to sacrifice led the audience to

[33]
donate three hundred Marks. Through this we were relieved of great anxiety. In those days the financial restriction was so

[32]
great that we did not even have the opportunity of having the leading principles of the movement printed, or

[32]
even leaflets published. Now the foundation was laid for a small fund from which then at least the barest necessi- ties and our

[32]
urgent needs could be covered. DEVELOPMENT OF THE N.S.G.W.P. 493 But the success of this first greater meeting was important also in

[32]
another direction. At that time I started to bring a number of fresh young forces to the committee. The many years

[33]
I had spent with the army made me acquainted with a great number of faithful comrades who now slowly began to join

[33]
the move- ment, moved by my persuasion. They were all energetic young men, accustomed to discipline, and in

[30]
their time in the army they had been educated according to the prin- ciple: nothing is impossible, and

[31]
everything can be done if one wants to. But how necessary such an influx of new blood was, I myself could

[31]
recognize after a few weeks' cooperation. The then first chairman of the party, Herr Harrer, was actually a

[30]
journalist and as such he was certainly exten- sively educated. He had, of course, a burden that was

[32]
exceedingly heavy for the leader of a party; he was not a speaker for the masses. No matter how painstakingly

[33]
exact he was in his work, yet it lacked, perhaps just in consequence of this lack of great oratorical talent, the great

[32]
sweep. Herr Drexler, who was then chairman of the local group of Munich, was a simple workman, as a speaker equally little

www.ingramcontent.com/pod-product-compliance
Lightning Source LLC
Chambersburg PA
CBHW020743020826
48980CB00019B/773/J

9780981462394